# Intellectual Virtue

*Perspectives from Ethics and Epistemology*

*Edited by*
Michael DePaul and Linda Zagzebski

CLARENDON PRESS · OXFORD

# OXFORD
**UNIVERSITY PRESS**

Great Clarendon Street, Oxford OX2 6DP

Oxford University Press is a department of the University of Oxford.
It furthers the University's objective of excellence in research, scholarship,
and education by publishing worldwide in

Oxford  New York

Auckland  Bangkok  Buenos Aires  Cape Town  Chennai
Dar es Salaam  Delhi  Hong Kong  Istanbul  Karachi  Kolkata
Kuala Lumpur  Madrid  Melbourne  Mexico City  Mumbai  Nairobi
São Paulo  Shanghai  Taipei  Tokyo  Toronto

Oxford is a registered trade mark of Oxford University Press
in the UK and in certain other countries

Published in the United States
by Oxford University Press Inc., New York

© the several contributors, 2003

The moral rights of the authors have been asserted
Database right Oxford University Press (maker)

First published 2003

All rights reserved. No part of this publication may be reproduced,
stored in a retrieval system, or transmitted, in any form or by any means,
without the prior permission in writing of Oxford University Press,
or as expressly permitted by law, or under terms agreed with the appropriate
reprographics rights organization. Enquiries concerning reproduction
outside the scope of the above should be sent to the Rights Department,
Oxford University Press, at the address above

You must not circulate this book in any other binding or cover
and you must impose this same condition on any acquirer

British Library Cataloguing in Publication Data

Data available

Library of Congress Cataloging in Publication Data

Data available

ISBN 0-19-925273-4

1 3 5 7 9 10 8 6 4 2

Typeset by Newgen Imaging Systems (P) Ltd., Chennai, India
Printed in Great Britain
on acid-free paper by
T. J. International Ltd.,
Padstow, Cornwall

# CONTENTS

| | |
|---|---|
| *List of Contributors* | vii |
| Introduction<br>**Linda Zagzebski and Michael DePaul** | 1 |
| PART ONE. CLASSICAL VIRTUE ETHICS AND VIRTUE EPISTEMOLOGY | 13 |
| 1. The Structure of Virtue<br>**Julia Annas** | 15 |
| 2. Intellectual Virtue: Emotions, Luck, and the Ancients<br>**Nancy Sherman and Heath White** | 34 |
| PART TWO. CONTEMPORARY VIRTUE ETHICS AND EPISTEMOLOGY | 55 |
| 3. Virtue Ethics: Radical or Routine?<br>**David Solomon** | 57 |
| 4. Practical Reason and its Virtues<br>**J. L. A. Garcia** | 81 |
| PART THREE. THE GOOD OF KNOWLEDGE | 109 |
| 5. Knowledge as Credit for True Belief<br>**John Greco** | 111 |
| 6. Intellectual Motivation and the Good of Truth<br>**Linda Zagzebski** | 135 |

7. The Place of Truth in Epistemology  155
  **Ernest Sosa**

PART FOUR. USING VIRTUE TO REDEFINE THE
PROBLEMS OF EPISTEMOLOGY  181

 8. How to be a Virtue Epistemologist  183
  **Christopher Hookway**

 9. Understanding 'Virtue' and the Virtue of Understanding  203
  **Wayne D. Riggs**

10. Knowing Cognitive Selves  227
  **Christine McKinnon**

PART FIVE. APPLYING VIRTUE TO EPISTEMOLOGY:
AN INTELLECTUAL VIRTUE EXAMINED  255

11. Humility and Epistemic Goods  257
  **Robert C. Roberts and W. Jay Wood**

*References*  281
*Index*  291

# CONTRIBUTORS

**Julia Annas**, Regents Professor of Philosophy, University of Arizona

**Michael DePaul**, Professor of Philosophy, University of Notre Dame

**J. L. A. Garcia**, Professor of Philosophy, Boston College

**John Greco**, Associate Professor of Philosophy, Fordham University

**Christopher Hookway**, Professor of Philosophy, University of Sheffield

**Christine McKinnon**, Associate Professor of Philosophy, Trent University

**Wayne D. Riggs**, Associate Professor of Philosophy, University of Oklahoma

**Robert C. Roberts**, Distinguished Professor of Ethics, Baylor University

**Nancy Sherman**, University Professor, Georgetown University

**David Solomon**, Associate Professor of Philosophy, University of Notre Dame; Director of the Notre Dame Center for Ethics and Culture

**Ernest Sosa**, Romeo Elton Professor of Natural Theology and Professor of Philosophy, Brown University; Distinguished Visiting Professor, Rutgers University

**Heath White**, Visiting Assistant Professor, Valparaiso University

**W. Jay Wood**, Associate Professor of Philosophy, Wheaton College

**Linda Zagzebski**, Kingfisher College Chair of the Philosophy of Religion and Ethics and Professor of Philosophy, University of Oklahoma

# Introduction

## Linda Zagzebski and Michael DePaul

The concept of a virtue has been enormously important in ethics since its beginning, but it has only recently been adopted by epistemologists. In 1980 Ernest Sosa introduced the idea of virtue into epistemological discourse in his paper 'The Raft and the Pyramid'.[1] Sosa's motive for an interest in virtue arose out of the epistemological concerns of the time, in particular, the dispute between foundationalists and coherentists, and it is quite different from the ethicist's motive. But Sosa's idea signalled the beginning of a movement that came to be called virtue epistemology. At a minimum, virtue epistemology is characterized by a shift in focus from properties of beliefs to the intellectual traits of agents. The primary bearer of epistemic value is a quality of the agent that enables her to act in a cognitively effective and commendable way. Some virtue epistemologists claim that traditional targets of epistemological investigation such as knowledge, rationality, or justification can be defined in terms of intellectual virtue, whereas others argue that the traditional targets themselves ought to be replaced by an investigation of virtue in the cognitive domain.

The earliest form of virtue epistemology was reliabilism. According to theories of this kind, the basic component of knowledge or justified belief is a

[1] Sosa (1980).

reliable belief-forming process[2] or faculty[3] or agent.[4] More robust forms of virtue epistemology make the fundamental bearer of epistemic value an epistemic or intellectual virtue in the sense of virtue used in ethics,[5] or they may even model the structure of an epistemological theory on virtue ethics.[6] The alternatives for this last approach are as diverse as the varieties of virtue ethics and most of them are as yet unexplored. There is also the alternative of eschewing theory altogether and adopting an anti-theory model for epistemology.[7]

Virtue epistemology is a recent movement, but virtue ethics is as old as Western philosophy. Ever since Plato, ethicists and historians of ethics have explored the nature of a virtue and the particular virtues, as well as the relationship between the concept of virtue and other key concepts in ethics such as that of a right act, a good motive, emotion, and happiness. Virtue epistemologists understandably concentrate on the ways the idea of a virtue can help resolve epistemological questions and leave the conceptual work of explaining value to ethics. Clearly, then, virtue epistemology needs virtue ethics. But the editors of this volume believe that virtue ethics also has something important to learn from virtue epistemology. Perhaps due to historical accident, virtue ethicists have had little to say about intellectual virtue. They generally take for granted that the moral and intellectual virtues are not only distinct, but relatively independent. Some may also think that it is the job of some other branch of philosophy to examine the intellectual virtues. Granted, Aristotle linked the moral virtues with the intellectual virtue of *phronesis*, or practical wisdom, and for that reason Aristotle scholars and ethicists influenced by Aristotle have attended to *phronesis* in their treatments of virtue, but their interest is generally limited by their concern with the connection of *phronesis* to the distinctively moral virtues. They typically give no attention to

---

[2] Alvin Goldman has proposed a form of process reliabilism. He does not use the term 'virtue' very often, but it appears in Goldman (1993*a*).

[3] Ernest Sosa has proposed versions of faculty reliabilism in many places. See Sosa (1991) for a collection of his papers. Alvin Plantinga's theory of warrant as proper function also appears in many places, in particular, Plantinga (1993*b*). Plantinga is sometimes classified as a virtue epistemologist, although he does not use the term 'virtue' for properly functioning faculties.

[4] John Greco has recently proposed a theory he calls agent reliabilism in Greco (1999*a*). In that paper Greco uses the term 'agent reliabilism' for a larger class of theories than his own, including Sosa's, Plantinga's, and Zagzebski's early theory.

[5] See Code (1987), Montmarquet (1993), and Zagzebski (1996). [6] See Zagzebski (1996).

[7] The anti-theory movement has had a following among virtue ethicists. For a collection of papers on this movement see Clarke and Simpson (1989).

such intellectual virtues as intellectual carefulness, thoroughness, humility, courage, trust, autonomy, or fairness. As a matter of fact, virtue epistemologists have not gone very far in investigating the individual intellectual virtues either, but they have taken the lead in addressing intellectual virtue as a topic of interest and importance apart from the relationship between *phronesis* and moral virtue, and some have begun a study of the relationship between the way in which we form beliefs and the way we conduct ourselves in our moral lives.

We believe that the nature of intellectual virtue and vice is critical for the purposes of both ethicists and epistemologists. It is therefore ironic that there has been so little interaction between them. In an effort to remedy this problem, Michael DePaul organized a conference at the University of Notre Dame in September 2000, which brought ethicists and epistemologists together to investigate the nature of intellectual virtue and its role in resolving disputes in ethics and epistemology. DePaul asked Linda Zagzebski to co-edit a book coming out of the conference, and additional papers by Wayne Riggs and Christine McKinnon were added to the nine papers presented there. This volume is the result of that project. Some of these essays are written by philosophers whose work is primarily in ethics: Julia Annas, David Solomon, Jorge Garcia, and Christine McKinnon. Some are written by philosophers whose work is primarily in epistemology: Ernest Sosa, John Greco, Christopher Hookway, and Wayne Riggs. One author (Linda Zagzebski) works in both epistemology and ethics. The final two chapters are co-authored, with one author in ethics and the other in epistemology (Nancy Sherman and Heath White, and Robert C. Roberts and W. Jay Wood).

The editors believe that intellectual virtue is one of the most promising topics in philosophy, but the literature on the topic is generally splintered into work that is primarily concerned with historical scholarship, work intended for moral philosophers, and work intended for epistemologists. As far as we know, these are the first essays written by virtue epistemologists and virtue ethicists in consultation with each other, including virtue ethicists with a historical orientation. Epistemologists and ethicists bring different knowledge and perspectives to the topic, and we think that the essays collected here demonstrate the benefit of each branch of philosophy to the other.

Traditional virtue ethics is usually associated with Plato and Aristotle, but Stoic virtue ethics gets at least as much attention from the ethicists in this volume (Annas, and Sherman and White), resulting in a chapter adopting a Stoic approach to virtue epistemology (Riggs). Two ethicists address contemporary virtue ethics, either in its debate with consequentialism (Garcia) or in its attempt to be interestingly different from traditional approaches

(Solomon). Advanced discussions by ethicists on virtue ethics and its place in the pantheon of ethical theories (or anti-theories) is important for virtue epistemologists who generally have not gone very far in investigating the place of the different forms of virtue epistemology in the taxonomy of normative epistemological theories.

Moral philosophers have traditionally investigated the individual virtues with great care, and in this volume Roberts and Wood's fascinating chapter on intellectual humility gives a detailed investigation of this virtue for the purposes of epistemology. We look forward to more inquiries of this kind.

The epistemological chapters in the volume focus on a number of questions that expand the topics typically addressed by epistemologists. One issue that gets considerable attention is the nature and scope of epistemic value. Two chapters (Sosa and Zagzebski) address the problem of what makes knowledge more valuable than mere true belief, and one other discusses it briefly (Greco). Some epistemologists are beginning to say that knowledge has received too much attention in contemporary epistemology, and other epistemic values have been neglected. In his chapter in this collection, Riggs argues that there is a need to expand the range of epistemic value to include understanding and wisdom.

The varieties of virtue epistemology and its potential for broadening the standard set of problems in the field are addressed by Christopher Hookway. Some virtue epistemologists have previously argued that the concept of intellectual virtue can be used in solving such traditional epistemological problems as the task of defining knowledge (Zagzebski, Greco, and Sosa) or answering scepticism (Greco), whereas others claim that the real virtue of virtue epistemology is the way it permits us to redefine the central questions. The chapters by Hookway and Riggs defend this position.

Christine McKinnon argues for the advantages of applying feminist ethics to epistemology since it permits an account of a broader range of cases of knowing than those standardly discussed, in particular, knowledge of oneself and others. She argues that a virtue approach in epistemology is better suited to giving an account of knowledge of persons than traditional approaches.

## 1. Summaries of Essays

*Julia Annas* begins her chapter, 'The Structure of Virtue', by acknowledging the interest of recent efforts to use a rich notion of virtue in epistemology. She is concerned, however, about reliance on Aristotle's particular version of virtue ethics to the exclusion of the rest of the ancient tradition. She examines two issues: the connection between virtue and skill and the relation of virtue to success. It turns out that the consensus position of ancient virtue ethics on these issues differs from Aristotle's in ways that are significant for the application of the notion of virtue in epistemology. Unlike Aristotle, the rest of the ancient tradition held that moral virtue is a kind of skill, according to the Stoics, the skill of living. Moral virtue shares the same intellectual structure as other skills. Intellectual virtues also share this structure, and hence are skills. But according to Annas the intellectual virtues are also importantly different from the moral virtues. While the moral virtues aim at doing the right thing, the intellectual virtues aim at truth. These aims might converge, but they need not—indeed, they can conflict. Hence, the intellectual virtues cannot simply be subsumed under the moral virtues; the relations between them are more complex. Virtue clearly requires success, but the issue is complicated since the virtuous person has two aims in acting. The overall aim, or *telos*, is to live a certain kind of life, one that is virtuous. But each particular action also has an immediate target, or *skopos*. Which aim must be attained for a person to have the kind of success necessary for virtue? Annas maintains Aristotle was confused here, but the Stoics were clear and answered that it is attainment of the ultimate aim. Knowledge is different. In order to know one must attain the immediate aim of forming a true belief. Hence, one cannot define knowledge simply in terms of virtue.

*Nancy Sherman and Heath White* point out that virtue epistemologists have underutilized some of the key resources of classical virtue ethics, in particular, the role of affect in intellectual virtue, and the role of luck and external goods in achieving knowledge. Their chapter, 'Intellectual Virtue: Emotions, Luck, and the Ancients', begins by exploring the role of emotion in intellectual virtue, and they defend the Aristotelian position that even though beliefs are not fully voluntary because the emotions that influence them are not fully voluntary, they are within the reach of responsibility. We are not primarily passive with respect to our emotions. Revising the cognitive core of emotions is one of the ways we revise emotions themselves. This is an Aristotelian point, but it is developed by the Stoics whose view of emotions was more thoroughly cognitive. The Stoics viewed emotions as voluntary assents to appearances of good and evil. They are judgements, but they are mistaken. How, then, could the Stoics endorse emotion as a central aspect of cognitive character? The answer, say Sherman and White, is that the sage can resist being taken in by appearances. Further, there are affective states that dispose the agent to make accurate judgements. To care about truth and certainty, in Stoic terms, is to be non-rash and non-careless in giving and withholding assent to the appearances. Since these are emotional attitudes, the affective component of intellectual virtue found in Aristotle survives even the Stoic revision. Aristotle and the Stoics had contrasting positions on the place of luck in happiness, however, since the Stoics maintained and Aristotle denied that virtue is sufficient for happiness. The Stoics even tried to deny the place of luck in knowledge. Cognitive virtues are sufficient for getting the truth. This position has been given up by modern epistemologists who almost always agree that there is a substantial amount of luck in getting truth. Sherman and White conclude that the difference between truth and happiness in the role of luck limits the extent to which virtue ethics and virtue epistemology can be unified.

In 'Virtue Ethics: Radical or Routine?' *David Solomon* sees the turn to virtue ethics in the latter half of the twentieth century as taking two different forms. One focuses on the ordering of evaluative concepts and argues that the concept of virtue is more basic than the concepts of a right act and a good state of affairs. Solomon calls this routine because of its focus on familiar arguments over theory construction. The other form focuses on deeper questions about the nature and ambition of modern ethics and its ability to satisfy our need for reflective guidance. This more radical approach includes such themes as a suspicion of rules and principles, the importance of the narrative structure of a human life, the importance of community, a critique of modernity, and sometimes a suspicion of moral theory itself. Debates over virtue ethics so far seem unresolvable because they are partly debates over the criteria by which an ethical theory should be judged. Virtue epistemologists should be aware that when they look to virtue ethics for a model, there are two very different models to which they can appeal. Solomon suggests that epistemologists might learn from the experience of moral philosophers about the variety of uses to which the language of virtue can be put and possible confusions about these uses.

*Jorge Garcia* argues in 'Practical Reason and its Virtues' that the instrumentalist conception of practical reasoning favoured by consequentialists is inadequate and incapable of protecting us against the moral horrors of the twentieth century. This is even true of the sophisticated consequentialism of Amartya Sen, who proposes that human sympathy in combination with instrumental reason is a safeguard against atrocities. But this leaves us with the need to justify acting from sympathy which, from the standpoint of instrumental reason, may seem imprudent. Sen maintains that the badness of rights-violations is an independent badness which makes acts that produce it wrong if not counterbalanced by good outcomes. Garcia argues that this still leaves us little protection against gross injustice, which almost always is seen as arising from a kind of sympathy—sympathy for humanity as a whole. The problem with that, Garcia argues, is that genuine sympathy is always for individuals, and it is individuals who are the bearers of rights.

Garcia's alternative is a theory of the moral life that has four characteristics: (1) It is role-centred, which means it makes all moral features (rights, virtues, duties) ones that a person has in virtue of being in role-relationships with others: friend, parent, fellow citizen, informant, and so on. (2) It is virtues-based, which means that it makes judgements of right and wrong, rights and duties depend on more fundamental judgements of attitudinal responses that are virtuous or vicious. (3) It is patient-focused in that the fundamental attitudes of virtue are those directed towards the person with whom the agent is related in the relevant role. (4) It is input-driven, which is to say that the moral status of an act is determined by its motivational input, not the physical structure of the act or its consequential output. Garcia argues that these features not only protect against tyranny but are sensitive to the moral significance of differentially demanding roles. This is true of our epistemic roles as well. The intellectual virtues are neither instrumentally nor intrinsically good. Like the moral virtues they are good-making in that they contribute towards our being good reasoners in the roles we have in our epistemic communities.

Two kinds of problem have plagued fallibilists regarding knowledge: the lottery problem and Gettier problems. In 'Knowledge as Credit for True Belief', *John Greco* argues that we can resolve both kinds of problem by attending to the illucutionary force of knowledge attributions, specifically, that they serve to give credit to the believer for getting things right. The idea is that in saying someone knows we are saying that the person has formed a true belief in virtue of her own effort and ability, and not because of some sort of good fortune. Greco begins his essay with sections devoted to each of the two kinds of problem and failed efforts to address them. He then takes up the task of developing his own account. Using work done by Joel Feinberg on blaming, which stresses the assignment of causal responsibility, Greco develops a general account of giving credit. According to this account giving credit crucially involves assigning causal responsibility to the agent, not in the sense that the agent is picked out as the sole cause, but in the sense that the agent is identified as a salient, or the most salient, part of the cause. Since salience is sensitive to context in various ways, Greco's resolution of Gettier and lottery problems inherits a significant contextual element. In addition to requiring that the agent be causally responsible for something in order to get credit for it, Greco requires that a relevant aspect of the agent's character play a significant causal role. A bumbling athlete who only rarely succeeds at some feat will not get credit even when she does, according to Greco, since the rare success will be attributed to good luck rather than the athlete's skill. What this comes to in the cognitive domain is that a believer's reliable cognitive character, or intellectual virtue, must be an important necessary element in the cause of a true belief for the believer to get credited with the true belief. After presenting his account, Greco tests it against a number of cases and closes with a brief consideration of how his account might help us understand the value of knowledge.

In previous work the editors of this volume have discussed the problem of what makes knowledge better than true belief.[8] Zagzebski calls this the value problem. In 'Intellectual Motivation and the Good of Truth', *Linda Zagzebski* investigates the value problem further. She distinguishes four ways a belief can be evaluated according to its relation to truth: (1) A belief can have value because truth is its consequence. (2) A belief can have teleological value in the Aristotelian sense, the kind of value something has when it is a component of a good natural end. On this account true belief would be intimately related to the good of *eudaimonia* or a good life. (3) A belief can be valuable in that truth is its end in the sense of an aim. Assuming that true belief is good, it is also good to aim at it. (4) A belief can be good because it arises from good motives, in particular, the motive of valuing truth or disvaluing falsehood. Since motives and aims are not the same thing, the fourth way in which the value of truth is related to the value of a given true belief does not reduce to the third. Zagzebski argues that the fourth way in which a given belief can be related to truth makes the belief better than either the first or the third way. She defends this claim by comparing beliefs to acts. An act that aims at relieving suffering is better than an act that merely leads to the relief of suffering, and an act that is motivated by a disvaluing of suffering is better still. Similarly, a belief that aims at the truth is better than one that merely leads to the truth, and one that is motivated by a valuing of truth is better still. Arguably, a belief that is

---

[8] See DePaul (1993: ch. 2) and (2001), and Zagzebski (1999a), expanded and reprinted in Axtell (2000).

motivated by a valuing of truth or a disvaluing of falsehood has the value that makes knowing better than mere true believing. Pursuing the belief/act analogy, Zagzebski concludes that true believing is not an end state analogous to the relief of suffering. Rather, true believing *is* an intellectual act, or at least, it is strongly analogous to an act.

The issue of how the reliabilist can handle the value problem is the topic of *Ernest Sosa's* essay, 'The Place of Truth in Epistemology'. Suppose we think that knowledge is belief that is both true and derives from intellectual virtue, where what makes a psychological feature an intellectual virtue is the reliable tendency of that feature to give rise to true beliefs. If we also assume that knowledge is more valuable than mere true belief, where does the value of knowledge in addition to truth come from? Sosa offers an answer to this question that retains the idea that truth is the only fundamental epistemic value (with some qualifications for values such as understanding that are not directly connected to knowledge). Sosa proposes that we prefer our own successes, epistemic and otherwise, to be attributable to our own doing, and this value can be intrinsic as well as instrumental. Furthermore, there is also what he calls 'performance value', the value of a belief performance that would normally produce true belief when operating in a suitable environment. A performance can have this value even when the ensuing belief is false. The chief intellectual goods involve hitting the mark of truth through the quality of one's performance.

In 'How to be a Virtue Epistemologist' *Christopher Hookway* begins his reflections with the schematic characterization of virtue epistemology as 'approaches to the most central problems of epistemology which give to states called "intellectual" or "epistemic" virtues a central or "primary" explanatory role'. This characterization contains three elements that require comment: the central problems of epistemology, the nature of epistemic virtue, and the explanatory primacy of virtue. Hookway addresses each of these elements, but what are perhaps his most interesting reflections concern the central problems of epistemology. He points out that standard versions of virtue epistemology accept the typical contemporary view of the central problems, i.e. that they are to analyse the concepts of knowledge and justification and address sceptical challenges by showing that it is possible for us to know, or at least have justified belief. Given this agreement with the rest of contemporary epistemology regarding the central problems, virtue epistemology is distinguished from other epistemologies only by the claim that the concepts of knowledge and justification must be analysed in terms of virtues. The acquiescence of most virtue epistemologists in the consensus view of the central problems stands in contrast to the position that has driven many contemporary advocates of virtue ethics. Virtue ethicists have tended to reject the contemporary consensus that the central problems of ethics concern the moral 'ought', arguing that we should instead concentrate on what is required to live well. Is there space for virtue epistemologists to mount a similar challenge? Hookway aims to show that there is, arguing that instead of focusing on static states such as belief and the evaluation of these as justified or knowledge, we might instead focus on evaluating and regulating the activities of inquiry and deliberation and the role of virtues in such evaluation and regulation.

*Wayne Riggs* proposes an alternative to standard truth-directed, success-oriented epistemological theories in 'Understanding "Virtue" and the Virtue of Understanding', arguing that the highest epistemic good is a state that includes much more than the achievement of true beliefs and the avoidance of false beliefs. In fact, it includes much more than knowledge: it requires understanding of important truths. So one way in which contemporary epistemology has been too limited is that it has focused on a less worthy goal than the highest epistemic good. Some of the intellectual virtues are best understood as directed at understanding rather than at truth or knowledge. Intellectual virtues are also usually construed as traits that require reliable success in reaching their goal, but Riggs argues that whether the goal is truth or understanding, reliable success cannot be necessary for intellectual virtue since some of the most intellectually virtuous persons, intellectual giants such as Aristotle, Newton, and Galileo, are not noted for their success. The intellectual virtues should therefore be understood in terms of the values at which they aim, not at the values they reliably bring about. When we give up truth-directed, success-orientated approaches in epistemology, the importance of intellectual virtue becomes much clearer.

*Christine McKinnon* argues in 'Knowing Cognitive Selves' that the standard epistemological requirements of impartiality on the part of the knower and passivity on the part of the thing under investigation exclude from the purview of epistemology a very important kind of knowledge: knowledge of persons. Feminist philosophers have focused on problems in explaining knowledge of *other* persons, but McKinnon suggests that the same considerations require a reorientation in the way we think of knowledge of ourselves. In this case the subjectivity of the knower is necessarily implicated, and the reflexive nature of the investigation means that what is known is unlikely to remain unaffected by the inquiry. Justifying the knowledge each of us has of our own selves poses enormous challenges to epistemology. These challenges can be met if we see methods of acquiring knowledge and justifying claims to know ourselves as continuous with the methods of acquiring and justifying our knowledge of other persons. Both are imbedded in social practices and both involve mastery of a theory and responsible exercise of certain cognitive capacities. There are asymmetries between first-person and third-person knowledge, but these asymmetries neither rest on traditional claims of first-person privileged access nor do they undermine the possibility of knowing others. The project of coming to know persons is a project of coming to know their moral and cognitive characters. The case of self-knowledge highlights some interesting points of intersection between virtue ethics and virtue epistemology and may illuminate some methodological issues in contemporary epistemology.

The most interesting parts of works from the virtue ethics tradition are often the detailed, perceptive treatments of specific virtues and vices. Our hope is that contemporary virtue epistemology will eventually produce similarly rich discussions of intellectual virtues and vices. In 'Humility and Epistemic Goods', *Robert Roberts* and *Jay Wood* provide a model for the kind of discussions we hope to see. They begin their treatment of intellectual humility by examining the broader, moral conception of humility. Their strategy is to situate humility in relation to its various opposing vices, which include arrogance, vanity, conceit, egotism, grandiosity, pretentiousness, snobbishness, impertinence, haughtiness, self-righteousness, domination, selfish ambition, and self-complacency. Roberts and Wood focus on vanity and arrogance in particular. They characterize vanity as an excessive concern with how one is regarded by other people and arrogance as a tendency to infer illicit entitlements from one's supposed superiorities. Humble as opposed to vain people are unconcerned with and inattentive to how they appear to others. This does not mean that humble people are ignorant of their good qualities, just that they are not particularly interested to be recognized for having these qualities. The reason for this is that their attention is focused on other, more important things. In the case of intellectual humility, one such thing would typically be the truth. Thus, for example, while vain persons might seek to hide their errors for fear of what others might think of them, the humble will be more concerned that any mistakes be brought to light so that they can correct their errors and get their inquiries back on track. Humble persons are not distinguished from arrogant persons by being unaware of or even unconcerned with entitlements. The distinction turns on what motivates the awareness or concern. Paradigmatic cases of arrogance involve an excessive interest in entitlements motivated by what Roberts and Wood call their ego-exalting potency. In contrast, when humble people do have an interest in some entitlement, the interest is pure, in the sense that they are concerned with the entitlement because it serves some valuable purpose or project. Roberts and Wood close their essay by considering a wide variety of ways in which intellectual humility promotes the acquisition of epistemic goods.

Over three decades ago Roderick Chisholm observed that 'many of the characteristics which philosophers and others have thought peculiar to ethical statements also hold of epistemic statements.'[9] These days we may be less inclined to focus on the linguistic form in which ideas are expressed than on the ideas themselves, but Chisholm's point still holds. Much of what moral philosophers talk about applies to epistemology, although epistemologists and ethicists usually formulate the problems of their respective fields differently. The problems of epistemology have evolved over the last few decades and the dispute between foundationalism and coherentism no longer dominates the field. Sosa's suggestion that the idea of an intellectual virtue can illuminate that dispute is no longer the main attraction to virtue in epistemology. The introduction of the idea of virtue into epistemological discourse has led to a new set of problems and issues for discussion in epistemology that overlap with value theory. A number of new directions for research are suggested by the chapters in this volume and we hope that this book will encourage further collaboration between virtue ethicists and virtue epistemologists.

[9] Chisholm (1969: 4).

# Part I

*Classical Virtue Ethics and Virtue Epistemology*

# 1

# The Structure of Virtue

## Julia Annas

### I

As a long-time worker in the field of virtue ethics I cannot but be pleased by its recent increased importance in ethical theory, and also by the recent emergence of a form of virtue epistemology which takes its inspiration from virtue ethics. This has been due to the work of Linda Zagzebski, especially her book *Virtues of the Mind*,[1] which has opened up many exciting paths of research exploring the links between virtue ethics and epistemology. This is a gripping and seminal book, which will surely change the contours of its field, and bring together two areas which have functioned in mutual isolation and can only gain from the discovery of their links. We all owe Zagzebski thanks for her pioneering work and its effects. My own contribution comes from the direction of virtue ethics, and I shall be exploring two aspects of the structure of virtue, as that has developed in the ancient virtue ethics tradition, which have implications for the relevance of virtue to epistemology. I shall have less to say about the details of the application, since epistemology, at least modern epistemology, is not my area of specialization; but I am fairly confident that they are central to the project of using a rich notion of virtue to illuminate epistemological issues.

---

[1] Zagzebski (1996). I shall also refer to Zagzebski (1999b) and to the exchange between her and various commentators in the Book Symposium on *Virtues of the Mind* in *Philosophy and Phenomenological Research*: Zagzebski (2000a) and (2000b), Greco (2000a), Alston (2000), Kvanvig (2000), Kornblith (2000), and Rorty (2000). Zagzebski usefully distinguishes her work from previous work in epistemology which featured terms such as 'intellectual virtue' or 'virtue epistemology' but which made no appeal to the notion of virtue as that has been developed in the virtue ethics tradition.

The issues I shall focus on are those of virtue and skill, and virtue and success. In both cases we get a clearer picture if we look at the whole ancient virtue tradition, rather than emphasizing Aristotle. For contingent historical reasons Aristotle's has been the theory on which most philosophers focus when they turn to virtue.[2] But treating Aristotle as authoritative for virtue ethics fails to do justice even to the ancient tradition. For hundreds of years different theories were proposed within the framework of happiness and virtue, and there was extensive inter-theory debate. As a result, we can separate the framework and main assumptions of virtue ethics from the specificities of Aristotle's own theory. Sometimes this can turn out to make a large difference as to what is implied by the use of a 'virtue ethics' approach, and I shall be arguing that for these two issues it does. In both cases, if we look at the whole virtue tradition, we find important implications for the relation of the moral to the intellectual virtues, and, hence, for the relation of ethics to epistemology.

## II

Aristotle rejects the idea that virtue is a skill. (Virtue here is moral virtue, as indeed is standardly assumed in ancient ethical discussion;[3] we shall get to intellectual virtue shortly.) This may strike us as unsurprising, indeed mere common sense. But it is significant that Aristotle is a lone voice here. The ancient virtue ethics tradition followed Plato and the Stoics in holding that virtue is a skill. That is, it is a kind of skill, there being other kinds as well; virtue is, as the Stoics put it, the skill of living. The claim that we should follow the ancient tradition rather than Aristotle may at first sound rather

---

[2] For one thing, Aristotle's lecture notes on ethics have come down to us in a more complete form than have those of other ancient schools like the Stoics and Epicureans. (This has not been an unmixed blessing, however, since the *Nicomachean Ethics* (hereafter *NE*)—though not, interestingly, the *Eudemian Ethics*—has been treated as though it were a continuous production, like a modern book, rather than a collection of notes, sometimes with differing treatments of the same issue.)

[3] Greco (2000a: 180–1) argues that virtue is a wider notion than that of moral virtue, covering the idea of excellence in general. In her reply, Zagzebski (2000b: 207–8), is inclined to think that the issue is merely verbal, and hence also the issue of whether reliabilist theories can be regarded as a type of virtue epistemology. However, within the ancient tradition of discussing virtue it was assumed that, while there was a broader use of 'virtue' to mean any excellence, the more proper use of the word was to apply it to moral virtue. For reference to passages making this point see Annas (1993: 129–31).

academic, but this issue of whether virtue is or is not a skill is not merely of historical interest: it raises philosophically crucial issues about the intellectual structure of virtue.

Aristotle says that there are many points of difference between a virtue and a skill. This is obvious enough, and modern writers have developed and modified the list of differences which he sets out.[4] For example, skill involves a mere capacity, can be forgotten, and is less precise than virtue is.[5] However, we can reasonably ask how much such differences matter: the thesis that virtue is a skill is a claim that virtue is one kind of skill, and thus that the idea of skill is central in helping us to understand what virtue is. Against this claim, pointing out obvious differences between virtues and skills is ineffective.[6]

How can virtue be a kind of skill? It has the intellectual structure of a practical skill. Even Aristotle recognizes this; it enters right at the start of his account of virtue, where he compares learning to be just with learning to be a builder. You have a role-model, and first you copy what he or she does, then come to understand for yourself what the point is of doing what that person does. Increase of understanding goes with increased autonomy of reflection and action. This is why, for both skill and virtue, you need a teacher to begin with, but then become able to act on your own independently.

Underlying this simple fact is a connected set of epistemologically interesting points about skill. First, a skill or expertise is teachable. There is some intellectual content to be conveyed, not just picked up by external mimicking. Where there are teachers and learners, we have something which at least in principle is an expertise, not just a matter of an empirical 'knack' to be picked up. Second, the expert is someone who has an understanding of her subject matter as a whole. This is a demanding condition. Someone learning, say, a language, will pick up bits of the subject here and there—the future tense, vocabulary, and so on. The expert in the language will have mastery of all that

---

[4] See e.g. Wallace (1978, 1988). Zagzebski follows Wallace fairly closely in (1996: 106–16).

[5] Skill involves a mere capacity, for knowledge can be used in ways opposed to the right ones, whereas a virtue cannot be used equally well for opposed ends (*NE* 1129$^a$11–16); virtue cannot be forgotten, whereas skills, being mere intellectual states, can (*NE* 1140$^b$28–30); with a skill the person who deliberately makes mistakes is preferable to the person who makes them without intending to, whereas the reverse is true with virtue (*NE* 1140$^b$22–8); virtue is more accurate than skill is (1106$^b$14–17).

[6] For a fuller discussion see Annas (1993: ch. 2, sect. 3, esp. 67–84; also Annas (1995). Aristotle makes the claim (*NE* 1105$^a$26–$^b$5, 1140$^a$2–6, 16–17, $^b$1–4, 6–7) that with skills all that matters is that the product be good, whereas with virtue actions cannot be appropriately judged without bringing in the agent's intentions. This is striking, but, as we shall see, not decisive.

is needed to understand the language, and, moreover, will see how it is all unified. Similarly, someone learning a practical skill like building will pick up bits of know-how and technique here and there; the expert, however, will have mastery of everything relevant to that kind of building, and will have unified that mastery so as to be able to understand his own and others' successes and mistakes, and to be able to apply his skill in new situations without further learning being required. And thirdly, an expert is able to articulate her understanding of her subject, able to 'give an account' of it, *logon didonai*, in the ancient way of looking at it. She is able not only to unify the various judgements she makes within her field, and the actions she does, but to explain them and, if necessary, justify them, in terms of whatever general principles are needed to express understanding of the subject.

These conditions are not independent of one another, since a teacher can scarcely teach if she is completely inarticulate about her subject, and what is taught must be a unified body of practical knowledge rather than a bunch of unconnected practical tips, if it is an expertise that we have.[7]

How is virtue a skill? It shares the intellectual structure of a skill in these three ways. This is visible in the account Aristotle gives of the acquisition of virtue,[8] but it can be seen most lucidly in the Socratic dialogues of Plato. There, Socrates challenges people who appear to be experts about some virtue, such as courage, but fail to unite their isolated beliefs[9] and to offer any articulate unified understanding of the matter; this shows that they lack understanding of the virtue in question. Laches, in the dialogue named after him, can give examples of courage by pointing to men fighting in battle. But at first he can provide no account at all of what this kind of action might have in common with other kinds of brave behaviour—coping bravely with illness or poverty, for example—and when he does, his suggestion is obviously hopeless at explaining how and why all the very diverse kinds of brave action are brave. Laches, who is supposed to be an expert in bravery, has failed to convey

---

[7] I have found that it is common at this point for some people to object that we commonsensically recognize kinds of expertise where these conditions are not met. I cannot go fully into the matter here, but I believe that, while these conditions are demanding, they are not alien to our intuitions, and that on reflection we do in fact deny that someone is an expert if she is inarticulate about her subject, unable to teach it, or unable to express more than isolated tips about its practice. [8] See Annas (1993: 67–69).

[9] Which may be correct; Socrates is not implying that Laches, e.g., in the *Laches*, is wrong about the kind of act which is brave. Where he fails is in having any unified understanding of courage; he fails the conditions for being an expert.

any articulate understanding of bravery; clearly he is, despite appearances, no expert in it. The same undermining of claims to expertise in moral matters occurs in other dialogues, and Plato scholarship has for some time now recognized that the kind of knowledge or understanding which is required and found lacking is the kind of knowledge that an expert possesses.[10] Indeed, Socrates is always appealing to practical skills such as those of the navigator, doctor, or farmer to illustrate the kind of practical understanding that he seeks in moral matters. Nor is this concern peculiar to Plato. The Stoics take over the thesis that virtue is a skill and develop it explicitly and at length, for the same reasons which appear in the Socratic dialogues.[11] It became so standard in ancient ethical theory that it could be taken for granted in any serious debate between ethical theories.

There are common objections at this point from modern philosophers. Kinds of practical expertise have ends which are fixed; it is clear and uncontroversial what counts as success in a skill like navigation, or car repair. And these ends are conditional in their hold on our motivation; our interest in exercising skills depends on our concern to obtain their ends. Can it then be reasonable to think of virtue as having the structure of a practical expertise, given that the end that virtue aims to achieve—a well-lived life—is one which is neither clear nor uncontroversial, and also one from which we cannot similarly become motivationally detached?

The answer to this in the ancient virtue ethics tradition is clear, and best put by the Stoics (though it can also be found in Plato). Virtue is 'the skill in living', and living your life is an end which everybody has, and which, short of suicide, is non-detachable. By the time you start to reflect about your life and the best way to live it, you already, as we put it, have a life. You already have a family context, for example, and a socio-economic context, with some kind of employment and income. You already are the product of some kind of education, including moral education, and have certain values and priorities. For the ancient virtue tradition, all this is your raw materials, on which you get to work as you develop virtue, aiming to make your life a product of understanding rather than conformity, something unified around pursuit of good values rather than driven by isolated desires or run by the values of others. Virtue, then, is a global expertise in your life, and will always differ from local kinds of expertise in just these two ways, namely that the end we seek in

---

[10] See Woodruff (1990) for good discussion of the issue.
[11] For the Stoics see Annas (1993: 69–70).

becoming virtuous is not antecedently fixed in the way that the end of car repair is, and also that living our life is not an end that we can cease to care about, as we can cease to care about having the car fixed. We can choose, of course, to live our lives in a thoughtless and random way rather than to live them in a way which tries to improve them in the light of unifying understanding; but this does not make the end of virtue detachable in the way the ends of local skills are.[12]

Moral virtue, then, is a skill in the ancient virtue tradition; it is an expertise, a kind of practical knowledge. Local, mundane skills serve as examples of the kind of unified practical understanding which, if we become virtuous, will order our lives in a unified way based on understanding.

How, then, does moral virtue relate to intellectual virtue? The right answer has been elegantly stated recently by Paul Bloomfield.[13] Moral virtue is one kind of skill, intellectual virtue is another. Moral virtue, as explained, is a kind of practical knowledge which is illuminated by practical kinds of expertise. Intellectual virtue is another kind of skill. Neither should be seen as a sub-kind of the other—although of course any realistic account of the moral life will find many complex connections between them.[14]

It is only to be expected that intellectual virtues should have a strong intellectual structure unified by understanding. Must an intellectual virtue, however, have the same intellectual structure as the moral virtues that we have seen sharing the structure of practical skills? If expertise is marked by the three conditions discussed above, of teachability, unified understanding of the field as a whole, and articulate ability to give an account of what is understood, then intellectual and moral virtues will share this structure. Intellectual virtues, however, appear to be more various in their structure than moral virtues are, in a way that doubtless owes something to the fact that theoretical skills are more various in their structure than practical skills are. Aristotle's intellectual virtues in *Nicomachean Ethics* VI are highly diverse. The virtue aiming

---

[12] Zagzebski (1996) is rather quick to dismiss what she calls a 'happiness-based' version of virtue ethics on the ground that the notion of happiness in question would have to be fixed and based on now unacceptable teleology (e.g. pp. 201–2). The constraints on eudaimonist theories are formal ones, and they allow for considerable rethinking of the aim of happiness in the light of the demands of the theory of virtue. This issue is discussed, with the ancient evidence, in Annas (1993: pts. 1, 4), and also in Annas (1998*a*).      [13] In Bloomfield (2000).

[14] Cf. Zagzebski (1996: 158–65). Zagzebski is also right that Aristotle's own discussion in *NE* VI does not give an adequate line of distinction between intellectual and moral virtues—although he does at points indicate where there might be conflicts.

for demonstrative knowledge, for example, is different in structure from the virtue aiming for non-demonstrative knowledge. The same goes for the Stoic subdivisions of wisdom, and for Plato's collection of intellectual virtues.[15] The structure of an intellectual virtue will naturally depend on the scope and type of the relevant intellectual skill; it would seem that we might have several differently structured intellectual virtues which all met the conditions for expertise.

It could be argued that the moral virtues essentially involve emotions and feelings in a way not true of the intellectual virtues. Indeed, moral virtue crucially involves in its development the progressive control and finally transformation of the person's emotive side.[16] But it would be a mistake to hold that development of an intellectual virtue like perseverance or intellectual honesty never involves such control and transformation of recalcitrant, not purely intellectual, elements of the person. Moreover, development of the intellectual virtues may straightforwardly require such transformation of the emotions and feelings by way of the development of a moral virtue. Honesty in some research, for example, requires that the person not be under the influence of greed for money; indeed, honesty seems to be the same moral virtue whether applied in handling money matters or in conducting research.

The real distinction emerges when we consider that moral virtue is essentially practical; it is the skill of living, where living, in the virtue tradition, is seen as essentially active, shaping your life so that it is ordered from within. The way you live is seen as actively reflecting and expressing your character and hence your choices. Intellectual virtue, on the other hand, is not essentially practical; it is theoretical in that it is directed at achieving aims other than good action. Particularly if we think of intellectual virtue as aimed at achieving truth, we can see that its aim is going to be distinct from that of moral virtue.

Of course, there might still be a close connection between the two kinds of virtue, and most virtue theories have thought that there is. One view frequently found attractive is that the intellectual virtues, whose aim is truth,

---

[15] At *Republic* 487a (and cf. 490c) we find that the ideal person to achieve knowledge, in ideal conditions, must, as well as having a good memory, be good at learning, large-minded, and 'elegant' (*eucharis*, probably meaning that he presents himself and his work in an attractive rather than harsh or gauche fashion). He or she must also be attracted to and 'akin to' truth, as well as having the moral virtues of justice, courage, and temperance. This is a collection of very different intellectual virtues. There would not seem to be any a priori reason why being large-minded, with a broad vision, should be structurally like having a drive to discover truth.

[16] See Annas (1993: ch. 2, sect. 2).

deepen the understanding which is the basis of the moral virtues. After all, the moral virtues are aimed at doing the *right* thing, and this can scarcely allow indifference to the truth of your beliefs about the matter. Even if the intellectual virtues enable us to discover truths about matters which are recondite and abstract, still our increased grasp of truth will serve to broaden and deepen the understanding at the basis of the kind of practical knowledge which is moral virtue. As Zagzebski puts it, '[I]f it turns out that the ultimate end of truth and the ultimate ends of the moral virtues are all components of a life of *eudaimonia*, then the moral and intellectual virtues do not even differ in their *ultimate* ultimate ends.'[17]

What, though, if this turns out not to be the case? In the virtue tradition there are two conflicting lines of thought on this, both of which are found appealing by both Plato and Aristotle. While they think most of the time that seeking truth will form part of a life well-ordered by moral virtue, they both at some points express a contrasting thought: seeking truth can become an end indifferent to or even conflicting with the end of living according to moral virtue.[18] The attractiveness of the intellectual search for truth, and the intrinsic appeal of its objects, can lead humans away from the aim of living a morally ordered life. It can lead them to aim to devote their energies entirely to the search for truth, to the point of wishing to transcend the boundaries of human life altogether and to try to 'become immortal', as Aristotle famously says in this connection. In this case the pursuit of happiness in a morally unified life will have been disrupted. Someone who seeks truth in a way which is indifferent to or conflicts with living a morally virtuous life is still, however, exercising the intellectual virtues. It is unconvincing to claim that someone whose intellectual pursuit of the truth conflicts with leading a moral life must really be lacking in intellectual virtue. (Indeed, it is likely to be the intellectually virtuous achievers, rather than the intellectually faulty, who have this problem.) The intellectual virtues can, though they need not, have a differing aim from the moral virtues, since the theoretical aim of truth can come into conflict with the aim of moral virtue, which is a practical type of knowledge.

The relation between intellectual and moral virtue that emerges from the virtue ethics tradition, at least in its developed ancient form, is that both are

---

[17] Zagzebski (2000a: 173).

[18] Plato expresses this memorably: see the picture of the philosopher's indifference to ordinary life and its virtues and vices in the 'digression' in the *Theaetetus*, and the way the 'Guardians' are forced to rule in the central books of the *Republic*. In Aristotle there is the well-known conflict between the body of the *NE* and the passage that has come down to us as the second part of 'Book 10'.

kinds of skill or expertise, whose aims can but need not converge. Taking virtue seriously in the epistemological framework of the intellectual virtues, then, does not give support to thinking of intellectual virtues as a subset of moral virtues, nor to taking epistemology to be properly subsumed under ethics.[19] Taking both kinds of virtue seriously, however, may be fruitful in other ways. For one thing, taking moral virtue seriously reveals how intellectual a structure it has, and this suggests that virtue ethics might get aid from epistemology, as well as epistemology benefiting from virtue ethics. Ethics and epistemology can produce mutual benefit from mutual study.

## III

The second issue is that of virtue and success. Zagzebski frequently insists that 'virtue is a success notion',[20] and in this she and others are following not only Aristotle, who insists that the virtuous person is successful (*katorthotikos*), but the Stoics, who call a virtuous action as performed by a virtuous person a success (*katorthoma*).[21]

The success element in virtue is important for anyone wishing to develop an epistemology in which virtue plays a basic or foundational role. For knowledge is a success term if any is. Knowledge is not the state you achieve by doing your best though you fail, but the state in which you actually succeed in getting your claim right, and succeed in meeting the required conditions,

---

[19] As Zagzebski (1996: ch. 7) claims. Her arguments, however, do support many weaker claims, for example that epistemology is more closely connected to ethics than many recent epistemologists and ethicists have thought. Epistemologists freely use ethical notions in developing their theories, and theories in epistemology frequently mirror ethical theories in their structure; Zagzebski is surely right that this should be done in a self-conscious and careful manner. I would add that writers in ethics have frequently had to develop a moral epistemology in isolation from modern developments in epistemology, which have focused on morality and moral epistemology only from their own perspective.

[20] Zagzebski (1996: 136–7, 176–84, 1999*b*: 107, 2000*a*: 174–5). At (2000*b*: 211) she responds to the objection of Alston and others that virtue may not be so closely connected with success with the irenic suggestion that reasonable people may differ as to the importance of the success element in moral assessment.

[21] Aristotle, *NE* 1104$^b$34, where the good person is said to be successful about the fine, the advantageous, and the pleasant, the three sources of motivation for choices and avoidances. *Katorthoma* in Stoic texts is usually translated by a different term from 'success' in English, to avoid confusion; thus Inwood and Gerson (1997) use '(morally) perfect action'. Long and Sedley (1987) translate it, rather weakly, as 'right action'.

whatever these may be. Zagzebski defines knowledge as a state of cognitive contact with reality arising out of acts of intellectual virtue,[22] and obviously 'act of virtue' must be a success term here, or it would not be knowledge that we were defining. Virtue, then, must be a success term in virtue epistemology.

When we look at the virtue ethics tradition, however, we find that the relation of virtue and success contains complexities, and that when these are examined we find that we must also introduce complexities into any attempt to make use of virtue in reaching a definition of knowledge.

The virtuous person must have the right motivation, and must also reliably succeed in what she does. An act which fails to achieve its aim can be said to 'lack[s] something morally desirable'.[23] But what is the virtuous person's aim in acting? She has two. One is her *telos* or overall aim, of living virtuously and acting from motives of virtue.[24] Virtue, after all, is a settled state of the person, with the overall aim of making the person's life as a whole be one way rather than another, virtuous rather than evil or complacent. (Living virtuously, further, either constitutes, or contributes to, happiness; but that is a distinct issue.) The virtuous person's other aim is what the Stoics call her *skopos* or immediate target, which is what is aimed at in any particular case of acting virtuously. The target of a just distribution will be everyone's getting what they are entitled to, that of a brave rescue will be the safe conveyance of people out of the burning building, and so on.

Plainly, someone can succeed in achieving the immediate target of an action on a particular occasion without achieving the overall aim of living virtuously. This will be the case if the person is not virtuous, and so does an action which is the kind of action which a virtuous person would characteristically do, but does not do it as a result of the virtuous person's motivation.[25] Equally plainly, a virtuous person can succeed in achieving the overall aim of

---

[22] Zagzebski (1996: 270–1, 1999b: 108–9, 2000a: 174–6). In all cases Zagzebski gives an alternative definition in terms of belief, which is narrower and links more directly to traditional definitions in terms of propositional belief.       [23] Zagzebski (1999b: 107).

[24] We should note that it is a mistake (often made) to think of this as egoistic. Her aim is to be an honest person, that is, to give others their due, to think of herself precisely as standing in *moral* relations to others. This is not egoistic, and has nothing to do with the condition of thinking that it is the state of your own character which matters, rather than other people and what you owe to them. It needs to be emphasized that ancient theories of virtue are not focused on the self rather than on making the world a better place.

[25] In such a case the Stoics say that the action is an appropriate action or *kathekon*, which is defined as an action such that you can offer a reasonable defence of having done it. Only an action done by a virtuous person from the right motivation is a *katorthoma*.

living virtuously by performing a virtuous act, even if, through no fault of her own, she fails to achieve the immediate target. If the brave rescuer does everything he can, takes the appropriate precautions, and so on, but the victims die anyway because they are shot on the way out by a deranged gunman who happens to be there, then the brave action has failed to achieve its immediate target, but not in a way which implies that the brave person has failed to achieve his overall aim of living virtuously and so acting, in this, case, bravely. It is crucial, therefore, in examining a virtuous act, to ask what kind of success is in question—success in achieving the overall goal or success in achieving the immediate target. For achieving the overall goal is a matter of having the right motivation (something, of course, which in a virtue ethics is the result of a lengthy and demanding process), and this is up to the agent, since it is she who makes her life be one kind of life rather than another. But success in achieving the immediate target may not be in this way up to the agent, and may depend on various kinds of moral luck.

From a virtue ethics point of view, which is the success that matters? Virtue ethics is concerned with the person's life as a whole, with character and the kind of person you are. The right perspective on an action, therefore, will for virtue ethics be the one which asks about success in achieving the overall goal, rather than success in achieving the immediate target. What matters is what the person's motivation was, and how this relates to her developed character and life as a whole; for this is her achievement, what she has made of her life. To the extent that success in achieving the immediate target depends on factors over which the person has no control—moral luck of various kinds—it will be of less interest to virtue ethics. Success or failure in achieving the immediate target will affect various judgements we make about the action, but if, like the Stoics, we distinguish clearly between the immediate target and the overall aim, it is achieving the latter, not the former, which will make the action a success, a *katorthoma*. Here virtue ethics parts company with theories like (most forms of) consequentialism, for which it is the actual results that matter for our evaluation of the agent,[26] and stands with Kantianism, for which what matters is the agent's motivation.[27]

---

[26] Modern versions of virtue ethics which align it with forms of consequentialism are thus abandoning the ancient virtue ethics tradition. This is perfectly reasonable, though it would avoid confusion if such theories made it clear that they are talking about a different sense of virtue from that found in the virtue ethics tradition.

[27] Though virtue ethics, because of its focus on the agent's character and life as a whole, has a richer conception of the agent's motivation than forms of Kantianism which focus on motivation at the time rather than on more established states like the virtues.

Virtue is a skill, in the virtue tradition, the skill of living your life in a way which turns your raw materials into a life lived with and from understanding. It is a global skill, as we have seen, and this explains why it is compatible with failure to foresee some particular circumstances. Our ordinary notion of skill goes some way towards making this point; we sometimes judge an expert by the exercise of her skill rather than by the product, as when an expert musical performer produces a better performance on a bad instrument than a lesser expert can on a good instrument, even if the latter can be said to sound better. Still, the Stoics insist that virtue is not to be judged by its actual results, like a skill which is judged by its products, but is more like performance skills, such as acting or dancing, where the excellence that is judged is the excellence in the activity and not in some separable result. For with virtue it is not the results which define success: 'actions initiated by virtue are to be judged right beginning from their first inception and not in their completion.'[28]

This is an issue where privileging Aristotle can lead to confusion, since on this point he is confused. On the one hand, he insists on the praiseworthiness of virtue, and the importance of choice as opposed to action in distinguishing characters.[29] But on the other hand he also stresses success in achieving the target in the practice of various virtues, sometimes in cases where this is explicitly not up to the agent, as with the 'virtue' of magnificence (the 'virtue' of spending money on civic projects), which only a rich person can exercise.[30] There is an unresolved internal tension in his theory as a result, mirroring his uncertainty as to the role of external goods in the virtuous life generally.[31] We can see the problem if we ask about the role of a 'virtue' like magnificence. To exercise it the person needs not only external goods, in this case money, whose possession is a matter of moral luck; he needs to be actually successful in his exercise of tasteful spending, producing what succeeds in impressing the audience without overwhelming them, and so on. Aristotle, however, also believes in the mutual reciprocity of the virtues; to have one you have to have them all. But he clearly does not believe that if you are fully brave, you have all the other virtues, and therefore have magnificence, and therefore have magically acquired lots of money and taste. This example shows that, since the virtues

---

[28] The spokesperson for Stoicism in Cicero, *On Moral Ends* (*De Finibus*) III 32. See Annas (1993: 403–5) for Stoic theses about virtue, skill, and success.   [29] *NE* 1111$^b$4–6.

[30] *NE* 1122$^b$26–9. Aristotle is scornful of 'silly' attempts to exercise the virtue without the correct amount of external goods.

[31] See Irwin (1990) and Annas (1996). Irwin's article brings out the tension very lucidly. My article tries to locate Aristotle's ambivalence on this issue within some larger issues in his ethics.

are mutually reciprocal, none of them can depend for their exercise on moral luck; hence magnificence, which does so depend, is not a real virtue. Aristotle fails to draw this conclusion because he is too respectful of conventional views which think of the activities of rich people, like magnificence, as virtues.

On this issue the Stoic view is much clearer and more defensible than Aristotle's. Of course it is often not up to me whether my action achieves the immediate target; but is it up to me whether I succeed or fail in acting virtuously—that is, with the right motives, from a developed disposition and with the right reasoning? If it is not, then it is not up to me whether or not I can become a moral person; and the Stoics are not alone in finding this an unacceptable position.[32]

It is sometimes urged that we feel more admiration for the act which, as well as being virtuous and thus succeeding in the overall aim, also actually does get its target; that this is the sense in which the act that fails here is morally lacking. But this seems not to be true. Take Socrates' defence speech, the *Apology*,[33] in which he uncompromisingly defends the values that he has lived by, and refuses to pander to the jury's values even at the risk of being executed for not doing so. Do we admire Socrates less because in fact he failed to swing the crucial thirty votes?[34] Do we think of him as a pathetic loser because he failed to express the degree of deference to the jury that would have secured his acquittal? Surely, rather than finding his action morally lacking, we admire him all the more for refusing on this occasion to compromise his values—if anything, his knowing refusal to do what was required to secure his immediate target makes us more convinced that he succeeded in achieving his overall aim of living a virtuous life.

It can be suggested[35] that we continue to praise the *agent*, but give the *act* less praise. This distinction can do work in some kinds of ethical theory, but in a virtue theory is problematic. For the suggestion here would be that we praise *Socrates* for being virtuous, living the life he does and having the character he does, but on this occasion we fault his action. Why, however, do we fault it? For being so uncompromising as to lead to failure in worldly terms. But this is

---

[32] There is, of course, a large debate here over the relative merits of the Aristotelian position versus the Platonic–Stoic one as wholes, and the entire issue of moral luck and its roles, if any, in ethics. What is relevant here is the point that the Stoics have much the stronger and more defensible position on virtue, skill, and success.

[33] I am here talking about Plato's version; Xenophon's *Apology* raises quite different issues.

[34] The jury consisted of 501 citizens; Socrates was condemned by a majority of 60.

[35] See Zagzebski (1996: 136–7, 1999b: 107, 2000a: 174).

to say that we fault it for being just the kind of act which this kind of person would do! To fault what Socrates did for its lack of success in achieving the target precisely is to fault Socrates for being the person he is, and for acting accordingly. Of course we can deplore the actual results of the action on this occasion. Virtue ethics can account as well as other theories for the fact that often we wish that the world had gone well and been improved in a way that did not happen.[36] We, as well as Socrates, can regret that the thirty votes went the wrong way; there is no reason to think that virtue ethics is more indifferent to the results of actions than other theories are. But the relevant point cannot be put, within a virtue ethics, by separating assessment of the agent from assessment of the act. In so far as it was a virtuous act, done by a virtuous person for reasons of virtue, it cannot be faulted from the virtue point of view. It is the jury we wish had been different, not Socrates' action.

It is also doubtless true that virtue is generally reliable in producing success in getting the immediate target. As Terence Irwin puts it:

> It is easy to see why, in favorable external conditions, virtuous people will have more objective success than other people will have. For they will have done all that can reasonably be expected of them; and if they do that, they will have tried to find all the relevant information that they could reasonably be expected to find, taken proper care, and so on. It is not surprising that action on these principles will often result in objective success.[37]

A virtue ethics approach can take all this into account; but when the virtuous person fails to get her target through no lack or fault of her own, a history of usual success here is not to the point. We have to choose which kind of success matters, and any virtue ethics in which the issue is clearly faced comes down on the side of success in achieving the overall aim, which is compatible with failure to achieve the immediate target.

How does this matter for the application of virtue theory to epistemology? As I mentioned, knowledge is a success term, and so a theory which defines knowledge in terms that feature virtue must take virtue to be a success term. Knowledge will, of course, be defined in terms of intellectual, not moral virtue, but for a theory which holds that these have the same structure or that the intellectual virtues are a subset of the moral ones this issue will be the

---

[36] Zagzebski (1996: 137) rightly stresses that 'morality is also in part a project of making the world a certain kind of place—a better place, we might say, or the kind of place good people want it to be.'  [37] Irwin (1990: 71).

same. So we must ask: what kind of success in intellectual virtue will be required for a workable definition of knowledge?

Here it looks as though the answer we get from ethics about moral virtue is the wrong one for epistemology. We surely do not want to define knowledge in terms of an overall disposition to succeed which is compatible with particular failures due to 'epistemic bad luck'. It would have the implication that I could have knowledge as a result of being intellectually virtuous, even though on this occasion, through no fault on my part, I am in fact wrong. A viable definition of knowledge in virtue terms must surely avoid this, and so must be aiming at success in achieving the immediate target. I have knowledge if I am right, say the truth (and also meet some further conditions). But, as we have just seen, this is not what a theory of ethical virtue demands; what is of most interest for it is success in achieving the overall goal. It looks as though the requirement for virtuous success in ethics—achieving the overall goal—is precisely what a virtue epistemology has to reject. Similarly, the requirement for virtuous success in epistemology—success in achieving the immediate target—is precisely what a virtue ethics has to reject.

It is because of this point, I think, that problems arise for attempts, such as Zagzebski's, to define knowledge as a state arising from acts of intellectual virtue. What is an act of virtue, in this theory? It is defined as follows:

An act is *an act of virtue A* if and only if it arises from the motivational component of A, is an act that persons with virtue A characteristically do in the circumstances, and is successful in bringing about the end of virtue A because of those features of the act.[38]

Zagzebski claims that 'the concept of an act of virtue is something we would want in an ethical theory anyway',[39] apart from its application in epistemology. This may be true, but what I am now concerned with is the issue of how well it fits a virtue-ethical theory in particular.

First, you do not need to have the virtue in question to perform an act of that virtue in the technical sense.[40] In the virtue ethics tradition, this would mean that the act is not an act of virtue at all; it is just an 'appropriate action'

---

[38] Zagzebski (1999b:108). The version at Zagzebski (1996: 248) adds a couple of complications which do not affect the present issue. Zagzebski (2000a: 175) gives a definition which includes the point, stated more generally, that 'the end of virtue A includes the ultimate end of virtue A as well as the proximate end.' But, as we have seen, this point is problematic.

[39] Zagzebski (2000a: 176).

[40] Zagzebski (2000b: 209), in response to Greco, is unwilling to require that an agent performing an act of virtue have the virtue in question on the grounds that this would make the grounds for having a virtue too weak.

such as anyone can perform when trying to become virtuous. An act performed by a non-virtuous person could not be a 'success', a *katorthoma*, and so could not be a starter as an act of virtue in any sense.

The impact of this, however, is somewhat softened by Zagzebski's requirement that to perform an act of virtue you need to have the virtuous motivation in question, at least the motivational component of it, although you are not virtuous. The idea is presumably that you have the virtuous motivation, but do not (yet) have it in a sufficiently robust, reliable, and integrated way to be virtuous. Hence you can perform an act of virtue in the technical sense, without having the virtue.

Here the problem is that this is the wrong story about virtuous motivation. For all versions of the virtue ethics tradition, the motivation of the non-virtuous person is *different* from that of the virtuous. Aristotle says that the virtuous person is motivated by the 'fine' (*kalon*) while those who are not yet virtuous are not—they are motivated by advantage or pleasure. Becoming virtuous is not a matter of already having a small amount of the right motivation which, so to speak, spreads and grows bigger; it is a matter of learning to *change*. Becoming virtuous is learning to *acquire* the right motivation; if you already had it, even on a small scale, becoming virtuous would be easier than it is. A virtue, in the virtue ethics tradition, is a complex matter, and coming to judge rightly and to be rightly motivated go in tandem, develop slowly and involve the person's becoming responsive to considerations which precisely do *not* resonate with the non-virtuous.[41] Someone without the virtue in question, then, cannot possess its motivational component. If an act can be performed by a person without the virtue in question, then it can be performed without being motivated in the way appropriate to that virtue. The technical notion of an act of virtue tries to combine the point that it can be performed by someone lacking the virtue in question with the point that it is nevertheless brought about by means of that virtue, since it is to be brought about by that virtue's motivational component. But these two points cannot be reconciled within a virtue theory, at least one in the virtue ethics tradition.

Second, an intellectually virtuous person, in this kind of virtue epistemology, may reason in a way that is virtuously motivated and follows the appropriate intellectually virtuous reasoning; but they may fail, because of epistemic bad luck, to get the right result, and in that case we do not have an act of virtue,

---

[41] For more detail, see Annas (1993: chs. 1–2) ('Making Sense of My Life as a Whole' and 'The Virtues').

in the technical sense. That is, a virtuous person may successfully achieve her overall aim, but fail to perform an act of virtue in the technical sense because she fails to achieve her immediate target. The person is virtuous, and acts virtuously, from virtuous motivation and reasoning. Yet the act fails to be an act of virtue in the technical sense because of facts that have nothing to do with virtue. This is surely a strange and undesirable result. Admittedly an act of virtue in the technical sense is a term of art; but surely it is strikingly odd that to succeed in performing one you need precisely what virtue does not supply.

This second problem makes it particularly clear that an act of virtue in the technical sense contains tensions which arise from the conflicting demands here of ethics and of epistemology. To serve in a definition of knowledge, the act of virtue in this sense must guarantee success in achieving its immediate target. But precisely this makes it utterly unlike acts of virtue within virtue ethics, for which the relevant kind of success is success in achieving the overall aim, even when the immediate target is unavoidably missed.

## IV

I have stressed two aspects of the structure of virtue, as that figures in the ancient virtue ethics tradition as a whole and not just in Aristotle. I have not here, of course, had the scope to develop them in a way adequate to make them appear appealing, still less compelling, though a fuller exposition would, I think, show that they both have individual advantages and form part of a powerful and attractive type of moral theory.

I have argued that if we take these two aspects of virtue—skill and success—seriously as they figure in the virtue ethics tradition, we find reason to doubt that virtue as it figures in that tradition can unproblematically be used as a basis for a traditional definition of knowledge. Tensions emerge between the structural requirements of virtue in the virtue ethics tradition and the structural requirements of virtue as it figures in virtue epistemology. In itself this is far from fatal to virtue epistemology, or to the project of defining knowledge in terms of intellectual virtue. It simply shows that virtue epistemology will have some problems as long as it works with the notion of moral virtue which comes from the ancient tradition of virtue ethics.

There are many possible responses to this. One might be to retain the goal of using virtue as the basis for a definition of knowledge, but to work with a notion of moral virtue which is explicitly a product of modern reflection, cutting ties to the ancient tradition. Some modern theorists of what they call 'virtue ethics' have already developed such notions.[42] Another version of this response might be to retain emphasis on moral virtue as it figures in the virtue ethics tradition, but to separate moral and intellectual virtue, treating them, for example, as distinct sub-kinds of skill, and to give an account of intellectual virtue which makes more of its differences from moral virtue. On either of these accounts, intellectual virtue as the basis for a definition of knowledge would not suffer from having to reflect the facts about success which make moral virtue in the ancient tradition problematic in application to epistemology.

Another response[43] might be to think of virtue not as the basis for a definition of knowledge guaranteeing success in achieving immediate targets, that is, appropriately achieved truths, but rather as the component of knowledge corresponding to justification or more broadly rationality, the analogue to the ethical overall aim of being virtuous. Intellectual virtue would on this view be what guarantees a global aim of being justified or having a rational approach, and would be thought of, like ancient moral virtue, as having succeeded if this overall aim were achieved, even if on occasion the immediate target were missed in circumstances of epistemic bad luck. This would mark a considerable divergence from traditional accounts of knowledge, for which the point of seeking knowledge is to guarantee the achievement of truth, in the right conditions. A radical approach might claim that these traditional accounts have proved unprofitable and that we would get more insight into knowledge by trying the above kind of intellectual virtue approach. A more moderate approach might claim that there is more to knowledge than traditional accounts have produced, and that we will gain from pursuing both approaches—aiming for the achievement of truths and aiming for overall rational justification, and taking them to be complementary rather than competing.

Intellectual virtue could on these approaches be seen to be of value in itself as constituting the epistemologically well-lived life. And it might also be of value as being our best strategy for success in achieving our immediate targets. The interest of this suggestion will of course depend on a number of

---

[42] Some of these theories have been consequentialist in inspiration (see n. 26), and it would be of interest to see whether their notions of virtue would function well in epistemology; using such notions would, however, undercut the spirit of recent virtue epistemology such as Zagzebski's. Most modern forms of virtue ethics, however, have harked back to the ancient tradition, particularly Aristotle.

[43] I owe my reflections on this to comments by Todd Stewart. I have also been helped by discussion and comments at the conference, particularly from Philip Quinn.

factors: whether intellectual virtue can have both these roles, and, if it cannot, whether it can have either, and which is of greater epistemological interest. Since, as I have stressed, epistemology is not my own field, I will leave these speculations to the epistemologists to criticize.

In the ancient, long, and rich virtue ethics tradition, moral virtue is not a more general concept which includes intellectual virtue, and the kind of success that virtue requires in ethics is radically different from the kind of success demanded by a notion of virtue which could serve to base knowledge. This shows only, of course, that in the virtue ethics tradition ethics did not serve as a basis for epistemology.[44] The idea that it might, and also the weaker idea that ethics might be illuminating for epistemology, are exciting ideas. I think, however, that they would be more defensible if we introduce, from the ancient virtue ethics tradition, complexities which make the application of ethics to epistemology more problematic and complicated, without reducing its interest, or its fruitfulness for further explorations.

[44] Ethics was a distinct 'part' of philosophy, while epistemology formed part of the 'logical' part.

# 2

# Intellectual Virtue: Emotions, Luck, and the Ancients

## Nancy Sherman and Heath White

> Cold theorems and maxims, dry and jejune disputes, lean syllogistical reasonings, could never yet of themselves beget the least glimpse of true heavenly light, the least sap of saving knowledge in any heart.
>
> (Cudworth, *Sermon* 92)

Part of the appeal of virtue epistemology is its shift in focus from the justification of individual beliefs to the overall status of the knower as a person of intellectual virtue. A belief is justified, for a virtue epistemologist, if it is believed in a way that an agent of intellectual virtue would believe it. Put this way, the idea parallels Aristotle's notion that an act is virtuous if the agent is in a certain condition when she does it (*Nicomachean Ethics* (henceforth *NE*) $1105^b1$). But the turn to virtue epistemology has underutilized some of the key resources of its analogue in virtue ethics. On the whole, virtue epistemologists have said too little about the role of affects[1] in intellectual virtue,[2] as well as the role of luck and external goods in achieving its objective of knowledge.

---

[1] Following Margaret Little we use 'affect' as a generic term to mean desires, emotions, and certain feelings of pleasure or pain that are like emotions, such as feelings of delight or taking pleasure in one's work, etc. Admittedly, the term is not ideal for it often connotes *felt* states, and we mean it to include unconscious emotions and motivations as well. But to speak just of emotions, as the first author has in past writings, excludes other kinds of affective states that are important to Aristotle's discussion and moral psychology, in general.

[2] Exceptions being Zagzebski (1996), Little (1995), Montmarquet (1992*a*) and (1987*a*).

Both themes are central to the ancient discussion of virtue and a matter of considerable debate between Aristotle and the Stoics. In the remarks that follow, we want to explore these themes in the hope of providing a more robust account of intellectual virtue.

In particular, we take up in section I the role emotions play in an Aristotelian account of moral virtue and what we might infer their role to be in the case of intellectual virtue. We also raise questions about the way we can be held responsible for our affects and how this bears on the notion of being responsible for beliefs. In section II, we explore the Stoics on affect and suggest that despite their inveighing against a life of emotional attachment, they still hold onto an element of affective sensitivity that has important implications for virtue epistemology. Finally, in section III we look at a tension between Aristotle and the Stoics on the role of success in happiness and discuss this in light of the role of extrinsic factors in the production of knowledge.

## I. Aristotle on intellectual virtues and affect

As is familiar to readers of the *Nicomachean Ethics*, Aristotle insists that moral virtue is concerned with right affect as well as right action. The virtuous person characteristically hits the mean with regard to both. So Aristotle states the formula: the virtuous person is one who feels 'both fear and confidence and appetite and anger and pity and in general pleasure and pain...at the right times, with reference to the right objects, towards the right people, with the right aim, and in the right way' (*NE* 1106$^b$15–22).[3] 'To stand well toward the affects', i.e. to have affects that are regulated and cultivated in the above ways, is characteristic of moral excellence. Aristotle tells us of the specific emotions concerned with specific virtues, e.g. courage with fear and confidence, and temperance with bodily appetite and pleasures and pains. And he insists that the habituation of affects will be as important to the project of moral education as the development of capacities of practical choice and reasoning.[4] But he doesn't specify the roles emotions like fear and confidence, delight and pity play in virtue such that they require regulation and cultivation. Still, we can fill in the lacunae along lines argued for elsewhere and here briefly summarized.[5]

---

[3] See also *NE* 1105$^b$26–8 for a list of emotions, and *Rhetoric* II for a fuller discussion of specific emotions and their analysis.     [4] See Sherman (1989: ch. 5).

[5] See Sherman (1997: ch. 2).

But first a note of caution: to include emotions in the constitution of intellectual virtue does not require that we think of emotions as always conscious states. Emotions can operate both consciously and unconsciously.[6] Indeed, to think of emotions as always conscious or as paradigmatically intense moments of affective peaks and troughs is to fail to appreciate the subtle flavour of most of our emotional life.

One primary role of emotions in the case of moral virtue is perceptual. Emotional sensitivities poise us to track moral saliences. If we have a sense of pity or compassion we are likely to notice suffering in a way that those who lack the sensitivity cannot. Moreover, as psychological research now suggests, we are likely to notice quickly and with a sense of urgency that may be requisite for action.[7] Generally put, emotions cue us to perceptual features of the external world—that there is something dangerous, or appealing, or worrisome, or threatening in our environment. To have emotions is to have antennae that track, not infallibly and not without proper tutoring, salience. In some cases, emotional cues will be self-disclosing, bringing to consciousness thoughts that we were not quite aware of before. For example, they may disclose that we are in fact bothered by how someone acted though we didn't think we were, that we are worried about a child's well-being, though we have been reassuring ourselves that all is okay, that a deadline is nagging at us, though it is vacation and we have resolved to put work aside. Without the trail of emotional feelings we might not access what is on our minds, and without their sensitivities we might not recognize the requirements situations impose on us.[8] We can bring these points back to Aristotle. Virtue requires a discernment of the particulars. Emotions as recognitional capacities or modes of attention are likely candidates to share the perceptual function of virtue.

Emotions are ways of noticing but they are also, simply put, ways of expressing ourselves. We undertake activities *with* certain manifest attitudes, which are sometimes in sync with our actions and choices, and sometimes in conflict with them. So we show delight, resentment, passion, annoyance, coolness, congeniality, interest, etc. The emotions convey to others what we care about and, to some extent, who we are. They convey the state of mind from which we perform an action. On an Aristotelian view, virtue requires

---

[6] See Freud (1926) on unconscious signal anxiety and its function as an early warning alarm system that allows us to defend against perceived danger.     [7] Oatley (1992).

[8] So McDowell (1979: 124) says virtue is 'an ability to recognize requirements which situations impose on one's behavior'. Our claim is that emotions help constitute these recognitional capacities.

that actions and overall bearing have the right emotional tone. How we comport ourselves emotionally matters morally.

Emotions are modes of attention and expression, but they are also modes of motivation. Thus, we often act 'from' or 'out of' an emotion. In a common-sense way, emotions seem to give us the 'oomph' or impulse that propels many actions. As Aristotle puts it in the *Rhetoric* II, emotions are beliefs, *phantasiai*, or construals about something, accompanied by pleasure and pain, and typically involving a desire to act. Of course, emotional motivations can be rash and impetuous, as in the case of a person who, hot with anger, desires to take immediate revenge. But the Aristotelian claim is that properly habituated emotional propensities will involve motivations to act[9] that are endorsed by later deliberation and reflection.

Much of the story about the role of emotions in moral virtue has become familiar territory. Less charted is how emotions, and affects, in general, figure in intellectual virtue. Before we take this up, however, let's quickly review some textual background. At the end of *NE* I Aristotle divides the psyche into rational and non-rational parts to which correspond excellences of intellect (practical and theoretical) and of character (i.e. moral virtues). Aristotle explicitly tells us that the non-rational part partakes of the rational in so far as the affects of the non-rational part can be brought under reason's sway (and we might add, following the *Rhetoric*, in so far as emotions are themselves partially cognitive states).[10] Left unstated is how the excellences of the rational part might themselves depend on the affects of the non-rational part. Aristotle makes explicit later that practical wisdom will involve deliberative desire and will itself be a part of the full constitution of each moral virtue.[11] But there is little anticipation here of the point that excellences of the theoretical or scientific intellect might also involve affective elements.

Apart from his account of deliberative choice in Book III, Aristotle postpones further discussion of the intellectual virtues until Book VI. There he offers a brief account of the virtues of practical and theoretical intellect. Under the first fall craft (*technē*), practical wisdom (*phronēsis*), judgement (*gnōmē*) and equity (*suggnōmē*); under the second, scientific understanding (*epistēmē*) involving inductive and deductive reasoning about necessary truths, comprehension

---

[9] Zagzebski's (1996) Aristotelian-inspired account of intellectual virtue capitalizes on this aspect of emotions. Thus, on her view, the emotional element of virtue is an action-directing motive. Emotional dispositions are the motivational component of virtue.

[10] Even more strongly, the virtues of the non-rational part are character states that themselves involve practical wisdom.     [11] *NE* 1113$^a$10 ff.; 1144$^b$18 ff.

(*nous*) involving a grasp of first principles, and contemplative wisdom (*sophia*), involving a combination of scientific understanding and comprehension. The *ergon* or function of these latter, in virtue of which they are excellences, is to grasp the truth.[12] They are concerned with 'affirmation and negation'. A 'good state' of intellect is one that arrives at the truth; a 'bad state' leads to falsehood or error.[13] Aristotle makes no mention of infallibility or even of the constancy or reliability of intellectual virtue to deliver the truth.

The list is fairly limited. As Linda Zagzebski notes, apart from the notions of calculative or deliberative reason, there is no specific discussion of the intellectual virtues of assessing contingent truths.[14] Aristotle's own focus within the theoretical sphere is on the unchanging and what cannot be otherwise. Moreover, Aristotle's list excludes mention of natural faculties (good memory or good eyesight) and cognitive processes that reliabilists tend to point to as intellectual virtues.[15] Nor does he mention character traits other contemporary virtue epistemologists point to as involved in the process of acquiring justified beliefs, such as fair-mindedness, perseverance, curiosity, impartiality before the evidence, conscientiousness, and autonomous judgement; nor intellectual forms of moral virtues, such as the courage of one's convictions or humility before the truth.[16] And, also, there is silence about the emotional dispositions we think of as typically associated with intellectual virtue, such as a passion for the truth, a delight in learning, excitement in discovery, pride in one's accomplishments, respect for good argument, repugnance at intellectual dishonesty, and in the case of empirical science, surprise at the disconfirmation of one's theory and joy at its verification.[17] Rather than regarding intellectual excellences as the competencies or traits or affects by which we are best positioned to pursue the truth, he views them as states that mark an intellectual grasp of the truth, in the sense of having arrived at scientific understanding, or wisdom of various sorts, or a grasp of foundational first principles. The emphasis on

---

[12] *NE* 1139$^a$29; 1139$^b$12.

[13] *NE* 1139$^a$22. Dancy (1995) raises the question of how reliabilist a gloss this definition demands. On the face of it, to say, as Aristotle does, that these virtues have truth as their function does seem another way of saying their end is to grasp the truth. Dancy, however, suggests that we might simply think of them as 'related' to the truth in a way that doesn't demand consequentialism and that allows for the inclusion of other kinds of intellectual virtues that are not at all related to bringing about the truth. The suggestion is appealing, though, as he himself acknowledges, it doesn't seem to be Aristotle's.

[14] Zagzebski (1996: 216).

[15] See Sosa (1991: ch. 8).

[16] Zagzebski (1996), Montmarquet (1987*a*), (1992*a*), (1992*b*), Dancy (1995).

[17] See I. Scheffler (1982), Polanyi (1958), Wood (1998).

achievement underscores a basic Aristotelian point about virtue, namely, that virtue is a cultivated and acquired state. Intellectual excellences will depend on natural powers, faculties, and receptivities as moral virtue does. But full virtue of either sort is never just a disposition or capacity;[18] it is a way of 'standing toward' dispositions and faculties that involve conscious shaping, regulation, and valuing as component parts in living well.

Aristotle claims that the acquisition of moral and intellectual virtues will differ in that the former are habituated, the latter acquired more didactically through teaching and study. The point is overdrawn.[19] Intellectual virtue will itself involve the example following and habituation of moral virtue: inspiration by role models will be important as will be learning through critical practice the habits of careful reasoning, methodical argument, and assessment of data. We study modes of reasoning and research, but we also practise them and model them.

We are now in a position to return to our primary question of how, despite Aristotle's silence, affect might figure in an Aristotelian account of intellectual virtue. First, are there supplemental texts we might draw on to fill out the picture? Second, can we apply his remarks about the affective components of moral virtue to those of intellectual virtue without damage to his overall view?

With respect to the first question, a few important texts help fill the lacunae. The *Metaphysics* famously opens with a statement of the delight humans take in using their discriminatory skills and suggests something of a natural human propensity for curiosity: 'All humans by nature desire to know. An indication of this is the delight we take in our senses; for even apart from their usefulness they are loved for themselves' ($980^a22$ ff.) In *NE* X. 3 Aristotle goes further, suggesting that even if we received no particular pleasure from exercising our discriminatory powers, the best life is still one in which those powers are cultivated and exercised: 'There are many things we would be keen about (*spoudēn poiēsaimeth'an*) even if they brought no pleasure, e.g., seeing, remembering, knowing, possessing the excellences' ($1174^a4$–6). And again: 'No one would choose to live with the intellect of a child throughout his life, however much he were to be pleased at the things that children are pleased at' ($1174^a1$–3). The suggestion, then, is that humans find intrinsic value in the activity of intellectual and sensory discrimination. In the best life, individuals take an interest in and

---

[18] *NE* II. 1; II. 6. As Aristotle puts it, it is a *hexis* (character state), not a *dunamis* (faculty).
[19] Zagzebski (1996) appreciates this. See Sherman (1989: ch. 5), which argues for an understanding of habituation that is more cognitive and instruction-based than our own notion of forming habits implies.

are committed to (*spoudēn*) the exercise and cultivation of these capacities. Here, interestingly, we do have mention of the more fundamental cognitive and sensory competencies as valued in the intellectual life in the way we value virtues. Though Aristotle has reason not to call them virtues, as we discussed above, he suggests that they are to be developed as part of the life of a good knower.

Aristotle's remarks on pleasure in Book X add to the picture. An activity performed in the best way and in optimal circumstances yields pleasure specific to and supervenient upon that activity. As Aristotle puts it, the pleasure completes and intensifies the activity: 'An activity is intensified by its proper pleasure, since each class of things is better judged of and brought to precision by those who engage in the activity with pleasure' ($1175^a30$). Moreover, to engage in an activity in a way that produces pleasure is to be focused, undistracted by competing activities, motivated to continue and pursue the activity more intensely. 'That is why when we enjoy anything very much we do not throw ourselves into anything else' ($1175^b9-11$).

The remarks are general but their application to intellectual activity is clear. To take delight in working out an argument, to find, on balance, more pleasure than pain in a day of writing, to be thrilled with the incremental discoveries of genome research is to be motivated to continue to invest one's energies and, in certain kinds of cases, to seek higher and more challenging levels of engagement.[20] Moreover, to be engaged in a way that yields pleasure is typically to be alive to one's work, alert to its challenges, attentive to its demands. In this sense, pleasure or delight exhibits the motivational and attentional roles of emotion, in general.

However, the pleasure supervenient on intellectual activity is, of course, only one small piece of an account of the affective components of intellectual virtue. Some points we can easily fill in from Aristotle's general positions. For example, it takes little to show Aristotle's commitment to the social nature of intellectual life and, correspondingly, to the social emotions of friendliness, mutuality, cooperativeness, perhaps trust and the reliance on mutual interest, requisite for discourse and understanding in general. Suggestive here are his books on friendship and his revealing remark in Book X that even leisurely contemplation, removed from the circles of social life, is most productive and continuous when it is pursued with others.[21] Indeed, one could easily interpret

---

[20] The psychological principle is what Rawls aptly called the Aristotelian principle.
[21] See *NE* $1175^a35$. Also, Sherman (1997: ch. 5).

his more general remarks that the best kind of life is one lived in the company of critical and reflective partners as a comment about the best kind of intellectual life.

But other remarks about the emotional quality of our lives as knowers are less forthcoming. That our lives as excellent knowers are emotionally laden,[22] filled with surprise and disappointment, competitive spirit and pride, eagerness and a degree of impatience, a zeal for truth and repugnance at deception, a healthy love of self and a zest for reaching what is humanly knowable is not something Aristotle hammers home, except in the few texts mentioned. Perhaps this absence of emotional talk in the intellectual sphere has to do with thinking of moral virtue as whipping the non-rational, affective (and sometimes animal) side of the self into shape in a way that Aristotle doesn't think has application when we are grasping for the truth (especially the lofty truth of what is unchanging), rather than our happiness. But clearly many of the emotions we experience as pursuers of the good, regarding having and losing, and what we wish for ourselves and others, and how aggressive or passive we are in pursuing our goals will also have their day as we apply ourselves as knowers.[23]

Still, Aristotle doesn't make the point. But would it misrepresent his view to make the point for him—to say, loosely speaking, that intellectual excellence is a way of comporting oneself well (i.e. in a way conducive to the function of grasping the truth) both with respect to beliefs *and* emotions? As such, to return to the familiar formula, intellectual excellence, like moral excellence, would require, among other things, that emotions be expressed in the right way, at the right time, towards the right persons, and so forth. At first glance, the point might seem strained. Take the case of a scientist on the verge of making an important breakthrough, whose diffidence holds him back from taking the last critical step. The step is within his reach, but he resists it because of not wanting to be in the limelight, or perhaps not wanting to discredit reigning authorities to whom he feels deferential. Our first reaction might be to fault him more for his overall moral character than for his intellectual character, qua scientist. He is a reasonable bench scientist, we might say; after all, he's careful, conscientious, judicious in assessing data and in subjecting his hypotheses to rigorous attempts at refutation. His problem is just that he is

---

[22] Aristotle of course makes the points with respect to practical wisdom.
[23] Perhaps some of Freud's remarks about transference have application here.

diffident. And this is more a flaw in his general character than in how he handles research.

But this misses the very point of virtue epistemology's reorientation. To focus on the criteria of a good knower rather than on knowledge is to open the door to new kinds of considerations, relevant to what it means to be in a position to know. If diffidence or caution stands in the way of exploring new frontiers, of asking bold questions, of submitting one's work to public scrutiny or acclaim, then it is an emotional defect in a knower. Similarly, if love of self turns into a grandiosity that makes listening to competing viewpoints difficult, if it squashes collaborative effort and makes teamwork a matter of hierarchical command, then such narcissism is, again, an emotional defect in a knower. Put this way, to require of the knower that she hit the mean with respect to emotions seems itself on the mark. Similar points can be made about emotional attitudes we typically take to be unequivocally conducive to the truth. Even a passion for the truth can lead one to distort evidence, to jump to conclusions, to be overly confident in a way that leads to dogmatism.[24] So too a zeal to know can lead to an impatience that cuts short discourse or frustrates the slow and methodical study often necessary for serious inquiry.[25] Thus, even putatively positive emotions crucial to the life of a knower can become excessive and counterproductive. They too may require the modulation and self-reflection requisite for apt or 'medial' emotions. The general point is that the Aristotelian claim that virtue is characterized by apt emotions holds in the intellectual sphere as well. Granted, hitting the mean with regard to emotions will be an individual matter, relative to external and internal circumstances, e.g. in the case of fear, how difficult the objective challenges are and whether one naturally leans towards bravado or caution. But this is no different from assessment in the case of moral virtue.

Still there may be a general worry, which we haven't yet addressed, in assigning emotions a central role in intellectual virtue. The worry is that it diminishes our responsibility as epistemic agents.[26] For emotions often seem to 'happen' to us, to be passive states we suffer. We can't easily start or stop emotions 'on a dime' as we think we can many actions. If, as we have been

---

[24] See Montmarquet (1987*a*).

[25] See Zagzebski (1996: 146–8) where she claims that a distinction between moral and intellectual virtue cannot rest on the notion that the former is involved in 'handling feelings' but the latter is not.

[26] But perhaps we might say no more so than in holding biological powers and cognitive processes to be intellectual virtues.

arguing, emotional character is an important part of intellectual character, then the non-voluntary quality of emotions might seem to indicate that our intellectual character is non-voluntary too. And this, in turn, might seem to remove responsibility for belief from the epistemic agent. Even if we concede that emotions are not fully voluntary, are the beliefs they influence outside the reach of our responsibility? With Aristotle, we suggest no.

On an Aristotelian view, responsibility for emotions, in general, will be indirect in so far as emotional habits follow from actions. In his lingo, we become by doing. We make ourselves into certain kinds of emotional creatures, not whole cloth, but by mediating our constitutions and natural receptivities. The idea that we are primarily passive with respect to our emotions is simply neither Aristotle's view nor that of contemporary developmental psychology. As young children we work on ways to self-soothe, ways to regulate our emotions through the sublimation of language, ways to play and pretend that help us come to know and experiment with our feelings. Even the youngest of infants, in early relationships with parents, struggle to learn ways to internalize images of parents and their positive feelings as ways of managing their own more destructive and fragmenting negative feelings. They learn ways of sustaining their good feelings, and ways of sharing them as parts of mutual and reciprocal games with parents. As adults, we shape our emotions in conscious ways, through reflection and self-study, through decisions to tweak this or watch out for that, through resolutions and self-monitoring. Friendships, as well as more explicitly therapeutic contexts, become places in which we assess not just what we have done, but what we feel, and the kinds of situations that make us happy or sad, proud or shameful, guilty or anxious. Revising the thoughts and beliefs that constitute our emotions are among the ways we revise emotions themselves. The point is an Aristotelian one, implicit in his claims about the cognitive core of emotion in the *Rhetoric*. It is a point that the Stoics develop more robustly, as they go on to define emotions as thoroughgoingly cognitive.

The general point has application in the epistemological arena. Emotional habits that affect one's effectiveness as a knower needn't be best construed as fixed traits. Diffidence, narcissism, or impatience to reach the truth may be entrenched, but that is not the same as unbudgeable.

Of course, *wanting to change* emotional habits is another story, and the social pressure to do so yet a further factor. Emotional habits may not change for the better simply because we often lack a social practice, outside circles of intimacy, of passing judgement on others' emotional characters. Even if we routinely judge others' intellectual characters, we seem a tad more guarded about assessing emotional traits that we view as epistemic boons or handicaps. So we openly talk about people's raw smartness or cleverness, their diligence or laziness, their conscientiousness or sloppiness. But do we freely talk about their zeal or cautiousness, their impetuousness or diffidence, their passion or lack of engagement? We think less so, and it probably has to do with the fact that we think that we are overstepping etiquette boundaries when we engage in these kinds of assessments. Moreover, we think these factors have less to do with intellectual output than more narrowly construed aspects of intellect.

However, we should not underestimate the emotional factors. How we approach our work—that is, with what emotional palette and appetite—has much to do with what we produce. Granted, we all have different emotional styles by which we conduct ourselves as learners and knowers. But it seems fair to say that some are more effective than others. Grandiosity is not a big win in a collaborative effort, nor timidity in most efforts that require taking on challenges and exploring new terrain.

In suggesting that emotions are constitutive of character, both moral and, as we have urged, intellectual, Aristotle implies that assessments of *emotional* character ought to be a part of general character appraisal. Moreover, the Aristotelian claim is that we can do things, through effort, study, discipline, and care, to shape our emotional lives, whether within the epistemic or ethical arena. On an Aristotelian reading, to include the emotions in a conception of intellectual virtue does not in an obvious way compromise our responsibility as epistemic agents.

## II. Stoic virtue and the emotions

The Stoics represent a historical development of Aristotelian ideas of virtue, and it will be worthwhile to examine what they have to say about the emotional aspect of intellectual character. At first, such an examination seems unpromising—after all, the Stoics advocate a life of *apatheia*, or freedom from the passions, precisely because, on their view, the emotions represent judgements that are mistaken, and once made, hard to let go of. We might think of the Stoic sage as the master of 'cold'—that is, unemotional—cognition. However, a closer examination of selected Stoic texts suggest that the Stoics do not fully renounce the emotions or the informational function they can serve. They recognize that interest and attention, that is, the recording of salience in general, are often emotionally processed, and that 'fine' or 'well-reasoned' versions of these capacities are worth cultivating. Even the sage has reason to cultivate these sensitivities as a part of the cultivation of wisdom.

Before going into this account, however, it is important to understand the Stoic position on the emotions more generally and its relation to their doctrine of indifferents. The Stoics view emotions as judgments (or beliefs) in so far as they are voluntary assents to appearances regarding goods and evils. Positive emotions, such as joy and desire, are directed at the appearance of a past, present, or future good; negative emotions, fear and distress, are directed at evils, again in the past, present, or future. All emotions are subspecies of these four.[27] Though emotions are cognitive on the Stoic view, they are nonetheless experienced with a kind of flutter or contraction of the mind, a cognitive arousal, that triggers *hormai*, or impulses to act on an emotion. Some accounts add that the judgement constitutive of an emotion is 'fresh' (*prosphaton*) or as the Latins put it, 'green', to capture the idea of immediacy and urgency of emotional experience.[28]

Now the emotions are judgements, but mistaken judgements. Put simply, they misappraise what is genuinely good and evil. Paradigmatically, they are judgements that express attachment to external items, such as health, wealth, fame, and friends, in ways that suggest those items matter to one's happiness. So to fear is to care about threats to one's health or property, to pity is to view undeserved loss as evils that diminish a person's well being, to love is to invest in something outside oneself which one cannot fully control. The Stoic claim is that while these items are natural advantages to be preferred (*elekton, seligendum*: *Fin*. III. 22), they are not genuine goods or to be chosen as constitutive of happiness. For genuine happiness, only virtue matters. The other advantages are 'indifferents'.[29] 'To prefer' rather than 'to choose' signals the demoted status. Thus a Stoic like Chrysippus demands a therapy to cure the soul of its emotional ills. *Apatheia* becomes a way of ridding the soul of false appraisals and attachments.

Yet there are significant texts that suggest Stoic education of the soul does not aim fully to root out the passions. And the claim is not just that some emotional residue is inevitable, but that emotional sensitivity can be a good thing. For the sage, no less than the plebeian, needs to be alerted to what is

---

[27] Stobaeus 2. 88, 8–90, 6 = L and S 65A.  [28] Andronicus, *On Passions* I = L and S 65B.
[29] Diogenes Laertius 7. 101–3 = L and S 58A. Stobaeus 2. 79, 18–80–13; 82, 20–1 = L and S 58C.

salient in his environment, to what is threatening or aberrant, to what is attractive or novel.

The doctrine of *eupatheiai* provides a way to understand how the Stoics could endorse emotions as a central part of virtuous intellectual character. The Stoics hold the view that there are good affective states that are themselves complete and well-reasoned responses to the external world. As Diogenes Laertius reports, the Stoics

> say that there are three good feelings (*eupatheiai*): joy (*charan*), watchfulness (*eulabeian*), wishing (*boulêsin*). Joy, they say, is the opposite of pleasure, consisting in well-reasoned swelling; and watchfulness is the opposite of fear, consisting in well-reasoned shrinking. For the wise man will not be afraid at all, but he will be watchful. They say that wishing is the opposite of appetite, consisting in well-reasoned stretching. Just as certain passions fall under the primary ones, so too with the primary good feelings. Under wishing: kindness, generosity, warmth, affection. Under watchfulness: respect, cleanliness. Under joy: delight, sociability, cheerfulness.[30]

The *eupatheiai* are emotional dispositions to make judgements that are not mistaken, like ordinary emotions, but accurate appraisals of what is truly good and evil. The sage, then, will have the *eupatheiai*—well-reasoned affective responses to the world—as part of his intellectual character.

There is a second doctrine, however, which is also important for understanding the Stoic's attitude to the role of emotions in intellectual virtue. Emotional preludes, or proto-emotions (*proludentia*), are preliminary tendencies to feel the early stages of an emotion. At such moments, the sage is involuntarily affected by the (false) appearances of external goods as real goods and evils, though he refrains from giving voluntary assent. That is, he resists being fully taken in by the appearance. In his analysis of the sequential stages of anger, Seneca suggests the possibility:

> Anger is undoubtedly set in motion by an appearance received of a wrong. But does it follow immediately on the appearance itself and break out without involvement of the mind? Or is some assent by the mind required for it to be set in motion? Our view is that it undertakes nothing on its own, but only with the mind's approval.

Seneca goes on to say that although the sage may involuntarily suffer 'that first mental jolt which affects us when we think ourselves wronged', he withholds voluntary assent from the appearance of injury. Indeed, he suggests that

---

[30] Diogenes Laertius 7. 116 = L and S 65F.

the sage resists the full-fledged emotion on many occasions. So he says, a prelude to anger

> steals upon us even while we are watching a performance on stage or reading of things that happened long ago. We have often a sense of being angry with Clodius as he drives Cicero into exile or with Antony as he kills him. Who remains unprovoked by the arms which Marius took up or by Sulla's proscriptions?... But these are not cases of anger, any more than it is grief which makes us frown at the sight of a shipwreck on stage or fear that runs through the reader's mind as Hannibal blockades the walls after the battle of Cannae... They are not emotions, but the preliminaries, the preludes (*proludentia*) to emotions... Thus, it is that even the bravest man often turns pale as he puts on his armour, that the knees of even the fiercest soldier tremble a little as the signal is given for battle.[31]

Thus, even the sage can be taken in by the appearances, manifest in a tremble of the knee or a pallor that falls on his face as he prepares for deadly battle. But it is important to be clear just what appearances the sage is reacting to. In so far as he *withholds* consent (*sunkatathesis*) to appearance, the appearances are presumably untutored appearances of good and evil, that is, views of the external goods as real benefits or harms to one's happiness. Thus, in the above cases, there is a gap between how things appear and how the sage knows they ought to be critically appraised. Even for the sage, the old ways of seeing things can insinuate themselves. At such times, virtue is only fortitude, a point Kant will exploit. For the Stoics, fortitude involves, among other things, active resistance to the suggestibility of certain impressions.[32]

From the point of view of a thoroughgoing Stoicism, we might think this a rather disappointing response. For it concedes that the sage cannot fully retool his perceptions of the world. If, as Aristotle says, 'the discrimination rests in perception', and if we are in some sense 'responsible for how things

---

[31] *De Ira*, II. 1–3 in Cooper and Procopé (1995). We have changed 'impression' to 'appearance'.

[32] The view is confirmed by Epictetus. He takes up the question of how a true sage can turn pale at the prospect of a shipwreck. He answers: 'Even the mind of a sage must necessarily be disturbed, must shrink and feel alarm, not from a preconceived idea of any danger, but from certain swift and unexpected attacks which overthrow the power of the mind and reason... They say that there is this difference between the mind of a foolish man and that of a wise man, that the foolish man thinks that such visions are in fact as dreadful and terrifying as they appear at the original impact of them on his mind, and by his assent he approves of such ideas as if they were rightly to be feared... But the wise man, after being affected for a short time and slightly in his colour and expression, does not assent, but retains the steadfastness and strength of the opinion which he has always had about visions of this kind, namely that they are in no wise to be feared but excite terror by a false appearance and vain alarms' (Rolfe 1927: XIX. 1. 17–18).

appear to us', then the above sorts of concessions suggest that the training of the emotions for virtue can only go so far. Transformation of the perceptual (or 'appearance') component of emotions will often lag behind the sage's more cognitive appraisals; in such cases, the sage must stand his ground through vigilant control and regulation. He must not succumb to first impressions or to the arousals and impulses they inspire. Even the sage must at times settle for a life of only continence.

But if at times, for the Stoic sage, fortitude is the only virtue, because of the incorrigibility of her proto-emotional responses, other Stoic epistemic virtues can make sure that fortitude at least is exercised. Consider 'non-precipitancy' and 'uncarelessness', characterized as virtues in the dialectical sphere.[33] Non-precipitancy (*aproptōsian*) is 'a disposition not to assent in advance of cognition'. One who is non-precipitate 'keeps control over his assents'.[34] Essentially, it is the 'science of when one should and not assent'.[35] Uncarelessness (*aneikaiotēta*) is a 'strong rational principle' involved in not 'giving in to what is merely plausible'.[36] The sage, then, whether engaged in dialectical argument or in the assessment of appearances relevant to the emotions, may entertain and be attracted by certain impressions, and even physiologically respond to them. Through the cultivation of virtues such as the above ones, however, he refrains from full assent.

As Seneca paints the picture with respect to the emotions, the sage engages in a two-step sequence—he is initially taken in by appearances, but then shows control in not actualizing the full emotional response. Still, to say the sage is 'taken in by the appearances' puts it somewhat misleadingly. For after all, the sage must remain alive to things that are important for his survival, namely the indifferents. It is just that he can't assent to them as proper goods or evils. The crucial difference between the sage and the plebeian is that the sage knows how to calibrate salience: he knows that not everything that is salient, or even important, in fact contributes to his happiness. He knows how to be guided by the emotions without being seduced by them.

If we integrate the earlier remarks about *eupatheia* with the discussion of emotional preludes, then we get what is probably a fairly developmentally

---

[33] Note that, on the Stoic view, dialectical argument is not primarily the art of persuasion, but the art of speaking what is 'true and fitting', and as such, is the proper profession only of the sage (Alexander, *On Aristotle's Topics* I. 89–14 = L and S 31D).

[34] Anonymous Stoic treatise (Herculaneum papyrus 1020 col. 4. col. 1) = L and S 41D.

[35] Diogenes Laertius 7. 46–8 = L and S 31B.

[36] Ibid. For further suggestive remarks, see Plutarch *On Stoic Self-contradictions* 1047A–B = L and S 31H. See Epictetus, *Discourses* 1. 7. 2–5, 10 = L and S 31R.

accurate picture: the sage who emerges is one who still, on occasion, has gut responses he must catch himself from fully indulging. (Perhaps they represent his blindspots or points of vulnerability. Perhaps they represent moments of regression that are part of the ebb and flow of human emotional life.) But in addition, he has moments when he sees and feels things immediately in a way that gets their valuation right. Thus, transformed emotional sensitivities will exist alongside more regressive emotional tendencies, which need to be kept in check by watchful observation. The upshot is that even a sage may, at times, be ambivalent, oscillating between appearances of, say, a shipwreck as really evil but also as merely dispreferred. More generally, even the sage must retain and cultivate emotional sensitivity to be able to navigate in the world. The epistemic and social advantages of living with the emotions appear to be still available to the sage, even at the end of an education that drastically reduces emotional vulnerability.

The point has application to the conduct of intellectual life, though the Stoics do not make it explicitly.[37] To investigate the world, to engage in dialectical argument with others, to understand theoretically and practically requires a responsiveness to emotional cues and emotionally conveyed information; cold cognition will simply not allow proper cognitive contact. However, it may be that the emotional aspects of cognition are never perfect. To counter this necessary imperfection, however, what are needed are not fewer affective dispositions but more. Indeed, to care about truth and certainty, in Stoic terms, to be non-rash and non-careless in the giving and withholding of assent to the appearances, are themselves emotional attitudes. The affective component of intellectual virtue, so important on an Aristotelian understanding of intellectual character, survives even a Stoic revision.

## III. Luck and knowledge

The ancient discussion of the role of emotions in virtue is a resource for contemporary virtue epistemology. But so too is the ancient debate about the role of luck and external goods in happiness. In what follows we want to suggest

---

[37] See the suggestive remarks about Chrysippus and the emotional tenor of dialectic in Plutarch, *On Stoic Self-contradictions* 1047A–B = L and S 31H. 'Furthermore, in Book 1 he [Chrysippus] has even written the following: "I think one should cultivate not just a frank and unaffected order but also, apart from the speech, the appropriate kinds of delivery in relation to the fitting tones of voice, facial expressions and gestures."'

that there is a revealing lack of parallelism in common-sense views about the luck requisite for happiness and the luck requisite for knowledge. By reflecting on a tension in Aristotle addressed by the Stoics, implications for the epistemological realm will emerge.

Aristotle's task in the *Nicomachean Ethics* is to specify the constituents of happiness. On the one hand, he is pulled by the Socratic view that happiness must reflect, above all else, our 'study and care'. It is the result of 'learning and training'. As he puts it, 'to enlist to chance what is greatest and most noble would be a defective arrangement'.[38] The consequence is that happiness will be predominantly constituted by virtue, or excellence, by the cultivation of our human nature in a way that involves the active exercise of our reason and is under our own control. On the other hand, Aristotle never fully rejects the archaic view, characterized by the Homeric heroes, that happiness is *eudaimonia* in a literal sense, having a good daimon or lucky charm. It cannot be devoid of a certain degree of unguaranteed success, prosperity, and fruition. Thus, on his view, external goods and luck find their way into a complete conception of happiness, both as instrumental means to the exercise of virtue and in some cases (as in having good children or good friends), as intrinsically valued goods in their own right, the lack of which would mar happiness.[39]

There are a few points to notice. First, on the Aristotelian view happiness, as the *telos* of moral virtue, is not antecedently specified. Correlatively, while virtue is conducive to happiness, it is not so as a means, but as a part or constituent that is itself intrinsically valuable. Thus his view of virtue is teleological—it has as its end the human good. But it is not consequentialist or externalist. There is no independently specified external end to which virtue conduces. Rather, happiness or the human good is something we dialectically set out to specify as reflective agents living a meaningful life. The *Nicomachean Ethics* is an example of that pursuit. This is not to suggest that the concept of happiness is fully open-ended. Aristotle takes it as a given that it will involve the flowering (or excellence) of our peculiarly human nature and in moderation, resources outside our nature—in the form of friendships, political structures, and goods, etc.—that allow for achieving our goals and in general enhance our well-being.

Second, while things outside our control will have a role in happiness, Aristotle struggles to minimize their impact. He agrees with common sense

---

[38] *NE* 1099$^b$10–25.
[39] *NE* I. 8–12, Irwin (1985*b*), Cooper (1985), Nussbaum (1986: chs. 11–12), Annas (1993: 364–84).

that happiness is a kind of prosperity, a kind of fruition or flourishing. And this typically involves luck. But happiness can't be only a matter of luck, or be snatched from someone by some slight piece of misfortune.[40] 'Small pieces of good fortune or of its opposite clearly do not weigh down the scales of life one way or the other, but a multitude of great events if they turn out well will make life more happy..., while if they turn out ill they crush and maim happiness.'[41] Thus while happiness is vulnerable to what is outside one's dominion, those external influences must be great in order to make a difference.

The Stoics, as we have seen, advance the Socratic half of Aristotle's picture in the extreme. Virtue, as the excellent use of our divine reason, is exhaustively constitutive of happiness. The indifferents that are according to nature—prosperity and flourishing, external goods of various kinds—are important to have, and virtue is a matter of wise selection of them. But they are not themselves constituents of happiness. Happiness resides in the life of virtue alone, and virtue is a matter of one's own effort. On the Stoic picture, happiness is not a matter of luck at all.

Now however counter-intuitive the Stoic position initially seems, there is still something terribly attractive about it. We do believe, with good reason, that while we suffer loss, we can (often) learn ways to survive loss that are healthy and not self-destructive; that while we become emotionally attached to ideas and people and causes, we can learn ways to detach, to get unstuck when and if it becomes reasonable. We think that there are internal victories in performing a skill flawlessly, or doing our duty unimpeachably, even when external victories have been snatched from us or are out of reach; that the yardstick for full success in certain parts of life is just our doing them well.[42] We may feel the tension Aristotle expresses—that this is not the whole of happiness—that how we are viewed by others, that whether our friends survive or regimes we live under are politically conducive to our welfare, that all this matters too; that earthquakes and wars, prisoner camps and inhuman treatment can reverse our fortunes and rob us of dignity in the matter of seconds. But still, even when we think of the worst, we often think we have some say in our happiness, that how we adapt and cope is still ours to contribute. Exhortations of Epictetus' type are not just edifying. We think they are true. We think we can often act well the part we are given, and that this is enough for happiness.

---

[40] *NE* 1100$^a$9–10.  [41] *NE* 1100$^b$22–25.

[42] This calls to mind the Stoic distinction between stochastic and non-stochastic virtues. On this, see Irwin (1998: 164–8) and Inwood (1986).

But the parallel point in virtue epistemology seems less feasible. The Stoics indeed try to make the parallel. They hold that cognitive skills can be honed in the right way as sufficient for the truth, that if we are non-careless and non-precipitous, non-casual and non-random in our assent to appearances, we can be infallible in our grasp of the truth.[43] So just as the sage's moral virtue is sufficient for his happiness, so too his epistemic virtue is sufficient for the truth. He will be free of error and infallibly avoid assent to mistaken appearances; he will be impervious to bad reasoning and unreliable sources; he will always have the internal powers and external place in history to access the truth perfectly.

Modern and contemporary epistemologists have felt the temptation of a Stoic view of knowledge and truth. Descartes, for instance, thought that attention to the clarity and distinctness of our ideas would be an infallible guide to avoiding error and assenting only to the truth. The appeal of such a view is that it places great power in the hands of the knower. The conclusion of the *Meditations* is that anyone, given proper leisure, can sit down and discover the deepest truths of the universe. But with such power comes responsibility; for a Cartesian, any assent to a falsehood is culpable, because it must have come about through insufficient attention to the clarity and distinctness of one's impressions. In short, on the Cartesian view as well as the Stoics', the availability of an infallible means for discerning the truth places knowledge squarely within the sphere of our own control.

Most contemporary epistemologists have given up on the idea that there is some method of justification, such as the Cartesian attention to clarity and distinctness, which guarantees truth. A different tactic has sometimes been advanced, however, for placing knowledge within our own power: defining truth in terms of some property we are able to control. For example, the coherence theory of truth holds, roughly, that a belief is true if it coheres (well enough) with other beliefs.[44] Presumably, anyone epistemically aware can tell if their beliefs are incoherent, and take steps to correct the mistake. Putnam and Dummett,[45] in their individual ways, have put forth the view that truth is a function of justification or verifiability—that whether a statement is true depends, in some sense, on whether (in suitably idealized settings) we can tell if it is true. On such views, like the Stoics', the ideal epistemic agent is infallible.

---

[43] Not that we can know every truth, but that we can avoid believing any falsehoods.
[44] See e.g. Bradley (1914).   [45] Putnam (1981); Dummett (1978).

The common thread running through all these epistemologies is that there need be no *luck* involved in believing the truth.

These views, and others like them, have had currency in contemporary epistemology. But the broad range of philosophers and laypersons have never been especially attracted to them; not attracted, that is, in the way that they are to the parallel Stoic picture of happiness. In the epistemological realm, by and large, we are naive realists about the external world. Truth is outside us to be grasped. And while justification and good reasoning, conscientiousness and care, good eyes and good memory, are our best shots at grasping the truth, they are only reliable, not infallible guides. We make mistakes and misperceive, we lack optimal techniques or placement in the power structure and history of theories, and we see from limited vantage points. Intellectual development is not the same as scientific progress.[46] As active and conscientious as we can be as knowers and informants, and as strengthened as we are by the social practices of knowledge, we still are vulnerable to error in our pursuit of knowledge. The stronger the realist we are, the more accepting we are of our passivity and our luck.

In contrast, we think happiness can be to a larger degree a matter of our making, that we can diminish the effect of luck without engaging in omnipotent thought or self-deception about our powers. We can conceive of happy people who have faced unspeakable tragedies and who have yet found ways of coping and even thriving; the Stoic conception of happiness, at least in its broad brushstroke, is something many of us embrace. Though the Stoics themselves argue for a unified thesis that demands a parallel between truth and happiness, we suggest that, at least on this issue, we do well to separate virtue epistemology from virtue ethics.

---

[46] Montmarquet makes the point in Montmarquet (1987a).

# Part Two

*Contemporary Virtue Ethics and Epistemology*

# 3

# Virtue Ethics: Radical or Routine?

## David Solomon

In recent years, epistemologists have turned increasingly to the taxonomies of normative theories sharpened within contemporary moral philosophy to illuminate the variety of possible views in epistemology. It is now almost as common to hear the language of virtue, deontology and consequentialism deployed in epistemology as in ethics. There are dangers, however, in this large-scale appropriation of the vocabulary of contemporary ethics by epistemologists. Within ethics itself, there are significant disagreements about how these categories are to be understood, and if these terms are problematic in the areas of inquiry where they were forged, it should not be surprising that exporting them to other areas of inquiry might cause more than a little confusion. I want to explore this possibility below with regard to the language of virtue as it has migrated from ethics into epistemology. I will argue that there is an important distinction between two forms of contemporary virtue ethics and that virtue epistemologists risk confusing themselves as well as others if they fail to attend to this distinction. My conclusion will not be that epistemologists should eschew the language of virtue, but rather that they should handle it carefully and with due appreciation for the deeply diverse range of views that have collected under the label 'virtue ethics' in contemporary moral philosophy.

## I

Since anglophone moral philosophers turned their attention once again to the exploration of large-scale normative theories a quarter of a century ago, ethics has become a very complicated place. After taking their lead from certain strands in G. E. Moore's thought and focusing their attention on tool-sharpening metaethical questions for most of the twentieth century, moral philosophers have in recent decades been influenced more by the model of John Rawls's *A Theory of Justice*.[1] It is not, of course, that they have all agreed with Rawls's broadly Kantian conclusions about normative theory,[2] but they have followed him in reopening the great questions of traditional normative theory and eschewing the normative minimalism that characterized most academic English-speaking ethics after the collapse of Sidgwick's consequentialism, Spencer's evolutionary naturalism, and Bradley's idealism under the critical fire of Moore and others. Since Rawls reopened these questions by rehabilitating a broadly neo-Kantian normative conception, a number of other moral philosophers have enriched the discussion by supporting alternative normative theories. There have been especially ambitious attempts to do for consequentialism and for neo-Aristotelian virtue theories what Rawls had done for neo-Kantianism, and there are now on offer a number of philosophically sophisticated and comprehensive reconstructions of traditional normative theories.[3] In this regard, the contemporary student of moral philosophy is confronted with an embarrassment of riches.

Current discussions in moral philosophy are dominated by the lively debates among proponents of these three competing normative theories. There are also, of course, debates among proponents of each one of these theories about how the theory is best formulated and defended. Frequently, these latter debates—among consequentialists, for example, about how consequentialism is best formulated—involve disagreements that are as deep, and sometimes as divisive, as those that arise across normative theories. The disagreements among proponents of an ethics of virtue are particularly complicated, involving disagreements along a number of different axes. Some virtue theorists see themselves in the Aristotelian tradition, others in the

---

[1] Rawls (1972).

[2] Nor have they given up, of course, addressing the traditional metaethical questions. It is rather that it is now impossible to take up narrowly metaethical issues without recognizing their relevance to normative theory.

[3] The most important proponents of neo-Kantianism are Rawls and his students such as Christine Korsgaard (1996), Barbara Herman (1993), Thomas Nagel (1986), Tom Hill (1992), and others. The most prominent consequentialists are Derek Parfit (1984), Samuel Scheffler (1982), and Shelly Kagan (1989). And among the most influential virtue theorists are Elizabeth Anscombe (1958), Philippa Foot (1978), Alasdair MacIntyre (1981), Martha Nussbaum (1986), and Rosalind Hursthouse (1999).

Humean tradition, and others yet feel more affinity with Nietzsche. Some virtue theorists regard their theories as essentially critical of central features of modernity; others feel comfortable regarding their theory as just another instance of a modern ethical theory. These deep and criss-crossing disagreements among virtue theorists have made some despair of giving a general characterization of virtue ethics. Others characterize it in a way that is hardly informative. Alasdair MacIntyre, for example, is reduced to this quite uninformative characterization of virtue ethics in an encyclopaedia entry he wrote on virtue ethics: 'Contemporary virtue ethics is in part a revival of some Greek preoccupations, transformed by the need to address the problems of modern moral philosophy'.[4]

The difficulty in giving a relatively determinate characterization of virtue ethics is especially troublesome, I think, for those in other areas of philosophy who have turned to virtue ethics for ideas or models for dealing with philosophical problems outside of ethics. These difficulties can be seen clearly, I think, in much of the work that has been done in the burgeoning field of virtue epistemology in recent years. Epistemologists, as is well known, have helped themselves recently to taxonomies, first developed for distinguishing among ethical theories and for dealing with distinctively ethical issues, in order to assist them in classifying their own approaches to epistemological problems. As a result, the language of deontology, consequentialism, and virtue is almost as familiar now to those working in epistemology as it is to those working in ethics. Indeed, the volume in which this chapter appears focuses on issues arising in contemporary virtue epistemology. One should not be surprised, however, that if moral philosophers fail to agree on a determinate characterization of virtue ethics, epistemologists might have some difficulty in making clear the distinctive features of virtue epistemology.

In this chapter, I hope to contribute to the understanding of some possible slips between the ethical cup and the epistemological lip with regard to matters of virtue. I am particularly interested in two quite different ways in which virtue ethics has been pursued which I will characterize as radical virtue ethics and routine virtue ethics. I am confident that the failure to recognize the distinction between the radical and routine with regard to virtue *ethics* has caused some confusion and misunderstanding among moral philosophers. I suspect that a similar distinction will have to be drawn within virtue *epistemology*.

---

[4] MacIntyre (2001: 1757). I am not suggesting, of course, that MacIntyre is unclear about what his *own* commitment to the project of virtue ethics amounts to.

My discussion here, however, is of the most preliminary sort, raising issues that will ultimately require a much more thorough treatment than they are given in this chapter. After initial comments about some general issues that arise concerning the relation of ethics and epistemology, I turn to a discussion of the emergence of virtue ethics within contemporary ethical theory. At the end of the chapter, I will return briefly to the implications of my discussion for the project of virtue epistemology.

## II

Although the focus of this chapter will be on a particular set of issues regarding the relation of ethics to epistemology, it is useful to begin by reminding ourselves of some of the more general difficulties that arise in understanding the relations of these two branches of philosophy. Most of these problems have their origin in the fact that epistemologists and moral philosophers pursue problems that tend to wander into the other's domain. Some of the most fundamental problems in ethics are, of course, epistemological problems: When, if ever, do we have knowledge in ethics? When are our moral beliefs justified or warranted? What is the nature of practical rationality? The heated discussions in recent years among moral philosophers about the adequacy of Rawls's method of reflective equilibrium cover much of the same territory as the more general epistemological debates about coherentism and foundationalism. And just as moral philosophers find themselves asking epistemological questions, epistemologists are centrally concerned with questions about our practical life. After all, the central problems of normative epistemology are problems about what to do. To believe or not to believe, that is the question—or at least one of them. Even the most avid naturalizers in epistemology must recognize the centrality of evaluations of ourselves and others to our epistemic life.

This shared territory of ethics and epistemology gives rise to difficult questions about the possibility of reducing one of these fields to the other—ethics might just turn into moral epistemology, a branch of general epistemology; or epistemology might just become the ethics of belief, a branch of general ethics. If these strong reductive programmes are seen to be objectionable, weaker relations may be pursued based on the more or less strong analogies between problems in the two areas or between key pieces of conceptual machinery found in both areas. It is easy, of course, to find such analogies.

(One might think that this is because both moral philosophers and epistemologists have so focused on the most abstract notions in their domains that it is no surprise that there is much overlap.) In recent years, certainly, epistemologists have helped themselves to explicitly ethical terminology more frequently than the other way around. That may be, however, because modern ethics has been so driven by epistemological concerns, that it can't take any more epistemic baggage on board. It is epistemically saturated.

Without altogether ignoring these larger issues about the relation between ethics and epistemology, I would like to focus my attention in this chapter on some issues about exactly how we should understand the turn to virtue on the part of many moral philosophers in recent years and what the implications of that turn might be both for ethics and epistemology. Surely, we can't sort out what epistemologists can learn from the revival of interest in the virtues until we get clear on what moral philosophers can learn from this revival. And, as will become clear, there are many disputed questions about what the virtue revival actually involves.

## III

One place to begin thinking seriously about the rise of virtue ethics is to look at it against the background of more general developments in ethics in the last half-century or so. It is not necessary to rehearse the well-known chronicle of figures and books that have followed—with some time lag—Elizabeth Anscombe's clarion call for the return to virtue—or at least a return to the discussion of virtue—in her remarkable 1958 paper, 'Modern Moral Philosophy'. This paper, which had little apparent impact on ethics for a decade or so after its publication, now seems prescient to a remarkable degree. Like many others, I suspect, I have found it important to reread it regularly just to be reminded of how much I have stolen from it. Instead then of attempting a simple history of the rise of virtue—and of providing yet another taxonomy of the different kinds of virtue ethics—I would like to focus on the question that the title of this chapter points to: has the turn to virtue in ethics involved a genuine revolution in ethics or have we simply been undergoing a slight course correction in ethical theory. Or as I put it in the title of this essay: 'Virtue Ethics: Radical or Routine?'

The terms, 'radical' or 'revolutionary' may sound a little over-wrought when applied to something as sedate and as irrelevant (for the most part) to larger cultural concerns as twentieth-century anglophone ethics. But we can surely speak, if we are careful, about some of the changes in the academic study of ethics with which we are familiar even in the twentieth century as, in important respects, revolutionary. These revolutions are typically marked by a piece of philosophy which divides pre- from post-revolutionary moral philosophy. Although there might be some disagreement among contemporary moral philosophers on the exact number of these radical changes, there would surely be a broad consensus that Moore's *Principia Ethica*,[5] Ayer's famous fifth chapter of *Language Truth and Logic*,[6] Rawls's *A Theory of Justice*,[7] and perhaps MacIntyre's *After Virtue*[8] mark such revolutionary developments. It is not the case that these works are themselves the first expression of new revolutionary thoughts. Indeed, in the case of each of these works, it is the culminating event in a kind of build-up to change. Moore's work is a natural response to the theoretical despair into which his teacher, Sidgwick, fell; Ayer brought his big idea back from Vienna; Rawls builds on the work of an already developing revival of traditional normative theory; and MacIntyre's work draws heavily on a renewed tradition of neo-Aristotelian thought which received its initial impetus almost twenty-five years before the publication of *After Virtue* in Elizabeth Anscombe's 'Modern Moral Philosophy'.

It is also not the case that these changes in direction within ethics are unrelated to the views that they aim to overturn. Moore's intuitionism prepares the way for emotivism (recall, for example, Stevenson's claim that 'non-natural properties are the shadow cast by emotive meaning'[9]), just as Hare's subtle elaboration of non-cognitivism in *Freedom and Reason* prepares the way for the full-blooded normative theorizing of Rawls.[10] Indeed, it is not uncommon for those philosophers who come before these revolutionary changes to interpret the change not as a radical change but rather as an extension of what has come before. In this way, non-cognitivism was seen by some as just another possible metaethical position alongside intuitionism, and Rawls's neo-Kantian views were taken by some of those he displaced as yet another metaethical theory. (This is surely the best way to understand Hare's remarkable review of *A Theory of Justice* in which he claims that Rawls is just another intuitionist—and not a very good one at that.[11]) There is always an attempt to draw revolutionaries back into the theoretical contexts from which they are attempting to escape.

Although I will not attempt to give necessary and sufficient conditions for determining when a change in ethics is revolutionary, it seems clear that these

---

[5] Moore (1903). [6] Ayer (1952). [7] Rawls (1972). [8] MacIntyre (1981).
[9] Stevenson (1944: 119). [10] Hare (1963). [11] Hare (1973a) and (1973b).

putative revolutionary works have in common an attempt to change in some substantial way the set of theoretical aims appropriate to moral philosophy. This can best be seen by looking briefly, and very inadequately, at the character of the changes these works introduced. The particular issues around which this revolutionary activity in twentieth-century ethics takes place (I will take it as understood from now on that I restrict myself to anglophone, broadly analytic, ethics—no Sartre, no Maritain, no Dewey) are complex. The three revolutions associated, roughly, with Moore, Ayer, and Rawls, however, might well be characterized as follows:

1. Moore's revolution focused on the rejection of the broad-scale normative theorizing characteristic of his nineteenth-century predecessors. There is a transition from moral philosophy dominated by Spencer, Bradley, and Sidgwick to moral philosophy dominated by Moore, Prichard, and Ross. The changes in the approach to ethics are almost palpable, although many of the arguments used by Moore would certainly have been familiar to Sidgwick and many other nineteenth-century figures. In the revolutionary work of Moore and those who follow, the ambitions of moral philosophy are curtailed in a number of different ways, and the cultural position of moral philosophy changes dramatically. Sidgwick caught the train to London regularly to discuss the affairs of the day with the prime minister.[12] It is unthinkable that Moore would catch that train.[13]

2. Ayer's revolution centrally involved the semantic turn as applied to ethics. There was a transition from a set of issues in ethics dominated by Moore, Prichard, and Ross to a set of issues dominated by Ayer, Stevenson, and Hare. Not only is large-scale theorizing about normative issues given up (as in the first revolutionary turn), but the normative is altogether expunged from moral philosophy. A sharp distinction is drawn between metaethics and normative ethics and moral philosophers are forbidden to trespass in the realm of the normative.[14] Moral philosophers, qua moral philosophers, are

---

[12] Schneewind (1977).

[13] The cultural involvement of Moore's ethics is, however, a complicated matter. Although he didn't talk to the prime minister, he talked as we know more than a little to the Bloomsbury Circle. Recall, also, his shock when he discovered on stopping by Westminster Palace to receive his knighthood that the king had never heard of Wittgenstein. Perhaps Moore thought that the king should have taken the train to Cambridge, rather than the philosopher to London.

[14] It might be thought that the distinction between the metaethical and the normative was already implicitly present in Moore's distinction between the questions 'What is the meaning of "good"?' and 'What kinds of things are good?' which he explores in the opening pages of *Principia Ethica*. But the full-blown distinction was surely not yet there. For one thing, Moore still regarded answers to the questions about what kinds of things are actually good as still part of the philosopher's

not even allowed with due Rossian sincerity to remind us that we ought to return our library books on time. Doing so is rather the task of those who actually use moral language (the familiar litany in books of the period—preachers, novelists, and ordinary people) and moral philosophers, qua moral philosophers, aren't allowed that privilege.

3. Rawls's revolution welcomes back a chastened but still robust normative theory. Moral philosophers are allowed to use their more sophisticated twentieth-century tools in pursuing once again the project of constructing large-scale normative theories. For the most part, this revolution does not attack those whose privileged positions within moral philosophy it usurps—it simply marches in and takes possession. Rawls barely mentions in *A Theory of Justice* his metaethical predecessors whose conception of the task of moral philosophy he utterly rejects. Hare's work, which had dominated discussion among moral philosophers for two decades, was dispatched by Rawls in two footnotes. The easy victory, no doubt, is partly to be explained by the exhaustion—both theoretically and practically—of classical metaethics.[15]

The Rawls revolution, though, was not just a revolution in favour of Rawls's favoured neo-Kantian style of normative ethical theory, but a revolution that opened the door, once again, to the construction of comprehensive normative theories of a variety of sorts. Moral philosophers could once again catch the train to London—or at least to Washington, D.C.—and they did. Rawls spawned an entire generation of students who pursued the elaboration of his favourite style of normative theory. The work of Rawls and his students, in turn, was confronted by ambitious theoretical work in defence of the consequentialist theories that Rawls had criticized in *A Theory of Justice*. In addition to the neo-Kantian and consequentialist efforts to revive traditional normative theory, there is a third kind of effort exemplified by the work of MacIntyre and others—the revival of neo-Aristotelian virtue theories. And this gives a kind

---

task, something denied by emotivists who put the distinction between the metaethical and the normative at the heart of their views. Also, Moore thought it was possible, in principle at least, that one's views about the meaning of 'good' might entail substantive normative views. This claim would also have been denied by the emotivists who adopted a strong version of the view that metaethical views *must* be morally neutral.

[15] This exhaustion also probably helps explain the ripple of enthusiasm that runs through relatively popular cultural organs at the return of normative theory. Recall Stuart Hampshire's (1974) celebratory review of *A Theory of Justice* in the *New York Review of Books* and Peter Singer's (1973) equally over-the-top article in the *New York Times Magazine*, 'Philosophers Back on the Job', which appeared shortly after the publication of Rawls's book. Both are variations on the theme: Ethics is back, and Harvard has got him.

of symmetry to our story of revolutionary activity in twentieth-century analytic ethics. Spencer, Bradley, and Sidgwick give way to Moore, Ross, and Prichard who, in turn, give way to Ayer, Stevenson, and Hare, who, finally, give way to Rawls, Parfit, and MacIntyre. The pursuit of this kind of trinitarian neatness has been known to mislead philosophers, however, and I think we do well to avoid it in this case also.

I suggested above that one might regard the emphasis on virtue exemplified in the work of MacIntyre and other neo-Aristotelians as itself revolutionary and not as a set of arguments responding to the same theoretical demands as their Kantian and consequentialist opponents. One might, however, see the revival of virtue ethics as structurally similar to the revival of neo-Kantian and consequentialist normative theories in that it is a return to the kinds of questions to which the comprehensive nineteenth-century normative theories were responding. It would then be operating on the same theoretical stage, as it were, with these other normative theories—asking the same questions, but giving different answers. In the terms suggested by the title of this chapter, it would be, relative to other normative theorizing, merely routine. It would be driven by the same theoretical demands but would be responding to these demands in different ways. Alternatively, as I suggested earlier, one could see the turn to virtue as harking back to the kind of classical approach to moral philosophy that characterized the aims of that enterprise in a quite different way from the way in which they are characterized typically within modern moral philosophy. This would make the turn to virtue radical indeed.

I believe that some of the work now being done in moral philosophy that is labelled 'virtue ethics' is merely routine, some is revolutionary, and perhaps some cannot make up its mind. I will not attempt here to name names (or at least not many names), but a brief preliminary survey of some of what is labelled 'virtue ethics' will be useful in fixing our ideas.

There is no doubt that Elizabeth Anscombe thought that the return to virtue she advocated in 'Modern Moral Philosophy' would be anything but routine. Her thundering indictment of twentieth-century analytic ethics as well as her claim that there was no substantial differences among all of the 'main' moral philosophers following Sidgwick should assure her of a place among the revolutionaries. Kurt Baier's attack on her paper—delivered a quarter of a century after it was written—characterized her views as an instance of 'Radical Virtue Ethics'.[16] Alasdair MacIntyre, also, has made his

---

[16] Baier (1988).

attempt to revive what he has called the 'tradition of the virtues', an integral part of a much broader attack on central features of modernity—and especially modern conceptions of practical rationality—which undergird much of the theory and practice of contemporary analytic normative theory. Among the many ways in which MacIntyre and Anscombe are similar is their tendency to downplay the differences from the point of view of an Aristotelian approach to ethics between deontological and consequentialist normative theories. The suggestion that deontological theories and consequentialist theories are simply minor variations on a style of modern moral theorizing to which an ethics of virtue is radically opposed is a common feature of those virtue theories which I would regard as radical.

If Anscombe and MacIntyre, as well as some others,[17] have promoted a return to virtue as a radical move within contemporary ethics, others have emphasized the virtues while working comfortably within the conventions of contemporary ethical theory. Here there are two kinds of cases. There are those like Michael Slote who describe themselves as doing virtue ethics, but who do ethics in such a way that their work fits neatly within the conventions of contemporary analytic normative theory[18] and others—here I would include consequentialists like Shelly Kagan and neo-Kantians like Barbara Herman—who are not doing virtue ethics, but struggle mightily and, in some cases, I think, brilliantly, to find a place for virtue and the concerns of those who have pushed virtue, within their own theories.[19] While rejecting virtue ethics, they have tried to assimilate virtue. There are, then, three broadly different kinds of ways to take virtue seriously in contemporary ethics, I think—a radical way, a routine way, and a way that merely accommodates it within a normative structure that doesn't give it a privileged place.

# IV

In this section of the chapter and the next I want to try to give some more substance to the distinction between what I am calling routine and radical virtue ethics. That there is such a distinction, and that it marks an important

---

[17] I have said I wouldn't name (too many) names, but some others who share some radical tendencies, I think, are Martha Nussbaum, Phillipa Foot, and Rosalind Hursthouse. However, Hursthouse (1999) suggests that she might not be quite as radical as she earlier appeared.

[18] I am thinking especially of the view developed in Slote (1992).

[19] See especially Herman (1993) and Kagan (1989).

difference between two ways of appropriating the language of virtue within ethics, becomes clear if we look at the different kinds of disagreements that arise between some proponents of virtue ethics and their neo-Kantian and consequentialist opponents. It is in the dialectical exchange among proponents of different moral theories that we come to understand the distinctive features of each theory. First, we will look in some detail at two quite different ways that the differences between an ethics of virtue and its opponents tend to be characterized in contemporary discussion. I will suggest, not surprisingly, that these two ways of characterizing the differences will be correlated with the distinction between the routine and the radical. Second, we will look, far too briefly, at a number of ways in which the opponents of an ethics of virtue have attempted to incorporate some of the insights of virtue ethics within their own theories. I will suggest that these strategies are reasonable only if the kind of theoretical insights they are attempting to assimilate arise within routine virtue ethics. Again, this will provide some insight into the difference between the radical and the routine.

So first we will consider two quite different ways of characterizing the nature of the disagreement between an ethics of virtue and its neo-Kantian or consequentialist opponents. The first way of characterizing the nature of the dispute is with reference to the question of which moral notion plays the primary role within the overall structure of a normative theory. This question gets its sense from a certain picture of how the three main kinds of competing normative theories—deontological, consequentialist, or virtue theory—might relate to one another. The picture suggests that each theory is specified by its relation to a key notion—deontological theories to rules, consequentialist theories to good states of affairs and virtue theories to virtues. And it is further suggested that the central dispute among these theories is a dispute about which of these key notions—the notion of a rule, an intrinsically good state of affairs, or a virtue—plays a primary structural role in the overall theory. A deontological theory will (in some sense to be specified) make rules the fundamental notion in the theory, while consequentialist theories will make intrinsically good states of affairs fundamental, and virtue theories will make virtues fundamental. The basic disputes among these theories then will be over this question of which notion has the privileged place.

Notice, however, that in thus characterizing the nature of the *differences* among competing normative theories, they are also treated as remarkably similar. Each theory will place *some* notion in the privileged place and presumably will have a structure similar to the other theories. There is certainly the suggestion that the fundamental notion in each theory will have to serve the same functions—essentially of motivating and justifying particular actions.[20] While there will certainly be differences among these different theories when characterized in this way, the differences do not seem to go very deep. They can be made to seem like matters of mere theoretical convenience as if we were choosing between alternative axiom sets for a formal system.

Now contrast this way of characterizing the differences between virtue ethics and its opponents with a second way which involves differences of much greater variety and depth. Many advocates of virtue ethics—including Alasdair MacIntyre and Elizabeth Anscombe—have drawn the contrast between virtue ethics and its modern opponents in a much more complicated way. Here are just some of the themes that run through much of contemporary virtue ethics and are seen by many of its advocates as central to their advocacy of virtue in preference to the neo-Kantian and consequentialist alternatives:

1. A **suspicion of rules and principles** as adequate to guiding human action in the complex and variegated situations in which human agents find themselves.
2. A **rejection of conscientiousness** as the appropriate motivational state in the best human action.
3. A turn for an understanding of the ethical life to **concrete terms** like the virtue terms in preference to more abstract terms like 'good', 'right', and 'ought'.
4. A **critique of modernity** and especially the models of practical rationality that underlie such Enlightenment theories as Kantian deontology and Benthamite consequentialism. This critique frequently extends to the bureaucratic and impersonal features of many central modern social practices.
5. An emphasis on the **importance of community**, especially local communities, both in introducing human beings to the ethical life and sustaining their practice of central features of that life. This emphasis is typically contrasted with the individualism that seems to many advocates of virtue ethics to permeate Kantian and consequentialist approaches to ethics.

---

[20] As we will see below, on this view the big disputes among these theories will frequently turn out to be disputes about which of these items—rules, virtues, or states of affairs—can best serve these functions. So, we will ask questions like: But can virtues guide actions as well as rules? And can the prospect of maximizing the good provide adequate grounds for doing our duty?

6. A focus on the importance of **the whole life** as the primary object of ethical evaluation in contrast to the tendency of Kantian and consequentialist theorists to give primacy to the evaluation of actions or more fragmented features of human lives.
7. An emphasis on **the narrative structure of human life** as opposed to the more episodic picture of human life found in neo-Kantian and consequentialist approaches to ethics. This narrative structure is especially important in understanding the special nature of human projects and human goods that can only be understood within the context of the story of a whole life.
8. An emphasis on **the centrality of contingently based special relationships**, especially with friends and family, for the ethical life in contrast to the tendency within neo-Kantian and consequentialist theories to downplay such relationships in favour of alienating ideals of universality.
9. **A suspicion of morality** understood as an abstract and distinctive grid of obligations and rights cut off from the more concrete features of human practical life.
10. A special emphasis on **thick moral education** understood as involving training in the virtues as opposed to models of moral education frequently associated with neo-Kantian and consequentialist moral theories which tend to emphasize growth in autonomy or in detached instrumental rationality.

I do not intend, of course, this laundry list of issues associated with contemporary virtue ethics to be in any way definitive of an ethics of virtue. Nor do I intend my brief characterization of each item to constitute anything like an argument for it. This list does, however, remind us of how diverse and rich are the differences between many contemporary advocates of the virtues and their neo-Kantian and consequentialist opponents. The attempt to reduce the difference between an ethics of virtue and its contemporary alternatives to a single, crucial issue—the place of the notion of virtue in the overall justificatory structure of a theory—is the mark of thinking of virtue ethics as routine. One might try to argue, of course, that this diverse and complex set of disagreements all derive from a more basic Ur-disagreement over which of the favoured notions—rule, virtue, or intrinsically good state of affairs—is to be taken as fundamental within a normative theory. But this doesn't seem very convincing—not least of all because this complex set of overlapping and intertwining disputes seems to involve a disagreement rather about the very idea of a normative theory within which something might be basic.

This way of characterizing an ethics of virtue also leads to the many attempts, especially current right now in ethics, to accommodate the demands of virtue ethics within the constraints of modern consequentialist and neo-Kantian theories. If the only question is: which notion is basic—rule, consequence, or virtue (or right action, good state of affairs, or personal excellence)—then surely there will be many ways to find some relatively basic position for virtue while keeping one's basic consequentialist or neo-Kantian commitments intact. These various attempts involve what I have called elsewhere forms of subordinating or—slightly more pejoratively—condescending to the virtues.[21] Indeed, it seems to me that we have recently seen a sea change in the way most opponents of virtue ethics have responded to it. While the original response tended to suggest that virtue ethics was just misguided or wrong (and we will explore some of those arguments below), more recently neo-Kantians and consequentialists have worked harder to find some place for virtue within their theories. Virtue has been invited into the house of contemporary normative theory, but told to stay in its place—typically some subordinate or secondary place within the overall structure of the theory.

These strategies of subordination, condescension, or assimilation come in a bewildering number of varieties. Some frequently encountered in and around applied ethics are of little theoretical interest, but are interesting nevertheless as illustrating how far the attempt to eliminate the distinctiveness of a virtue approach to ethics might be taken. The least interesting of these are what might be called projects of *mere assimilation*. Mere assimilationists argue that there need be no deep conflict between the traditional competing normative theories. Indeed, they claim that the neo-Kantian, the consequentialist, and the neo-Aristotelian are rather developing different aspects of the ethical, and the goal of ethical theory should be to bring these different aspects into a kind of harmony. Sometimes, it is argued that the views are interchangeable in that there is a kind of material equivalence to the views.[22] The question of whether one chooses to put rules, virtues, or consequences at the focal point of one's

---

[21] Solomon (1999).

[22] The well-known textbook in medical ethics by Beauchamp and Childress (2001) illustrates this strategy well. They have retained through a number of editions of this textbook a chart which claims to show how the language of rules and the language of virtues are simply alternative ways of talking about the same normative phenomena.

reflection is one to be settled by mere preference. Other times it is argued that there must be a division of labour among the various conceptual items. Rules do part of the job and virtues another. Professor Frankena's well-known remark that 'rules without virtues are impotent; virtues without rules are blind' exemplifies this approach.[23]

Among other philosophers who have defended this sort of strategy are Tom Beauchamp and Edmund Pellegrino. Beauchamp says that:

> there is no reason to suppose that we need to dispatch or minimize the importance of principles and rules in order to embrace these virtues. The two kinds of theory have different emphases, but they are compatible. A moral philosophy is simply more complete if the virtues are integrated with principles...*we have grounds to declare virtue theory and principlism* [his term for a particular kind of rule-based theory] *partners rather than competitors.*[24]

Pellegrino, who regards himself as a proponent of virtue ethics, says:

> what is evident is that full accounts of the moral life, particularly as it regards judgments of accountability and justification, require an integrated assessment of the four elements of a moral event—i.e., the agent, the act, the circumstance, and the consequence—in relation to each other. *Today's challenge is not how to demonstrate the superiority of one normative theory over the other, but rather how to relate each to the other in a matrix that does justice to each and assigns to each its proper normative force.*[25]

And he goes on to say:

> I am not suggesting a feeble eclecticism, a cafeteria-style ethics, that would add a spoonful of virtue here, a principle there, and a dash of consequence in another place. Nor do I suggest a formless syncretism based in egregious compromises for the sake of a unity that enervates conflicting theories. Rather, the strength of each theory must be preserved, drawn upon, and placed in dynamic equilibrium with the others in order to accommodate the intricacy, variety, and particularity of human moral acts.

Whether either Beauchamp or Pellegrino is guilty of producing a 'feeble eclecticism' or a 'formless syncretism', I will leave to others to decide. What is clear though is that these irenic suggestions do not do justice either to the variety or to the complexity of the kinds of deep disputes discussed above.

In addition to the various forms of mere assimilationism, there are a number of other ways of subordinating virtue which fall into certain regular patterns.

---

[23] Frankena (1963: 89).   [24] Beauchamp (1995: 195); my emphasis.
[25] Pellegrino (1995: 273); my emphasis.

One can discern certain characteristic techniques within both deontological and consequentialist theories for locating virtue but displacing it from the centre of normative attention. These *patterns of subordination*, as we might call them, represent ways in which Kantians and consequentialists make their ethical worlds safe from virtue—safe, that is, from any tendency on the part of virtue to take ethical centre stage.

These patterns of subordination may take two broadly different forms both in consequentialist views and in neo-Kantian views. The first form, *master subordination*, tends to identify one state of character, specified with reference to the fundamental evaluative orientation of either neo-Kantianism or consequentialism, as the fundamental motivational state to be associated with the theory. This form tends to force such theories towards an emphasis on *virtue* as opposed to the *virtues*. The central idea in master subordination is that there is a state of character, the *master virtue*, which is specified by the overall orientation of the ethical theory and which, in some sense to be specified, will be the most important state of character for agents to possess. This form of subordination can be seen in the tendency of some consequentialists to make *benevolence* the central, or perhaps the only, virtue. In a similar manner, Kantians are often accused of (or praised for) giving *conscientiousness* a dominant role within their account of character. This resort to a master virtue involves subordination of virtue because both the content of the virtue and the defence of its motivational centrality are derivative from other, more fundamental, components of the ethical theory.[26]

In the second form of subordination, *distributed subordination*, the opponents of an ethics of virtue are inclined to speak of virtues, rather than virtue, and they are prepared frequently to admit a rich and diverse family of states of character that qualify for this description. Where master subordination singles out a single motivational state that lies at the heart of excellence of character, distributed subordination points rather to a diverse set of ethically valuable dispositions of agents that contribute to the overall ethical well-functioning of the agent. Kantians and consequentialists again will distribute subordination differently,

---

[26] One might argue, of course, as some have, that according to classical virtue theory, the virtues are also subordinated to some other more fundamental value to be specified by the theory. Thus, some have thought that on Aristotle's view the goodness of the virtues is exhaustively explained by their role in promoting some distinct good state, *eudaimonia*. Isn't this a form of subordination, too? It would be, of course, if the relation of the virtues to the final good had this broadly instrumental character. It is hardly necessary to argue, however, in light of the sustained criticism of this instrumentalist view by Aristotelian scholars, for the inadequacy of this view.

however. Kantians, characteristically, regard virtues as certain relatively determinate states of character that embody motivation to act in accordance with certain principles while consequentialists regard them as states of character the possession of which in the members of a community tend to maximize the chances of bringing about whatever instrinsically good states of affairs are identified within the theory.

These various strategies to downplay the differences among normative theories are of course motivated by a number of different considerations. Some moral philosophers clearly think that the real world conflicts over moral issues (e.g. disagreements over the moral legitimacy of abortion, the details of just systems of distributing wealth and power, and affirmative action programmes) will be more likely to be resolved if the apparently deeper disagreements among normative theories are shown to be not quite so deep. Others seem to operate out of a kind of congenital optimism that deep theoretical differences among moral philosophers will be overcome. Whatever their motives, however, in pursuing various of these strategies of assimilation, the tendency of those philosophers to pursue them with regard to virtue ethics is, I think, a sure sign that we are in the realm of the routine and not the radical.

## V

A second way of appreciating the radical nature of virtue ethics (when it is radical) is by looking at the kinds of objections brought against it. I have suggested elsewhere that the most important objections are a set of three objections which I have called internal objections—internal because they come from inside ethics.[27] These objections to virtue ethics are found quite frequently in the literature of moral philosophy and proponents of virtue ethics have responded to them quite frequently. And there is the puzzle. Why do the same objections continually arise, where the objectors feel that no adequate response is made? Alternatively, why do virtue ethicists persist in defending an ethics of virtue which, from the point of view of their critics, is a futile effort, shown to be futile by these powerful objections. One explanation, of course, is that one side in this debate is just philosophically obtuse, unable to determine when they have been soundly refuted. Another more reasonable explanation,

---

[27] I give a much lengthier discussion of these objections in Solomon (1988).

I think, is that the disagreement between virtue ethicists (of a radical sort) and their critics is more complicated at least than the critics realize. The three criticisms make demands of an ethics of virtue that the critics take to be appropriate demands to be made of any ethical theory. They seem unable to accept that any ethical theory worthy of the name would reject these demands.

What are the objections? I take it that they are familiar to anyone who has followed the debate over virtue theory in the last couple of decades. They are:

(a) The action-guiding objection which claims that a virtue theory fails to give adequate guidance in situations of practical perplexity. The rules and principles characteristic of deontological and consequentialist theories are alleged to guide action more effectively and more determinately.

(b) The self-centredness objection that claims that an ethics of virtue is insufficiently other-regarding. It alleges that virtue theories in their classical form ground the need for virtue on the part of agents in the desire of agents for their own fulfilment or satisfaction and that this seems to turn ethics upside down. Instead of my needing to be good in order to benefit others, I am required to be the sort of person who benefits others in order to be fulfilled myself. Virtue seems to be itself compromised by a kind of vanity or prissiness.

(c) The conscientiousness objection that claims that an ethics of virtue fails to do justice to the special kind of motivation peculiar to the moral. Genuine goodness, according to this objection, must involve acting under a certain kind of constraint. The perfectly virtuous person apparently finds it easy to do what he or she ought, but this seems to fly in the face of any realistic moral phenomenology.

Each of these objections presupposes that a certain kind of demand is appropriate for any adequate ethical theory. In particular, it is presupposed that any adequate ethical theory must:

(a) Guide action in a particular kind of direct way. The theory itself must yield some devices that are directly and concretely motivating.

(b) Provide some conduit from self to other. Indeed, it is claimed that the problem of the ethical is how the agent can leap from egoism to altruism—or, even if the move from egoism to altruism is, as Bernard Williams says, 'a gentle slide' instead of a leap, how to accomplish that slide.[28]

[28] Williams (1973a).

(c) Identify some distinctive motivational state appropriate to the realm of the moral. This motivational state must be qualitatively discontinuous with the normal motivational states in other non-moral practical cases.

What is missed in this discussion, it seems to me, is that the virtue theories—in so far as they are radical—reject these demands, at least in the terms in which they tend to be made in modern ethics. It is not that an ethics of virtue utterly ignores the need to guide action; or the need to notice the existence of others; or the specialness of certain kinds of special demands on human beings—demands, for example, to tell the truth, to resist (at least sometimes) the lure of bodily desires, the need to handle the debilitating influence of fear, the importance of treating others decently. It is rather that virtue theories tend to deal with these matters in quite (radically) different ways from many modern theories. (To take just one example: virtue theorists think that action should be guided not by action-guiding devices entailed by principles in the theory—but rather by the virtues themselves.) It is because virtue theories are radical in their conception of the demands of an adequate ethical theory that the dialectic between these theorists and their opponents has been so untidy.

My suggestion, then, is that the radical nature of virtue ethics (when it is radical) is manifested in these two different ways. First, the range of disagreements between proponents of virtue ethics and their contemporary opponents is much greater than one would expect if the disagreements were just over the question of whether virtues, rules, or consequences should be basic in the theory. Second, the kinds of objections raised to virtue ethics by its opponents are typically question-begging in their confrontation with virtue ethics. In making these objections typical modern opponents of an ethics of virtue suppose that they share with proponents of virtue ethics a similar view of the criteria for adequacy in a normative ethical theory. In so far as an ethics of virtue is radical, I am suggesting, the dispute is over the criteria themselves—or at least over how they are to be interpreted.

## VI

Let me conclude with some even more general remarks about the overall project of reviving the virtues in contemporary ethics.[29] One can think of the

---

[29] Much of this section is adapted from Solomon (1999).

recent revival of virtue ethics in two quite different ways. On the one hand there is a narrow attempt to find a place for the concept of virtue (or of the particular virtues) within a conceptual map of the practical life. This is a relatively focused conceptual problem of finding a place for virtue. Typically, consequentialists will want to subordinate the virtues to some notion of a 'good state of affairs' and deontologists will want to subordinate it to some notion of a right or obligatory action. Virtue ethicists will strive to give the virtues a more foundational role. But in all cases the exercise will be a relatively narrow one of conceptual ordering. The pursuit of this narrow task has occupied much of the time of moral philosophers who have attempted to accommodate virtue. It is technical, narrowly focused, relatively removed from the larger questions of moral philosophy, and always in danger, I would say, of begging certain larger questions which form both the background for this narrow task as well as its motivation.

These larger questions frame a much more ambitious project which is also associated with the revival of virtue ethics. Here the question is not how to locate the concept of virtue within the local economy of practical life, but rather how to accommodate certain fundamental commitments of classical ethical theory within the relatively restricted—and restricting—agenda of modern moral philosophy. Those philosophers who are most responsible for bringing virtue theory back into currency—Anscombe, Geach,[30] Foot, MacIntyre, and others—were not interested primarily in a reordering of the central concepts in practical life. Rather they were concerned with certain larger questions both about the moral life and about the role of general philosophical thinking in that life. They thought that there were certain deep difficulties in modern moral theory connected both to the history of modernity as well as to certain features of modern life. Modern moral philosophy was misleading not only in its answers, but also in its questions. It focused our attention on features of our practical life which are not central to the project of successful human living and it encouraged us to have certain ambitions for philosophical reflection or practice almost Promethean in their reach. The modern demands for impartiality and objectivity seemed to these critics excessive and unattainable by creatures like us. But their unattainability was not as serious a problem as the fact that their presence distorted our lives in ways that were inimical both to personal success and to social order.

In this push for virtue theory, the focus was not on relatively technical questions of the ordering of normative and evaluative concepts, but on deeper

---

[30] Geach (1956).

questions about the nature and ambition of modern ethics and its ability to satisfy our need for reflective guidance. The separability of this broader push for virtue from the narrower argument is confirmed, I think, by the use of these broader attacks on modern moral theory by philosophers like Bernard Williams who have no interest in promoting a virtue theory more narrowly conceived.[31] Indeed, some of these arguments are shared by a number of philosophers who have been called anti-theorists because of their reluctance to take any positive view in ethical theory.[32]

We can distinguish, then, a broader agenda for virtue ethics from a narrower one. The former involves, in many cases, a rich and diverse set of objections to the very project of modern moral philosophy. It looks to the ancient world for an alternative model for such theory. The latter agenda, however, is more directly involved in the contemporary problematic of analytic—largely English-speaking—ethics. It looks to play the game of contemporary normative theory but to place virtue in the place of privilege in the received theoretical models for the ordering of ethical concepts.

There are, then, two different conflicts going on between so-called virtue ethicists and their contemporary opponents. There is a narrower conflict which is a battle over the ordering of concepts. Here virtue ethicists struggle to plant the concept of virtue at the conceptual heart of ethics—and the opponents develop ingenious arguments and strategies to displace it. This really is a relatively parochial conflict within contemporary analytic ethics. Then there is a much grander conflict between the ambitions and agenda of modern ethics—and its classical opponents. Here the debate ranges over much deeper questions about the very nature and status of ethical reflection. Here it is probably misleading to speak of a single broader conflict. Rather, the battle ranges along a ragged front which separates the classical and the modern. This too is misleading as an analogy, since one of the areas of the front is a battle over the very question of whether there really is a front—that is, many philosophers have recently argued that the very idea that there is a divide (or at least a sharp divide) between the classical and the modern is itself a mistake.

Much of the difficulty in knowing what is exactly at stake in the debate over virtue ethics grows out of the interplay between these two different conflicts—and their two different (broader vs. narrower) conceptions of what virtue ethics is. This explains why so many philosophers complain that they are not sure what an ethics of virtue is. It also explains, I think, why so many clashes over the prospects for an ethics of virtue are 'unclear'. It is precisely

---

[31] See Williams (1985).   [32] See, e.g., Clarke and Simpson (1989).

because an opponent of the narrow virtue agenda encounters a proponent of the broader agenda—or an opponent of the broader conception encounters a proponent of the narrower conception.

Of course, one must not exaggerate the difference between these two conceptions of virtue ethics. They are clearly connected in a number of different ways. Proponents of the broader agenda will typically also promote the narrower one. But it is certainly not the case that proponents of the narrower agenda will even typically promote the broader agenda. Indeed they occasionally seem a bit embarrassed by it. It seems to me likely that the debates between the friends of the virtues and their opponents will remain untidy and relatively ill-defined until more attention is paid to the interaction between these two quite different agendas.

## VII

But what does all this have to do finally with the contemporary project of virtue epistemology? It certainly is not intended as an argument to show that virtue epistemologists should aim to be radical, rather than routine. Nor is it an argument to show that virtue epistemologists have eschewed the radical and adopted the routine in attempting to learn from virtue theorists in ethics. Rather, it seems to me that epistemologists should attend to these matters in order to avoid some of the confusion that has attended the virtue revolution among moral philosophers. Much of the recent discussion about how ethical discussions might relate to epistemological ones has focused on questions about whether there are useful analogies between particular argumentative moves—or theoretical structures—in ethics and in epistemology. The style of argument here might be called 'virtue to the rescue'. Questions asked by epistemologists in this vein include questions like these: Can the use of virtue help reliabilism stay afloat and fend off its critics armed with one more devastating counterexample? Or can virtue help provide an irenic middle ground between the first-personal austerity of externalism in epistemology and the baroque richness of internalism? The hope lying behind these questions, I think, is that some of the insights developed in discussions of virtue within moral philosophy might be put to use in epistemology. The suggestion of this chapter is simply that epistemologists might also learn from the experience of moral philosophers something about the variety of uses to which the language of virtue can be put—and possible confusions attendant on not being clear about these different uses.

In particular, epistemologists should be aware that when they turn to contemporary ethics for insight into the nature of the virtues and normative theories that take them seriously, what they get may be just routine. The virtue epistemologies that result from drawing upon work in ethics, therefore, may also be routine, and may fail to get to the root of the problems that motivated the turn to virtue in the first place. Let me illustrate with a few examples.[33]

Ernest Sosa, one of the founders of contemporary virtue epistemology, seems to me to have fallen into the pattern of distributed assimilation.[34] His virtues are faculties or dispositions by which a subject can reliably distinguish the true from the false within a field of propositions (thus his view is seen as a form of 'virtue reliabilism'; his own term for his view is 'virtue perspectivism'). There is an independent standard of reliability which serves as the measure of the various faculties and dispositions, and determines their status as virtues, or not. As has often been noted, reliabilism is similar in some respects to consequentialism. We could construct an ethical theory called virtue consequentialism, in which those traits are virtues which tend to produce the best overall results, which would be parallel to Sosa's theory. Thus Sosa's virtue epistemology remains a form of reliabilism which has assimilated virtue in a distributed pattern.

Another main style of virtue epistemology on the market, virtue responsibilism, is largely inspired by the work of Lorraine Code. Code claims that 'epistemic responsibility is a central virtue from which other virtues radiate'.[35] In a similar vein, James Montmarquet writes: 'The fundamental epistemic virtue—what I call (epistemic) conscientiousness: the desire to attain truth and avoid error—has been widely recognized by philosophers interested in the notion of epistemic responsibility'.[36] Virtue responsibilism, I think it is clear, is in danger of falling into a master pattern of assimilation. (I will remain agnostic as to whether Code or Montmarquet actually fall into this pattern, as that would require a sustained analysis of what Code has to say about practical wisdom, and Montmarquet about the regulative virtues of impartiality, sobriety, and courage.)

There are other virtue epistemologies on the market, of course. But even if they do not fall into patterns of assimilation, they may well be just routine. For example, they may take as given the same problematic that reliabilists and internalists address, may see the goal of epistemology as giving an analysis of

---

[33] I would like to thank Chris Toner for suggestions on this section of the chapter. I have also benefited from discussions with him and with Margaret Watkins Tate on the chapter as a whole.
[34] See, e.g., Sosa (1994).    [35] Code (1984: 34).    [36] Montmarquet (1993: viii).

knowledge, taken univocally and in terms of necessary and sufficient conditions. Calling virtue epistemology routine, of course, does not itself constitute a devastating objection to it—nor, for that matter, any kind of objection at all. Surely, epistemologists have as much of a right to be routine as do moral philosophers. But if the point of turning to virtue was to find a new approach to epistemology, it ought at least to give us pause.

Can we say anything about what a radical virtue epistemology would look like? Happily, it is not the job of the moral philosopher to attempt to answer that question. But we are all entitled to our opinion and I would suggest that such a radical virtue epistemology would have some of the following features. It would not be belief-based; it would be agent- or end-based in that virtue would be more basic than belief. It would focus on the cognitive life of the agent rather than on episodes of cognitive activity in isolation. It would view inquiry as a practice, or a set of practices, always with a determinate form influenced by the historical and social circumstance within which the inquiry was carried out. It would strive for historical specificity of inquiry without falling into relativism. In this respect, it would draw more closely to much recent philosophy of science while also making use of insights from radical virtue ethics. Among contemporary philosophers who have written on epistemology, a few seem to be moving in the direction of the radical: Jonathan Kvanvig,[37] Linda Zagzebski,[38] and Alasdair MacIntyre.[39]

As a moral philosopher with a strong commitment to the radical style of virtue ethics, I am inclined to root for similarly radical views in epistemology. My only point here, however, is that we would do well to attend to the distinction between these two (radically?) different approaches to the virtues both in ethics and in epistemology. Failure to do so has costs of a number of different sorts, I suspect, not the least of which is that conversations about the role of the virtues and character generally in matters of ethics and epistemology are difficult to carry on in a clear-headed way. And the desire for a clear and disciplined discussion of these matters is surely common to all of those interested in the virtues, however radical their ultimate agenda may be.

---

[37] Kvanvig (1992), although this is largely promissory.

[38] Zagzebski (1996), although I think she waffles a bit between the radical and the routine, in both her ethical discussions and her epistemological ones.

[39] MacIntyre (1990), who is radical in both his ethics and his epistemology.

# 4
# Practical Reason and its Virtues

## J. L. A. Garcia

Alasdair MacIntyre holds that traditions of inquiry develop and mature through processes of internal debate and confrontation with alien modes of thought.[1] Accordingly, this essay seeks to assist the recent rethinking of the role of virtues in normative theory by critical reflection on some recent philosophical writings by the economist Amartya Sen. Sen is a good focus for such examination because his philosophical work, itself a model of creativity, builds on the careful, influential, Nobel Prize-winning work he has done in decision-theoretic accounts of rational choice. My hope here is both to show the need for revising our understanding of the operation of practical reasoning in moral thinking, in favour of an understanding in which virtues play a central role, and to begin sketching elements of such an understanding.

My focus will be on reason, especially practical reason, and on Sen's views of its proper relation to feelings and to firm moral convictions. Sen maintains that moral reason needs to work with sympathy to avoid the kinds of misery that fanaticism and totalitarianism visited on humanity during the past century. In these and other writings, however, Sen manifests an instrumentalist conception of practical reason, as is characteristic of rational choice theory. I argue such a conception of reason provides no genuine bulwark against oppression. The chapter develops an alternative idea to show how sympathy,

---

I am grateful to Douglas Portmore, Henry Richardson, Amartya Sen, and Linda Zagzebski for offering to share their writing with me, and to Zagzebski, Jason Taylor, Michael Formichelli, and an anonymous referee for suggestions on revising the text.

[1] See, most recently, MacIntyre (1999).

with its inherent individualism, suggests a different way of reasoning in situations of conflict. In the process, I draw both on the role-centred, virtues-based, patient-focused, and partially input-driven account of moral life that I have sketched elsewhere, and on Henry Richardson's influential notion of 'norm-specification' as an alternative to the 'values-balancing' usually invoked to resolve conflicts. Such a view eschews simple result-optimization for a kind of minimax strategy, on the grounds that thus minimizing the agent's maximum deviation from virtue towards anyone may afford greater protection to those placed at risk in pursuing social projects than does merely instrumental rationality. Such an approach, I maintain, also better captures the proper distribution of our moral concern than does the position-relative value theory Sen's consequentialism deploys for the same purpose. Sen's recent writings also treat the relationships of reason to firm moral convictions and even faith. In the course of my discussion, I hope to manifest the inadequacy of his accounts of such strong belief by comparison with approaches more consonant with a virtues-based approach. At the end, I suggest some implications this approach to the intellectual virtue of excellent practical reasoning may have for broader issues in epistemology.

Excellence in practical reasoning, and what counts as doing such reasoning well, has traditionally been called *phronesis*. Following Aristotle's classification of *phronesis* (at *NE*, bk. 6), Aquinas considers what he calls *prudentia* to be one of the most important intellectual virtues.[2] Aquinas writes of prudence that it 'is essentially an intellectual virtue', though one having 'something in common with the moral virtues', for which reason he thinks it can also properly be 'reckoned with the moral virtues'.[3] As there seems little reason to challenge this ancient and medieval classification, it follows that I am here exploring what has been recognized to be a central and crucial intellectual virtue.

## I. Sen on sympathetic feelings and respect

Reflecting on some of the last century's tragedies, and especially mindful of the horrors—some purposive, some bumbling—wrought by its totalitarian regimes, Sen observes that 'our hope for the future must, to a considerable

---

[2] But not *the* most important of them. See *ST*, 1a–2ae, q. 66, art. 5, where Aquinas argues that wisdom is the greatest of the intellectual virtues, and especially *ad* 1, where he argues specifically wisdom's superiority to prudence, which 'serves' it.    [3] Ibid., q. 58, art. 3.

extent, depend on the sympathy and respect with which we respond to things happening to others'. 'Spontaneous' responses, 'human responses' of 'respect and sympathy' need to be 'cultivat[ed]'. Quoting Jonathan Glover, Sen affirms that, as the millennium opens, '[i]t is to psychology that we must now turn'. Not just to the psychology of feelings and sentiment, however. In fact, Sen takes exception to Glover's criticisms of the Enlightenment, and finds David Hume and Adam Smith exemplary in seeing 'reason and feeling as deeply interrelated activities'. Whether or not Hume was right to see reason merely as passion's 'slave' (and whether or not either is really an 'activit[y]'), Sen maintains that the two must work together. This is unexceptionable, perhaps because it is so unexceptional, but the examples of this cooperation that Sen offers are not so reassuring. Sen turns to Smith to remind us that, first, our feelings of approval and disapproval, directed towards helpful and harmful conduct respectively, depend 'on our reasoned understanding of causal connections between conduct and consequences', and, second, that affective reactions can and should change in light of reason's discovery when 'one object is the means of attaining some other'.[4]

## II. Avoiding outrages

I find this pair of illustrations unsettling because, standing alone as they do, they suggest that Sen thinks what the future of humanity chiefly requires, in order to avoid a third-millennium repetition of the twentieth century's atrocities, is to abet sympathetic response with instrumental reason. This is objectionable for at least two reasons. The first is that this would leave the 'choice' of sympathy (and respect) unjustified. Why is morality so tied to sympathy rather than to hostility, or to indifference, or to (narrower or wider) self-interest? Reason—and even, broadly conceived, practical reason—ought to be able to go a considerable distance towards answering this question, but it will not be instrumental reason. Even if sympathy's link to morality is said to be conceptual, we are left to ask what justifies *caring about* or *acting from* sympathy rather than from hostility, or from indifference, or from selfishness?[5] Why is such behaviour not monumental imprudence, a repudiation of prudence sometimes so great

---

[4] All quotations are from Sen (2000a: 34).
[5] Michael Perry talks, disapprovingly, of a 'definitional strategy' for justifying human rights by claiming certain things morally ought or ought not be done simply as a matter of what we

that it threatens, as Henry Sidgwick saw, to turn practical reason against itself? Sorting this out may be a task for some form of reason, but even if it is broadly 'practical' it cannot be narrow and instrumental. I return to this matter below.

The second ground for concern is that instrumental reason coupled to sympathy does not seem up to the task of precluding totalitarian-style outrages. In light of Stalin's gimlet-eyed recognition of the need to break eggs to make omelettes (means–end rationality), such reason offers little protection against the totalitarian inhumanity that Glover fears. The problem is not that the programmes of a Hitler or a Stalin have no connection to human sympathy. On some conceptions of sympathy, such as the utilitarians', it is concern for humanity as a whole. Sen himself follows Glover in glossing sympathy as 'caring about the miseries and happiness of others'. So understood, sympathy affords little protection to individuals against the schemes instrumental reason may devise for maximizing happiness or achieving a net reduction in misery. Respect offers more protection, but only in so far as it involves no attempt at net maximization across individuals. If a form of practical reasoning allows the sort of trade-off in which some may be treated disrespectfully in the hope of achieving more respected lives for others or, still worse, allows us to trade disrespecting some to gain others greater happiness (or to spare them further misery), then respect becomes less a bulwark against victimization than it is a new threat, a new maximand in whose pursuit individuals may be abused or sacrificed.

In this connection, it is worth noting that Sen has steadfastly maintained, defended, and developed a moral theory that, in its most recent statement, explicitly (and even proudly) insists that, with even such moral rights as it acknowledges, 'there can be "trade-offs" between rights, and…between the goodness of rights fulfillment and other good consequences.'[6] This 'consequentialism of rights' allows that an act of rights-violation may have disvalue independently of its further effects on human pleasure or satisfaction. However, on Sen's approach, this disvalue takes on what we might call 'wrong-making force' only by diminishing the overall value of the act's

---

mean by 'the moral point of view' (Perry 1998: 29–32). (I am not sure Perry is right to see James Griffin as employing such a strategy.) What I envision here is someone arguing, similarly but more broadly, that morality requires sympathy simply in virtue of its definition. Perry rightly notes that this leaves untouched the question of how to justify moral concern. However, he shows little appreciation of the way in which the demand to 'justify' morality is fishy, the moral being already a mode of justification. (We should, for example, see moral concern as no more in need of justification than is narrow self-interest.)

[6] Sen (2000*b*: 499 n.).

'comprehensive outcome', which may also include other valuable and offsetting 'feature[s]' including pleasures won, preferences satisfied, and goals advanced. For Sen, the fact that these gains are achieved through the violation of someone's rights, her victimization and disrespect is simply another, albeit disvaluable, fact to be thrown on the scales. Wrong action is still determined—not just for practical purposes, but in principle—by somehow commensurating (or, at least, comparing) the various and opposed values and disvalues to determine the 'comprehensive' outcome's total value-score. Hence, Sen's consistent willingness to describe his approach as a form of consequentialism.[7]

I think all this is deeply wrong-headed. Genuine sympathy, feeling with, is for *individual* persons, for only they have feelings that we can imaginatively share. Likewise, genuine respect is owed only to individuals, who alone possess the bases of human dignity. (What Sen calls the 'future of humanity' as such seems to me beneath moral notice, though *each* person's welfare matters greatly.) This underdetermines 'imperfect theory', broadly understood not as theory for worlds in which some immorality is performed, but theory for worlds (such as the actual) where not all morally admirable inclinations are perfectly realized, i.e. lived out. How ought someone to act when she cannot help everyone in every way? There is little reason to assume she is then required to maximize total good ('happiness') across persons or (differently, we should note) to minimize total evil ('misery'). I suggest sympathy's individualism points imperfect theory and conflict-resolution in a different direction. As we cannot always respond in action to each person in the way sympathy and respect would incline us, abstracting from the context's practical exigencies, one approach, which appealingly manifests the way that sympathy and respect are directed always at individuals, is to seek to act so as to minimize the extent to which we depart from sympathy or respect in our response to anyone.[8]

## III. A different approach

Adam Smith, whom, we noted, Sen approvingly and repeatedly cites, thinks we judge an action's 'propriety' by our feeling (or lack) of sympathy with

---

[7] Sen (ibid.: 47f.) notes that some will be unwilling to call his view 'consequentialist' owing to their narrow view of consequences as including only what he calls 'culminating outcomes'. Nonetheless, Sen himself explicitly rejects that view of outcomes as too narrow, and fashions his essay as a defence of 'consequential evaluation', as he conceives it, as the key to, and sole method of, proper practical reason.

[8] Elsewhere, I argue that this helps explain why it is wrong intentionally to bring significant harm even to one undeserving person for the sake of any goal, no matter how lofty. See Garcia (1993).

its agent's discerned motives, and judge an agent's and her action's merit by our sympathy (or lack of it) with (hypothetical) reactions of those it affects.[9] Therein, Smith recognizes a fact nowadays forgotten, that actions are morally important chiefly for their inputs, and that what is crucial there is how they stand vis-à-vis virtue and vice. Moreover, Smith sees that the moral life does not pursue some overall good, rather, virtue directs our concern differently to different people, depending on how they are situated relative to us.[10] We should note that our reactions to the acts of others that affect us may differ according to whether their effects on us were foreseen by the agent, or were foreseeable, intended, or accidental. The level and kind of solicitude that you owe your friend, that it would be vicious not to have towards her, is different from that you owe a stranger, though, of course, you owe both *some* solicitude. This sort of approach opens the possibility that moral reasoning will be non-consequentialist, because it is focused on inputs (agent's motives, expectations, intentions) rather than on outcomes, and also that it will centre on the different role-relationships in which different persons stand towards someone.

Such a possibility can be fulfilled in an account of moral life that is *role-centred, virtues-based, patient-focused*, and is also *input-driven* in its account of the permissibility of actions. As I use the terms, a conception of the moral life is *role-centred* when it makes all moral features (rights, virtues, duties, etc.) ones that someone has *in* (relative to, and in virtue of) certain role-relationships, which roles we can thus call 'morally constitutive' or 'morally determinative', because they determine someone's moral features by constituting/forming her moral life. (This contrasts with conceiving these duties etc. as held independently, for example, from Sidgwick's 'point of view of the universe'.) Among the chief role-relationships that constitute a person's moral life are those of friend, confidant, fellow, citizen, spouse, parent, child, informant, and so on. I will not try to justify this partial list here nor to delineate in any detail the content of particular roles. Nevertheless, intuitively, we can see that each such role is an analogue of friendship, even a form of it, involving a commitment to the good of some person, either her good as a whole (as in parental devotion) or some aspect or part of her good (as your informant normally seeks that you have the good of some information). They are personal roles, tying a person to a person, involving her in the latter's life, even if only as a distant well-wisher.

---

[9] For the first point, see Smith (1976: pt. I, sec. I, chs. 3, 4); for the second, see ibid. pt. II, sec. I, chs. 1–3.   [10] Ibid. pt. VI, sec. II.

I call an account *virtues-based* when it understands judgements about rights, duties, etc. in terms of more fundamental judgements of some attitudinal responses as virtuous—and other such responses therefore, vicious in light of their departure from these—(rather than making them independent of virtues-judgements, for example, or making virtues-judgements depend on rights- or duties-judgements). Each of the morally determinative roles I mentioned is one a person can fulfil well or ill, and this is chiefly a matter of whether she is committed in suitable ways and at some suitable levels to the good of each of those in whose life she plays the role. Some traits will constitute fulfilling the role, acquitting oneself well in it; others will in general only causally contribute to such fulfilment.

It is *patient-focused* when the interests and needs chiefly dispositive in determining the fundamental moral features (virtues within a virtues-based view) of a subject and her action are those of the persons to whom she is pertinently related (rather than their always being the desires or needs of, for example, the agent herself). For me to be a good friend to you in the ways that amount to a moral virtue is for me to be suitably devoted to your welfare. A good friend to someone—someone good as (and at being) her friend—is a loving friend. Of course, one sign of the kind of devotion that is good friendship is a desire and effort to be (more) loving. Still, if I succeed in this effort, then what I will ultimately be devoted to and aiming at is your good, not my being loving.[11] To see if you are a good friend to person A, a good fellow to B, a good spouse to C, etc. in the ways that amount to your being morally virtuous, we must look to what you care about, what you want for each.[12] What you as a good friend care about, however, what is the focus and centre of your concern, is the welfare of A, and of B, and of C, et al. In this way, the focus is on the patient's (the other person's) good, not the agent's. (I except such roles, which little concern us here, where agent and patient are the same person—the self-regarding morally constitutive roles.) Of course, you know (or are in a position to know) that part of A's faring well is her having good friends, of B's is her having good fellow travellers in life's journey, of C's is her having good

---

[11] So here I depart from a view some Stoics may have held, according to Julia Annas. See Annas (2000). On it, the chief aim of the virtuous person is her own virtue. Such a view strikes us as self-centred precisely in the part of life where we have the best opportunity for overcoming self-centredness. I think a similar response should be made to views according to which the chief value of friendship is as an occasion for learning more about oneself.

[12] And, of course, how you care about it. However, that introduces complications, some of which I try to treat below.

spouses.[13] So, *secondarily*, you should as a friend try to be loving, try to be a good friend and to avoid being a bad one, try to be virtuous in your responses to each and avoid falling into vicious responses—good friendship and, therein, moral virtue, will involve that.[14] Still, these virtues are other-regarding, patient-focused. This will become important later as we consider practical deliberation and moral reasoning.

Finally, an account of morally right action is *input-driven* when it makes a course of action's moral status depend on its motivational input (rather than on its physical structure, or on the resultant state of the world, or on its causal effects, etc.).[15] I suggested that some of the most salient morally determinative roles are analogues or forms of friendship, and that good friendship is chiefly a matter of suitable concern for—really, devotion to—one's friend. So, here, and I think more generally, the constitutive virtues in these roles are internal, psychological conditions. They are orientations of the heart, and it is an action's (or omission's) relation to these that chiefly determines, even constitutes, its status as morally permissible, required, or forbidden.[16]

Any adequate account of the moral virtues will need a battery of other distinctions that I cannot explore here. Nevertheless, we should note that, whereas an analysis of the moral virtues of the sort just sketched will foreground truthfulness, loyalty, confidentiality, justice, and other forms of good will as the principal constitutive virtues within the various role-relationships that make up our moral lives, it will also need to acknowledge the contribution of courage, various forms of temperance, and other classical virtues, usually deemed self-regarding and self-improving in enabling someone to fulfil her roles. These traits, which we may call contributive virtues in our other-regarding relationships, may also be constitutive virtues in those morally constitutive roles, such as that of self-stewardship, that each of us plays within her own life.

---

[13] My talk of having 'good spouses' in the plural does not imply that I think polyandrous or polygamous societies better, or as good as, monogamous ones in their social arrangements. I simply do not presuppose the contrary here, and I assume that even within polyandrous or polygamous societies, someone is better off with good spouses than bad ones.

[14] However, if I am right, that is never the ultimate goal of the virtuous.

[15] What I here call input-drive(nness) is in keeping with a strict interpretation of Mark 7: 21–23: 'For from within, out of the hearts of men, proceed the evil thoughts and fornications, thefts, murders, adulteries, deeds of coveting and wickedness, as well as deceit, sensuality, envy, slander, pride and foolishness.' In the sort of view taken here, it is not merely that these acts originate in our choices and preferences, but they are evil *because* of the choices, preferences, likes, desires, intentions, etc. that they express and from which they spring.

[16] Here, I treat each of these theoretical features—role-centring, virtues-basing, etc.—as categorical (non-scalar). However, we might instead talk of a conception's being role-centred *to the extent*

So, in this sort of moral theory, the other-regarding virtues of benevolence take a proper prominence denied them in antiquity, but the classical virtues of courage and of temperance in its different forms also have an important place.

We should point out, *pace* Rosalind Hursthouse and others, that making duty and right action logically dependent on character does not suffice to distinguish what she calls 'virtue ethics' from utilitarian or neo-Kantian accounts.[17] For a utilitarian may allow that a right act is one that a(ny fully) virtuous agent would perform, taking a virtuous agent to be one who consistently maximizes the good as a matter of character. The neo-Kantian might say the same, taking a (fully) virtuous agent to be one who always acts in accord with the Categorical Imperative. On any *virtues-based* view in the sense of the one taken here, however, these approaches are ruled out, because each utilizes a conception of virtue that itself depends on an axiological or deontic concept at least as fundamental.[18]

I should add a remark about the relation between reason and the virtues. There is some basis for maintaining that a conception of reason—especially, of practical reason—must be prior to that of the moral virtues, because any such virtue needs to be understood, in part, in terms of reason's operation. It may seem, then, that not just any love for others, or commitment to the truth, or devotion to community suffices for moral virtue, for example, but only such love, commitment, and devotion as are reasonable. And similarly for the other moral virtues. Plainly, there is truth in this argument's premiss, which expresses Aristotle's insight that, for our passions, desires, and choices to become virtuous, they must be under the guidance of practical reason. Similarly, Aquinas maintains that 'Moral virtue cannot be without prudence...[T]here can be no moral virtue without prudence...For it is by the virtue of understanding that we know self-evident principles both in speculative and in practical matters.'[19]

---

*that* it conceives someone's moral life as constituted by her roles, or virtues-based *in so far as* it regards virtues-judgements as more fundamental than judgements about rights or duties, and so on.

[17] Hursthouse (1996) holds that in virtue ethics an act is morally just when a virtuous agent would characteristically perform an act of that type, where such an agent is one who exercises the virtues. She leaves it open how the virtue ethicist conceives the traits that count as virtues.

[18] A problem with this response: suppose the utilitarian defines virtue in terms of maximizing pleasure or happiness rather than 'the good' and the neo-Kantian defines it in terms of universalizable maxims rather than an imperative? Will not a theory using these seemingly neutral notions then pass muster as a form of virtue ethics? Probably not. The distinction is artificial, pre-textual, and forced, since there is no way of justifying the importance of pleasure (etc.) or of maxims except by reference to their axiological or deontic significance. And, my claim is, on the best analysis those notions rely on more fundamental virtues-concepts and judgments. In any case, I think it better to talk of some normative systems being 'virtues-based' in the sense explicated, than of their being (forms of?) 'virtue ethics'.    [19] Aquinas, *ST*, 1a–2ae, q. 58, art. 4.

Still, things are more complicated than such arguments make it appear, and it does not follow as a conclusion that practical reason is whole and comprehensible prior to and independently of any of the moral virtues. For proper and improper exercises of reason are best characterized in terms of certain intellectual virtues and vices. We are inclined to say the person who goes too far (or not far enough) in this sort of love, commitment, or devotion is being rash, timid, vain, lazy, biased, and so on, in her thinking. The deliberation of someone who gets things right we want to call sensitive, careful, fair. More generally, we reason poorly when we are vain, gullible, pusillanimous, impatient, etc., in our reasoning, and better to the extent that we are therein modest, trusting, courageous, perseverant in it, etc. Yet it is quite difficult to draw a sharp and convincing line between these intellectual vices and virtues and familiar moral virtues and vices, both constitutive and contributive. Indeed, it has been suggested that there may be no such sharp boundary.[20] If practical wisdom is internal to moral virtue, it appears, then so too many moral virtues are internal to practical wisdom, and thus to intellectual virtue and practical rationality themselves.[21] The two may well be locked in such a conceptual embrace that neither can adequately be understood save through the other. It would follow that they can be understood, if at all, only together. All this suggests that the old utilitarian dream of reducing morality to the broader application of a supposedly independent personal prudence, understood as instrumental rationality, may rest on a mistake. In so far as instrumental rationality is real rationality, it seems to need analysis through the intellectual virtues, which themselves appear inextricably tied to the moral virtues. Practical reason, including instrumental reason, is a human faculty, susceptible to a kind of excellence, virtue, that cannot be understood independently of moral fulfilment.

## IV. Position-relative evaluation

I have criticized Sen's view for its consequentialism, maintaining that it leaves the door open for the kinds of atrocities that characterized much of the

---

[20] See Zagzebski (1996).

[21] Aquinas seems also to have held this, though perhaps for somewhat different reasons. Immediately following his argument that moral virtue cannot exist without prudence, he proceeds to argue that 'prudence cannot be without moral virtue'. He reasons that 'in order that he [someone] be rightly disposed with regard to the particular principles of action, viz. the ends, he needs to be perfected by certain habits, whereby it becomes connatural, as it were, to man to judge aright of the end of virtue' (*ST*: q. 58, art. 5).

twentieth century. Sen thinks that a consequentialist account of right action can be made more sensitive to the concerns of anti-consequentialists by allying itself with a position-relative value theory. On such a theory the impersonal value (perhaps even the intrinsic value) of a state of affairs can vary across persons according to the different ways in which each is situated, especially, how she is situated relative to the state of affairs. This permits such a theory to accommodate some anti-consequentialist concerns because it allows that, say, my death and the occurrence of your act of killing me are worse things relative to you (situated as you are, i.e. as causal agent) than they are relative to the uninvolved stranger who happens to sit next to you on the bus. In this way Sen hopes to make room within an act-consequentialist theory of right action for a kind of agent-relativity, a feature Thomas Nagel and others have faulted consequentialism for excluding.[22] Sen excludes direct agent-relativity from his theory of right action, but incorporates it into his value theory, whence it indirectly impacts the determination of right action. Because your killing me might be a worse thing relative to you than is two strangers' dying of plague, you might be justified, as anti-consequentialists have maintained and some consequentialists have felt they had to deny, in refusing to kill me to make a serum from my body that could help the plague-ridden strangers. I find this position-relative value theory appealing for reasons quite independent of its supposed usefulness to consequentialists. We want to say you are justified in feeling worse about your sister's dying in the plane crash than you do about mine, and I am justified in feeling worse about mine's dying than I do about yours. Sen's position-relativity gives us the formal apparatus to affirm such things.

What is less clear is how this could work, how *im*personal value can vary across persons. Shortly after Sen first advanced this proposal, I suggested it could be well (and, quite likely, best) accommodated within what I call a role-centred and (at least partly) virtues-based moral theory.[23] Suppose that we adopt virtues-basing at least far enough to analyse the claim that a state of affairs is impersonally bad, that is, undesirable, as a claim that desiring it would (normally) be morally bad, in the sense of being bad-making, morally vicious. Next suppose we further adopt role-centring by saying that being vicious is always being vicious in one or more of certain role-relationships such as friend, fellow, citizen, kinsperson, etc. Now allow that different roles may have different standards of moral adequacy, so that some have higher thresholds of

---

[22] Nagel (1986: ch. 9); Sen (1982), (1985), (1999a: ch. 3), (2000b); Portmore (2001).
[23] Garcia (1986).

what counts as minimally virtuous while others permit much lower levels of sympathy and concern without falling into vice. This could enable us to say that your sister's dying is very bad, highly undesirable, in respect to you, and is worse relative to you than is my sister's death. For it enables us to gloss this last claim as maintaining that you would be more vicious, be worse (as a sibling) to your sister in desiring her death than you would be vicious to mine, a stranger to you, in wanting my sister's death. And, *mutatis mutandis*, the same holds about me in relation to my sister's death and yours respectively. Notice, however, that the sort of position-relativity this account explains is rooted in the relative position of *persons*, really in their personal and interpersonal relationships.[24]

Thus far, some form of agentive position-relativity may be vindicated. However, other problems attend it. Why are such motives as cruelty, etc., bad-making features of a state-of-affairs (i.e. motives that tend to make them bad), except that they are, prior and independently, wrong-making features of actions?[25] Using position-relativity within consequentialism here gets things backwards. True, cruel acts 'result' in instances of cruelty-being-in-the-world. However, their having that result is not what makes the acts wrong. Non-cruel acts may also have such 'results', as when your forgiving me so enrages me that I treat you or another cruelly, or when your wearing a white suit does so. Cruelty is more intuitively, more plausibly, and more revealingly (i.e. better) theorized as a wrong-making *input* feature of action. This is easily accomplished if we adopt a strongly virtues-based theory, which collapses wrongdoing into viciously informed behaviour. Of course, the mode of connection between action and result could itself be incorporated into the state of affairs, or as a value-shaping feature of it. Again, however, that appears to be spinning epicycles in a desperate effort to save a consequentialist account of the right. Any theory that regards an action's cruel motivation simply as a part of its resulting state of affair's (position-relative) objective/impersonal value is therein tendentious, and *ad hoc*. The proponent of such a view owes us some account of what it is that supposedly makes it *substantively* consequentialist, rather than

---

[24] It is less clear whether it secures the moral import of the sort of agentive position that interests Sen. Still, it is not wildly unreasonable to think that if you (viciously) cause my death, you should be especially troubled by it. Such differential value as this does not fall neatly out of role-centring, and needs some independent theoretical grounding. Yet we cannot rule out such a defence in principle. So, it could be true that it is even worse for you to desire or take pleasure in my death than it is for others, and in that sense, we can say it is worse relative to you in virtue of your position.

[25] More strictly, they do not themselves logically suffice for an action's wrongness, nor is the relation merely causal. Rather, these features of an action *count towards* its being wrong.

one that saves the term by calling its non-consequentialist elements parts of its account of the good.[26]

In any case, once Sen allows that a state of affairs can have such value, so that your death is impersonally worse with respect to me if (and *because*) it results from my maliciously shooting you with intent to kill than if it results from my accidentally shooting you, and much worse than if it comes about from natural causes unaffected by me, then it is difficult to see what possible justified objection there can be to the *more* intuitive position that my act's wrongness can likewise be input-sensitive. Obviously, it cannot be that inputs do not count towards assessments. That would be mere question-begging. So we are entitled to ask just what makes it legitimate for Sen to count an action's cruel motivation towards its resultant states of affairs' badness, but objectionable to allow that input a direct role in determining whether the action is wrong.[27]

Sen talks of rights-violations as *bad* independently of their further effects on welfare, etc., but not independently *wrong*. The most it seems he could allow is that an act's being a rights-violation has inherent 'wrong-making force' in that the disvalue of its occurring would suffice to make it wrong if its outcome had no counterbalancing good features. Yet I think this view problematic. A rights-violation's being bad can be analysed as its being undesirable: desiring it to have happened is a bad-making, that is, a vicious, desire.[28] But then that viciousness also directly infects the act from its input side. Its occurrence is

---

[26] I have in mind any theory that, like Sen's, says that a cruelly motivated action's occurrence counts morally only as a morally disvaluable feature of the action's effect, a bad thing that results from the action and thereby counts against it morally, rather than as a feature that counts against it on the input side.

[27] Remember that these are prospective action-assessments, so it is not really even concrete act-particulars that are being evaluated, but only something abstract, such as the state of affairs that this or that act is done.

[28] See Garcia (1987) for such an analysis of judgements of impersonal value. My account is offered in the context of denying any intrinsic value independent of virtue. Note, however, that Zimmerman, in the course of defending such value, suggests an analysis of it according to which for something to have intrinsic value is for it to be obligatory for someone to favour it, where this obligation is said to express an 'ideal ought' that is scalar and consists in an appropriateness or fitness of the favouring response. There is plainly a movement towards convergence here. Zimmerman's view is that for your being healthy, say, to have intrinsic value is for it to be more or less suitable or appropriate of someone S to favour it, and I say that we should construe the claim that it is good that you are healthy as the proposition that S's wanting you to be healthy is virtuous within (suits, is appropriate to) one or more morally determinative roles. The differences between these positions are less striking than the similarities, and my view can be seen as adding detail to, by spelling out the concept of suitability within, a position like Zimmerman's. See Zimmerman (2001: ch. 4, esp. sec. 4, 5).

a bad—that is, a bad-making—thing to be glad has happened, a vicious thing to want for someone idly to wish or to hope for; finally and especially, it is bad to choose, prefer, and intend its occurrence. This is true quite independently of the act's being part of what Sen calls its own 'comprehensive outcome'.[29] Sen is correct closely to tie moral rightness to goodness and wrongness to badness. However, he doesn't go far enough. Moral right and wrong need to be understood in terms of an action's (and, therefore, an agent's) being morally virtuous and vicious, and being morally virtuous or vicious is only plausibly seen as a matter of an action's inputs, not its outputs.[30] The same viciousness that attaches to the desire for the killing, enabling Sen (somewhat misleadingly) to say that the killing is impersonally bad/undesirable, already pollutes the act as it comes into reality from a vicious choice, preference, decision, and intent that an action of that type happen.[31]

The input-driven approach to act-permissibility taken here has some advantages over Sen's act-consequentialism. It lends a theory *unity* and *simplicity* because, just as a particular action emerges from motives, decisions, expectations, intentions (and reflects them in certain ways) that legitimate its moral categorization, so too in it, *how* that action reflects those internal states and events, and *which* ones it reflects, determine the categories to which it belongs. In addition, it sharply *limits the import of result-luck* (for act-permissibility, though not for some kinds of responsibility).[32] Like consequentialism, it closely ties the

---

[29] '[M]otivation can be seen to be part and parcel of part of what is happening and may well be taken into account when a state of affairs is judged...[T]he reach of consequential reasoning can incorporate processes of choice [including motivation]...I have argued for the importance of paying particular attention to "comprehensive outcomes" (including actions undertaken, processes involved, and the like, along with final outcomes).' (Sen 2000b: 491 n.).

[30] *Pace* Thomson (1997) and (1999).

[31] In fact, I think an action's moral wrongness is not just input-sensitive but input-*determined* (in conjunction with facts about surrounding circumstances, and about alternative inputs and actions). However, that is a stronger claim that I will not fully defend here. It is tied to the fact that I think all features of a person, of her mental states or her actions that are of direct moral import, are either intrinsic (driven by human sociality and by the nature of our mental states) or input-determined: the rightness or wrongness of actions, the virtue or vice of attitudinal stances, etc.

[32] Virtues-based moral theory, of course, is not immune from all forms of luck. There is an element of luck involved just in what dispositions one finds occasion to cultivate and in the ease with which that cultivation is accomplished. Still, for the most part, the less a theory makes moral status dependent on luck the better, because a person's moral status, and that of her actions and reactions, should reflect what she is and chooses, not what merely happens beyond her control. As the moral virtues are traditionally seen as acquired by a programme of habituation voluntarily sustained, the influence of luck in the virtues is always tempered by choice. That is much less true of the influence of luck in what happens as a result of chosen actions.

rightness and wrongness of actions to the goodness and badness of what is associated with them. However, where Sen and consequentialists tie an action's being morally wrong or right to what they see as the *non*moral value of its effects, this approach derives moral right and wrong from the moral virtue and vice of its motivational input. An act is wrong because it stems from what is bad, in the sense of being bad-making, that is, because it comes from what tends to corrupt 'the thing and its work', in Aristotle's phrase. Moreover, in the spirit of Sen's own repeated emphasis on agency, it focuses on agency— that is, on motives, decisions, expectations, intentions—in assessment of actions.[33]

In contrast, to the extent that an approach to act-rightness and wrongness is sensitive to an action's actual consequences, it therein (a) holds an action's being morally right and wrong hostage to result-luck; (b) it divorces it from agency in the agent's preferences, choices, expectations, commitments, etc.; (c) it divorces it from moral virtue and vice; (d) it divorces it from the bases for moral praise and blame; (e) it dehumanizes human actions and agents by viewing them as mere mechanisms for the production of valued results; and thus (f) it introduces unnecessary complexity into moral assessments, which must already look to inputs for judgements of actions' (and agents') virtue and vice. This last point is worth exploring a little more fully, since Sen sees 'the need to take responsibility for the consequences of one's choice' (in its actions and results) as a key to consequentialism.[34] The theorist who, like myself, denies that an action's being right or wrong is sensitive to its consequences, of course, need not *refuse* to take responsibility for the effects of her choices, nor deny other agents' responsibility for theirs. However, she does not see agents as blameworthy for the bad effects of their refusal to treat others unsympathetically, or disrespectfully, or otherwise viciously. More important, when moral

---

[33] See Sen (1985) and (1982). We should note, in passing, some further problems in act-consequentialism. Anna Stubblefield (2000) objects to results-based accounts of the immorality of racial oppression on the grounds that any such view must find little moral objection to oppressive environments when their oppression motivates oppressed people to overcome its effects. Stubblefield thinks the oppression objectionable nonetheless, because it unjustly poses greater obstacles to flourishing to some people than to others. I think she is right, but hold also that the injustice should not be understood simply in terms of effects. The point is generalizable against act-consequentialism, which, after all, has difficulty classifying my cruelly harming you as morally wrong when it motivates you to avoid the harm's lasting effects or when a benevolent being intervenes to cancel harms. Even indirect consequentialism faces a similar problem when a benevolent being or our own psychology acts systematically (at least, regularly) to counteract and prevent (or quickly to end) such harms.    [34] Sen (2000*b*: 477, 502).

theorists talk about 'moral responsibility', they usually mean praiseworthiness or blameworthiness. Actions, however, merit *moral* praise and blame not on the basis of their effects but because of the virtuous feelings, preferences, aspirations, and so on, that inform them.

The role-centring and patient-focus of the account proceed by explicating the *roles* at play in the case in light of the personal purposes and needs they advance (causally or constitutively) in the life of each moral 'patient', identifying and elaborating each role's *virtues* (inherent and instrumental), and delineating how in light of its motivational input (the choices, preferences, expectations, etc. from which it comes), each of the agent's available courses of action would place/distance her (the agent) relative to those role-virtues.[35] However, this sort of global ranking pays too little attention to the agent's situation to *suffice* to settle quandaries, 'norm'-conflicts. (Even if it is insufficient to the purpose of resolving conflict, can it be relevant to an apparent conflict between the demands of being virtuous in R1 and in R2 that, say, R1 is somehow 'more important' than R2? I do not rule this out in principle, but I should need to see how any proposed metric of commensuration is supposed to work.)

## V. The irrelevance of consequences

What of consequences, then? My approach can be called consequence-insensitive. Can that be plausible? Can it be that morality is indifferent to effects, that it tells us to ignore what happens?[36] I think we can see how to answer this by reflecting on, and generalizing from, what we earlier observed about friends. Certainly, in their practical deliberation, agents should (and virtuous ones

---

[35] Ultimately, these roles also need integration into a coherent life, and this can be done (perhaps most efficiently, appealingly) through a comprehensive role-relationship that incorporates and interrelates the others. Someone's role-relationship (as creature) to God, her fulfilling which requires her to be good in her other role-relationships to human persons, seems best to fit this bill. Maybe some roles are somehow more important than others seen in this way under the aspect of eternity.

[36] For doubts, see, for one example, Thomson (2001: 153): 'I know of no philosophers who have said it is never relevant to the question whether we ought to do a thing what the consequences of our doing it would be.' There are several issues to be distinguished, however. Whether an agent considers the consequences of actions is surely relevant to whether she acts kindly or callously, and thus to whether she acts virtuously or viciously, permissibly or impermissibly. A fortiori, it is relevant what effects she intends to achieve. It does not follow that the effects her action actually has, or would probably have, are relevant. Plainly, we do not think whether the action is kind or thoughtful or truthful, etc. so depend, and it needs to be argued that what happens is relevant to permissibility. Here, I argue the opposite.

would) attend to prospective results of their conduct. That is what it is to be motivated by such sentiments as love and compassion, and such sentiments include an inherent inclination to action. In so far as she has even rudimentary understanding, the virtuous agent will also see that to a significant extent the prospective patients of her action thrive or are set back precisely in that they have good or bad friends, fellows, and occupants of the other morally-determinative roles. So, she will also strive thematically to fulfil her roles (to fulfil them as such), to be good in her roles, and to avoid being a failure in any of them, at least to minimize the extent of any such failing. In this way, the virtuous agent's deliberation, teleologically directed ultimately at the other's welfare, *secondarily* becomes reflective, self-scrutinizing. Therein, it also becomes *moral* reflection. Not all moral reasoning is practical in the sense of being deliberative, action-orientated, nor is all practical thinking moral. However, the virtuous person's practical reasoning and deliberation will become morally informed. Thus, she has two reasons to try not to hurt you. First, because, as virtuous in one or more relevant roles vis-à-vis you, her goal is for you to fare well, and hurting you would set that back directly. Second, because her goal is to help, i.e., for her to be helpful, and because her trying to hurt you would make her bad in one or more of the morally determinative roles that she plays in your life, her failing you in that respect (failing you as your R, for some pertinent value of R) would constitute an additional setback to your welfare.

Thus, virtuous deliberation looks to prospective outcomes. Notice, however, that in the specifically and thematically *moral* part of her deliberation (the part concerned with fulfilling her role to you or failing you in it), the fully virtuous agent looked only at the impact of her *trying* to hurt you, her *intended* outcome, not any actual result. That is what matters morally, as also can failures to adopt certain intentions. Turn now from the agent's deliberation to the spectator's moral judgement. The latter must look to whether the agent is responding virtuously or viciously to her situation. I think we should see that as a matter of what she chooses, prefers, decides, and intends, and of what she fails to choose, prefer, decide, intend. An action's actual effects, then, may matter to other parts of our moral consideration, especially in determining for what an agent is responsible, but they are irrelevant to her action's moral viciousness, and therein to wrongdoing, permissibility.[37]

---

[37] My position is the polar opposite of that of Thomson, who proposes what she calls '*The Irrelevance-of-Intention-to-Permissibility Thesis*: It is irrelevant to the question whether X may do *alpha* what intention X would do *alpha* with if he or she did it' (Thomson 1991: 294).

## VI. Conflict and specification

A moral system with even a single fundamental command can generate what at least appear to be conflicts. An approach such as Sen's, with its pluralist axiology according independent value to freedom and rights as well as to various components of well-being, opens the possibility for still deeper and seemingly intractable and permanent conflict.[38] So too will a view such as that I have suggested, in which an agent stands in a multiplicity of morally-determinative role-relationships, each grounding responses of preference whose external realization cannot always be jointly realized. Someone assessing how an agent has handled her situation will need to 'specify' the responses that her role-virtues ground in the agent's situation. The goal, I think, should be to provide her with the information she needs to minimize the extent to which she need depart in her agency (her behaviour's motivational background/input) from the virtues in any of the role-relationships that determine and (in fact) constitute her moral life. Why ought *this* to be the standard in cases of apparent conflicts among the 'norms' of virtue? Because, I think, this best captures, incorporates, and responds to the inherent individualism of our moral lives—the way they divide our moral concern and differentially call for us to distribute it over different persons according to how they stand in relation to us. It will become manifest that, as conceived here, anyone's moral life is a matter of how she acquits herself in certain role-relationships. If that is true, then it becomes reasonable that what she is chiefly to avoid (or to minimize the depth of) is any departure from virtuous response to anyone in any of the role-relationships she occupies. Thus, the approach taken here will help justify the (I think) intuitively appealing suggestion made above that we should resolve norm-conflicts by minimizing the badness of action, while its input-driven account of good/bad action enables it nonetheless to avoid commitment to any consequentialism.[39]

---

[38] Sen is straightforward about this problem, describing his own view as 'inescapably pluralist', pluralist for several reasons. One reason stems from the problem 'of what weight to attach' to such values as freedom as compared to those such as functioning (Sen 1999a: 76). He is also forthright about his own dependence on 'balancing' to resolve conflicts. Arguing for a 'democratic' over a 'technocratic' approach to determining 'how the weights are to be selected', he maintains that the weights that the balancing procedure requires are to emerge from determined 'public discussion and critical scrutiny' (ibid.: 78–79, 81).

[39] In Garcia (1993), I urged serial consideration of conflicts in order to defend against the claim that we ought to countenance violating rights, sympathy, and respect as the number of those who suffer because of our restraint grows. In any case, it is unclear how to add the depth of someone's

We have talked of conflicts, norms, and specification. These terms bring to mind the pioneering, insightful, and influential recent work of Henry Richardson on what he calls 'norm-specification'.[40] Richardson proposes that in case of apparent conflict we 'specify' the relevant norms, in a certain technical sense, articulating each in such a way that it no longer conflicts with the other. He believes such a procedure has important theoretical advantages over the 'balancing', so often invoked but little articulated, as the way to resolve moral quandaries. Richardson thinks murky talk in the literature of 'balancing' radically different values and principles provides little more than the appearance of rationality for choices that are in fact unprincipled and may be driven more by bias, sentimentality, arbitrariness, caprice, or other unacknowledged and illegitimate factors, than by reason. (Or, I should add, by virtue.)

Sen's own theory—marked by a variety of independent kinds of human good: rights, freedom, perhaps dignity, in addition to well-being and its components—is rife with potential conflicts. These offer no evident mode of commensuration and Sen suggests little on how to resolve the conflicts save by some form of the balancing Richardson rightly views with suspicion. What concerns Richardson is that the practitioners and proponents of balancing seem unable to articulate what determines one result over another.

What is important for our purposes is how specification might apply to the virtues. What Richardson himself says on this is unsatisfactory, for reasons that need not detain us.[41] My suggestion is that moral virtues are internal to what are considered to be moral principles and rules, with what we call the moral rule against lying, for example, being interpretable as classifying lies as vicious in that they are dishonest.[42] Virtues-basing suggests that

---

departure from virtue(s) in role R1 to that of her departure in role R2 (whether or not she plays them in the life of the same person). That is, it is unclear what sense to make of this sort of addition.

[40] See Richardson (2000).

[41] Richardson considers 'the case of a conflict between the virtues of generosity and tolerance and a duty (perhaps of justice) which calls for outrage and punishment'. Richardson suggests that an important distinction needs 'to be incorporated into our interpretation of these virtues,... [moving us] from "be generous and tolerant" to "be generous and tolerant towards all persons... but [not always] towards behavior"' that warrants punishment. (Richardson (2000: 300).) The details need not concern us. What matters is that virtues are traditionally and properly seen as dispositions, not, *contra* Richardson, imperatives. Nor do they neatly yield imperatival norms.

[42] I also think someone's moral virtues are dispositions to respond that make her good as occupant of some personal role-relationship, but will not here explore the details of this approach. In my view, we should try to resolve moral conflicts (that is, apparent conflicts between one course of action, in performing which I would tend to live up to a virtue, and another) about what to do by determining which course of action in its motivation, intention, and choice would

action-'norms' are better formulated with internal virtue- and vice-terms ('Lying is dishonest') rather than imperatively ('Don't lie') or with 'thin' moral language ('Lying is wrong'). This conception of norms allows the relevant virtues' and roles' nature, content, and point to guide the process of specification. It also allows a more nuanced, contextual consideration of conflicts than does abstracted, lexical ordering of virtues or roles. So understood, what Richardson calls 'norm-specification' might better be understood as a process of articulating the practical implications of virtuous response to a situation, so as to eliminate what, prior to this scrutiny, appears to be a conflict.[43]

Consider Bernard Williams's unfortunate Jim, or Kant's unlucky rescuer at the door when the would-be murderer comes calling. Or consider us as spectators reflecting on their predicaments.[44] As seen here, what the moral judge must do is reflect on each pertinent role the agent occupies and its point and internal contribution to the life of the person in whose life he occupies the role, and the internal virtues it generates and that in part define it. What would constitute justice and charity from Jim even to the one selected for possible execution? To what extent would Jim fall short of the mark in the morally determinative role-relationships he plays within that person's life by killing him, in comparison to the extent he would fall short in respect to any one of the others in refusing to prevent her death? What would be minimally honest and truthful even to the prospective killer? I will not here try to defend answers to these questions.[45] I am interested now in how to think about the process of consideration. Properly understood, the task is less norm-specification than it is grasping the relevant modes of virtuous response, and the kinds of behavioural responses they ground and normally motivate.

This procedure appears to work well in at least some cases. Sen suggests that we say your welfare and life are more important than my property right in such a way that, in an emergency, it is morally permissible for someone S to infringe my property rights to use some food and shelter to save you.[46] However, it seems more intuitive and less dangerous to say in such a case that when, after reflecting on the role-relationship, we properly specified the practical

---

more greatly deviate in the circumstances from the pertinent virtues (in the agent's relevant roles).

[43] I will not here argue that, perhaps excepting some cases of innocently misinformed conscience, such conflicts can always be made thus to disappear.

[44] See Williams (1973b: 98–118); Kant (1994).

[45] For my treatment of the killing cases, see Garcia (1993); on lying, see Garcia (1998).

[46] Sen (2000b: 499).

implications of S's being just to me (in her role as my fellow), we would see that S wouldn't be acting unjustly towards me in so using my property. Such use by S manifests none of the disrespect, contempt, callousness, or ill will towards me that would make it unjust. This fits our intuition that S's action is not a permissible violation of my moral rights—would Sen consider this a violation of moral rights that is somehow not unjust? or an injustice that morality nonetheless somehow permits?—but rather an act beyond the scope of my moral rights in this property because, in it, S expresses no attitudes contrary to justice.[47]

In contrast, S's killing me to make a serum for you from my body would disrespectfully, and thus unjustly, and therein immorally, treat me as a mere means. Suppose we consider whether it is always wrong intentionally to kill an innocent, and thus wrong for an agent, Alice, to kill an innocent victim, Val, even when otherwise another agent, Anna, will kill two other victims, Victor and Vincent. In judging Alice's actions, we must look at *her* alternatives, which are her killing Val or not killing Val. Anna's killings, of course, are not among Alice's alternatives. What Anna does is only a probable result, an output, of one of Alice's options. That plainly does not render it wholly irrelevant, but what moral relevance it possesses is indirect. When Alice decides against killing Val, as a result of which omission Victor gets killed by Anna, we can say Alice fails to act for the sake of securing to Victor the good of life. This refusal opens Alice to the charge that she has behaved viciously towards Victor, has failed him morally. (The same charge, *mutatis mutandis*, could be made on behalf of Vincent, of course.) However, if Alice were to kill Val, she would therein open herself to the graver charge that she has acted in a still more vicious way towards Val. For she would have acted for the sake of preventing Val from having the good of life, and therein more greatly distanced herself from the virtuous stance of willing Val's good. (She would not intend this harm for its own sake, of course, but Val's death is still a goal that Alice needs and strives to attain in pursuit of her further goals of saving Victor and Vincent. It is intended by her as a sort of building block in the execution of her plan to save them.)

When an agent acts with the expectation, but not the intention, that someone S will not have a beneficial property P, then the stance of her will is less

---

[47] Thomson might call this an 'infringement' of my rights that is not a violation of them, because she reserves the latter term for 'infringements' that are morally objectionable. See Thomson (1991). However, that is confusing, and it is better to say that you act consistently with my rights as they exist in the situation, in the sense that you observe everything that your being just in your treatment of me here demands.

opposed to the virtuous one of intending that S have P than it is when she acts with the intention that S not have P (whether or not she also acts with the expectation that, because of her behaviour, S will not have P). To see this, consider the fact that someone's acting with the mere expectation that S will have P does not rationally exclude her also taking steps intended to prevent S from having P. In contrast, it is obvious that no rational person could take such steps while also doing something that she not merely expects but actually *intends* to result in S's having P. That would be asinine. For example, I may (intentionally) enter the baby's room with the mere expectation that I will wake her. Doing this is rationally compatible with my simultaneously doing something else, e.g. tiptoeing, to avoid waking her. In contrast, if I enter her room with the intention of waking her (say, to administer a medication), then it is not rational for me also to take steps to avoid waking her. To enter her room with the intention of waking the baby while also doing something to prevent myself from waking her would be foolish, for it would mean adopting aims (whether instrumental or ultimate) diametrically opposed to each other. This pattern holds true whether or not P is something impersonally good.[48]

Those with residual sympathy for consequentialism may complain that even if this shows that Alice's killing Val here would be worse than her letting Victor be killed and that her killing Val would also be worse than her letting Vincent be killed, it does not show that it is worse than Alice's letting *both* Victor and Vincent die. Yet even if everyone should count for one, that does not tell us *how* each should be counted. A moral method taking seriously the fact that someone's moral duties are always duties owed this or that person on account of the role(s) she fills in the person's life, should require that the cases for and against acting to prolong the life of each interested party be made one at a time. What I have in mind can be made clearer if we model moral reasoning as an adversary proceeding in a kind of courtroom. In my view, the proper way to organize these moral hearings, the way most consistent with a role-centred

---

[48] It is true that when I do not just expect but positively *know* that my action will have a certain undesirable result, then I cannot rationally take steps to prevent that result while I perform the action. Here, however, the interference comes from my *cognitive* stance towards the undesirable result. It remains true that the attitude of my *will* by itself is not so fixed on the undesirable result that *it* (by itself) rationally excludes my taking steps to thwart that result. My claim has been that only inputs justify actions and, among inputs, that cognitive attitudes are relevant primarily as indicators of the agent's volitional and desiderative stance. Nothing in our treatment of the special case of situations in which the agent is sure of the bad result undermines that claim, nor the more fecund claim that action done with the mere expectation of certain bad results is not so bad as action done with the intention that such results ensue.

conception of moral life, is to demand that, in the case just considered, Victor come before the bar *alone* to make the case for Alice's saving his life from Anna's threat by Alice's taking Val's. Only after that case is adjudicated does Vincent then get to come before the bar to make the case for saving his life. Each of these litigants will meet Val as adversary. Each will, in turn, try to show that the moral case against Alice's letting him die is stronger than that against her killing Val. Only such a procedure as this will remain faithful to the fact that for anyone to act wrongly is *to wrong someone* by the former's violating her relationship with the latter and that, for this reason, anyone's acting more wrongly in doing one thing than doing that must consist in her wronging some*one* more gravely by doing this than she would otherwise wrong anyone by doing that. Of course, my contention is that Val will win each such contest, since Alice's intentionally killing him wrongs Val more gravely than her refusing to kill him (and therein letting them be killed) wrongs either Victor or Vincent.

Thus, virtues-basing, role-centring, patient-focus, and input-drive combine with Richardsonian specification to defend a conclusion sharply at variance with standard consequentialism. Moreover, the conclusion in its absolutist implications is plainly also at variance with Sen's more sophisticated position-relative brand of output-driven ethical theory. Sen's position-relative value theory may approximate some analogue of role-centring, but the sort of input-driven account of action-justification that emerges from virtues-based moral theory, with its focus on the welfare of each moral patient, seems beyond the reach of Sen's theory.

## VII. Sen on reason and strong belief

Let us briefly return to our point above that instrumental reason is an inadequate supplement to sympathy because sympathy needs reason to justify it, not just to implement it. The kind of reason that can justify sympathy would need to be different from that which calculates means to ends. In the philosophical literature, some of the main options have been reason as intuitive (or, perhaps, inferential) grasp (i) of first principles ('reason sees sympathy is better'), or (ii) of natures, especially of human nature and what develops it (Aristotelian), or (iii) of the nature of values and what suits them (e.g. Max Scheler), or (iv) of feelings and when they are appropriate (e.g. Franz Brentano). In so far as each of these uses of reason tends to yield well established or even apodictic propositions, it tends to justify the 'strong[er] belief' that worries Sen, though none fits Sen's term 'instinct', in so far as instinct is essentially nonrational. Moreover, moral feelings can be important indicators of morality's 'first principles', and serve as an important check on their theoretical reconstruction. Perhaps these are not, *pace* Brentano and Alexius Meinong, incorrigibly 'experienced as correct', and perhaps reason needs to assess them by investigating the nature and location of value, the value inherent in persons (including the moral subject) and elsewhere, and the point and structure of feelings, sentiments, and other modes of value response. Still, Sen seems not to appreciate this epistemic role of feelings as important (and perhaps indispensable). Some have preferred to ground sympathy in hypothetical contracts or accounts of the nature of morality. My own approach notes that such things as someone's relief from suffering, the improvement of her condition, her moral development, and so on, cannot plausibly be seen as merely instrumentally desirable. Because being 'desirable' in this use is best understood as being what it is morally good/virtuous to desire, this means that the virtues cannot be instrumental and that attachment to the welfare of persons is virtuous independently of its actual, general, or probable results.

Whatever approach is taken to grounding sympathy, sympathy for each individual is a fundamental moral datum. This is surely an appropriate content of firm and unwavering belief. What Sen repeatedly calls 'blind belief' may well be the enemy of reasoned inquiry and of moral action that Sen worries it is.[49] Yet this is not the whole story. What chiefly poses danger to moral conduct is *what* moral beliefs someone has, not their shielding from criticism or the firmness with which they are held. Steadfast moral convictions, grounded in reasoned speculation about humanity's nature, sociality, origin, and destiny, and perhaps also in apodictic, emotionally presented intuitions, are probably an indispensable part of a bulwark against the kinds of victimization totalitarians practised in the last century. That is not to deny that fanaticism is a threat, but to remind ourselves that, contrary to Richard Hare's notorious treatment, fanaticism is manifested in unyielding attachment to ends, a willingness to take any means to them.[50] It is the distinguishing characteristic, the essential hallmark, of consequentialists not, as Hare imagines, of their intellectual and moral adversaries. That this evil is promoted to moral principle in consequentialism is part of what makes that 'discipline' (as Sen calls it) unfit for use in moral reflection, deliberation, or action.

[49] See, especially, Sen (2000*a*).
[50] See, among other discussions, that in Hare (1963: ch. 9).

Sen has extended his strictures against deferring to strong belief also to anyone's relying in her practical reasoning on social tradition or so-called group identities.[51] I will not pursue those arguments of his here. We need not reject Sen's claims that neither tradition nor group identity can be autonomous with respect to reason, because a reasonable person can and should rationally evaluate a tradition's practices and modes of thought and the claims someone's affiliation with any ethnic or racial group is presumed to make on her loyalty, conformity, and service.[52] Yet this does not show that one's moral life can be adequately conceived or conducted on the basis of merely instrumental rationality. On the view I have suggested, whatever moral virtues or vices a person has, as well as any moral rights or obligations devolved upon her therefrom, are ones that she has *as* occupying one or another morally determinative role-relationship in the life of some person or persons. These role-relationships may or may not be recognized in a given system of belief, set of traditions, or group's self-conception. Nevertheless, there is little reason to think that the role-relationships that constitute our moral lives are mere inventions—'constructions' in the fashionable term—of social groups.

In the end, then, I think that where reflection on the roles of strong belief, tradition, and group identity in practical rationality leads is consideration of what we can learn from what I termed 'role-centring'. If we follow today's common, though misleading and objectionable, practice of calling a person's 'identities' the categories that mean the most to her in her deliberation and self-image, or those that matter most to others in their treatment of her, then we ought to say that, morally, anyone's identity ought, in the first instance, at least, to be multiple. The personal and interpersonal categories that matter most—that determine her moral virtues, duties, etc.—are those of friend, of fellow, of citizen, spouse, parent, child, and so on, whether or not she or her social group happens to realize, recognize, or like that fact.[53] These morally determinative roles are analogues of friendship, most of them forms of friendship. Some of these we choose to enter and occupy. Some we discover ourselves already to occupy. All of them pose choices. That discovery is a kind of

---

[51] See Sen (1999*b*), (2000*a*) and (2000*c*).

[52] The MacIntyrean position that reason itself must turn to traditions of inquiry for its standards and criteria, if not for its basic principles, merits more serious engagement than Sen's strategy of branding it relativist and dismissing it on that basis. See, especially, Sen (1999*b*) and (2000*a*). For more on this aspect of MacIntyre's thought, see my contribution to Murphy (forthcoming).

[53] Some of us think the most important one of these roles, incorporating the rest, is that of creature. I hope to pursue that more theological development of the theory on another occasion.

achievement of reason, to be sure. However, it is not unaided reason, but reason informed by what Smith (and perhaps Hume) might call 'sympathy'.

That sympathy, feeling what the other feels, is a starting point. In an adequate theory, the Scotsmen's 'sympathy' needs to transform itself into a critical benevolence, where we want (and are therein motivated to seek) for each person, not for any average or typical human (let alone for humanity's future), simply what normal and informed people would want in her place, not what she happens to want, but what is objectively beneficial to her, rooted in a reflective understanding of human beings, our needs and capacities. This reflection on being human will involve intellectual virtues that may themselves be forms of moral virtues or interdefinable with them. Merely instrumental reason and consequence-driven evaluation are not up to this task. Sympathy, then, and respect, need supplementation and justification beyond what can be provided by the instrumental rationality that Sen seems to have in mind. That project will need theoretical reflection on fundamental forms of human relationships, as I suggested above.[54]

## VIII. Virtues-based moral theory and the place of virtues in epistemology

Linda Zagzebski and Abrol Fairweather list several questions that should be addressed in the recent approach to epistemology that stresses the intellectual virtues.

> Which of the many notions of virtue is best suited for epistemic evaluation? Are the moral and intellectual virtues unified?...Are certain affective states intrinsically praiseworthy, or only insofar as they bring about true beliefs?...How do we balance epistemic principles and virtue in our theory of knowledge?[55]

The sort of virtues-based moral theory here sketched may also suggest some lines of response to these epistemological problems. The understanding of virtue we have employed is centred in differentially demanding roles. Adapting that to epistemology might yield a theory in which different levels of scrutiny, care, and so on might be minimally virtuous in different roles an

---

[54] It probably will also require revivified study of human nature—informed by the natural and social sciences, but resolutely philosophical—perhaps of the sort recently undertaken in MacIntyre (1999). [55] Fairweather and Zagzebski (2001: 12).

epistemic subject occupies. Of course, that exacerbates the problems of disunity and conflict that the plurality of virtues already poses, and suggests that in epistemology, as in ethics, unity may require development of a coherent theory of the subject as a unified self. That suggests that philosophical anthropology and psychology may be no less necessary to epistemology than to ethics. As to how the virtues are good, intrinsically or instrumentally (what they 'bring about'), this approach indicates another option. Such moral virtues as compassion are not good merely instrumentally, because they would count towards their bearer being a good friend, fellow, etc., even in the absence of usual or contextual desirable results. Nor are they good intrinsically; for they are not so much themselves good as they are good-*making*. Such moral virtues are, rather, constitutively good-making—they are that in which being a good friend, etc. consists. Perhaps we might profitably say something similar of many of the intellectual virtues—epistemic patience, courage, boldness, humility, trust, and so on. They are neither good in themselves nor merely good for their results. Rather, they are constitutively good-making, counting as such towards our being good reasoners in this or that capacity.

Finally, the approach taken here to moral duty, right, and wrong, and therein to moral principle, treats those features as definable through the virtues and vices. What is wrong is what it would be vicious to do. Similarly, talk of epistemic principle and requirement might be reducible to discourse about the intellectual virtues and vices. For someone to violate her epistemic duty might be understood as her doxastic states expressing and emerging from epistemically vicious mental states or operations, that is, ones that count towards her being bad in some epistemically central roles. Plainly, our lack of voluntary control over our epistemic states and the scalar nature of epistemic justification calls for some such interpretation of epistemic duty.

I leave it to the epistemologists to determine whether these suggestions prove promising to their enterprise. If so, all the better. Even if not, the suitability of a role-centred, patient-focused, input-driven, virtues-based approach to moral theory needs to be assessed in its own right. My project here has been to suggest how it can both illuminate and offer alternative approaches to problems inherent even in sophisticated consequentialist understandings of practical reason and its excellence.

Part Three

*The Good of Knowledge*

# 5

# Knowledge as Credit for True Belief

## John Greco

I begin by reviewing two kinds of problem for fallibilism about knowledge. The first is the lottery problem, or the problem of explaining why fallible evidence, though otherwise excellent, is not enough to know that one will lose the lottery. The second kind of problem is Gettier problems. I will argue that both kinds of problem can be resolved if we note an important illocutionary force of knowledge attributions: namely, that when we attribute knowledge to someone we mean to give the person credit for getting things right. Put another way, we imply that the person is responsible for getting things right. The key idea here is not that knowledge requires responsibility *in* one's conduct, although that might also be the case, but that knowledge requires responsibility *for* true belief. Again, to say that someone knows is to say that his believing the truth can be credited to him. It is to say that the person got things right owing to his own abilities, efforts, and actions, rather than owing to dumb luck, or blind chance, or something else.[1]

---

I would like to thank Robert Audi, Heather Battaly, Michael Bergmann, Stewart Cohen, Keith DeRose, Tamar Gendler, Stephen Grimm, Daniel Nolan, Philip Quinn, Wayne Riggs, Ted Sider, Eleonore Stump, Ernest Sosa, Fritz Warfield, and Linda Zagzebski for their helpful comments in discussion and on earlier versions of the chapter.

[1] The idea that knowledge entails credit for true belief can be found in Sosa (1988) and (1991), and Zagzebski (1996) and (1999*b*). More explicitly, Wayne Riggs argues that in cases of knowledge 'we deserve credit for arriving at true belief non-accidentally'. See Riggs (2002: 95).

# I. The lottery problem

The lottery problem for fallibilism is stated nicely by Stewart Cohen.[2] On the one hand, fallibilists want to say that there can be knowledge by inductive reasoning. Thus fallibilists define themselves against rationalists, who hold that only deductive grounds can give rise to knowledge. On the other hand, it seems that a ticket holder does not know that she will lose the lottery, even if the odds are heavily in favour of her losing. So here is the problem for fallibilism: how is it that in general one can know through inductive grounds, but in the lottery case one fails to know, though one's inductive grounds are excellent?

To sharpen the problem, consider two cases of inductive reasoning.

Case 1. On the way to the elevator S drops a trash bag down the garbage chute of her apartment building. A few minutes later, reasoning on the basis of past experience and relevant background knowledge, S forms the true belief that the bag is in the basement garbage room. Of course her grounds for so believing are merely inductive: it is possible that the trash bag somehow gets hung up in the chute, although this is extremely unlikely.[3]

Case 2. S buys a ticket for a lottery in which the chances of winning are ten million to one. A few minutes later, reasoning on the basis of past experience and relevant background knowledge, S forms the true belief that she will lose the lottery. Of course her grounds for so believing are merely inductive: it is possible that she buys the winning ticket, although this is extremely unlikely.

Many will have the intuition that S knows in Case 1 but not in Case 2. But how so, given that her reasons are excellent in both cases? This is what the fallibilist needs to explain.

## A. Nozick's tracking account

The difficulty of the problem is illustrated by some accounts that fail to solve it. According to Robert Nozick, S knows $p$ just in case S's believing $p$ tracks the truth.[4] Complications aside, this amounts to the following:

S knows $p$ just in case

1. $p$ is true.

---

[2] Cohen (1988) and (forthcoming).
[3] The example is from Sosa (2000a). We can imagine that the bag's getting hung up is extremely unlikely because everything would have to go just right for that to occur, including the trajectory of the bag, its contents, the distribution of its weight, etc.    [4] See Nozick (1981).

2. If *p* were true then S would believe *p*.
3. If *p* were false then S would not believe *p*.

Nozick's account does a good job explaining why S does not know in the lottery case: if S were going to win the lottery, she would still believe that she is going to lose. However, the tracking account rules incorrectly in the garbage chute case. This is because it is possible, although an extremely unlikely occurrence, that the trash bag gets hung up in the chute. But if the bag did get hung up, S would still believe that the bag is in the basement, and so S fails to satisfy clause (3) of Nozick's account. In fact, the garbage chute case and ones like it were originally formulated as counterexamples to Nozick's account.[5]

## B. Sosa's safety account

Let us say that one's belief is sensitive to the truth just in case it satisfies Nozick's clause (3). Ernest Sosa suggests that a belief is better safe than sensitive, where a belief is safe just in case one would have it only if it were true.[6] Complications aside, Sosa's suggestion amounts to the following:

S knows *p* just in case

1. *p* is true.
2. S believes *p*.
3. S would believe *p* only if *p* were true. Alternatively, S would not believe *p* unless *p* were true.

Sosa's clause (3) is ambiguous between the following two interpretations:

Strong Safety: In close worlds, always if S believes *p* then *p* is true. Alternatively, in close worlds never does S believe *p* and *p* is false.

Weak Safety: In close worlds, usually if S believes *p* then *p* is true. Alternatively, in close worlds, almost never does S believe *p* and *p* is false.

---

[5] Here is another counterexample to Nozick's account, due to Jonathan Vogel (1987: 212): 'Suppose two policemen confront a mugger, who is standing some distance away with a drawn gun. One of the officers, a rookie, attempts to disarm the mugger by shooting a bullet down the barrel of the mugger's gun. (I assume that the chances of doing this are virtually nil.) Imagine that the rookie's veteran partner knows what the rookie is trying to do. The veteran sees him fire, but is screened from seeing the result. Aware that his partner is trying something that is all but impossible, the veteran thinks (correctly as it turns out) [that the] rookie missed.'

[6] See Sosa (2000a), (1999a) and (1999b).

But now there is a problem. If Sosa means to endorse strong safety as a condition on knowledge, then his account does no better than Nozick's with Case 1: S would believe that the bag is in the basement even if it were hung up in the chute, and so S fails to satisfy a strong safety condition on knowledge.[7] This suggests that Sosa means his safety condition to be interpreted as weak safety. But now his account rules incorrectly that there is knowledge in Case 2: it is true that in close worlds, usually if S believes she will lose the lottery then it is true that she will lose, and so in the lottery case S satisfies a weak safety condition.

That is how Sosa's account rules on the lottery case when complications are set aside. When complications are not set aside, Sosa adds that there are other conditions required for knowledge, or at least for full-blooded, reflective knowledge. For example, in one place Sosa says that a belief's safety 'must be fundamentally through the exercise of an intellectual virtue', where an intellectual virtue is a reliable or trustworthy source of truth.[8] In another place he says: 'For reflective knowledge one not only must believe out of virtue. One must also be aware of doing so.'[9] But it seems clear that these added requirements do not make a difference in the lottery case, for there S *does* believe through reliable inductive reasoning, and might even be aware that she does.

## C. Cohen's contextualism

Finally, consider Cohen's own solution to the lottery problem. According to Cohen, the problem is solved by recognizing that attributions of knowledge are sensitive to context, and, more specifically, that the standards for knowledge are sensitive to context. We have knowledge in cases of ordinary inductive reasoning, such as that employed in the garbage chute case, because the standards that are operative in ordinary contexts are low enough to admit such cases as counting for knowledge. We do not have knowledge in the lottery case, however, because in that context the standards for knowledge are raised—the possibility of winning the lottery becomes salient, and our inductive evidence, as good as it is, does not rule out this possibility.[10]

I do not wish to deny Cohen's general point that the standards for knowledge are sensitive to context—it seems to me that they are. What is less clear is how this is supposed to solve the lottery problem for fallibilism. The problem is that Cohen gives us no explanation why the standards for knowledge should

---

[7] Here I am assuming that there is a close world in which the bag gets hung up in the chute. If that seems wrong, we can invoke Vogel's rookie cop example from n. 5. There it seems uncontroversial that there is a close world where the rookie's bullet enters the mugger's barrel.

[8] Sosa (1999a: 383, n. 7). [9] Sosa (1991: 278). [10] Cohen (1988: 106–7).

get raised so high in the lottery case. More specifically: he gives no explanation why the standards should be raised beyond S's capacities to meet them. Cohen is quite explicit that he means to remain within the framework of fallibilism. Moreover, in the lottery case it is stipulated that S has excellent (although fallible) reasons for believing that she will lose. So why, on a fallibilist account of knowledge, does S fail to know that she will lose? To be clear, I am not claiming that S *does* know in the lottery case—I agree that she does not. My complaint is that nothing in Cohen's account explains *why* S does not know.

The same problem can be viewed from a different angle. Cohen says that when S reasons about the odds, the very form of her reasoning makes the possibility that S wins salient. And once made salient, Cohen says, that possibility cannot be ruled out. But again, why can't it be? Why isn't S's reasoning about the odds good enough to rule out the possibility of winning, even once made salient? It has been stipulated that S has excellent reasons for thinking she will not win the lottery, so why doesn't she know that she will not win? In sum, Cohen's contextualism does not explain what it was supposed to explain: given that we are fallibilists about knowledge, and given that we think inductive grounds are good enough to know in other cases, why are S's grounds not good enough to know in the lottery case?[11]

## II. Gettier problems

It has long been understood that fallibilist accounts of justification give rise to Gettier problems. For example, consider the following.

> Case 3. On the basis of excellent (although fallible) reasons, S believes that her co-worker Mr Nogot owns a Ford: Nogot testifies that he owns a Ford,

---

[11] My claim is not that standards contextualism cannot explain the lottery case in principle. Rather, I restrict myself to the weaker claim that Cohen's contextualism does not in fact explain it. What are the prospects for other versions of standards contextualism? The trick, of course, is for the standards contextualist to explain why S does not have knowledge in the lottery case, while at the same time preserving the intuition that S does have knowledge in other cases of inductive reasoning. But this will be hard to do. For example, Keith DeRose argues that S has knowledge if her belief matches the truth out to the nearest world where a salient alternative possibility is actual. However, the matching requirement ensures that DeRose's account rules incorrectly in the garbage chute case and in the rookie cop case from n. 5. This is because these cases are designed so that not-p worlds are very, very close, and so no matter how weak the standards for knowledge are being set, S's belief will not match the truth far enough out into alternative possible worlds. In other words, no matter how close the nearest world where a salient possibility is actual, S's belief will not match the truth out to that world. See DeRose (1995).

and this is confirmed by S's own relevant observations. From this S infers that someone in her office owns a Ford. As it turns out, S's evidence is misleading, and Nogot does not in fact own a Ford. However, another person in S's office, Mr Havit, does own a Ford, although S has no reason for believing this.[12]

Clearly S does not know that someone in her office owns a Ford. The problem for the fallibilist is to explain why this is so, given that S has excellent evidence for this true proposition.

## III. A proposal for resolving the two problems for fallibilism

We may distinguish two questions one might try to answer when giving an account of knowledge. The first is the 'What is knowledge?' question. This question asks what conditions a person must satisfy to count as knowing. The second is the 'What are we doing?' question. This question asks what illocutionary act is being performed when we say that someone knows. I will have more to say about the 'What is knowledge?' question below. But I think that the key to solving our two problems for fallibilism lies in the 'What are we doing?' question.

So what are we doing when we attribute knowledge to someone? Clearly, we might be doing any number of things. But one of the central functions of knowledge attributions is to give credit for true belief. When we say that S knows p, we imply that it is not just an accident that S believes the truth with respect to p. On the contrary, we mean to say that S gets things right with respect to p because S has reasoned in an appropriate way, or perceived things accurately, or remembered things well, etc. We mean to say that getting it right can be put down to S's own abilities, rather than to dumb luck, or blind chance, or something else. But then this gives us a resource for solving the two problems for fallibilism reviewed above. For in the lottery case, it *does* seem to be just a matter of chance that S gets it right when S believes that she will lose the lottery. And in Case 3 (the Gettier case), it seems just a matter of luck that S gets it right that someone in her office owns a Ford. In the garbage chute case, however, we think that it is owing to S's good reasoning that she gets things right—we give S credit for arriving at the truth in this case, and we are therefore willing to say that she knows.

[12] The example is from Lehrer (1965: 169–70).

This is the main idea that I want to pursue.[13] The idea needs to be developed, however. For one, my treatment of the two problems has remained largely intuitive so far. More importantly, the main idea I am proposing is faced with the following problem. First, I have said that we are willing to give S credit for her true belief in cases of knowledge, but not in the lottery case or in Gettier cases. Second, I have said that this is because in the former, but not in the latter, S's arriving at the truth is owing to her own efforts and actions, or more exactly, to her own abilities. But it is not clear why the various cases can be distinguished in this way. Consider that in the lottery case, S uses excellent reasons to draw the conclusion that she will lose. And in the Gettier case, S reasons flawlessly to the conclusion that someone in her office owns a Ford. But then it seems that S arrives at the truth because of her abilities in all of the cases above, and not only in the cases where we judge that S has knowledge. Clearly, more needs to be said.

By way of saying more, I will draw on some important work in moral theory. Specifically, I want to look at Joel Feinberg's fascinating discussion of attributions of moral blame.[14] From this it will be easy enough to construct a general theory of credit attribution, and a theory of intellectual credit attribution in particular. With this groundwork in place, it will be possible to explain why it is appropriate to give S credit for her true belief in cases of knowledge, and appropriate to withhold such credit in the lottery case and Gettier cases. More specifically, it will be possible to explain why, in cases of knowledge, it is appropriate to say that S gets things right *because* of her own abilities, whereas in the lottery case and Gettier cases, it is appropriate to deny this.

## A. Feinberg on blaming

Feinberg's account of moral blaming takes off from the following central idea: when we attribute blame to a person for some occurrence, part of what we are

---

[13] I first suggested a solution to Gettier problems along these lines in Greco (1994). Linda Zagzebski develops the idea in a different direction in Zagzebski (1996) and (1999a), and Keith Lehrer develops a similar idea in Lehrer (2000). Earlier than any of this, Sosa writes that in cases of knowledge one's belief must 'non-accidentally reflect the truth of P through the exercise of... a virtue'. However, he does not suggest that this idea can be used to address Gettier problems. See Sosa (1988: 184). See also Sosa (1991: 277).

[14] Feinberg's discussion takes place over three papers, 'Problematic Responsibility in Law and Morals', 'Action and Responsibility', and 'Causing Voluntary Actions', all of which are collected in Feinberg (1970). My account of Feinberg's account of blaming is a reconstruction—I have taken parts of what he says from each of his three papers and put them together in a way that suits my present purposes.

doing is assigning causal responsibility to that person for the occurrence. Put another way, when we blame S for X's occurring, we imply that S figures importantly in a correct causal explanation of why X occurred. To get further insight into our practices of blaming, therefore, Feinberg makes some observations about the pragmatics of causal explanations in general. One important aspect of causal explanation language is this: in general, when we say that Y occurs because X occurs, or that Y's occurring is due to X's occurring, we mark out X's occurring as a particularly important or salient part of the causal story behind Y's occurring. For example, to say that the fire occurred because of the explosion is not to say that the explosion caused the fire all by itself. Rather, it is to say that the explosion is a particularly important part, perhaps the most important part, of the whole story. Or to change the example: to say that the fire occurred because of S's negligence is not to say that S's negligence caused the fire all by itself. Rather, it is to say that S's negligence is a particularly salient part, perhaps the most salient part, of the set of relevant factors that caused the fire.[15]

What determines salience? Any number of things might, but Feinberg cites two kinds of consideration as particularly important. First, among the various necessary parts of a complete causal process, an explanation will often pick out what is abnormal in the case, or what is contrary to expectations. For example, we will say that sparks caused the fire if the presence of sparks in the area is not normal. That explanation would misfire, however, if we were trying to explain the cause of a fire in a welding shop, where sparks are flying all the time. Or suppose that a white elephant walks into a room and causes a panic. Of course the white elephant entering the room is not sufficient all by itself to cause the panic—it would not if the room were part of a zoo and the people inside were animal trainers. But if the room is a place where white elephants are not expected to be, and if the people inside *are* as we would expect them to be, we have no trouble picking out the elephant as 'the' cause of the commotion.

Another major factor governing salience is our interests and purposes. For example, often when we are looking for something's cause we are looking

---

[15] It is tempting to follow Feinberg and to put things this way: when we say that Y occurs because X occurs, or that Y's occurring is due to X's occurring, we mark out X's occurring as a particularly important or salient part of a sufficient condition for Y's occurring (Feinberg 1970: 177). This assumes, however, that all causes can be understood as sufficient conditions. Since I do not want to deny either (a) the possibility of agent causation or (b) the possibility of indeterminate causation, I employ the looser language above.

for something that we can manipulate to good effect. If the thing to be explained is smoke coming from the engine, for example, we will look for a part that needs to be replaced. Here it is perfectly appropriate to say that the cause of the smoke is the malfunctioning carburettor, although clearly a faulty carburettor cannot cause smoke all by itself. Or witness the various explanations of New York City's plunging crime rate. The police attribute it to good policing, the mayor attributes it to broader social policy, and opposing politicians attribute it to things over which the mayor has no control, such as an upturn in the national economy. Of course any honest person would admit that the crime rate is influenced by all of these things. But different people have different interests, and so highlight different parts of the causal conditions that were together sufficient for the drop in crime.

None of this need be insincere, nor is salience something that is merely subjective. The argument over 'the' cause of the drop in crime is an argument over which of many causal factors should be deemed most important, given our collective interests and given what we know about human behaviour, how we want to spend limited resources, what policies have what costs, etc. Likewise, a correct explanation of what caused a panic focuses on what is in fact abnormal about the situation. As was noted above, if the presence of elephants in the room were not in fact abnormal, then a correct explanation would have to focus elsewhere. In sum, correct causal explanations pick out some salient necessary part of a total set of causal factors, where salience is determined by a number of factors, including what is in fact normal and what are our actual interests.[16]

We may now revisit Feinberg's point that attributions of blame imply causal explanations. This is most obvious in cases where the thing for which the person is blamed is a consequence of the person's actions. For example, to blame someone for the fire is to imply that her actions caused it: she is the one who struck the match, or who did not pay attention, or who did pay the arsonist. Alternatively, we can blame a person for the action itself, implying that she herself was the action's cause, or perhaps that her choice was or her efforts were. As Feinberg notes, the distinction between blaming someone for her action and blaming someone for a consequence of her action is often merely

---

[16] Another example: sports fans will argue endlessly over why we lost the big game. Was it because we gave up too many points or because we didn't score enough? Obviously, the outcome of a game is a function of both points allowed and points scored. The real argument here is over what was the most important factor in the loss. And *that* is a function of what one can normally expect, what could have been done differently, etc.

verbal. For example, we can say either 'She caused the fire by striking the match', or 'She started the fire'. Likewise, 'She caused his death by poisoning his food' substitutes for 'She killed him'.

Finally, Feinberg argues that when we blame someone for an action we imply that the action reveals something important about the person himself: 'In general, I should think, a person's faulty act is registerable only if it reveals what sort of person he is in some respect about which others have a practical interest in being informed.'[17] Feinberg's position is perhaps too strong on this point; it would seem that people can be rightfully blamed for actions that are out of character. Nevertheless, there does seem to be a *kind* of blame that Feinberg is right about. In other words, even if not all blaming implies that the person's action reveals a faulty character, there is a strong sort of blame, which is common enough, that does. Moreover, this strong sort of blame has a counterpart in a strong sort of credit. Often enough, credit for an action implies a judgement about the person as well, implying not only that the person is responsible for doing something good, but that this is a manifestation of virtuous character.

Putting all this together, Feinberg's account of blame for an action can be summed up as follows.

A person S is morally to blame for action A only if
   a. A is a morally faulty action,
   b. A can be ascribed to S, and
   c. A reveals S's faulty moral character.

Feinberg concludes that attributions of blame share the same pragmatics as causal explanations. His argument for this emphasizes clause (b) of the above account: attributing blame involves ascribing action, and ascribing action involves causal citation. What I want to emphasize, however, is that clause (c) acts the same way. Clause (c) also ensures that attributions of blame involve causal citation, for what does it mean to say that an action reveals character, other than that the action results from character? In other words, clause (c) can be read:

c'. S did A *because* S has a faulty moral character.

This might seem too strong, and it is if we read (c') as saying that S's character was sufficient all by itself to cause S's action. Similarly, it is too strong if we read (c')

---

[17] Feinberg (1970: 126).

as saying that, given S's character, S had to do A. But it is not too strong if we remember the pragmatics of causal explanation language reviewed above. For according to that account, to say that S's action is a result of her character is to say that S's character is an important part, perhaps the most important part, of the story. Taken this way, (c′) is not too strong at all, but rather reflects our common-sense attitudes about the sources of human action. The fact is, we cite character in explanations of human behaviour all the time, as when we say that he made the remark because he is insensitive (as opposed to having a bad day), or that she failed to spend the money because she is cheap (as opposed to hard up for cash at the moment).[18] Feinberg's analysis reveals that such explanations are implied in attributions of blame, or at least in attributions of a certain sort of blame. And this implies that attributions of blame (of that special sort) will inherit the pragmatics of causal explanations. Clearly, any action will be the result of a number of factors, including a person's character. But sometimes we want to say that character is particularly salient—that it is an important part, perhaps the most important part, of the story behind why the person acted as he did.

## B. A general theory of credit attribution

Feinberg's account of moral blaming can easily be broadened in two ways. First, I have already noted that the counterpart of blame for an action is credit for an action. In fact, we can use credit as the general term, and talk about positive credit (i.e. praise) and negative credit (i.e. blame) for an action. Second, there are kinds of credit other than moral.[19] For example, we credit athletes for athletic feats and thinkers for intellectual ones. Accordingly, I propose the following as a general theory of credit.

> A person S deserves credit of kind K for action A only if
> a. A has value of kind K,
> b. A can be ascribed to S, and
> c. A reveals S's K-relevant character. Alternatively: S's K-relevant character is an important necessary part of the total set of causal factors that give rise to S's doing A.

---

[18] Some recent work in social psychology suggests that common sense is flawed in this respect. For example, see Ross and Nisbett (1991). For a persuasive argument against such a conclusion, see DePaul (2000). [19] Feinberg's own discussion is at times aimed at other kinds of blame.

Two examples will illustrate this account.

> Case 4. Ken Griffey Jr. runs full speed toward the center field wall, leaps with outstretched glove, and catches the ball while diving to the ground. The home team crowd, just robbed of a game-winning double, shake their respective heads in admiration of Griffey's spectacular catch.
>
> Case 5. Griffey Jr. runs full speed toward the center field wall, trips, and falls face down on the ground. The ball bounces off his head, goes straight in the air, and comes down in his glove. The home team crowd, just robbed of a game-winning double, shake their respective heads in disgust.

In both cases, the action in question has clear athletic value—catching the ball before it hits the ground is essential to winning baseball games. Moreover, in both cases the catch is ascribable to Griffey—we can be sure that a broadcaster announcing the game will be yelling, 'Griffey caught the ball! Griffey caught the ball!' But only in Case 4 will Griffey be given credit for catching the ball, and that is because in Case 4 Griffey's catching the ball is the result of his relevant character, i.e. his great athletic abilities. In Case 5 Griffey's catching the ball was just dumb luck, and so the home team crowd is not just a bunch of sore losers. They are right to be disgusted.

A similar phenomenon occurs when a poor fielder makes a spectacular catch. In this case he will be given credit of a sort—he will get pats on the back from his teammates and applause from the crowd. But it won't be the same kind of credit that Griffey gets. *Griffey* makes spectacular catches all the time—*his* catches manifest his great skills. Not so when Albert Belle makes such a catch. If the catch is difficult, it is almost just good luck that he makes it. And opposing fans will treat it that way, withholding the credit they would readily give to Griffey. Or consider Bucky Dent's infamous home run to knock the Red Sox out of the play-offs. To this day Boston fans do not give Dent credit for the home run or the Yankees credit for the win. Dent was just a singles hitter, and his fly ball would have been a routine out in any park but Fenway. The home run was just bad luck, Boston fans think, having little to do with Dent's abilities as a hitter.

Finally, it is interesting that the case can be viewed in more than one way. Yankee fans *do* give Dent credit for the home run—to them, he will always be considered a great hero. This is because Yankee fans don't think that Dent's home run was just a matter of luck. Their thinking emphasizes the idea that *some* luck is always involved in sports, but Dent got his bat on the ball, he was strong enough to muscle it out there, and he was able to take advantage of Fenway's short left field. In other words, their account of the home run downplays luck and emphasizes Dent's abilities. This is a common enough phenomenon in sports: losers try to deny credit by emphasizing the role of luck, and winners try to take credit by putting the emphasis back on ability. Hence the attractive but dubious claims that 'Good teams make their own luck' and 'It all comes out even in the end'.

## C. A theory of intellectual credit attribution

When we attribute knowledge to someone we imply that it is to his credit that he got things right. It is not because the person is lucky that he believes the truth—it is because of his own cognitive abilities. He figured it out, or remembered it correctly, or perceived that it was so. Applying the account of credit attribution above, we have:

> S deserves intellectual credit for believing the truth regarding $p$ only if
> a. believing the truth regarding $p$ has intellectual value,
> b. believing the truth regarding $p$ can be ascribed to S, and
> c. believing the truth regarding $p$ reveals S's reliable cognitive character. Alternatively: S's reliable cognitive character is an important necessary part of the total set of causal factors that give rise to S's believing the truth regarding $p$.

And hence:

> S knows $p$ only if believing the truth regarding $p$ reveals S's reliable cognitive character. Alternatively: only if S's reliable cognitive character is an important necessary part of the total set of causal factors that give rise to S's believing the truth regarding $p$.

We are now in a position to apply these results to the two problems for fallibilism.

# IV. The lottery problem solved: chance undermines credit

The application to the lottery problem is initially straightforward: knowledge attributions imply attributions of intellectual credit for true belief, and intellectual credit implies that the true belief is the result of S's own intellectual abilities. But here as in other cases, salient chance undermines credit. In the lottery case, but not in the garbage chute case, it seems just a matter of chance that S believes the truth. In the garbage chute case, but not in the lottery case, S's true belief is appropriately credited to her, i.e., to her intellectual abilities.

This was our initial treatment of the case. But this initial treatment gave rise to the following problem: S employs admirable inductive reasoning no less in the lottery case than in the garbage chute case. In both cases, therefore, S's abilities make up a necessary part, but only a part, of the whole story regarding S's believing the truth. The present account of credit solves this problem. For it is only in the garbage chute case that S's abilities are a *salient* part of the story. In the lottery case, what is most salient is the element of chance.

Why does the element of chance become salient in the lottery case? I would suggest that the very idea of a lottery has the idea of chance built right into it. Here is the way we think of the lottery case: first, S reasons on the basis of excellent grounds that she will lose the lottery. Second, the lottery is held and reality either does or does not match up with S's belief—it's just a matter of chance. Notice that things are different if S believes that she lost the lottery because she reads the results in the newspaper.[20] Here again her evidence is merely inductive, but now the role of chance does not play an important part in the story. Here is the most natural way to think of the newspaper case: first the lottery is held and the facts are fixed. Second, S infers from a reliable source that she has lost the lottery. Now it is not just a matter of chance that she believes the truth—she believes the truth because she has the good sense to believe what she reads about the results.

Two more cases help to explore the implications of the present account.

> Case 6. On the basis of excellent evidence, S believes that her friend will meet her in New York City for lunch. However, S's friend has bought a ticket in the lottery, and if he were to win then he would be in New Jersey to collect his winnings. In fact, the friend loses the lottery and meets S for lunch.[21]

Intuitively, people can know things about their friends even when, unknown to them, their friends have bought tickets in the lottery and would behave differently if they won. On the other hand, there is some intuitive pull towards thinking that S does not know in Case 6, since if her friend were to

---

[20] This point is made in Cohen (1988).
[21] This kind of case is discussed in Cohen (1988) and in Harman (1974).

win the lottery then he would not meet her for lunch. The present account explains these conflicting intuitions by distinguishing contexts of attribution. In contexts where considerations about the lottery are not important, the salience of chance is low and so attributions of knowledge can still be appropriate. However, in contexts where considerations about the lottery are important, the salience of chance rises, and therefore knowledge attributions are undermined. Handling Case 6 this way allows us to say that knowledge is closed under known entailment. Taking a page from the book of standards contextualists, we may note that there is no single context relative to which (a) S knows that her friend will meet her for lunch, (b) S knows that her friend will meet her for lunch only if he loses the lottery, and (c) S does not know that her friend will lose the lottery. If the context does not make chance salient, then relative to that context S can know that her friend will meet her for lunch. But if the context does make chance salient, then relative to that context S knows neither that her friend will meet her for lunch nor that he will lose the lottery.[22]

Now consider another case.

> Case 7. S is visiting from another culture and knows nothing about lotteries. However, over a long period of time S observes many people exchanging dollar bills for small slips of paper, which they invariably discard after a brief examination. On the basis of excellent inductive reasoning, S concludes that the next person in line will soon discard his slip of paper. And in fact S's belief is true.[23]

This case threatens a counterintuitive result: that relative to S's context, S knows that the next person in line will discard his ticket. Put another way, if S were to express a knowledge claim, then, relative to S's own context of attribution, his claim would be true. This result threatens because S understands nothing about the workings of lotteries. And therefore, it seems, chance could not be a salient factor in S's context. However, this way of interpreting the case assumes that salience is a psychological phenomenon—that salience is a function of where someone's attention is, or how he is thinking about things. This is admittedly one meaning of the term, but it is not the one that we want here. On the contrary, I have argued that salience is a function of (a) what is in fact

---

[22] Cohen and DeRose have both argued that contextualists need not run into closure problems. See Cohen (1988) and DeRose (1995). For an early discussion of relevant issues, see Stine (1976). [23] This sort of case was raised by Phillip Quinn in discussion.

normal or abnormal in the case, and (b) what interests and purposes are in fact operative in the context of attribution. Therefore, whether something is salient relative to a context of attribution, in the sense intended here, is not a question about how anyone is thinking.

What we are looking for is not psychological salience but explanatory salience. The way to identify what is salient in this sense is to ask where a correct explanation would have to focus. As noted above, a correct explanation of a car fire might properly focus on sparks coming from the engine, whereas a correct explanation of a fire in a welding shop must focus somewhere else. But this has nothing to do with how people are thinking about the cases. Rather, it has to do with what is in fact normal and abnormal in cars and welding shops. Likewise, if a drunk driver runs a light and is involved in a collision, then almost always a correct explanation will focus on the driver's impaired condition. Given the interests and purposes that are usually in place, other explanations of the collision are almost always inappropriate.

These considerations explain why it is correct to say that S does not have knowledge in Case 7, even relative to S's own context of attribution. For although the role of chance has no psychological salience for S, it does have explanatory salience; that is, any correct explanation of why S believes the truth would have to refer to the lottery. This is because playing the lottery is pretty much the only thing going on here. Relative to almost any context we can imagine, including S's own, an explanation that did not refer to the lottery would leave the most important thing out. This is in contrast to Case 6. In that case any number of factors contribute to S's believing the truth regarding her friend meeting her for lunch. And relative to most contexts that we can imagine, the fact that her friend loses the lottery will play no important part in a correct explanation of why she believes the truth.

Finally, it will be helpful to compare the present account with standards contextualism. First, both accounts are contextualist; that is, they both make the truth conditions of knowledge claims relative to the context of attribution. But the way this works in the two accounts is different. According to standards contextualism, the context of attribution determines the standards for knowledge, so that standards are higher or lower relative to different contexts. On the present account, however, the context of attribution determines the salience of various contributing causal factors, thus determining responsibility for true belief. Standards are not raised or lowered according to context; rather, responsibility for a complex event (someone's believing the truth) is creditable or not creditable to the believer according to context.

Second, I argued above that familiar versions of standards contextualism do not explain why S's inductive reasoning does not allow her to know that she will lose the lottery. The standards contextualist says that in the lottery case the standards for knowing get raised because the possibility of winning becomes salient. But this does not tell us why S's reasoning fails to meet those standards, even if raised. The present account does better in this respect. The very idea of a lottery involves the idea of chance, and so we have an explanation why chance is salient in cases where the lottery is salient. We can then apply a familiar general principle of credit attribution: that salient chance undermines credit.

## V. Gettier problems solved: abnormality trumps interest

Recently I have argued that the following conditions are necessary for knowledge.[24]

S knows p only if

1. S's believing p is *subjectively* justified in the following sense: S's believing p is the result of dispositions that S manifests when S is trying to believe the truth, and

2. S's believing p is *objectively* justified in the following sense: the dispositions that result in S's believing p make S reliable in believing p. Alternatively, the dispositions that result in S's believing p constitute intellectual abilities, or powers, or virtues.

The thinking behind the subjective justification condition is that knowledge requires that belief be appropriate from the knower's point of view. More specifically, the knower must have some awareness that a belief so formed has a good likelihood of being true. Some authors have required that the knower *believe* that this is so, but I have resisted this way of understanding the kind of awareness in question. It seems that people rarely have beliefs about the genesis of their beliefs, and so it would be too strong to require that they always have one in cases of knowledge. Accordingly, I have stated the subjective justification condition in terms of dispositions to believe rather than actual

---

[24] See Greco (2000*b*) and (1999*a*).

beliefs, or even dispositional beliefs. People manifest highly specific, finely tuned dispositions to form beliefs in some ways rather than others. And this fact, I take it, amounts to an implicit awareness of the reliability of those dispositions.

The objective justification condition can be interpreted along the lines of Sosa's weak safety condition above: to say that S is reliable in believing *p* is to say that, at least in relevantly close worlds, usually if S believes *p* then *p* is true. Notice that clause (2) makes the knower the seat of reliability: it says that S is reliable, not that some process is, or that S's method is, or that S's evidence is. The thinking here is that knowledge must be grounded in the knower. That is, it must be grounded in the knower's own abilities, rather than in a process or method that might be engaged in accidentally, or on evidence that might be trusted on a whim.

I now want to add a third condition on knowledge, understanding knowledge attributions to imply attributions of intellectual credit, and understanding intellectual credit along the lines above. I propose that adding this third condition makes the three sufficient as well as necessary for knowledge.

> 3. S believes the truth regarding *p because* S is reliable in believing *p*. Alternatively: the intellectual abilities (i.e., powers or virtues) that result in S's believing the truth regarding *p* are an important necessary part of the total set of causal factors that give rise to S's believing the truth regarding *p*.

I claimed above that clause (3) allows us to handle a range of Gettier cases. Intuitively, in cases of knowledge S's reliable character has salience in an explanation of how S comes to get things right. In Gettier cases, S's reliable character loses its salience in favour of something else. What we want now is an account of why this is so. Hence we have two questions before us: first, why is it that S's cognitive abilities have salience in cases of knowledge? Second, why is it that they do not have salience in Gettier cases?[25]

---

[25] What is a Gettier case? Zagzebski has argued that all Gettier cases are ones where bad epistemic luck is cancelled out by good epistemic luck. For example, in Case 3 S's evidence is deceptive (bad luck), but someone else in S's office owns a Ford (good luck). This analysis suggests that we can treat Gettier cases in the same way that we treated the lottery problem above—we can say that Gettier cases involve salient luck, and salient luck undermines credit. In my opinion this assessment is correct, but it is not as informative as we would like. This is because in Gettier cases, to say that S believes the truth because of good luck is very close to saying that S believes the truth for some reason other than her own abilities. And although that seems true, it is not more informative than what we already have—which is that clause (3) is violated. (In the lottery case, we said that the clause is violated because of the role of salient chance. That explanation *is* informative, however, because we have an independent grasp of what we mean by chance in a lottery.)

## Knowledge as Credit for True Belief / 129

To answer the first question we may turn to a point that has been emphasized by Sosa. He writes:

> All kinds of justification involve the cognitive or intellectual virtues, faculties, or aptitudes of the subject. We care about justification because it tends to indicate a state of the subject that is important and of interest to his community, a state of great interest and importance to an information-sharing social species. What sort of state? Presumably, the state of being a dependable source of information over a certain field in certain circumstances.[26]

For present purposes Sosa's point may be glossed this way: for beings like us, dependability (or reliability) of cognitive character is of fundamental social importance. But this implies that cognitive character will have a kind of default salience in the explanation of true belief. Unless something else is present that trumps the salience of S's cognitive abilities, those will be the most important part of the story, or at least a very important part of the story.

We may now turn to the second question: why is it that S's cognitive abilities are not salient in Gettier cases? Gettier cases seem to fall into three categories in this respect. First, there are cases where S's abilities are not salient in an explanation of true belief because S's abilities are not involved at all. Here is one such case.

> Case 8. Charlie has excellent reasons to believe that he will make his connection in Chicago. However, Charlie does not recognize these reasons for what they are, nor does he base his belief on them. Rather, he believes that he will make his connection because he is overcome with wishful thinking at the prospects of seeing his fiancée. As it turns out, his belief is true.

Here it is straightforward that Charlie does not believe the truth because of his intellectual abilities, since his abilities are not involved at all in the production or maintenance of his belief. As I have described the case, he believes the truth entirely out of wishful thinking.

Second, there are cases where S's belief is produced by faculties that would normally be considered abilities, but where S is not reliable in the environment where those faculties are used. Here are two.

> Case 9. Henry is driving in the countryside and sees a barn ahead in clear view. On this basis he believes that the object he sees is a barn. Unknown to

---

[26] Sosa (1991: 281–2).

Henry, however, the area is dotted with barn façades that are indistinguishable from real barns from the road. However, Henry happens to be looking at the one real barn in the area.[27]

Case 10. Rene is the victim of an evil demon who causes him to be systematically deceived. Despite admirable intellectual care and responsibility, almost all of Rene's beliefs are false. However, his belief that he is sitting by the fire, which is based on appropriate sensations and background beliefs, happens to be true.[28]

In Case 9 S's belief is the result of perception, and normally S's perception would constitute a cognitive virtue, i.e., a reliable ability or power. However, reliability is relative to an environment, and S's perception is not reliable relative to the environment in the example. Similar things can be said about Case 10—Rene's beliefs are caused by his cognitive faculties, and in a normal environment these faculties would constitute abilities or powers. But in Rene's actual environment his faculties are unreliable.

Finally, there are Gettier cases where S does use reliable abilities or powers to arrive at her belief, but where this is not the most salient aspect of the case. Case 3 regarding the Ford is one. Here are two others.

Case 11. A man *takes* there to be a sheep in the field and does so under conditions which are such that, when a man *does* thus take there to be a sheep in the field, then it is *evident* to him that there is a sheep in the field. The man, however, has mistaken a dog for a sheep and so what he sees is not a sheep at all. Nevertheless, unsuspected by the man, there *is* a sheep in another part of the field.[29]

Case 12. Smith looks at his watch and forms the belief that it is 3 o'clock. In fact, Smith's watch is broken. But by a remarkable coincidence, it has stopped running exactly twelve hours earlier, and so shows the correct time when Smith looks at it.[30]

In all three of these cases, reliable cognitive character gives rise to the belief in question—Lehrer's office worker reasons from her evidence, Chisholm's sheep-watcher trusts his vision, and Russell's time-teller trusts his watch. But in none of these cases does the person believe the truth because of reliable character. On the contrary, an explanation of how the person comes to get

---

[27] The example is from Goldman (1976). Reprinted in Goldman (1992).
[28] The example is from Sosa (1995).
[29] The example is quoted from Chisholm (1977: 105).
[30] The watch example is due to Bertrand Russell (1948). The example is cited by Chisholm (1977: 104–5), where he points out that it is a Gettier case.

things right would have to focus somewhere else. In Case 3, S believes the truth because someone else in her office owns a Ford. Chisholm's sheep-watcher believes the truth because there is a sheep in another part of the field. Russell's time-teller believes the truth because his watch has stopped running exactly twelve hours before he looked at it. In each of the cases, there is something else that is more salient than S's cognitive abilities in the explanation of how S came to get things right.

Why is that so in this third category of Gettier cases? I propose that, in at least many such cases, there is something odd or unexpected about the way that S comes to believe the truth, and that the salience of the abnormality trumps the default salience of S's cognitive abilities. We have already seen that the salience of abnormalities is a general phenomenon. When a white elephant enters the room, all bets are off for other explanations regarding why the room emptied out. The odd or the unexpected undermines the salience of other factors involved in the event. In fact, Gettier cases are often told so as to increase this effect. Typically, there is a first part of the case where an entirely normal scene is described. Then comes the 'big surprise' part of the case, where we get the odd twist: what S sees is actually a dog, but there happens to be a sheep in another part of the field; S's evidence is misleading, but someone else in the office owns a Ford.

Not all abnormalities undermine the salience of cognitive character, however. For example, an unlikely coincidence reminds the detective of evidence he has neglected, and this missing piece of the puzzle allows him to solve the crime. Less dramatically, an unusual noise causes someone to turn her head, and something else comes into plain view. We would like an account of which abnormalities undermine the salience of character in the explanation of true belief and which do not. Here is a suggestion that seems to handle the above cases well: abnormalities in the way one *gets* one's evidence do not undermine credit, whereas abnormalities regarding the way one gets a true belief, given that one has the evidence that one does, do undermine credit. Put another way, in cases where something unusual does take away the salience of character, it seems just a matter of good luck that S ends up with a true belief, *even given that she has the evidence that she does*.[31]

We may understand this point in a way that generalizes to other kinds of credit: we may say that, in general, situational luck does not undermine

---

[31] The distinction employed here is similar to Mylan Engel's distinction between verific and evidential luck, in Engel (1992). I thank Michael Bergmann for pointing out to me that Engel's distinction is helpful in the present context.

credit. In other words, luck in the way that one gets into one's situation does not undermine credit for what one does once in that situation. This, I take it, is one of the lessons of the literature on moral luck. A general prohibition on luck shrinks the sphere of moral responsibility to nothing, and hence an adequate theory of moral responsibility must allow for the influence of some kinds of luck but not others.[32]

In sum, the present account goes some way towards explicating the content and pragmatics of knowledge attributions, although we must recognize that it does not go all the way. It goes some way because it analyses knowledge in terms of credit attribution and credit attribution in terms of the content and pragmatics of causal explanations. It does not go all the way, however, because the pragmatics of causal explanations, and especially those concerning the salience of partial causes, are not fully understood. For example, the account given above in this regard is clearly only a partial account.[33] Nevertheless, our intuitions about knowledge seem to follow our intuitions about causal explanation: in cases of knowledge, we think that S believes the truth because she is reliable, whereas in Gettier cases we think that S's believing the truth must be explained in some other way.

## VI. Concluding remarks

I would like to end with two considerations that lend further support to the account of knowledge that has been offered here. First, the account predicts certain phenomena that do in fact take place. Second, the account suggests a solution to the value problem for knowledge.

### A. Conflicting knowledge attributions

If the preceding account of knowledge is correct, then there should be arguments over knowledge attribution that mirror arguments over other kinds of credit attribution. More specifically, there should be cases where disagreements over whether someone has knowledge reflect different emphases on

---

[32] In this regard, see Nagel (1979), Walker (1991), and Greco (1995).

[33] We can imagine Gettier-type cases, for example, where the problem is not abnormality in the way that S comes to believe the truth, but the interference of another agent, such as a 'helpful demon'. Here, as in other cases, credit for true belief and hence knowledge is undermined. And, here again, this seems to be a general phenomenon regarding credit. So, for example, the influence of a helpful demon would undermine moral credit as well. I thank Daniel Nolan and Tamar Gendler for raising this kind of concern.

# Knowledge as Credit for True Belief / 133

the relative importance of S's contribution to arriving at the truth. This is in fact the case. For example, consider the following conversation between a gambler and his wife.

GAMBLER: I told you so, Honey! I knew that horse would win!

WIFE: You knew no such thing, you idiot! That horse could have lost—you nearly threw away our rent money again!

GAMBLER: No—I knew she would win! I've been watching that horse for months now, and I knew that she would run great in these conditions.

WIFE: You son-of-a-bitch.

The conversation lends itself to the following interpretation: the gambler is trying to take credit for his true belief that the horse would win, and his wife is trying to deny him credit. In doing so, he tries to emphasize his ability to pick winning horses, and she tries to emphasize the role of luck.

In the context set by the above example I would tend to agree with the wife. But perhaps there are other contexts relative to which the gambler's claim to know is correct. Consider a conversation that might take place among gambling buddies.

FIRST GAMBLER: How did you know that horse was going to win?

SECOND GAMBLER: Are you kidding? I've seen her run in mud before, and the only horse in the race that could touch her was pulled just before post time. When I saw that, I ran to the betting window.

FIRST GAMBLER: You son-of-a-bitch.

In this context the claim to know is accepted by all involved. Perhaps this is because gamblers are deluded about the relative importance of luck and ability in picking horses. Alternatively, in the present context the role of luck is taken for granted, and so all emphasis is rightly put on the relative abilities among the gamblers. If the 'amateur' in the next row also picked the winner, he *wouldn't* be given credit for his true belief.

## B. The value problem

Recently, Linda Zagzebski has called attention to the value problem for knowledge.[34] An adequate account of knowledge, she points out, ought to

---

[34] Zagzebski raises the problem in (1996: 300–2), and in a more extended way in (1999*a*), reprinted in expanded form in Axtell (2000). See also Zagzebski's contribution to this volume.

explain why knowledge is more valuable than mere true belief. In closing, I will suggest how the present account solves that problem.

In Book II of the *Nicomachean Ethics*, Aristotle makes a distinction between (a) morally virtuous action and (b) action that is merely as if morally virtuous. One important difference, says Aristotle, is that morally virtuous actions 'proceed from a firm and unchangeable character' (II. 4). Moreover, it is morally virtuous action, as opposed to action that is as if virtuous, that is both intrinsically valuable and constitutive of the good life: 'human good turns out to be activity of soul exhibiting excellence' (I. 7). The same point holds for intellectually virtuous action, where the distinction between 'virtuous action' and 'action as if virtuous' translates to a distinction between knowledge and mere true belief. Following Aristotle, therefore, we get an answer to the value problem: as is the case regarding moral goods, getting the truth as a result of one's virtues is more valuable than getting it on the cheap.[35]

---

[35] Riggs takes a similar approach to the value problem. He writes, 'When a true belief is achieved non-accidentally, the person derives epistemic credit for this that she would not be due had she only accidentally happened upon a true belief.... The difference that makes a *value* difference here is the variation in the degree to which a person's abilities, powers, and skills are causally responsible for the outcome, believing truly that *p*' (Riggs 2002: 93–4).

# 6

# Intellectual Motivation and the Good of Truth

## Linda Zagzebski

## I. Introduction

According to the medieval doctrine of the Transcendentals there is a fundamental unity between the good and the true. We still think of truth as good, but we use the concept of truth differently than our predecessors did. To us truth is not a property of a belief. At best, it is a property of the object of belief—a proposition. In a deflationary theory truth does not even get the status of a property at all. Either way, truth is not a form of good. A true proposition is not like a good person or a good state of affairs. It is not even like a good thief since a true proposition is not better *as* a proposition than a false one. So when we speak of the good of true belief, we do not mean that truth is a good property for something to have. What we mean is that the relation that obtains between the believer and the proposition believed in a case of true belief is a good one. We can put the point another way without mentioning truth at all: roughly, what is good about a true belief is that the mind fits reality. Slightly less roughly, the agent's propositional representation of reality is accurate. Not all mental representations are propositional in form and not all representations aim to be accurate. Believing aims at accurately representing some part of reality propositionally.[1] When a belief is true it *is* accurate.[2]

To the medieval philosophers truth was identified as the property a *judgment* has when it is accurate; it is not a property of a proposition. So if accuracy in one's intentional aim is a form of good, they were right to speak of truth as a good. We continue to speak of the value of truth because of this history, but even though we are right to think that beliefs are good when they have true objects, the goodness of a true belief is not in the truth. The thing we think is good—the state of belief—is not true. The thing that is true—the proposition—is not good. But as long as we are clear about this distinction, I doubt that there is anything wrong with speaking about the good of truth.

We have made another change in traditional terminology that hopefully does not unduly complicate the issue of the value of true belief. Our category of belief is broader than the medieval category of judgement. When we speak of true beliefs we usually include dispositional states as well as judgements, where a judgement is a mental act but a belief may not be. True beliefs include dispositions to have accurate propositional representations, where being accurate is the aim of the representation. A true belief is therefore good because it is successful in its representational aim or is a disposition to be successful.

One part of the world we represent is ourselves representing the world. We represent ourselves representing accurately or inaccurately. We are therefore able to ask about the truth of our beliefs at the second order level while simultaneously believing them at the first. Beliefs aim at truth just because they are beliefs, but our ability to represent ourselves having false beliefs makes it possible for us to raise the question of whether our beliefs are true and hence good. We would not have an idea of good and bad believing if we did not have the second order capacity to represent ourselves representing and to think that we could do it accurately or inaccurately. Nor would we have the idea of knowledge, which is the form of good believing that has most captivated the imaginations of Western philosophers since Plato. Nor would there be an issue

---

[1] Not every propositional representation is a belief because not every such representation has the aim of representing reality accurately. Wishes, hopes, and fears are in this category. Wishes aim at making reality correspond to the propositional content of the wish. In contrast, beliefs aim at making their propositional content correspond to reality. (If I am right about this, corresponding is not a symmetrical relation. Correspondence has a direction.) This difference in the aim of these intentional states may explain why it is problematic to speak of an accurate wish even when you get what you wish for.

[2] Compare David Velleman's claim that a belief is accepting something as true with the aim of getting truth in Velleman (2000: ch. 11).

of responsibility for beliefs which, like responsibility for acts, requires the ability to examine our beliefs as objects. To have a belief is to think it is true; otherwise it would not be a belief. But even though we think every one of our beliefs is true, it can still be the case that we should not have thought so and we are quite capable of wondering if we should think so even while thinking so. We wouldn't be responsible for our beliefs if we couldn't wonder in this way.

The situation is similar but not identical in the evaluation of our acts. Aquinas thought that we always do an act 'under the aspect of good'.[3] But thinking that our acts are good does not in itself relieve us of responsibility if they are not good. We are responsible for our acts because we can reflect upon them. Similarly, when we have a belief we *ipso facto* think the belief is true, but it does not follow that we have no responsibility for believing what is true. Even while having a belief and thereby thinking it is true, we can, and sometimes should, ask ourselves whether it is true. Our responsibility for that portion of our cognitive activity that leads to belief arises out of the fact that we have this ability.

Our responsibility for our belief states suggests that there is a parallel between beliefs and acts. The degree to which beliefs *are* acts is an important issue in the philosophy of the mind and I do not insist that beliefs are literally acts. Nonetheless, I think it aids our understanding of the evaluative status of beliefs to see them as at least analogous to acts. As I mentioned, we tend to include dispositions in the category of beliefs, in which case beliefs ought to be considered acts and dispositions to perform acts of a cognitive nature. The focus of this chapter is on the evaluation of such acts and the cognitive activity that generates them. In particular, I am interested in the kind of evaluation that can function as useful advice in the way we conduct ourselves cognitively.[4] Since cognitive acts of this kind aim at true belief and since true belief is good, the good of true belief is bound to play a significant role in the evaluation of cognitive acts. Similarly, the production of good states of affairs is the aim of much of our overt activity. But since there are many ways in which the good of acts is related to the good of the outcomes of acts, there are also many ways in which the good of acts of belief can be related to the good of true belief. In the next

---

[3] *ST* I–II, q. 19, a. 1.
[4] This raises the issue of cognitive control. It might be that we are only responsible for our cognitive activity to the extent to which we can control it. If so, this leads to my requirement that the kind of cognitive evaluation relevant to our responsibility to have true beliefs is something we can use in making ourselves better cognizers. I will leave aside the control issue for this chapter, however, relying on the intuition that if we are responsible for our cognitive conduct, then there must be a kind of evaluation of it that we can use in such conduct. That is the sort of evaluation that interests me in the next four sections of this chapter.

four sections I will discuss four ways in which the value of cognitive acts can be related to the value of true belief. I will raise the issue of knowledge briefly when we get to section VI, but it is not the primary focus of this chapter.

## II. Consequentialist value

One way our cognitive activity could be evaluated is in terms of its consequences. We could take accuracy of propositional representations, or to return to the terminology of truth, true belief to be the basic epistemic good and false belief the basic epistemic bad. We could then say that cognitive activity is good just in case it is successful in its aim of reaching truth and avoiding falsehood. This is parallel to the evaluation of acts in consequentialist moral theories, in particular, hedonistic utilitarianism. Mill acknowledges that hedonist value is more complex than it appears, however, because pursuing pleasure and avoiding pain are different strategies. Mill does not find this problematic, but concludes that there are two kinds of happy lives:

> The main constituents of a satisfied life appear to be two, either of which is often found sufficient for the purpose: tranquillity and excitement. With much tranquillity, many find that they can be content with very little pleasure: with much excitement, many can reconcile themselves to a considerable quantity of pain.[5]

There is an epistemic parallel to Mill's tranquil life and exciting life, as William James pointed out.[6] A person who successfully avoids false beliefs may be content with few true beliefs, whereas with many true beliefs she may be able to reconcile herself to a number of false ones.

Simple reliabilism is epistemic consequentialism. Reliabilists say we want to maximize the ratio of true to false beliefs, but we also want lots of the former. One problem with this approach is that it is not at all obvious how we are to weigh the two values against each other. Is 85 per cent accuracy with many beliefs better or worse than 87 per cent accuracy with somewhat fewer beliefs? We could, I suppose, say that a preference for safety from falsehood over acquiring truth is just a matter of personal taste and epistemic temperament. Perhaps, like Mill, we could just agree that it doesn't matter. If Mill is right that there are two kinds of happy lives, perhaps there are two kinds of epistemically happy lives too—two ways of being epistemically good. Could we get away with the epistemic position parallel to Mill's—that quantity and

[5] Mill (1957: 18).  [6] James (1979).

a high accuracy ratio are both ways of being epistemically good and favouring one over the other is up to the individual?

It seems to me that in spite of any virtues that position may have in ethics, its epistemic parallel makes epistemic value too much a matter of personal preference. Any set of beliefs that either includes a lot of true beliefs or has a 'high' ratio of true to false beliefs would count as good, and we would be forced to permit an enormous range of variation in recognition of the two values. Epistemologists rarely have been so tolerant. Assuming we are right to find this unacceptable, we need a procedure to adjudicate the two. I will leave that question for others to investigate.

In spite of these difficulties, I think it is tendentious to deny that consequentialist value is a value. The real issue is whether it is the most important or the most interesting value and, as in debates over ethical consequentialism, we need to look at cases of epistemic value conflict to test that. I will mention two.

First, there is the problem that on the consequentialist/reliabilist approach no substantive activity is automatically evaluated positively, whether it be weighing evidence, following established logical procedures, or trusting that most authorities in one's epistemic community are reliable until proven otherwise. It is an empirical question whether any of these activities leads to truth and away from falsehood or furthers the goals of inquiry. None of these behaviours is epistemically valuable unless it is reliable, and it is valuable only because it is reliable. (Elsewhere I call this the alignment problem.[7]) Some utilitarians worry about the parallel problem in ethics and some do not. Is it good to be a kind and generous person? Shouldn't we know that it is in advance of looking at the evidence for the consequences of such behaviour? But a committed utilitarian will be unmoved by this difficulty. One can always remain a consistent utilitarian if one is willing to make some adjustments—sometimes rather serious—in prior intuitions about what is good and bad behaviour, and it is possible to be a consistent reliabilist in the same way. Some people are willing to let it be an open question whether kind behaviour is a good thing. And for the same reason, they can let it be an open question whether it is a good thing to weigh evidence, or be intellectually fair, impartial, thorough, and careful.

A related problem is that what happens and what we try to make happen can come apart on the consequentialist approach. A conscious aim for the good does not necessarily have good consequences; in fact, it has sometimes been suggested that better consequences result from a different aim. As

---

[7] Zagzebski (1999c); revised and reprinted as Zagzebski (2000c).

Sidgwick says, 'Happiness is likely to be better attained if the extent to which we set ourselves consciously to aim at it be carefully restricted.'[8] This is another test of how consequentialist a theorist really is. We can evaluate a person's intentions either by the value of their consequences, or by the value of the ends at which she aims. Suppose the epistemic position parallel to Sidgwick's is right—that we are more likely to get true beliefs if we do not consciously aim at truth. What if aiming at falsehood is more truth-conducive than aiming at truth? Here is another way in which maintaining consequentialism consistently comes with a price. If we cannot assume in advance a connection between aiming for truth and getting truth, then reliabilism does not give us any epistemic advice, and so reliabilism does not help us with the kind of evaluation pertinent to our responsibility to have true beliefs whether or not it is a good theory of knowledge. As long as it is an open question whether anything in particular is reliable, the advice can't be to be reliable. It is to do what we independently find out is reliable. So if the reliabilist approach is to be helpful, we need a reason to think there is a connection between reliability and trying to get the truth. Hopefully, there *is* such a connection, as John Greco has argued,[9] but then the latter is doing the work. This leads us away from consequentialism to another way in which the value of cognitive activity can be related to true belief: the teleological approach.

## III. Teleological value 1: natural ends

Instead of evaluating our cognitive activity by the extent to which true belief is a consequence, we could evaluate it in terms of whether true belief is its end. True belief can be a teleological value rather than a consequentialist one. That in turn could mean either a natural end or an intentional end—that is, what we move towards by nature, or what we consciously aim at. An end in either sense and a consequence are not the same thing.

Let us start with the first sense of 'end'—a natural end rather than an intentional aim. Could the value of true belief contribute to the value of cognitive activity as the natural end of that activity? Perhaps we can tell an Aristotelian story supporting this approach. (I do not mean a story from Aristotelian epistemology; I mean Aristotelian ethics.) The shortest version of the story would be something like this: having true beliefs is part of one's natural end, living a life of *eudaimonia*. Good cognitive activity contributes to the natural end of human life in the same way as good moral activity.

---

[8] Sidgwick (1966: 405).   [9] Greco (1990).

Now I have no interest in arguing that this approach won't work. In fact, I hope it does. In spite of the problems with natural teleology, it is hard to deny the sensibleness of the basic value idea of natural teleology, namely, that some things are *good for* us, and they're good for us just because we are the kinds of beings that we are and the world is the way it is.

We have already seen that truth is the intentional object of the state of belief and there is a sense in which we call that end good; it is a natural good in that it is the aim of belief. Of course, that is not sufficient to show that true belief is good *for* us. Nevertheless, it *is* reasonable to think that true beliefs are (in general) good for us. If so, it seems reasonable to evaluate cognitive activity according to how well it gets us what is good for us: true belief. Such activity would then be good for us in a derivative sense—like nutritious food and sufficient sleep. But this threatens to collapse into the first position, the consequentialist one. Is the value of cognitive activity anything over and above its tendency to have a good consequence, something that is good for us in a non-derivative sense? Presumably, Aristotle thought that moral and intellectual virtues are constituents of *eudaimonia*, and since *eudaimonia* is an active state, it includes components of morally and intellectually virtuous acts. So acts of intellectually virtuous true belief may be components of *eudaimonia* in roughly the same way morally virtuous and successful acts are components of *eudaimonia*. But this raises questions about the need for the success component. *Eudaimonia* no doubt includes lots of virtuous acts, both moral and intellectual, but there is no reason to think it is limited to virtuous acts that are successful in their ends—truth in the case of believing, many other ends in the case of moral acts. Do acts of intellectually virtuous true believing have a special place in a life of *eudaimonia*? The intellectually virtuous contemplation of truth does seem to be the central part of the good life as Aristotle describes it in Book X of the *Nicomachean Ethics*, but since the contemporary model of cognitive activity is inquiry rather than contemplation, this approach would probably have to be modified in many ways to fit it comfortably into contemporary discourse. I think, then, that this route has promise, but it is complicated. Let me move on.

## IV. Teleological value 2: intentional ends

The second sense in which true belief can be an end of cognitive activity is as an intentional aim. If true belief is good, whether good as a final end or as a means to some other good, cognitive activity might derive value from being intentionally aimed at true belief. This is different from the consequentialist approach for the same reason that evaluating an act according to whether it aims at utility is different from evaluating an act according to whether it leads to utility. It differs from the first teleological approach in that it does not appeal to natural ends or what is good for us. Note that on this approach true belief can either be instrumentally good or good as a final end.

There is reason to think that we do evaluate positively acts that intentionally aim at goods, including the good of true belief. We commend people who make others happy, and we also commend people who try to make others happy. We praise even more the people who do both. And we praise the most people who make others happy in part because they try to do so. It is the same with the value of true belief. We commend people who have true beliefs, and we also commend people who try to have true beliefs. We praise even more people who do both, those who both have true beliefs and try to do so. Most of all we praise people who not only have true beliefs and try to do so, but who have true beliefs in part *because* they try to do so. This is something I've argued before.[10]

Ernest Sosa has recently made some critical comments about aiming for the truth 'as such'.[11] Aiming for the truth as such is not the same as aiming at the truth for its own sake (as a final end), and I think he is right about that. Sosa explains the distinction as follows. Someone could want the truth as such even though she wants it as a means to some other end. For example, Sosa says he may want to open a door as such even though he wants to open it in order to enter a certain room. To do that he may want a key with a certain shape, but he does not want a key with that shape as such. What he wants as such is to open that door. Similarly, he may want to know the number of the winning lottery ticket as such even though knowing that is not something he wants for its own sake, but rather as a means to the end of winning the big money. Now I find Sosa's teminology confusing because he takes himself to be objecting to the idea that getting truth should be an epistemic *motive*, whereas it seems to me that the actual object of his criticism is the view that getting true belief should be an intentional aim. I will therefore take Sosa's objections to apply to the approach of this section and will address the value of motives in the next section.

Could cognitive acts get value from aiming at truth as such? One way the aim of truth could govern our belief-forming activities would be that we resolve to act on a maxim to believe $p$ just in case $p$ is true. But Sosa objects that

---

[10] Zagzebski (1996: p. II, sec. 6).    [11] Sosa (2001).

# Intellectual Motivation and the Good of Truth / 143

if we are in a position to apply the maxim, then we already believe *p*. Such a maxim is useless. We might instead try to adopt a maxim to use practices that are truth-conducive, but that gets us into a vicious regress because we are led into a hierarchy of practices each of which is adopted because of a prior belief that propositions of sort *F* are likely to be true. So if it makes sense intentionally to aim at true beliefs in one's cognitive activity, it cannot be by adopting one of these maxims. I agree with Sosa about that.

Nonetheless, as we saw in the first section, our ability to reflect about the truth of our beliefs at the second order level makes it possible for us to consider the issue of whether our beliefs are true even while believing them. I suggested that one of the reasons we ought to reflect about our beliefs is that we have responsibility for them and for the cognitive activity that leads to them. There are many kinds of responsibility and they have different functions in our ethical practices, but one of the ways in which responsibility for our beliefs arises is from our responsibility to others to be accurate informants. Given the plausible assumption that human beings are naturally garrulous and that we often reveal our beliefs involuntarily, we cannot be accurate informants unless we have mostly true beliefs. Hence, we have a responsibility to others to have accurate beliefs. Assuming that the kind of evaluation relevant to our responsibility for our beliefs is something we can take as advice, something we can act upon, it follows that there must be something we are able to do consciously, i.e. advice we can follow, to satisfy our responsibility to others to have true beliefs. Clearly, the advice 'Have true beliefs' is no advice at all, but the advice 'Try to have true beliefs' is something many of us think we can follow and, vague as it is, it captures the essence of our epistemic responsibility to others. But since Sosa is right that we cannot do that by following the practical syllogisms he describes, we must be able to do it in some other way.[12]

Sosa proposes a case that we can use to test the suggestion of this section that cognitive activity gets extra value from having truth as an intentional end. He asks us to consider his belief that his parents cared for him. It is possible that his desire that the belief be true disposes him to discount or ignore evidence

---

[12] Notice that if we think of cognitive evaluation as arising primarily from our responsibility to others, that tends to make our responsibility not to have false beliefs stronger than our responsibility to have true beliefs. I would conjecture that this is related to the fact that we have a greater responsibility not to harm others than to do them good. Social responsibility therefore favours a conservative approach. This is probably a mistake, but it is an understandable one.

that his parents did not care for him. But since there is no such evidence, his non-virtuous disposition is never engaged. He believes that they cared for him because he has plenty of evidence that they did. Sosa wants to say two things about this case: (1) his belief has epistemic value, even the kind that gives him knowledge (although knowledge is not my topic in this section); (2) he does not believe in a way that aims at truth as such since he might still have believed it had it been false. But it seems to me that Sosa's description of the case is not one in which he does not believe with the aim of getting truth as such; rather, it is a case that shows that aiming to get truth and aiming to avoid falsehood are not the same thing, as James showed us. Let me illustrate with a different example.

Here's what it would be like not to aim at truth as such: suppose I need to buy a new bathroom scale and I announce to my friends that I want to buy a scale that says I have lost 5 lbs. Why do they laugh? Because if we assume that it is reasonable for me to want to lose 5 lbs, then I should want a scale that indicates I have lost the weight because I *have* lost the weight. But if I simply want a scale that says I have lost 5 lbs, I do not want the truth of the belief as such. I want the pleasure of the belief rather than the truth of the matter, and that is silly. But if the scale indicates I have lost the weight, the belief that I have is probably true, assuming most new scales are reasonably accurate, so I probably wouldn't be able to get the belief unless it was true. But I do not want the truth as such because I want a true belief only in so far as such a belief is one I enjoy having. I don't really care about accuracy. What I care about is the enjoyment of having the belief. I want the belief qua enjoyable, not qua true. This is like Sosa's example of wanting a key with a certain shape as one that opens a certain door. He wants the key qua key that opens that door, not qua key with the shape that it has. He doesn't really care that the key has that shape, and I don't really care that my belief is true. But a key with that shape is the one he wants (one that opens the door), and a true belief is the one I want (one I enjoy having).

Now let us return to Sosa's belief that his parents loved him. As he describes the case, it seems to me that he *does* care if it's true, and he does aim at having a true belief as such. It's not that he wants to enjoy having the belief. But he is much more motivated to believe accurately if the belief is true than if it's false. And the same situation could apply to my believing that I've lost 5 lbs. Let's suppose now that I *do* want to know if I've lost 5 lbs—that is, if I've lost the weight, I want to know it. But maybe I do not want to know if I have not lost

# Intellectual Motivation and the Good of Truth / 145

weight, and I especially do not want to know if I have gained 5 lbs instead. But that does not mean that if I want to know the truth when I've lost 5 lbs I am not motivated by the aim of getting that true belief as such. After all, I do not want to miss the fact that I've lost 5 lbs if I have, and I want that *as such*. It is like wanting there to be a God, and wanting not to miss finding out if there is one, but being much less motivated to find out if there isn't one. So it seems to me that Sosa and I *are* aiming to get at the truth as such in these cases, even though we're much less motivated to get at the truth as such if the negations of our beliefs are true instead. Now we may be epistemically criticizable, of course, but I don't see that either of us can be criticized on the grounds that we are not aiming at truth as such.[13]

The moral is that valuing truly believing some proposition $p$ as such is compatible with not putting equal value on truly believing *not p* should *not p* be true instead. And it is compatible with not putting equal disvalue on falsely believing $p$. So I may not disvalue falsehood to the same extent that I value truth about some proposition, but James already alerted us to that possibility. It is rather common to value believing truths about matters of concern to us more than believing their negations should the negations be true, but that does not mean that we do not aim at the truth as such. It just means that we do not value the truth as such and disvalue falsehood as such across the board. Very little of what we value is across the board anyway.

So I can aim for truth as such in my belief formation, although Sosa is right that we cannot form our beliefs as the result of a practical syllogism the major premiss of which is either 'Believe what is true' or 'Adopt belief-forming practices that are truth-conducive'. It is highly doubtful that I follow any such syllogism, even implicitly, but this should not be too surprising when we consider that many things at which we aim do not typically appear as a major premiss in a practical syllogism, for example, our own happiness. Like true belief, happiness is an aim we have for ourselves. But for the most part, I doubt that we follow a practical syllogism: (1) Be happy. (2) X leads to happiness. (3) Do X. I seriously doubt that we use any such syllogism for most of what we

---

[13] Sosa's footnote on this starts out right and then goes into an example that does not apply to our case here. He construes the desire that if $p$, I believe $p$ as the desire that it not be the case that $p$ and I don't believe $p$. His example is one where that is satisfied because I don't want $p$ to be true. But the bathroom scale case is not like that. I want $p$ to be true and I want to make sure that if it is, I take notice.

do, even implicitly. But that does not mean that we do not have the intentional end of being happy. More importantly, valuing happiness and truth typically operate in our psychology not as ends in any sense, but as motives. Let us turn, then, to the fourth way in which the value of true belief can contribute to the value of cognitive activity—as a motive.

## V. The value of motives

Motives and ends are not the same thing. A motive is not the same thing as the intention to bring about a certain end. More than one motive can have the same end and the same motive can aim at different ends. For example, the end of giving someone a gift could be variously motivated by love, pity, or gratitude. And a motive such as love can cause an agent to aim at different ends, even at the same time. I take a motive to be a certain kind of psychic state in the agent that causes her to act and which can explain or make intelligible the acts it motivates. An end, in the sense discussed in the last section, is a state of affairs the agent tries to bring about through her act. A desire or intention to bring about an end is a psychic state, and these states are commonly associated with particular motives, but neither one is identical with a motive; a motive is not even the same kind of state as either a desire or an intention to bring about a certain end. Nonetheless, knowing that an agent aims at a certain end is often sufficient to identify her motive. So when we say that an agent's motive for her searching behaviour is to find her keys, we understand the typical motivational state associated with the end of finding one's keys, even though there is more *in* the motive than a state directed towards that end.

In my view motives are emotional states that move us because they are ways of representing the world affectively. However, my position on the nature of emotion and the way it motivates us is not important for my points in this chapter. I want to focus on the way motives can add to the value of the acts they motivate. The motives I will use for illustration are non-controversial examples of motives. These are the emotions of compassion and love. Neither is a determinate emotion, but they have many forms arising from the nature of their intentional objects. The love of true belief differs significantly from other forms of love and it is no part of my project to distinguish love of truth from, say, appreciation of truth. My point in this section depends only on the position that love of true belief is a psychic state that includes the valuing of true belief, and that it can motivate cognitive activity. For comparison I will

## Intellectual Motivation and the Good of Truth / 147

discuss compassion, which is a disvaluing of the suffering of another person, and which also can motivate action. For brevity I will sometimes speak of the love of truth, but given my remarks at the beginning of this chapter, I will take that to mean love of true belief since truth itself is not a good.

What kind of value does the love of true belief have? Presumably it at least has extrinsic value derived from the value of true belief. This might be due to a general principle that love of something valuable is itself valuable. Love of truth might also be good *for* us. Robert Adams has recently argued that what is good for a person is a life characterized by enjoyment of the excellent.[14] Presumably, he also thinks it is good for us to act in ways motivated by enjoyment of the excellent. If we applied Adams's approach to cognitive activity we could say something like this: (1) True belief is an excellence. (2) It is good for us to appreciate true belief. (3) Cognitive activity motivated by such an appreciation is good for us.

My own preference is for a non-teleological approach, but I do not deny that it is good for us to be motivated by love of truth, nor do I deny that love of truth gets some of its value from the value of true belief. I also think love of truth has intrinsic value, by which I mean value that is not derived from the value of anything else. But what I am particularly interested in here is whether the love of truth has a kind of value that is capable of conferring additional value on the acts it motivates, and I want to argue that it does. Whether it can do that without being intrinsically valuable is an issue in the metaphysics of value that I will discuss only briefly in this chapter.

One way to defend the position that love of truth can confer value on the acts it motivates without going very far into the metaphysics of value is by example. Let me use an analogy between the value of cognitive acts motivated by love of truth and the value of overt acts motivated by compassion. Apart from what compassion motivates a person to do and the ends it aims to accomplish, and apart from the consequences of acting on it, compassion is a good state because it is an accurate emotional fit with its intentional object, a suffering person. It is a disvaluing or aversion to the suffering of others. Acts motivated by compassion are better than acts arising from just any reliable process or faculty for relieving suffering. For example, suppose suffering persons were helped just by being around other people and hearing them talk,

---

[14] Adams (1999: 93). Adams's view on excellence seems to blur the distinction between intrinsic goods and final goods. He says an excellence is a non-instrumental good, good as an end, but he also says an excellence is a type of intrinsic good (ibid. 14).

that the sound of the human voice eased their pain. And suppose also that people were not aware of that connection. Talking when around a suffering person would have consequential value, but we would not evaluate it the same way we would evaluate an act with the same consequence that is motivated by compassion. An act motivated by compassion is better than an act that merely has the consequence that the suffering of another is relieved.

An act motivated by compassion is also better than an act that aims at alleviating suffering but without the motive of compassion. Suppose I am the sort of person who gets nauseated at the sight of a person suffering, so I aim to eliminate their suffering. I do not really disvalue their suffering as such; I just don't like to be nauseated. I would think that an act with such a motive is not as laudable as an act motivated by compassion. The conclusion is that, other things being equal, an act motivated by compassion is more valuable than an act that has the aim of compassion but without the motive, and is more valuable than an act that has the consequence at which compassion aims but without either the motive or the aim.

Compassion is a disvaluing or aversion to the suffering of others. The most straightforward epistemic parallel is an aversion to false beliefs. I maintain that such an aversion is a good thing quite apart from the fact that it motivates a person to act cognitively in ways that lead away from false beliefs. It is better for the same reason that compassion is better than the propensity to do something that happens to relieve suffering. This makes cognitive acts motivated by an aversion to falsehood better than those that arise from processes that lead away from falsehood but without such a motive. Furthermore, cognitive acts motivated by an aversion to falsehood are better than those acts that aim to avoid falsehood, not because the agent actually disvalues false beliefs as such, but for some other reason. Maybe, as in the compassion case, I get nauseated every time I have a false belief and, realizing the connection, I aim to shun false beliefs. More realistically, I might aim to avoid false beliefs because false beliefs give me a bad reputation. In these cases I would not be motivated by an aversion to false belief as such. I suggest that acts motivated by an aversion to a bad reputation are not as good as acts motivated by an aversion to falsehood as such. It follows that acts motivated by compassion or the aversion to false belief confer value on the acts they motivate in addition to any other value the acts have because of their ends or consequences.

The aversion to falsehood and the aversion to human suffering are negative motives, but positive motives can also confer value on the acts they motivate,

# Intellectual Motivation and the Good of Truth / 149

in particular love. I propose that love of truth is a motive that confers value on acts of belief in addition to any other value such acts might have. Here we might pause for a moment to take a closer look at the motives of love of truth and aversion to falsehood because I have sometimes heard it said that the motive for truth is so natural and automatic that it is trivially satisfied. We have already seen one reason why that cannot be the case—the aim to get truth and the aim to avoid falsehood are two different aims, and it is unlikely that they arise from the same motive. A love of truth is not the same as a dislike of falsehood any more than a love of comfort is the same as a dislike of discomfort. We will return to the problem of a potential clash of epistemic motives. But first I want to say that neither one of these motives is trivially satisfied. To think so does not do justice to the commonality of wishful thinking. There is a sense in which everyone wants to believe the truth, but there is a difference between someone who wants to believe $p$ if $p$ is true, and someone who wants $p$ to be true and wants to believe it. When we indulge in wishful thinking, we believe $p$ because we want $p$ to be true, and we want $p$ to be true because we want to believe it. The love of truth as such does not operate as a motive for the belief. The typical motive in wishful thinking is closer to love of the possible state of affairs of a certain proposition's being true.

One difficulty mentioned in section II on consequential value is that getting truth and avoiding falsehood are not only distinct values, but they are sometimes in tension. Unless we are willing to settle for a very high degree of personal preference in weighing the two, we need a way to adjudicate between them. This problem arises in all four of the approaches we have considered, including the motivational approach I am supporting. An appreciation for true belief can be at odds with an aversion to false belief. The parallel phenomenon is well known in ethics. The value of autonomy can be at odds with the value of trust in others, and there is similar tension between the values of perseverance and flexibility, open-mindedness and steadfastness, honesty and kindness, and many others. In other work I have suggested that one of the functions of the Aristotelian virtue of *phronesis*, or practical wisdom, is to adjudicate among the competing demands of different virtues and the different values relevant to a given situation. I propose that the *phronimos* not only has good judgement about the extent to which in a given situation autonomy should be balanced against trust in others, or perseverance against flexibility, or honesty against kindness, but he is also the standard of good judgement about the extent to which it is worth risking falsehood in order to get a true belief concerning some proposition.[15] It is very doubtful that there is any rule or decision procedure that captures such good judgement. What ultimately counts as good motives, whether cognitive or moral, are the motives of a practically wise person. The motivational approach I endorse can therefore avoid the need for a third value by adopting this virtue-ethical approach to resolving moral quandaries. A quandary requires practically wise judgement.

## VI. The value of knowledge

In the last section we looked at the way the value of a motive can add value to the act it motivates. Given two acts, both of which are successful in their ends, the acts can differ in value because of a difference in their motive. In this section I want to address briefly the question of whether the value of the motive can explain the value that knowledge has in addition to the truth of the belief.

Before proceeding, let me say that I have become increasingly sceptical that the question of what constitutes knowledge can be resolved since the concept of knowledge has been made to serve so many different philosophical purposes. Sometimes knowledge is thought to be no more than the minimum state we expect out of a reasonable person with respect to a given proposition, but sometimes it represents the pinnacle of our cognitive aspirations. The value I am talking about in this chapter is unlikely to be the pinnacle, but it is probably more than the minimum we can get away with. I don't know how it could be demonstrated that the value of a cognitive state is of the right sort to convert true belief into knowledge, but for the purposes of this chapter I want to argue only that if we think of knowledge in the way I will describe, we can explain why knowledge is more valuable than true belief.

Many times I have claimed that moral discourse can aid us in understanding the evaluative aspects of our cognitive behaviour, but I used to think that this strategy does not help in the analysis of knowledge since, as far as I could tell, knowledge has no ethical analogue. There are parallels between moral motives and cognitive motives, moral acts and cognitive acts, and morally good outcomes analogous to true beliefs, but how can moral outcomes be converted into something more valuable the way true belief is said to be converted into knowledge? My position now is that I was thinking of knowledge

---

[15] See Zagzebski (1996: p. II, sec. 5.2).

# Intellectual Motivation and the Good of Truth / 151

on the wrong analogy. It's true that a good outcome such as relief of suffering cannot be made better by the act that produced it, much less by the motive of the act that produced it, but that's because the outcome is a state of affairs separate from the act. In the case of acts of belief, the intended outcome is a property of the act itself. The closest moral analogy would be an act that aims at having a certain property, a property that is determined by something outside the agent. I don't know if there are acts like that, but I suggest that if there are, they are the closest analogues to the state of knowing. They are good when they are successful in achieving the intended property, but they are even better when they arise from the right motive.

Let us return to the bathroom scale cases to test whether acts of true belief motivated by love for truth have the value that makes knowledge better than mere true belief. Recall that in the first bathroom scale case I believe what the scale says and since the scale is accurate, I am unlikely to have the belief unless it is true, but I don't care whether it is true or not. What I want is to enjoy believing that I have lost 5 lbs. Let us suppose the belief is true, that I have lost 5 lbs. Do I know that I have? The scale is reliable and its reading is good evidence, but I care neither about the reliability of the scale nor its evidential support of my belief. Still, I am not so irrational that I can believe what I want at will, and so there is *some* connection between the fact that there is good evidence for the belief and my belief. After all, I cannot believe a proposition unless I think it is true, and I cannot think it is true if there is no indication of its truth. But I do not care about the indicators of the truth as such. I care only about having whatever it takes to enjoy believing that I've lost weight. I doubt that very many of us are able to manufacture a belief out of thin air; we cannot form a belief without indicators of its truth. But I doubt that that means we are incapable of wishful thinking. In the first scenario I believe I have lost weight because I want to. The evidence for the truth of my belief plays no role except to make it psychologically possible for me to form the belief at all. It thus shields me from the most extreme form of irrationality, but it hardly makes me grasp the truth in a good way. My getting the truth is a matter of luck in a certain sense of luck. In a way, it is not an *accident* that I got the truth since it is not accidental that I believe what the scale says and it is not accidental that the scale is accurate. Still, from a certain point of view it *is* an accident that I got the truth.[16] I don't get *credit* for getting the truth. I suspect that that is sufficient to deprive me of knowing, but I don't know to what extent we can

[16] See Riggs (1998).

really expect to settle the matter. My point is just that my act of true belief arising in this way is not as good as an act of true belief arising out of the right motive.

In the second bathroom scale case I do value the truth as such with respect to believing that I've lost 5 lbs, but I do not equally value the truth as such with respect to believing that I have not lost weight. And I might not disvalue believing that I've lost weight falsely as much as I value believing that I've lost weight truly. This means that I do not impartially value truth and disvalue falsehood about the matter of my weight. Nonetheless, I do value believing that I've lost weight truly. In fact, I value it highly. My cognitive activity in this case therefore has the following virtues: I value believing that I've lost weight if it's true that I have, I use a reliable process and good evidence in forming the belief because of my valuing the truth in this case, and I get to the truth in part because of my motive and the processes to which it gives rise. From my point of view, the accuracy of the scale is not accidental, as it is in the first case. Granted, I do not get as much credit as I would if I valued truth more impartially and consistently, but it does seem to me that I get credit for believing the truth, and that is probably sufficient to attribute knowledge to me. Sosa's case of believing that his parents cared for him is similar. In both cases we care about the truth of a particular proposition, we care about the evidence *as* evidence, and our believing seems to be knowing, although not unqualifiedly. Again, I'm not sure whether we can settle the matter, but my primary point is that my belief state in the second bathroom scale case is better than in the first.

In *Virtues of the Mind* I defined a category of act I called 'an act of virtue'. An act of virtue V is an act motivated by a V-motive, is an act a person with virtue V would characteristically do in the circumstances, and is successful in reaching the end of virtue V because of these other good-making features of the act. When this schema is applied to intellectual virtue, we can say that an act of intellectual virtue is an act motivated by the motivational component of intellectual virtue, is an act an intellectually virtuous person would characteristically do in these epistemic circumstances, and is successful in reaching the truth because of these other features of the act. I then argued that knowledge can be defined as true belief arising out of acts of intellectual virtue, and showed how this definition avoids Gettier problems.[17] Now I think that this definition can also solve the value problem, but to do so the schema of acts

---

[17] Zagzebski (1996: 248 and 270–1).

and outcomes needs to be modified. True belief is not an end state analogous to relief of suffering that is the product of intellectual acts. True believing *is* an intellectual act, or at least, it is strongly analogous to an act. Of course, it is an act that is in part generated by a series of previous acts. Nonetheless, it is enough like an act to make a comparison with overt acts illuminating. I propose, then, to modify my definition of knowledge as follows: knowledge is an act of intellectual virtue.

## VII. Conclusion

Ever since the ancient Greeks Western thinkers have admired those who are relentless in the pursuit of truth. Such people are thought to be noble, certainly beyond the ordinary. I suspect that the source of this idea also comes from the Greeks—the pervasive suspicion that much of what we take to be true isn't really true. When left to our own devices and the conventions of our various cultures, we do not do a very good job of getting at the truth.[18] We are unreliable, both individually and collectively. Of course, we are much more reliable about some things than others. That is why there has been so much emphasis in modern epistemology on clear perception of medium-sized objects. But the wide disagreements in practical, moral, religious, and philosophical beliefs, as well as many categories of scientific beliefs, is evidence that reliability about many important matters is not widely distributed among the general human population. This makes the desire for truth a desire to rise above the common lot. Traditionally, that desire led to a search for one or two inspired people who have the truth and can become one's mentors. Nowadays we are less likely to think that such a search will be successful, and so we rely upon ourselves. And that often means flouting convention. In any case, it takes special effort. John Dewey is probably right that human beings are naturally credulous, which means that all too often learning the truth involves unlearning a falsehood. And that is what is noble about the desire for truth: we often have to give something up. If I'm right about this, the difficulty in getting at truth means that the right way to behave cognitively requires the motives needed when there are internal or external obstacles to overcome, the motives constitutive of autonomy, courage, perseverance, humility, fairness,

---

[18] Not only philosophers have this suspicion. It is standard among educators to say that they aim to train the young to learn how to learn, implying, of course, that the young won't do it right if they are not trained.

open-mindedness, and other intellectual virtues. In this chapter I have concentrated only on the motive of valuing truth, which is probably primary, but I suspect that for many categories of truth we are not going to get truth at all unless we have the motives that are constituents of these other virtues. Within some domains the situation is not just that some people get the truth through virtuous activity and others by non-virtuous but reliable processes and we credit the former more than the latter. Rather, it's that the latter don't exist at all. Reliability in getting many of the most valuable truths requires dispositions to have virtuous motives. If so, the criteria given by reliabilism coincide with virtue criteria in these domains. I have argued that virtuous motives give the beliefs they produce a value that mere reliability cannot. What *makes* the thinking agent reliable is what is really valuable.[19] It is also what makes the resulting belief truly her own.

---

[19] I have defended this point in another way in Zagzebski (2001a). I argue that reliability is not strictly necessary for knowledge, but it is a good sign of what is necessary: the presence of agency.

# 7

# The Place of Truth in Epistemology

## Ernest Sosa

> [Human] good turns out to be activity of soul in accordance with virtue, and if there are more than one virtue, in accordance with the best and most complete. (Aristotle, *Nichomachean Ethics*, bk. I, sec. 7)
>
> With those who identify happiness [faring happily or well] with virtue or some one virtue our account is in harmony; for to virtue belongs virtuous activity. But it makes, perhaps, no small difference whether we place the chief good in possession or in use, in state of mind or in activity. For the state of mind may exist without producing any good result, as in a man who is asleep or in some other way quite inactive, but the activity cannot; for one who has the activity will of necessity be acting, and acting well. And as in the Olympic Games it is not the most beautiful and the strongest that are crowned but those who compete (for it is some of these that are victorious), so those who act win, and rightly win, the noble and good things in life. (Ibid., bk. I, sec. 8)
>
> [Of] the intellect which is contemplative, not practical nor productive, the good and the bad state are truth and falsity respectively (for this is the work of everything intellectual). (Ibid., bk. VI, sec. 2)\*

## I

In order to qualify as knowledge, a belief needs to be not only true but also 'apt' (*epistemically* apt). What is this additional requirement and what role might

---

\* My essay may amount to little more than a partial reading of these three passages by Aristotle (partial, perhaps, in more than one sense).

truth play in determining it? Is a belief apt in so far as it promotes some truth-involving goal? If so, which goal?

Knowledge is surely better than mere true belief. If so, in what way is it better? How does our conception of epistemic aptness help explain why it is better to have an *apt* true belief than a mere true belief?

A true belief does not count as relevantly apt (and thereby knowledge) simply because it promotes the goal of having true beliefs. A belief that a certain book is a good source of information may be ill-grounded and inapt though in fact true and, when acted upon, a source of much further true belief. A true belief can promote a massive acquisition of true beliefs without thereby becoming apt (without thereby becoming knowledge).

We do well to replace that diachronic goal, therefore, perhaps with a synchronic goal of *now* having true beliefs (and no false ones). But this threatens a *reductio*—all and only one's present true beliefs might then be epistemically rational, by promoting one's goal of *now* having true beliefs.

We might try replacing the simple synchronic goal with a subjunctive synchronic goal:

G   Being such that, for any given proposition, one would now believe it if and only if it were true.

This avoids the *reductio*. Not every true belief is such that one *would* believe it if and only if true.

These truth goals nonetheless all share a problem: namely, how implausible it is to suppose that we either do or should have any such goal. We are, it is true, said to want the truth as intellectual beings. But what does this mean? It might mean that we want true beliefs, any true beliefs, since among the features that make a belief desirable is its plain truth. If so, is our time and energy always well used, or at least not wholly ineffectual, in acquiring true beliefs, *any* true beliefs?

At the beach on a lazy summer afternoon, we might scoop up a handful of sand and carefully count the grains. This would give us an otherwise unremarked truth, something that on the view before us is at least a positive good, other things equal. This view is hard to take seriously. The number of grains would not interest most of us in the slightest. Absent any such antecedent interest, moreover, it is hard to see any sort of *value* in one's having that truth.[1]

---

[1] It might be replied that the value is indeed there, though nearly indiscernibly slight. This I am not inclined to dispute, since what I have to say could be cast about as well in terms of vanishingly slight value, irrespective of whether its magnitude is epsilon or zero.

# The Place of Truth in Epistemology / 157

*Are* we then properly motivated to acquire true beliefs *simply under the aspect of their being true*? More plausible seems the view that, for any arbitrary belief of ours, we would prefer that it be true rather than not true, other things equal. In other words,

(a) So far as truth goes, we'd rather have it in any given belief that we actually hold.

However, this does not entail that

(b) If all a potential belief has to be said for it is that it is true, then we prefer to have it than not to have it.

Nor does this follow even if we add that the belief is evaluatively neutral in every respect other than its truth.

To want the answer to a question, for its practical value or simply to satisfy our curiosity, is to want to know a truth. If I want to know whether *p*, for example, I want this: *to know that p, if p*, and *to know that not-p, if not-p*. And to want *to know that p, if p*, is to want *to know that it is true that p, if it is true that p*; and similarly for *not-p*. So our desire for truths is largely coordinate with our desire for answers to our various questions.

Just as we want that our food be nutritious, so we want that our beliefs be true, other things being equal. Indeed, in pursuing the answer to a question we are automatically pursuing the truth on that question. But this does not mean we must value the truth *as* the truth, in the sense that, for any of the vast set of truths available, one must value one's having it at least in the respect that it is a truth. This no more follows for true propositions than does its correlate for nutritious food.

That distinction bears emphasis. I can want food that is nutritious, in this sense: that *if*, for whatever reason, perhaps because I find it savory, I want to have—with my next meal, or just regularly and in general—bread, I would prefer that my bread be nutritious; which does not mean that I want, in itself and independently of its being otherwise desired, nutritious food simply for its nutritive value. In fact, of course, most of us do want nutritious food, as its own separable desideratum. Nevertheless, from (a) the premiss that we want the food we *do* eat to be nutritious rather than not, we cannot validly draw (b) the conclusion that we have a separable desire that we eat nutritious food, an objective of next, or regularly, doing so, regardless of whatever *other* desires we may or may not have for sorts of food.

To put it more formally, the fallacy is as follows:

P1  I want Fs of sort G.
P2  I want that *if* I have an F of sort G, it be also of sort H.
C   Therefore, I want Fs of sort H.

Thus here are our instances of the fallacy:

P1  I want savoury food.
P2  I want that *if* I have savoury food, it be also nutritious.
C   Therefore, I want nutritious food.

P1  I want beliefs that answer my questions.
P2  I want that *if* I have an answer to a question of mine, it be true!
C   Therefore, I want true beliefs.

We may want true beliefs, in this sense: that *if*, for whatever reason, we are interested in a certain question, we would prefer to believe a correct rather than an incorrect answer to that question; but this does not mean that we want, in itself and independently of our wanting our questions answered, that we have true answers to them simply for the truth this would give us.

What then of our belief formation? What do we hope for in that regard? In so far as we seek to answer questions of interest to us, we of course aim at truth, trivially so, as we have seen. But which questions *should* we want answered, if any? Some questions we can hardly avoid: our very survival turns on them. Other questions we want answered for the sake of our comfort, and so on. Even once we put aside the most mundane questions, that still leaves a lot open. We shall be interested in a huge variety of questions, as family members, as citizens, and just as rational, naturally curious beings. Is there anything general to be said here? Can some general desire for the truth be recommended? It is hard to see what it could be. Remember, we have no desire for truths per se. When we have a desire for the truth, this is because that desire is implicated in our desire for an answer to a particular question or for answers to questions of some restricted sort. But our interest in the truth in such a case is just our interest in the question(s). If we can generalize beyond this to a recommendable desire for truth, accordingly, it must involve a generalization to a sort of questions that *should* draw our interest. But is there such a thing? Can we at least pick out a *sort* of truth that *should* interest us (apart from the sort 'truths that should interest us' or variants of this)?

Your life goals may quite properly be different from mine once we move beyond the most abstract level of *living a good life* or *living a good life in the company of good fellow human beings in a good society*, or the like. Each of us may have such a goal, but great differences set in once we determine more specifically the shape of its realization in a life, given the constitution and context of that particular human being. Won't our intellectual goals be subject to this same kind of difficulty? Our interest in the truth is an interest in certain questions or in certain sorts of questions. What questions interest a given thinker may properly differ, moreover, from those that interest others.

It might be replied that we do or at least should have truth as our goal, if only with near-vanishing intensity when the truth is unimportant enough. Take again the synchronic goal:

G   Being such that, for any given proposition, one would now believe it if and only if it were true.

If G includes the multitude of trivial truths of vanishingly small interest and importance to us, it will presumably induce a correspondingly diminished desire that we satisfy *this* goal, as opposed to the goal that, for any given *important* truth, one would now believe it if and only if it were true. And consider now the implication for the account of epistemic aptness through *pursuit of synchronic goal G*. If G is insignificant, the means to it cannot derive high epistemic status thereby. But the epistemic rationality and aptness of a belief in a triviality is *not* proportional to how well that belief furthers our goal G. The trivial truth may be one we only negligibly desire *to believe if and only if it were true*. Irrespective of that, however, it may be epistemically rational to the highest degree. The problem here is that the way in which the truth goal bears on our retail believing is wildly out of step with the degrees of epistemic justification of our unimportant beliefs. Accordingly, the epistemic normative status of *these* beliefs is not plausibly derivable from our interest in believing truths, or from any standing motive towards the truth.

Perhaps we should weaken goal G to G′: *Being such that, for any given proposition, one would believe it only if it were true.* This would be what elsewhere I call *safety* and defend as preferable to its contraposed *sensitivity*. (A safe belief is one that you would have only if it were true, whereas a sensitive belief is one that you would *not* have if it were *not* true.) There is a lot to be said for requiring safety of any belief candidate for the title of knowledge. Actually, the true requirement will have to be somewhat more complex, since a belief might be unsafe because overdetermined, and yet amount to knowledge.[2]

---

[2] This point is due to Juan Comesaña. Sosa (2000b) contains a further reason why a belief might amount to knowledge despite being unsafe.

Regardless of how the safety goal is to be delineated, a problem remains. If the objective is to explain the epistemic rationality relevant to whether a belief amounts to knowledge, and if the goal-theoretic strategy is that of understanding such epistemic rationality as a variety of means–ends rationality, then the goal invoked had better be one that potential knowers in fact do have, and the positive normative status of our beliefs had better be explicable through their promoting or being thought to promote the goal in question. But how does our hosting a belief promote the goal of having safe beliefs, goal G′ above? It is quite obscure how one promotes such a goal by having any particular belief. Whether we have or do *not* have the belief seems irrelevant to whether we satisfy that goal with respect to the proposition believed. That is to say, the following two things seem independent of each other: (a) whether you do or do not attain this goal: that *you would believe that p only if it were true that p*, and (b) whether you do or do not actually believe that *p*. Indeed, *not* believing that *p* would seem *less* risky with regard to making sure you do not fall short of that goal.

In any case, there is now this question: Why think of the epistemically normative status that turns a true belief into knowledge in terms of a *goal*? Why not just say that the belief needs to be safe in order to be knowledge, while making no commitment on whether safety is or is not anyone's goal?

## II

Perhaps truth has a role to play *not* as a goal or as a component of a goal but more plausibly as a value in terms of which we can assess beliefs, whether anyone does or should have a corresponding goal or not. We come thus to the value that beliefs have in virtue of being true. Let us suppose, for the sake of argument, that truth is the only distinctively cognitive or intellectual intrinsic value or, at least, the only such *fundamental* value. If so, then cognitive methods, processes, faculties, virtues, etc., will have value only derivatively, perhaps in virtue of their efficacy in yielding beliefs that are true. This approach to epistemology is distinctively 'reliabilist'. And now, it is argued, we may see how poorly such reliabilism fits our intuitive conviction that knowledge and epistemically rational true belief are more valuable than mere true belief. In brief the argument is as follows.

## The Anti-reliabilist Argument

1. To believe that *p* correctly *and* with epistemic rationality is more valuable than merely to believe that *p* and be right.
2. The additional value of epistemically rational belief over mere true belief would have to derive from the value imported by the belief's additional property of being thus rational.
3. According to reliabilist accounts of epistemic rationality, a belief is epistemically rational through deriving from a method, or process, or faculty, or virtue that is reliable, one that generally yields beliefs that are true.
4. But in that case how can being yielded by such a source add any further value to a belief over and above the value that it has simply in virtue of being true? How can a true belief obtain further value, beyond the value of its truth, by deriving from such a source, when the whole point of using the source is to get beliefs that are true? This would be as absurd as a hedonist supposing that the value of a pleasure could depend on the reliability of its pleasure-source.[3]

With this argument we focus on epistemic rationality, at most one component of epistemic aptness, of what a belief needs in order to qualify as knowledge. I will not here try to relate epistemic rationality more specifically to epistemic aptness. However these are related, since truth is by hypothesis the only fundamental epistemic value, the value of epistemic rationality must itself be explained in terms of truth.[4]

In considering our argument let us first distinguish between two sorts of value: the intrinsic and the instrumental. Let us assume monistic hedonism,

---

[3] The issues of epistemic normativity involved in this argument are discussed in a growing literature that includes the following, all of which I have found helpful and suggestive, as will be clear to those in the know (of course I would not have written this essay had I not been left with a question or two): Jones (1997); Kvanvig (1998); Zagzebski (1999a), reprinted in Axtell (2000); David (2001); DePaul (2001); Riggs (2002). The approach to the value problem developed here is sketched in Sosa (1988) and (1997), reprinted in Steup (2001). John Greco also treats related issues in his contribution to this volume, with a persuasive contextualist approach.

[4] My value-monistic assumption is only a working assumption. I doubt that the value of understanding can be reduced to that of truth. I should also recognize that my use of 'rationality' here is very broad, and does not pertain only to the proper operation of reason in any narrow sense. It pertains rather more broadly to the proper operation of one's cognitive systems, skin-inwards, or, better, mind-inwards. So epistemic 'adroitness' might better capture my sense.

and consider events Y and Z, each an instance of pleasure. Suppose event Y also brings about much future pleasure, while Z does not. Y is then better (in at least one important respect) than Z, even if it is no better *intrinsically*. Moreover, an event X may not be an instance of pleasure, and hence *not* good intrinsically, while yet it is still good instrumentally, because of the pleasure it yields. All of this we may appreciate, as good hedonists, from a judicial, spectatorial stance that evaluates how matters stand, past, present, and future.

Take now two situations, or even two worlds, wherein the only evaluatively relevant aspects are as follows, for X, Y, and Z as described above. Both worlds contain this sequence: X occurs, then Y occurs, then Z occurs. In world W1 each member causes its successor if any. In world W2 no member causes any other member. Is world W1 better than world W2? Not according to hedonism, whose only source of intrinsic value is pleasure, for there is no more pleasure in W1 than in W2. And yet the X of W1, call it X1, is anyhow better than the X of W2, call it X2. X1 is better than X2 since X1 brings into the world the intrinsic value that it entrains by causing Y1 and, indirectly, Z1, whereas X2 entrains nothing. And so, X1 is better than X2, and Y1 is better than Y2. And Z1 is the same in value as Z2. And yet W1 is no better than W2. How can this be?

The explanation: worlds are evaluated by total intrinsic value, but particular events are not. Particular events are also evaluated by their instrumental value, a sort of value with its own distinctive status. True, it is not a fundamental kind of value, since it involves rather the amount of intrinsic value that an event *causes*. So instrumental value is logically constituted by causation plus intrinsic value. The instrumental value of an event derives from the intrinsic value found in the causal progeny of that event. Nevertheless, events can have a distinctively instrumental value over and above any intrinsic value that they may also have. When we assess an event from the judicial stance, we may assess it as intrinsically valuable, and also, separately, as instrumentally valuable.

An agent A may bring about an event E. The bringing about of E by A may then itself be assessed. This event, call it E′, may not have any intrinsic value beyond the intrinsic value contained already in E, but it will have instrumental value proper to the special relation involved in E's happening because of E′. Call this special sort of instrumental value *praxical value*, the sort of instrumental value in actions of bringing about something valuable. Now, for the hedonist, an event of someone's being pleased does contain some measure of intrinsic value. Supposing someone brings about that pleasure, is there also value in this further event? For our hedonist there is here no distinctive intrinsic value, no intrinsic value *beyond* that found in the pleasure brought about. But even a monistic hedonist may yet find in that action some degree of praxical value.

A world does not enhance its total value by containing not only intrinsically valuable but also instrumentally valuable states. Praxical value is in this respect just like any other variety of instrumental value. But, again, from this it does not follow that a particular event with praxical value is not itself valuable through the praxical value that it contains. Here again praxical value is like instrumental value in general. Instrumentally valuable events do have their proper value, their own sort of *instrumental* value.

## III

Take a case of someone's knowing something in particular. Do we attribute to such knowledge any value over and above whatever value it has through being a true belief? When a thing has value it has it in respect of having a certain property or satisfying a certain condition. More precisely, then, our question is this: when you have a true belief that $p$ and thereby know that $p$, does your belief have some value in a respect other than being a true belief? It would seem so, it would seem that there is extra value to knowledge over and above the constitutive true belief. But how could you possibly explain this if you thought that any such extra value would have to derive from the belief's manifesting an intellectual virtue, understood as a psychological mechanism that would deliver a high enough preponderance of true beliefs (over false ones), at least in normal circumstances. This is hard to see as a respect in which a true belief could then be enhanced, any more than espresso itself is enhanced simply through the reliability of its source.

If persuaded that knowledge must have some value beyond that of its constitutive true belief, therefore, one may well take the Anti-reliabilist Argument to refute the following sort of virtue epistemology:

VE (i) A belief's epistemic worth is constituted at least in important part through its deriving appropriately from an intellectual virtue, and
 (ii) what makes a feature of a subject's psychology an 'intellectual virtue' is the reliable tendency of that feature to give rise to true beliefs on the part of that subject.

Is VE refuted by the value problem?

Within the sport of archery we aim to hit the bull's-eye, an end intrinsic to that sort of activity. When engaged in the activity, don't we also prefer to hit the bull's-eye by means of skill and not just by luck? A gust of wind might come along and guide our arrow to the bull's-eye, but this will not be as sweet a hit as one unaided by such luck. Of course a hit that through skill compensates for the wind might be sweeter yet. Accordingly, the notion of a good, skilful shot goes beyond that of a mere winning or accurate shot. A winning, accurate shot may have been just lucky and not at all skilful, and not in that sense a good shot. In archery we want accurate, winning shots, but we also want shots that are good and skilful. Are the goodness and skill that we want in our shots qualities that we want merely as means? Maybe so, but it seems unlikely. We would not be fully satisfied even with many accurate, winning shots, if they all derived from sheer luck, and manifested no skill, despite our gaining *some* satisfaction through hitting the mark (not to speak of prizes, fame, etc.).

Whether or not we want such goodness and skill only as means, anyhow, a perfectly understandable concept of a good, skilful shot includes *both* hitting the mark *and* doing so through skill appropriate to the circumstances. Can there be any doubt that we have such a concept concerning archery? Surely we do, along with many analogous concepts in other sports, *mutatis mutandis*. What precludes our conceiving of knowledge in a similar way, as a desideratum that includes an intrinsic success component, a hitting of the mark of truth, along with *how* one accomplishes that, how one succeeds in hitting the mark of truth? On this conception, knowledge is not just hitting the mark but hitting the mark somehow through means proper and skilful enough. There seems nothing 'incoherent' in any pejorative sense in such a desideratum of 'knowledge', and there are plenty of analogous desiderata throughout the wide gamut of human endeavours.

That may well be so, moreover, even if no additional *intrinsic* or *fundamental* value could account for the value in the skilful shot over and above the mere hitting of the bull's-eye. The further value might rather be just *praxical* value or the like. Can VE deal with the value problem through the praxical value of intellectual skill's hitting the mark of truth?

# IV

In a *very* weak sense even a puppet 'does' something under the control of the puppeteer, and even to stumble across a stage unintentionally is to 'do' something. These are cases of 'behaviour' or even 'action' in correspondingly weak senses. Still a puppet's performance can be assessed. A puppet can be said to perform well or not, depending for example on whether its hinges are rusty and tend to stick. And the movements of the stumbling ballerina might be, as mere motions, indistinguishable from a lovely pas, though less admirable nonetheless.

Greater independence is displayed by a temperature control system consisting of a thermostat with two triggers, one for a heater and one for a cooler. The system normally keeps the temperature in a given space within certain bounds. If it gets too hot, the system triggers the cooler, if it gets too cool, it triggers the heater, and otherwise it idles. What makes it a good system for that space, moreover, is how it *would* perform in normal conditions, not just how it *does* perform. How the system would perform relative to that space derives, finally, from two factors: (a) from its internal constitution and character, and (b) from its relation to the space. In virtue of how it is stably constituted and related, the system is, at least in a minimal sense, a properly operative system of temperature control for that space.

If it is so constituted and related by sheer accident, the system then falls short in respect of how properly operative it is for that space. At least it falls short in a certain stronger sense of what is required in such a system. A properly operative temperature-control system for a given space over a certain interval is not one that *accidentally* remains so constituted and related that it would keep the temperature in that space within the desired bounds.

We can of course assess the system independently of its relation to the space. We might naturally assess how well it *would* control the temperature of such spaces if suitably related to them (in a way perhaps in which one can standardly make such systems be related to such spaces). One can of course then assess such a system independently of whether it then happens to be appropriately installed. It might be sitting in a display room in a store. The evaluation would then focus on whether it is so constituted that, if also suitably installed, it would reliably control the temperature of that space.

Whether such a system performs well would then go beyond whether by virtue of its performance it does or does not contribute causally to keeping the temperature within proper bounds. A good system might perform in such a way that it does so contribute, *not* because it is working right, however, but only because, although it does *not* then work right, luck enables it to cause the right outcome anyhow. Thus the system may suffer a glitch, while yet, coincidentally, an insect alights on a crucial component of its internal mechanism so that the cooler is triggered as it should be if the system is to keep the temperature within the proper bounds. Only because of that bit of luck does the system then contribute causally to keeping the temperature within the proper bounds. Had it not been for the insect, then, the system would not have triggered the cooler. So it would be false to say that it 'worked right' on that occasion, when it just suffers a glitch. It is a good enough system nevertheless, since it does work right in the great majority of circumstances where it is normally called on to operate.[5]

This example shows that for a system to work right or perform well, in ways that are creditable, more is required than just (a) that it be a good system (in the relevant respects), and (b) that it then contribute causally to the desired outcome. For it may contribute causally to that outcome only through some fluke, in which case it then contributes despite *not* working right or performing well.

A system works right or performs well on a particular occasion, then, only if it unflukily enters a state that would lead in the relevant circumstances to the desired outcome. Accordingly, what the system does in entering that state, unaided by luck, must be sufficient to produce the desired outcome, given perhaps its normal relation to its relevant space. In our example the system did enter such a state, but only because of the insect *in machina*.

## V

We might evaluate an artefact by how well it serves us on the whole. Or we might evaluate it independently of how well installed it is, if installed at all. Or we might evaluate its operation on a particular occasion: does it work right or perform well on that occasion? So there is the 'agent' in a broad sense that includes mechanical agents of various degrees of sophistication, with various ranges of intended activity. There is the 'performance' of that agent on a particular occasion. And sometimes there is also a performance-distinct situation or object or quantity of stuff that such an agent brings about or produces through its performance, a performance-distinct result that might also be

---

[5] It might be replied that the system did work right, *with the help of the insect*. And I am in some linguistic sympathy with this reply. Perhaps, I am willing to grant, 'working right' is at least ambiguous, and in one sense it does permit this reply. In any case, there would presumably remain the sense in which the system itself does not really work right, which is tantamount to its not working *well* on that occasion, and 'working well' lends itself less well to the present reply, as it seems less subject to the ambiguity that affects 'working right'.

entirely performance-transcendent, as when some physical product is produced while in no way *constituted* by the performance.

None of our three evaluations of aspects of such a situation, wherein an agent performs, uniquely determines any of the others. An agent could be a fine agent and perform poorly on a particular occasion, which in turn is compatible with the performance-distinct product being of high quality or of low quality or of any quality in between. Or the agent could be a mediocre or worse agent and yet perform well on a given occasion. It is even possible that a poor performance by a poor agent may lead to an excellent performance-distinct outcome. So the three dimensions of evaluation seem largely independent of each other—but not entirely, or so I now argue.

Performances relate in one direction to the agents involved, and in another direction to their performance-distinct products, if any. So they might be evaluated with a view towards one direction, or towards the other. An agent might be nearly incompetent and yet perform most effectively on a particular occasion. This evaluates the performance in the light of its wonderful outcome. Someone with a barely competent tennis serve may blast an ace past his opponent at 130 mph. This is a most effective serve given its outcome: a ball streaking past the receiver untouched, having bounced within the service court. But from another point of view it may not have been so positively evaluable after all. If the player is a rank beginner, for example, one most unlikely to reproduce that performance or anything close to it, then one may reasonably withhold one's encomium. It was still a wonderfully *effective* serve, but hardly *skilful*. Performances are in this way double-faced. So the evaluation of a performance seems not after all independent of the evaluation of the other two components of the performance situation. The evaluation is either agent-involving or outcome-involving (or both). Creditable performances must be attributable to the agent's skills and virtues, and thus attributable to the agent himself.

## VI

In evaluating the Anti-reliabilist Argument it will help to have in view the categories of praxis, of human doings and actions. To get something done you do not need much sophistication. Water flows downhill, for example, supermarket doors open when people approach, your knee jerks under the doctor's mallet, and so on. Distinctively human action is on a higher plane. A rational agent's action is controlled and informed by reason. At a minimum one must know what one is doing and must do it for a reason. Bees dance, it is true, perhaps guided not only by instincts but also by 'reasons', unlike puppets. Higher up the animal kingdom, in any case, and well before we reach humanity, much behaviour is less and less plausibly explained by appeal to mere instinct. Differences of degree are still differences, however, and the rational animal stands head and shoulders above the rest.

*Three sorts of agency.* The dimension of agency divides into at least three divisions, corresponding to at least three ways of ø-ing. First, there is *plain* ø-ing, however autonomously or informedly, or even attributably. Second, there is ø-ing intentionally, perhaps deliberately. Third, there is ø-ing *attributably*, in a way that makes one's ø-ing attributable to oneself as agent, as one's own doing. Just as it is fallacious to infer that an agent ø-s intentionally from the fact that he ø-s, since he might ø unintentionally, so it is a fallacy to infer that an agent ø-s attributably from the fact that he ø-s, since he might ø unattributably, as when someone *falls*, having been pushed off a roof, where one's falling is not at all one's own doing, and is hence not attributable to oneself as agent. All intentional ø-ings are attributable, but the converse is false; and all attributable ø-ings are plain ø-ings, but again the converse is false. One's plain falling is something one 'does', since one *does* fall, but it is not something one does attributably to oneself as agent, as one's *own* doing.

*Three forms of evaluation.* With regard to instruments, tools, mechanisms, and useful artefacts, methods, and procedures in general, there are three interestingly different forms of evaluation, positive or negative, whether the evaluation takes the form of approval, favouring, or admiring, or the form of disapproval, disfavouring, or deploring. A useful cultural device is normally meant to help secure goods that we value independently of the device. Thus we value conveyance to one's destination, ambient temperature within certain bounds, savoury and nourishing food, etc. And we also value devices whose normal operation will enable us to secure those goods, and also particular instances where the operation of the device secures one of its characteristic goods.

We favour and approve of good performance in our devices. We admire and even 'praise' such performance. On the flip side, we disfavour and disapprove of malfunction, and deplore poor performance, and may even 'blame' it on the device. Such evaluations of performance, whether positive or negative, go beyond the evaluation of goods produced by the performance, whether it be conveyance to one's destination, ambient temperature within certain bounds, savoury and nutritious food, etc. And they also go beyond evaluation of the artefact and of its general reliability. The evaluation of a particular performance is distinct from the evaluation of the artefact that then performs and of any performance-transcendent product of the performance. A first-rate artefact may yield an excellent product despite the very low quality of its performance itself on that occasion.[6]

Why do we evaluate not only devices and their products, but also, separately, their performances? Well, why do we evaluate not only intrinsic value but also extrinsic value? Presumably we have concepts of instrumental value because it is useful for us to keep track of the levers of useful power. We bend nature to our ends, and in doing so we rely on what works, on what leads causally to our desiderata. Thus the importance of suitable concepts that help us keep track of what does work, of what has value through its causal powers. These are often states we can control more directly, whereby we secure more remote effects, as when we switch on the light by flipping the switch. But an extrinsically evaluable state need *not* be such a potential instrument relative to human capacities. A hurricane can be awful even if uncontrollable. The more general concept is the concept of what brings about value or disvalue, a concept clearly important to agents whose wills must work indirectly in securing goods and avoiding evils. And it also seems important to those who need to ward off perceived danger, even in the absence of full control. Thus the hurricane; we can at least control our relationship to it.

Tools, instruments, mechanisms, and other artefacts and devices, draw our interest primarily for the goods secured through their use. Efficiently smooth operation may of course be admired in its own right, apart from its utilitarian implications. For the most part, nonetheless, what we care about in our artefacts is that they serve us well by helping produce desired goods.

Derivatively from that, we evaluate also the artefacts themselves relative to how reliably they operate in respectively normal circumstances. We keep track of the reliability of our thermostats, cars, airplanes, etc., with concepts, including evaluative concepts, that enable discrimination of the reliable from the unreliable. And we evaluate the *performances* of our artefacts, using similar categories of evaluation. What is the *point* of such evaluation? If we already know (a) that the performance-transcendent product of the performance has a certain value, and (b) that the performing artefact also is reliable up to a

---

[6] And things can come unravelled in other ways too. Thus an excellent performance may have an unfortunate outcome owing to unfavourable circumstances.

certain level, why then are we *also* interested in (c) how worthy the particular performance is?

It is hard to see what interest there could be in such evaluation except through its implications for assessment of the performing artefacts. We have an important interest in the reliable quality of our artefacts, and from this interest derives rationally our interest in the quality of their particular performances (still leaving aside any purely aesthetic interest that artefactual performances may acquire). Artefacts are 'agents', however, only weakly, perhaps in an extended and even metaphorical sense. And this is of a piece with our treating them as mere means (except when we treat them as objects of aesthetic appreciation). Correlatively, our approval, admiration, and even praise for their performances is also qualified by the standing of the performers as mere tools at the service of our ends.

## VII

*Wise action.* Suppose your raft glides downstream and comes to a fork. Down the right effluent there's treasure, down the left effluent only mud. Knowing this, and having control of the rudder, you take the right effluent and reach your reward. What you do and your attainment are then attributable to you, and properly admirable and praiseworthy. The reward is something you win through your own well-directed rational effort.

Consider now some ways of falling short:

(a) The raft might be completely beyond your control, either because someone else controls its rudder and disregards your preferences, or because it drifts rudderless.

(b) You might not know that you are taking the right effluent, or that it is better to take that direction.

If either (a) or (b) is true of you, then even if you *do* go down the right effluent and reach the prize, this will be something that *happens* to you, by luck, *not* something properly attributable to you as your rational doing, something admirable of you, deserving of praise.

Again, in a *very* broad sense you *do* something when you 'go down the right effluent tied down and blindfolded'. You do something at least in the way water does something when it flows, or the knee does something when it jerks. Take an arbitrary 'doing' of yours, in this very general sense. What conditions must it satisfy to be a proper object not only of admiration (as one may admire the swelling flow of Niagara) but of praise or blame, credit or discredit? One condition would require that it be autonomous enough, another that it be sufficiently well informed.

What is true of our doings generally is true of our believings in particular. Beliefs or belief-like states may be found up and down the evolutionary scale, and perhaps even below. A door may 'think' somebody is approaching when a garbage can blows by. A dog may think it's about to be fed when it hears a clatter in the kitchen. Man is rational when his belief is controlled and informed by reason (and 'adroit' through his properly operating cognitive systems). A belief may also be instilled, however, through mere subliminal suggestion, or through hypnosis, or brainwashing. Such a belief is insufficiently derived from the exercise of the subject's distinctively intellectual capacities and abilities, his faculties, cognitive methods, and intellectual virtues (irrespective of whether its adoption counts as *voluntary*). The believing is hence not attributable to the subject, not even in the way in which the circulation of the blood is attributable to the subject's heart and thereby, indirectly, to the subject as well. You may believe something, again, in a way that does not derive from the exercise of your intellectual excellences, but only from some external source not appropriately under your cognitive control. If so, then the believing in question may not be properly attributable to you as your doing. It may be something you *do* only as weakly as does the puppet dance when the puppeteer makes it do so.

## VIII

Even when one attributively believes something in particular, it remains to be seen whether its being a *true* believing is also attributable to oneself as one's own doing. The following is, again, fallacious:

1. Attributably to S as S's doing, S ø-s.
2. S ø-s in way W.
3. Therefore, attributably to S as S's doing, S ø-s in way W.

Consider:

1a. Attributably to your heart as its doing, it pumps blood through your body.
2a. Your heart pumps blood in this building (pointing to the building where you are).
3a. Therefore, attributably to your heart as its doing, it pumps blood in this building.

Your heart's pumping blood in this building is perhaps your doing, since for one thing you could easily have been elsewhere, but that the pumping takes place in this building is not attributable to your heart as *its* doing.

Analogously, the following would also be fallacious.

1b. Attributably to you as your doing, you believe that *p*.
2b. You believe that *p* correctly (with truth).
3b. Therefore, attributably to you as your doing, you believe that *p* correctly.

In order for *correct* belief to be attributable to you as your doing, the being true of your believing must derive sufficiently from 'yourself', which involves its deriving from constitutive features of your cognitive character, and of your psychology more generally.

If truth has its own cognitive or intellectual value, then bringing about one's believing truly will have its corresponding praxical value, a distinctive sort of instrumental value. Compatibly with this, truth may still have a special role in explaining the normativity of belief. For the hedonist, similarly, pleasure has a special role in explaining the normativity of action, even if there are many things with value besides instances of pleasure. Eating savoury food will have value instrumentally by promoting pleasure, for example, and the bringing about of pleasure will have its own distinctive value, different from the intrinsic value of the pleasure brought about, but value nonetheless, praxical value.

Does the bringing about of pleasure have value over and above the value of the contained pleasure? Well, it does have a different sort of value, one distinct from the value of the pleasure brought about. So a world where that pleasure is present uncaused will have the same intrinsic value as this one, but it will be missing something present here, which does here have value of a sort, praxical value. This is rather like the comparison between the world where the X–Y–Z sequence occurs unaided by any causation, and hence with no instrumental value in the X or the Y components, by comparison with the world where Y causes Z and X causes Y, wherein there is the same intrinsic value present in the three items, but wherein also (a) it's a good thing X happens, *not* because of any intrinsic value of its own but because of the intrinsic value that it yields by causing Y and Z, and (b) it's a good thing Y happens, not *only* because of its own intrinsic value but also because of the intrinsic value that it yields by causing Z.

Similarly, in the world where an agent brings about some pleasure, there is not only the intrinsic value of the pleasure but also the distinctive value of the agent's action. It's a good thing that action is done, at least in the respect that it brings about some pleasure, which is intrinsically good. So there is this praxically good action in the world in addition to the intrinsically good pleasure that it brings about.

Consider now a case where a true belief, a *true* believing, is attributable to you as your doing. We may now say that, besides the epistemic good in that true belief, there is further the praxical good in your action of bringing it about. And this arguably involves your exercise of excellences constitutive of your cognitive character.

That is a way in which truth can have a distinctively important and fundamental place in explaining epistemic normativity, compatibly with knowledge having epistemic worth over and above the worth of mere true belief. We can see the good that attaches to an epistemic action creditable to the agent, who brings about that good for himself, and is more than just the recipient of blind epistemic luck.[7]

## IX

However, the account of the extra value of knowledge in terms of the praxical value that it contains does not go far enough. For this praxical value does not explain the fact that we would prefer a life of knowing, where we gain truth through our own intellectual performance, to a life where we are visited with just as much truth but through mere external agency (brainwashing, hypnosis, subliminal suggestion, etc.). This might be the work of a less malevolent evil demon, who allows a world out there pretty much as we believe it to be, but one that fits our beliefs only through happenstance, through the demon's deigning to give us true beliefs although he might more easily have given us false ones.[8]

If we prefer a life in which we gain our truths through our own performances, then the value of our apt performances cannot be mere praxical value. For if

---

[7] In fact the account here of praxical value is only a first approximation, perhaps sufficient unto the day. A more adequate account, in any case, would allow the possibility of a performance with praxical value that does *not* succeed in securing its characteristic inherent value. Even if some bad luck robs it of its expectable fruits, an action may still be a wonderful performance, and properly admirable, and correspondingly valuable, *praxically* valuable in our richer sense. (Delineating that sense should be within reach, and what follows is one attempt.)

[8] Nor does the account explain how the virtuous bringing about of a true belief is better than the accidental bringing about of that belief even if the two bringings about are otherwise the same to the greatest possible extent.

it were, then the value of our performances would derive entirely from their causing the value in the true believings that they bring about. In that case, and if true believing is the only intrinsically valuable epistemic good, then two worlds containing the same true believings could hardly differ in overall value, even if in one of them there is a lot more praxical value. Compare the case of extrinsic value more generally, and the two X–Y–Z worlds above.

So if we rationally prefer a world in which our true beliefs derive from our own cognitive performances to one with the same true beliefs, now courtesy of the less malevolent demon, then there must be some further value involved in the first world not exhausted merely by the praxical value that it contains. What could this further value be?

When Aristotle speaks of the 'chief good' as activity that goes beyond the state of mind producing it since 'the state of mind may exist without producing any good result' it seems clear that in his view performances creditable to an agent as her own are the components of *eudaimonia*, of human good or faring well, which 'turns out to be activity of soul in accordance with virtue'. In purely theoretical activity, moreover, truth and falsity are the good and bad state respectively, and the work of everything intellectual.

According to the Aristotelian view, then, passive reception of truth is not enough to count as human good, or at least not as the chief human good. Our preference is not just the presence of truth, then, however it may have arrived there. We prefer truth whose presence is the work of our intellect, truth that derives from our own virtuous performance. We do not want just truth that is given to us by happenstance, or by some alien agency, where we are given a belief that hits the mark of truth *not* through our own performance, not through any accomplishment creditable to us.[9]

We have reached the following result. Truth-connected epistemology might grant the value of truth, of *true believing*, might grant its intrinsic value, while allowing also the praxical extrinsic value of one's attributably hitting the mark of truth. This praxical extrinsic value would reside in such attributable intellectual deeds. But in addition to the extrinsic praxical value, we seem

---

[9] When I presented these ideas at Notre Dame, Alvin Plantinga wondered what would be so bad about being the beneficiary of divine revelation, where there are no special faculties, really, that set one apart; where one is just visited by the overpowering light of the revealed truth. In response it seemed to me that even if, with Aristotle, one finds the de facto chief human good in active virtuous attainments of one's own, this need not prevent one from granting that there may be other ways to the truth that might be just as desirable and even admirable. Much of our epistemology and epistemic value theory can be isolated from such issues of rational theology.

plausibly committed to the *intrinsic* value of such intellectual deeds. So the grasping of the truth central to truth-connected epistemology is not just the truth that may be visited upon our beliefs by happenstance or external agency. We want rather to attain truth by our own performance, which seems a reflectively defensible desire for a good preferable not just extrinsically but intrinsically. *What we prefer is the deed of true believing, where not only the believing but also its truth is attributable to the agent as his or her own doing.*

Does this adequately account in truth-connected terms for the value of knowledge over and above its contained true belief? Is the additional value simply the value contained in the attributable, creditable attaining of the truth, as opposed to the mere presence of truth (which might conceivably derive from happenstance or external agency)? The foregoing considerations go quite far, but *not* all the way to the required full account of epistemic value within truth-connected epistemology. At least one further step is needed and that is the aim of our next section.

## X

Compare two evil demon victims. The first victim takes in fully and flawlessly the import of her sense experience and other states of consciousness, to an extent rarely matched by any human, and reasons therefrom with equal prowess to conclusions beyond the reach of most people, and retains her results in memory well beyond the normal. The other victim is on the contrary extensively handicapped in her cognitive faculties and performs with singular ineptness. Clearly one of these victims is better off than the other; you would prefer to be and perform like the first and unlike the second. However, neither one attains truth at all, not even as a doing, through being visited with truth; much less does either one attain truth as a deed, by hitting the mark of truth through the excellence of their performance. So the epistemic value of the intellectual conduct of the first victim, the value that lifts her performance over that of the second victim, is not to be explained in the terms of our earlier account. Neither subject hits the mark of truth at all, whether attributably and creditably or not. So how can one of them still attain more value than the other? What sort of value can this be?

Recall the temperature-control device, with the two triggers. Suppose it is taken off the shelf in the display room for a demonstration, and a situation is simulated wherein it should activate the cooling trigger, and then a second situation is simulated wherein it should activate the warming trigger. In such a test the device might either perform well or not. But the quality of its performance is not to be assessed through how well it actually brings about the goods that it is meant to bring about in its normal operation. For in the display room it brings about neither the cooling nor the heating of any space. And yet we can and do assess the quality (and in a sense the 'value') of its performance. What we are doing is quite obvious: we are assessing whether it performs in ways that would enable it to bring about the expected goods once it was properly installed, i.e. properly related to the target of its operation. We might call this sort of value 'performance value'. The performance value of a performance is the degree of positive or negative quality attained by that operation, measured by how well the performance enables the 'agent' to operate, by entering various states in various circumstances, so as to be such that, if suitably installed, it would in fact bring about the expected goods in its target (where of course the 'agent' and 'target' might be the same).

It does not require an imaginative leap to conceive of our cognitive systems as devices that operate normally with the expected result: truths of certain sorts acquired by the host organism. There are various ways of conceptualizing this, but one way might include *the visual system, the auditory system*, and so on. Alternatively, we might have *the brain-including nervous system, together with sense organs*. Alternatively, we might have *the animal*, or *the human being*. In any case, there would be the system or organism on one side, and the normal environments in which it operates on the other. And we can evaluate the performances of the organism independently of its proper emplacement in a suitable environment. This would be similar to what we do in evaluating the performance of the temperature-control device in the display room. Consider then the deliverings of our cognitive systems, of whatever level of complexity we pick, including the top, total-human, level. Such deliverings can be assessed for performance value, through assessing how well the performance would enable the system to deliver the expected goods if it were 'properly installed' in a suitable environment.

Recall the greater epistemic value, the higher epistemic quality, found in the performance of the first of our two victims of the less malevolent demon. We may now say that this higher value is performance value. It is like the higher value of the glitch-free performance of the temperature control device in the display room under simulation. If this is correct, then we have a way to understand the value of the epistemic justification that we find in the beliefs of the properly 'perceiving' and reasoning victim of the evil demon. It is performance value, and what is good about this performance value is still to be understood in a truth-connected way. What is good about that performance value cannot be understood independently of the fundamental value of true believing, and especially of true believing that hits the mark of truth attributably to the agent. For *this* is the good that the relevant system is expected to deliver through its operation when 'properly installed' in a suitable environment, and the good that may thus be credited to the organism as a whole, in virtue of the proper operation of its cognitive architecture.

Does that sufficiently identify the sorts of epistemic values that an adequate epistemology should be able to explain? We have identified: (a) the value of bare true believing (since we do prefer to be given truth rather than falsehood, even when it comes through happenstance or external agency); (b) the *praxical, extrinsic* value of true believing where the agent brings about the belief; (c) the *eudaimonist, intrinsic* value of true believing where the agent hits the mark of truth as his own attributable deed, one that is hence creditable to the agent as his own doing; and (d) the performance value of a deliverance-induced believing, present even when the belief induced is false, so long as the performance is high on the quality scale for such performances, as measured by how well the performance would provide its expected goods, if the system were properly installed. Are we able to account for all our intuitions concerning epistemic evaluation, epistemic quality, and value, in terms of these four concepts of epistemic normative or evaluative status?

It might be objected now again that our preference for the life of the first of the two demon victims, the one who 'perceives' and reasons properly, is not explained exhaustively merely through appeal to the performance value of the believings of that victim. For if it were mere performance value, then we would *not* hold that world and that life to be intrinsically better than the life and world of the other victim. But we do think it to be thus intrinsically better, do we not?

Surely we care about our devices performing well in display rooms not intrinsically (again, leaving aside aesthetic evaluation) but only because that shows them to be devices suitable for delivering the goods. But it is the goods to be delivered that we really care about. Of course the goods to be delivered need not be performance-transcendent. And indeed, on the Aristotelian view, in our intellectual lives the goods to be delivered by our cognitive systems are not performance-transcendent. The 'chief' intellectual goods involve attributable truth-attainment, where one does hit the mark of truth through the quality of one's performance. Nevertheless, one cares about cognitive systems in good working order not for their own sake, but for the truth-attaining performances that they enable. Much less does one care about good performances by cognitive systems 'in display rooms' isolated from the environments within which they would enable one attributably to attain the truth. Such good performances are valued presumably only for their implications about the worth of the operative systems, so their value is partly epistemic; they manifest within our view the worth of the operative systems. But partly it is a distinctive value of its own, even independently of what they enable us to know. Even if there is no one around to see it, the good performance by a system is somehow better than its poor performance; and this is presumably at least in part a matter of the more-than-accidental connection between the quality of the performance and the quality of the system. To the extent that the system performs poorly, to that extent is it a lesser system than it might be.

In any case, whether through its epistemic value or through its connection with the worth of the performing system, the value of simulational good performance is, like extrinsic value, not of fundamental, intrinsic import. The world with such good performances is no better epistemically on the whole than the one without them, so long as the two worlds contain all the same intrinsically valuable epistemic goods.

That being so, those who defend the fundamental status of truth or truth attainment as the basis of epistemic value would seem committed to denying that the good performance of the superior victim is of a higher intrinsic order than the poor performance of the other victim. They are different in quality, true enough, those two performances, but the difference is to be explained in terms of performance value, and hence not in terms of intrinsic value. That is how it would seem on the eudaimonistic account, and that is how it seems to me.[10]

## XI

Eudaimonist virtue epistemology gives pride of place to truth, as Aristotle explains. But the truth that matters is not just the truth of true propositions in splendid isolation. What matters is your *having* the truth. And what matters most importantly, 'the chief good', is your grasping the truth attributably to your intellectual virtues acting in concert conducted by reason, and thus

---

[10] However, a fuller treatment would advert to the intrinsic value of reflective coherence, with its correlative measure of understanding.

attributably to you as epistemic agent. Nevertheless, other epistemic values may be understood in terms of this 'chief' good and of its contained lesser, though still intrinsic, good, namely truth itself, however acquired. (We would intrinsically prefer to be fed truth rather than error, presumably, and prefer to chance upon the truth rather than error.) Thus there is the praxical, extrinsic value of what leads to true beliefs, especially to true beliefs fully attributable to the subject. And there is also the performance value of good cognitive performance, even when poor positioning robs it of its reward.

These are distinct epistemic values, and values of distinct sorts. But they may all be understood through their various relations to the truth. Moreover, they are compatible with the sort of virtue epistemology sketched as VE above. For, VE allows a sort of value to be found in knowledge over and above the value of its constitutive true belief. Indeed, VE comports especially well with that special value if it amounts to the eudamoinistic value constituted by a deed of true believing attributable to the agent because attributable to that agent's establishment of intellectual virtues.[11]

[11] Much of our reflection in epistemology seems applicable to ethics, *mutatis mutandis*.

# Part Four

*Using Virtue to Redefine the Problems of Epistemology*

# 8

# How to be a Virtue Epistemologist

## Christopher Hookway

## I. Introduction: locating virtue epistemology

Over the last twenty years, a number of people have advanced positions that have been described as versions of 'virtue epistemology'.[1] This approach to the theory of knowledge is now sufficiently well established that there are conferences and anthologies of contributions devoted to it.[2] What do these positions have in common? A schematic answer can be given by saying that they are all:

1. Approaches to the most central problems of epistemology
2. which give to states called 'intellectual' or 'epistemic' virtues
3. a central or 'primary' explanatory role.

There is scope for debate about just what the 'central problems of epistemology' are, about the nature of intellectual virtues, and also about the sort of explanatory primacy that is at issue, so it is easy to see that a wide variety of views, many quite different in content and spirit, could fall under this general characterization. Indeed, each of these three clauses raises interesting questions and requires further examination.

It is one indication of this variety that Alvin Goldman sees an appeal to epistemic virtues as a way of vindicating a strongly naturalistic approach to epistemology,[3] while for others it is associated with an approach to epistemology,

---

[1] See e.g. Sosa (1991) and Zagzebski (1996).
[2] See e.g. Axtell (2000) and Fairweather and Zagzebski (2001).
[3] Goldman (1992: ch. 9).

inspired by Aristotle's work in ethics, which could emphasize the irreducibility or ineliminability of the normative and of talk about reasons.[4] Although motivations for giving a central role to epistemic virtues can differ, it is reasonable to say that most who do so are attracted by the fact that it permits a motivated sensitivity to the complex interplay of internalist and externalist considerations in our practice of epistemic evaluation. This is because virtues are typically capacities, habits, or states of character that combine being internal to the agent with being such that their operations are largely opaque to reflection or introspection. Consider an ethical example: when a generous person acts out of her generosity, she is likely to be motivated by a concern for the welfare of others which is habitual, part of her character. She will not need to (and may not be able to) reflect carefully on the details of different courses of action and decide on the basis of abstractly formulated principles. But since her generosity is part of her *character*, the merits of the act can properly be imputed to her. It is probably no accident that virtue epistemology emerged during a period when the conflict between unsustainable forms of internalism and apparently problematic externalist alternatives dominated epistemological discussion. Appeal to virtues offered a way of explaining how we are not alienated from our beliefs and inquiries in spite of the fact that we do not (and perhaps cannot) formulate or provide a non-circular vindication for the normative standards which guide them. We can be praised for our cognitive successes and (sometimes) blamed for our failures even if we have no access to, or control over, the methods of belief formation and traits of cognitive character which contribute to them.

The way we characterized the trend towards virtue epistemology above helps us to see that someone could allow that there are epistemic or intellectual virtues, and admit that they are important for dealing with a range of problems about epistemic evaluation, without being a full-blooded virtue epistemologist. Their importance may not lie in solving the 'central' problems of epistemology, or they may not possess the required kind of explanatory 'primacy'. For example, someone might argue that although possession of epistemic virtue is not strictly necessary for getting into a good epistemic position, it is, for human inquirers, a valuable means towards doing so efficiently or speedily. Alternatively, it could be argued that we will only understand some distinctive kinds of human *irrationality* by recognizing the role that states such as virtues have in our practice of epistemic evaluation.[5] In either case,

---

[4] This might fit the work of Linda Zagzebski (1996).   [5] See Hookway (2001).

virtues may be important for the study of epistemic evaluation without having a 'primary' role in solving the 'central' problems of epistemology. This raises the questions of what makes epistemological problems 'central'. I shall say more about this below. For the present, we can say that it is sufficient for a problem being central that it is among the problems that *give rise* to the inquiries carried out by epistemologists. If epistemology begins with the questions 'What is knowledge?' and 'Do we have any?', so that an inquiry that did not address these questions was not, properly speaking, epistemological at all, then these questions about knowledge would be suitably 'central'. If we can do epistemology without addressing those questions, then they are not 'central'.[6]

The literature on virtue epistemology has tended to focus on a fairly limited number of ways of filling out our schematic characterization of virtue epistemology. Most significantly, it identifies the 'central problems of epistemology' and 'explanatory primacy' in ways that were established before virtue epistemology emerged as a serious option. For example, virtues are introduced in order to find new solutions to the Gettier problem or to show how we can block the regress of justification. By contrast, the revival in virtue ethics among mainstream analytical moral philosophers which has been growing since the 1950s has often involved the claim that other moral philosophers have been mistaken about what should be the primary focus of the subject, questioning, for example, the suggestion that the central problem of ethics is to explain the nature of moral obligation or the moral 'ought'. Some virtue ethicists find the whole idea of moral obligation problematic; and others hold that emphasizing questions of responsibility and holding people to account for their actions reflects a distorted perspective that taking virtues seriously can help us to overcome. I shall argue that we ought to be open to the possibility that something similar could occur in epistemology. Virtue epistemology has proposed ways of rethinking, and perhaps overcoming, familiar distinctions found in the study of justification or warrant; for example, the distinctions between foundationalist and coherentist, and between internalist and externalist, theories of justification. Should it also lead to a rethinking of just what the central problems of epistemology are: is a concern with analysing knowledge, providing theories of justification, and defeating scepticism simply a mistake?[7]

---

[6] It may be better to give this a normative formulation: if we *should* do epistemology without addressing those problems, then they are not, properly speaking, central.

[7] There are two different ways in which such an approach to epistemology could identify an error in our epistemological practice. It could allow that the concept of knowledge is indeed central to our practice of epistemic evaluation, and argue that our practice should be changed so

The standard approach, then, takes the central tasks of epistemology to be concerned with the concepts of *knowledge* and *justified belief*. We need to provide analyses of these concepts, and, in the face of sceptical challenges, we need to establish whether we are in fact capable of obtaining knowledge and justified belief. Thus virtue epistemologists typically appeal to intellectual or epistemic virtues in providing these analyses and in showing how we can resist these challenges. Moreover, the sort of explanatory primacy invoked is *conceptual*: we can analyse or define *knowledge* or *justified belief* in terms of the virtues. For example: knowledge is true belief which is produced or sustained through the exercise of our intellectual virtues. As Guy Axtell has documented, virtue epistemology emerges from a change in the direction of analysis: where earlier epistemologists might take virtues seriously by defining them as traits which are conducive to the obtaining of knowledge, virtue epistemologists define knowledge as belief which depends upon the traits we describe as virtues.[8]

The later sections of this chapter examine each of the three clauses of our schematic characterization. After examining how we should understand the notion of an epistemic virtue (section II) and what sort of 'primacy' virtues can have in virtue epistemology (section III), we turn to the question of how we should understand the central problems of epistemology. After discussing what I call the 'standard' view of the central problems of epistemology, the chapter suggests that virtue epistemology should identify the central problems in a different way. This allows for the possibility that what are now taken to be the central problems might turn out to be of marginal interest or, indeed, of no importance at all, although it does not *require* that this be the case. My aim is not to defend this approach in detail but rather to use it as a way of suggesting that we should be open to the possibility that the emphasis on intellectual and epistemic virtue should lead us to consider some non-standard views about the central problems of epistemology.

## II. Virtues

If we think of virtues as 'excellences' then it is apparent that they will be many and varied: from the sharpness of a knife to the ruthlessness of a hired killer,

---

that it no longer rests on this mistake. Alternatively, it could claim that it is the epistemologists who make a mistake: the concept of knowledge is not, in fact, central to our practice, but epistemologists falsely believe that it is.

[8] Axtell (2000: Introduction).

and on to the trace of sympathy for others which impairs the killer's efficient execution of his duties. In epistemology, those who take intellectual and epistemic virtues seriously have appealed to states of two distinct kinds.[9]

First, there are specific skills and capacities, innate and learned, for example, good eyesight or memory (perhaps specified by reference to the particular range of circumstances over which the skill or capacity is good or reliable). The ability to keep track of complex structures of argument is another example. We might also include subject-specific skills: someone may have learned to be good at bird or plane recognition; or she may have extensive and accessible knowledge of some subject matter. These are undeniably excellences, and thus 'virtues'. And their excellence consists in their reliability: someone with a good memory accurately describes what she has seen or heard, reliably recalls what she has learned; and our skilled bird watcher generally identifies the birds he sees correctly.

Although Aristotle's 'intellectual virtues' are often of this kind, the states fundamental to his virtue ethics are rather different. The epistemological analogue of the latter would be traits and capacities that are manifested in the use or exercise of skills of the first kind in deliberation and inquiry. If someone is *observant*, he uses his good eyesight and his recognitional capacities appropriately. His *open-mindedness* is reflected in his readiness to admit appropriate or relevant questions and challenges to his views. His carefulness is manifested in the fact that he knows when to check inferences and observations and rarely makes mistakes. And his intellectual *perseverance* is shown in, for example, his ability to acknowledge the consequences of his views without wavering. Such virtues regulate the ways in which we carry out such activities as inquiry and deliberation; they enable us to use our faculties, our skills, and our expertise well in pursuit of our cognitive goals. The description 'trait of character' applies to these virtues, although it does not naturally apply to a good memory or to expert knowledge of warblers. Thus we can adopt a two-tier picture: we would not be reliable seekers after the truth or effective solvers of theoretical problems if we did not possess specific skills and capacities: good eyesight and hearing, a reliable memory, good knowledge of specific subject matters and so

---

[9] It is possible that my abstract characterization of virtue epistemology is still not abstract enough, because it required that our epistemological explanation appeal to states which could count as virtues. I suppose that there could be a version of virtue epistemology which appealed to the 'virtue' of the knower, to 'how virtuous she is', without explaining this in terms of the possession of distinct virtues.

on; but our success also requires us to possess traits of character which enable us to use our skills and capacities effectively when inquiring and deliberating.

Both kinds of 'virtues' can contribute to our reliability or to our cognitive success. The first kind are more like the virtues of mechanisms, of calculators, or of visual sensors. Virtues of the second kind are more like virtues of character: their exercise involves *judgement* and equips us to deal with the *holistic* character of most epistemic evaluation. To borrow a phrase from John Greco,[10] virtues of the second kind contribute to our *reliability as agents*; they enable us to deploy reliable faculties and mechanisms to good effect. How good I am at investigating matters and at forming well-grounded beliefs is a function of how well I make use of my cognitive skills and resources. This is reflected in another difference between the two sorts of virtues. The acuity of someone's eyesight is, indeed, an excellence, but in commenting upon it, we praise her eyesight, and we do not necessarily praise her. She deserves praise only if she makes good use of this resource. When someone is described as observant or as open-minded, the implied praise can attach to the agent directly.[11]

In the introduction to his valuable new collection of papers on virtue epistemology, Guy Axtell contrasts two kinds of virtue epistemology. 'Reliabilist' virtue epistemology might define 'justified belief' in terms of 'virtuous character' and then explain virtuous character in terms of 'successful and stable dispositions to form true beliefs'.[12] The alternative approach, designated by Axtell as 'responsibilist', emphasizes the role of epistemic virtues in guiding agents in carrying out activities such as inquiries (myself and Linda Zagzebski are among the cited followers of this approach). This distinction does not correspond to the distinction between the two kinds of virtues. As we have just seen, both sorts of virtues are relevant to our reliability as believers, to the likelihood that our beliefs will be true. And our ability to inquire responsibly depends upon our using skills and capacities in an observant, open-minded, and perseverant way.[13]

---

[10] Greco (1999*a*).

[11] It is an interesting question why this should be, but it will not be considered further here.

[12] Axtell (2000: xiii). The characterization is taken from Greco.

[13] I am unsure that the label 'responsibilist' is a good one. Those who belong to the second approach wish to exploit analogies with Aristotelian ethics and thus regard the second kind of virtue as the paradigm of an epistemic virtue. They may, but need not, be reluctant to call excellences of the first kind 'virtues' at all. But it would be wrong to deny that the 'reliabilist' camp are concerned with epistemic responsibility. Ernest Sosa, for example, defends a form of 'virtue perspectivalism', and the role of the 'perspective' is to capture the internalist aspect of justification which is connected to ideas of epistemic responsibility.

For the present I want to note one significant mark of these differences in approach, however it is described. Although Axtell's reliabilist can take note of the difference between two kinds of virtue that I described above, and can allow that the second kind may have a special kind of significance for reflective agents like us, the epistemic importance of the two kinds is much the same: each is of value because, in different ways, they contribute to the reliability of the agent's beliefs. For the second kind of virtue epistemologist, the *second* kind of virtue has theoretical primacy: the second kind of virtue is directly manifested in our capacity to inquire well and responsibly. Indeed someone who favours the 'responsibilist' approach may hesitate to describe the first kind of excellence as a virtue at all, feeling that the use of the same term may obscure differences that are of fundamental philosophical importance. Our true epistemic virtue, we might suppose, is manifested in our ability to inquire successfully through exploiting our 'virtues' of the first kind. This terminology enables us to maintain the parallels between virtue epistemology and virtue ethics. Moreover, each usage can claim the authority of Aristotle, I suspect: his general use of 'virtue' to refer to any excellence (and some of his remarks about intellectual virtues) support a readiness to acknowledge a wide range of traits, skills, and capacities as virtues; but someone who seeks an approach to epistemology which parallels Aristotelian approaches to ethics is likely to place a special emphasis on states that regulate the processes of inquiry and deliberation. But we shall return to these (and related) distinctions as the chapter proceeds.

Before we continue, other kinds of epistemic virtue must be acknowledged. The examples considered all appeal to the virtues of individuals: it is people that possess good eyesight, skills at bird recognition, open-mindedness, and so on. It is easy to see that communities may also possess virtues—facilitating debate and regulating the progress of investigations—which may not be reducible to the virtues of the individuals who belong to them. Moreover, this possibility complicates what we can say about individual virtues. A research team may benefit from having some members who are dogmatic, and unwilling to take on board new possibilities, while others are much more ready to take seriously seemingly wild speculations. What would be vices in individual inquirers may be virtues when possessed by members of a team. We also talk of the virtues of theories and hypotheses.[14] That a new theory is simple, that it

---

[14] This paragraph acknowledges a remark made by Ernan McMullin during discussion of this essay at the conference at Notre Dame.

avoids known anomalies, that it invokes mechanisms analogous to those that are successful in related areas: all of these are excellences in theories, features whose presence should recommend the theory to us. Whether they are excellences because they are reliable indicators of truth, or whether theories are true partly in virtue of possessing these excellences, is a controversial matter. It is clear that sensitivity to the virtues of hypotheses would be a personal virtue, but it is not obvious that this requires acceptance of what I have called a virtue epistemology.

## III. The priority of virtue

Within a virtue theory, we noticed, explanations (and evaluations) in terms of virtues must have a distinctive kind of *priority*. What sort of priority is involved? The 'standard view' that we sketched in the first section held that the appropriate kind of priority is *conceptual:* we can analyse fundamental terms of epistemic appraisal in ways that make reference to epistemic virtues. However, we do not have to depart from the 'standard view' to see that this is not the only possibility. Even if we do not need to appeal to virtues in providing analyses of knowledge and justified belief, they may have an ineliminable role in carrying out the second central task of epistemology, explaining how knowledge, or justified belief, is, in fact, possible.

An example may help us to see what this might involve. Suppose we accept a relevant alternatives account of knowledge: someone knows some proposition if and only if they can rule out all relevant alternatives to it. And let us also assume that our analysis of what makes a possibility 'relevant' can be explained without reference to epistemic or intellectual virtues. In that case, we might suppose, the first, definitional, part of the epistemological enterprise can be completed without appeal to epistemic virtues. (Note that this is intended purely as an illustrative example: I am not defending a relevant alternatives theory of knowledge, nor am I convinced that virtues may not have a role in explaining when alternative possibilities are 'relevant'.)

Whether an alternative possibility is 'relevant' to whether I know some proposition can depend upon a wide range of factors: it may depend upon the context, and it may be sensitive to the many factors which influence the probability of the alternative being realized. If the responsible search for knowledge required us to list all possible alternatives, assessing which of them are 'relevant' in the light of this extensive array of considerations would be extremely difficult, if not simply impossible. In that case, we may conclude that our confidence that we can obtain knowledge depends upon our possessing a warranted confidence that any alternatives that occur to us are likely to be relevant and that those alternatives that do not occur to us are generally not relevant. Unless we can generally trust our 'instinctive' judgements about relevance, the responsible search for knowledge would impose demands for reflective monitoring of our progress that we could not reasonably expect to comply with. If we can trust our intuitive doubts and be confident in our habitual certainties, and if we are right to do this, then knowledge is possible; but unless we can trust these things, we may have no confidence that knowledge is available to us at all. Possession of evaluative habits of the sort described in the last section may then have an irreducible role in explaining how it is possible for this confidence not to be misplaced. The centrality of virtues for epistemology may be found in the need to appeal to them in order to explain how knowledge (or perhaps just human knowledge) is possible at all.

In the introduction to his anthology, Guy Axtell characterizes virtue epistemology by reference to a shift to a 'new direction of analysis'. Other approaches to epistemology can allow that there are such states as epistemic virtues, but will characterize them as traits that help us to acquire justified beliefs or knowledge: virtues are means to the acquisition of knowledge. The new approach defines justified belief as belief that is expressive of virtuous character, perhaps defining virtuous character traits as those that are conducive to the acquisition of true belief: 'Virtue epistemologists typically define not only justified belief but also knowledge through essential reference to their source in intellectual virtues.'[15]

This section of my chapter suggests that it is possible to be a virtue epistemologist without adopting this shift in the direction of analysis. Virtues may have a fundamental role in explaining, not what knowledge is, but rather how knowledge is possible. If this explanatory problem is itself one of the *central* problems of epistemology, then that is enough for virtues to be relevant to the central problems. Indeed, such an explanation may have a role in defending an analysis of knowledge that does not itself refer to the virtues. Someone might argue that a relevant alternatives analysis of knowledge could be plausible only if it was possible to combine it with an adequate account of the role of the virtues in epistemic evaluation.

[15] Axtell (2000: xiii).

This discussion has been hypothetical and abstract, and it will be useful to collect our thoughts. If we accept the standard view of the central problems of epistemology, then virtues can have a primary role in our responses to them in several ways:

(i) Virtues can be referred to in the analysans for knowledge or justified belief: knowledge may be explained as virtuously acquired true belief.
(ii) Virtues may be invoked in our defence of some analysis that does not refer to them: it is only because we believe that the regulation of our deliberations and inquiries can be regulated by epistemic virtues that we find it plausible to accept an analysis of knowledge as requiring the elimination of relevant alternatives.
(iii) This role of the virtues in the regulation of inquiries and deliberations may have a fundamental role in our response to scepticism, in our explanation of how knowledge is possible.

(iii) may be combined with either (i) or (ii), but it is also possible to accept (iii) without accepting either of the other theses. Given our initial characterization of virtue epistemology, it is reasonable to treat any of these positions as versions of virtue epistemology. Our next task is to ask whether accepting one or other of these theses is necessary for being a virtue epistemologist: are there ways of understanding the central tasks of epistemology that enable one to abandon the standard view?

## IV. The epistemological project

The third element in our characterization of virtue epistemology was the 'central' or fundamental problem of epistemology: what is the task or goal of epistemological inquiry? The standard view suggests a familiar answer to this question:

**Answer I:** to explain what knowledge and justified belief are, and to investigate how far we are able to possess states of knowledge and justified belief.

We could instead begin with a less specific answer:

**Answer II:** to describe and explain our practice of epistemic evaluation; to investigate how far our epistemic goals are appropriate and how far our evaluative practice enables us to achieve our epistemic ends. (This may also involve proposing amendments to our evaluative practice.)

The first answer is a refinement of the second: it takes a specific stand on the vocabulary we should use in describing our practice of epistemic evaluation, employing terms such as 'knowledge' and 'justified belief'. In this section, we shall consider some reasons for thinking that Answer II is to be preferred.

Why might we prefer Answer II? One reason, perhaps suggested by Ernest Sosa's recent writings, is that there is more to our practice of epistemic evaluation than the assessment of beliefs as justified or as cases of knowledge. Answer II allows us to take seriously a wider range of issues about epistemic evaluation than those formulated in these terms. It is compatible with this that issues of knowledge and justification are still the fundamental, most central ones, in which case our approach would not count as 'virtue epistemology'. Another reason, a more radical one, is that adopting Answer II forces us to address the question of just how central and fundamental the issues about *knowledge* and *justification* are. Perhaps these are more specialized, less fundamental, terms of epistemic appraisal than the recent epistemological tradition has supposed. In other words, if we start by adopting Answer II, we can then ask: is the proper analysis of knowledge and justified belief a fundamental epistemological question? And, if so, why? There is a good reason to consider this possibility when our concern is with the bearing of virtue theories upon epistemological matters. Traditionally, much ethical theory assumed that the most important issues of ethics concerned the nature of obligation, the force of the moral 'ought'. And some of the most important contributions to virtue ethics have claimed that this was a mistake, that taking virtues seriously enables us to turn aside from these questions and concentrate upon questions of how to act and live well. Virtue ethics encourages a change in how the most central questions for ethics are formulated. It would be a mistake to set up the questions for epistemology in a way that ruled out from the beginning the possibility that we might conclude that 'knowledge' and 'justification' are less central to its concerns than had been supposed.

We can immediately notice one special merit of Answer II. We can distinguish two systems of epistemic evaluation that we make use of. First, we can evaluate people's cognitive *states*. Some beliefs, we suppose, are warranted or legitimate; they are justified. Some beliefs may count as instances of *knowledge*. We might also consider the rationality of people's *doubts* and of the appropriateness of their agnostic stances with respect to some propositions. I shall refer to these as *static* evaluations—evaluations of states. Answer I restricts its attention to static evaluations. But there are other epistemic evaluations that are not static. We evaluate and regulate activities of inquiry and deliberation.

I shall assume that inquiries (and deliberations) are goal-directed activities, attempts to find things out. These activities can be carried out well or poorly; and many important epistemic norms are concerned with how we should carry out activities of this kind. How reflective should we be when we carry out inquiries and deliberations? What form should our monitoring reflections take? What role have the concepts of *knowledge* and *justification* in the ways in which we regulate our inquiries? Indeed, need they have any fundamental role at all?[16]

Once Answer II is taken seriously, we find room for another kind of 'virtue epistemology'. The notions of a 'well-conducted inquiry' or of a 'well-managed system of opinions' emerge as important foci for what seems to be a form of epistemic evaluation. And, as we shall see further below, states such as virtues may well have an important role in the evaluations we make use of when ordering inquiries and managing our beliefs. Indeed, since we are here concerned with the regulation of an activity, and with the regulation of the deliberations that guide the actions involved in carrying out these cognitive activities, we would not be surprised if clear parallels could be found between proposals drawn from virtue ethics and strategies within virtue epistemology. Thus virtue epistemology might fall into place as an account of the evaluations required for well-regulated inquiries and theoretical deliberations. We should emphasize why this is especially congenial to virtue epistemology. Aristotelian virtues are manifested in the regulation of conduct and practical reasoning. They determine which considerations are salient when we are deliberating about what to do. The second system of epistemic evaluation is tied to the regulation of the activity of inquiry. If the fundamental role of virtues lies in regulating activity, it would be unsurprising if they had a similar role in regulating epistemic activities or inquiry and deliberation. Hence the focus on virtues leads us to attend to the evaluations involved in this second system rather than those (cast in terms of *knowledge* and *justified belief*) which are involved in the first. Indeed it may not be an accident that the concepts of knowledge and justified belief often have very little role in epistemological work in the philosophy of science, which tends to be concerned with activities of inquiry.

It may be objected that, developed in this way, Answer II does not provide a serious alternative to Answer I: it either falls into place as a version of Answer I, or it fails to be a characterization of what I called the central questions of epistemology. We land on the first horn of this dilemma if we propose to

---

[16] Hookway (1999) explores this contrast between two systems of epistemic evaluation in more detail.

define knowledge or justified belief as belief which results from, or is sustained by, good inquiry and effective cognitive management.[17] For, in that case, we appeal to the regulation of inquiry in explaining what knowledge is or how it is possible. If we deny that the account of good inquiry has such a role in explaining knowledge or justified belief, then, while making an interesting contribution to the study of epistemic rationality, it does not engage with the defining questions for epistemology.

An adequate response to this complaint suggests a necessary condition for developing virtue epistemology along the lines suggested: we need to provide a characterization of the fundamental problems of epistemology which does not give a central role to the analysis of knowledge (or perhaps justified belief). We might suppose that this is impossible: if epistemology is the theory of *knowledge*, a concern with the analysis of knowledge cannot fail to be fundamental to its concerns. The remainder of this chapter is an attempt to show that this is a mistake. It is at least possible that we can give an account of epistemology that does not lead Answer II either to collapse into Answer I or to fail to engage with central epistemological concerns. As noted below, it is not clear that we do have to set the task of epistemology in the standard way. Moreover, the long history of failed attempts to provide accounts of knowledge which are impervious to Gettier-style challenges may encourage the suspicion that this concept is flawed, not serving as a vehicle for evaluations which are central to epistemological concerns. The history of attempts to construct an adequate inductive logic may similarly cast doubt on the integrity of the concept of justified belief. A parallel with ethics is pertinent here. Even those who question the value of the concept of *moral obligation* will recognize that we can acquire obligations in special cases: by making promises or by signing contracts, for example. Their objection is to the applicability of the concept of obligation to cases which lack a special legal or institutional backing. We might also make sense of a specialized use the word 'knows' to identify sources of reliable testimony, or of speaking of justification in special cases when I am able to justify my belief to my fellows. It does not follow from this that interesting concepts of knowledge and justification apply more generally, that all secure beliefs that we are right not to question count as justified and, if true, as knowledge. Answer I rests on some substantial assumptions about the character and vocabulary of epistemic evaluation, and a virtue approach

---

[17] This is what appears to occur in Hookway (1999).

together with reliance upon Answer II contributes to making those assumptions controversial.

We still need to understand how the result could be viewed as engaging with the central problems of epistemology. We shall approach this indirectly. First, note that Answer I's view of the goal of epistemology has two components: the first was to provide an account of knowledge and justified belief; and the second was to defend the claim that we possess knowledge and justified belief against sceptical challenges. We might view each of these components as a version of a more abstract project. We desire, first, to describe and clarify our practice of epistemic evaluation, and, second, to understand how our practice is successful, to the degree that it is. Answer I describes our practice in terms of *knowledge* and *justified belief*; it therefore characterizes the second component in terms of explaining how we obtain knowledge and justified belief. It then makes the additional claim that we can meet this explanatory demand only if we can answer familiar sceptical challenges to knowledge and justified belief. We can envisage a position that meets the more abstract characterization, yet rejects all three of these components of Answer I's view. This *need* not involve refusing to take scepticism seriously—so long as the scepticism in question is not directed against knowledge or justified belief. But, equally, the task of understanding the success of our evaluative practice need not require us to engage with sceptical arguments at all, beyond, perhaps, explaining why others are wrong to take them seriously.

The history of epistemology helps to clarify this. We often introduce the subject to our students by telling the story of Descartes's *Meditations*: we tell them that he is concerned with the possibility of knowledge, or perhaps of certainty because, he supposed, certainty was required for knowledge; and the familiar sceptical challenges suggest that the senses are less reliable as a source of knowledge than common sense supposed. The upshot of trial through scepticism is then supposed to be that we can, indeed, possess knowledge. Whatever its didactic merits, this way of presenting his views has little support from the texts: his aim is reassurance that he can make contributions in the sciences that are going to last, and the modern concern with 'knows' and its cognates is almost entirely absent. His aim seems to be to show that he can contribute to scientific inquiry successfully, without being committed to unrealizable demands for a reflective defence of his strategies. In a similar way, the Pyrrhonists use sceptical challenges to undermine our confidence, not that we can possess knowledge or justification, but rather than we can take responsibility for the success of our inquiries at all. Exposure to their wiles is supposed to leave us suspecting that no matter how careful we are in our inquiries, we can be forced to acknowledge burdens of reflection that cannot all be discharged. We can be forced to suspend judgment on any proposition we are disposed to believe. Once again, the concepts of knowledge and justification are wholly absent; the concern is with how reflection interacts with deliberation and inquiry.[18]

Sceptical challenges suggest that the evaluative practice is somehow self-defeating, that its use will prevent our achieving the goals that its use was intended to serve. It places upon us burdens of reflection that we cannot discharge: it requires us to reflect upon various sceptical possibilities, and it fails to provide resources for dealing with them. This encourages us to conclude that our confidence in our practices has not been earned; it is illegitimate. So it is possible for us to encounter sceptical problems even if we reject Answer I. That is why I have been careful to describe scepticism without using the concepts of 'knowledge' and 'justified belief'. If we think that *knowledge* can be clarified successfully and can be used to identify our goal in inquiry, then, indeed, Answer II may lead on to Answer I. But, as noted above, if their ordinary use is more specialized than that, then Answer I can be resisted. Answer II allows us to leave this question open, as a question for epistemology rather than as something that is already settled when epistemology begins. And it leaves open the possibility that other forms of scepticism may become pressing. But our understanding of the tasks of epistemology gives us no reason to suppose that they will.

I have suggested that virtue epistemology encourages a focus on the second of the two systems of epistemic evaluation that I described, as well as, or even instead of, the first. Virtues regulate inquiries and deliberations and only indirectly regulate beliefs. They can also affect our attitude towards how far the meeting of sceptical challenges should have a role in our explanations of the successes of our practice of epistemic evaluation. Sceptical arguments emerge when our practice of epistemic evaluation imposes burdens of reflection. They arise when epistemic responsibility calls upon us to reflect upon the grounds of our beliefs and control the standards we employ in the course of such reflection. If the regulation of inquiry is entirely driven by reflection, then it is unsurprising that sceptical challenges emerge as pressing. But virtue theories deny that regulation of inquiry is entirely driven by reflection; traits of

---

[18] A fuller defence of the interpretations of Descartes and Pyrrhonism defended here can be found in Hookway (1990: chs. 1–4).

character, habits and capacities, can regulate inquiries and deliberations even if we have no access to how they do so. In that case, a virtue epistemologist may be able to resist the claim that responding to scepticism is central to the epistemological task. When philosophers leave the study, they resemble everyone else in treating sceptical challenges as irrelevant to their cognitive evaluations. On returning to their work, they may suspect that this is an error, that we *ought* to take such challenges seriously as they call for reflection which is relevant to whether we possess knowledge or inquire successfully. Virtue epistemologists may view this professional reaction as the result of a flawed understanding of our practice of epistemic evaluation, one that assigns too great a role to reflection.

## V. Virtue epistemology

My own interest in virtue epistemology grew from some ideas I developed during the 1980s and sketched in a small book on scepticism.[19] In line with the view offered in the last section, I urged that the primary focus of epistemic evaluation is the activities of inquiry and deliberation, attempts to find things out. It enables us to inquire well and effectively, subjecting our inquiries to a degree of control and taking responsibility for how well they go. So a fundamental problem for epistemology concerns how it is possible for us to carry out the investigations required for effective and responsible inquiry.

On this basis—and inspired by readings of both Descartes and the Pyrrhonists—I argued that sceptical arguments emerge from the reflections we carry out in the course of pursuing inquiries and threaten the possibility of our being able to take responsibility for whether we inquire and deliberate well. (I put this, unfortunately I now think, by saying that we needed to be able to carry out our inquiries 'autonomously', directing them in the light of the information we possess. In that case, sceptical arguments challenge the possibility of a distinctive kind of autonomous inquiry.) I then claimed that sceptical arguments could be resisted only if we could make sense of a way in which the role of *reflection* in the control of inquiry could be limited. Our investigations depend upon what I thought of as a body of largely acquired habits, whose internal operations were opaque to us. And we had to think of the operation of such habits as 'internal': awareness of their role should not lead

[19] Hookway (1990).

to a sense that our deliberations are subject to influences we can think of as alien, perhaps as heteronomous. I began writing about epistemic virtues in the search for a better way of expressing the ideas sketched in that book; and this led me to focus on their role in the regulation of inquiry and deliberation. I took it that the primary focus of epistemic evaluation was regulation of activities of deliberation and inquiry, rather than the (largely third person) evaluation of states of belief as 'justified' or as 'knowledge'. So in so far as I defended a form of virtue epistemology this was based on the claim not that we should define 'justified belief' in terms of the virtues, but, rather, that we shall only understand how we can regulate deliberations and inquiries, only understand how we can control our opinions and inquire well to the degree that we do, by giving a central role to states such as virtues.[20] Indeed, the role of virtues in 'theoretical' deliberation (in identifying reasons for belief, for example) paralleled the role of virtues in practical deliberation (in identifying reasons for action). Thus, although at times I have been tempted to explain justified belief as belief that issues from a good deliberation or inquiry (or from a proper lack of deliberation), that is not essential to the project.

Why should virtues have a role in these explanations? A necessary condition for avoiding scepticism is that we can be *confident* that we can carry out inquiries in ways that are appropriately regulated by norms. Sceptical arguments can undermine this confidence. Indeed some forms of epistemological externalism also have difficulty vindicating this confidence. The mere fact that my beliefs are formed in a reliable manner, for example, is not sufficient to give me a legitimate confidence that they do so—some of BonJour's examples concerning clairvoyance illustrate this.[21] In order to consider how such confidence is possible, we must ask what normative tasks we must be able to carry out. Here is a partial list:

(a) Identifying good strategies for carrying out inquiries.
(b) Recognizing when we possess an answer to our question or a solution to our problem.
(c) Assessing how good our evidence for some proposition is.
(d) Judging when we have taken account of all or most relevant lines of investigation, and so on.

We have identified inquiry as an attempt to answer a question. The normative regulation of inquiry involves raising further questions about the progress of

---

[20] However, I should admit that this was not evident from at least some of my writings on the topic. See Hookway (1994) and (1999).  [21] BonJour (1985: ch. 3).

our inquiry: Should I have considered other possibilities? Should I have checked my reasoning or repeated my experiments; and so on. We can persevere with our inquiries only if we are confident that we will ask the *right* subordinate questions, that our reflection will take appropriate routes.

Inquiry would be impossible if we had to consider every possible subordinate question and ask, concerning it, whether we need to answer it as a means to achieving our cognitive goal. Many familiar sceptical arguments exploit this alarming possibility. In our ordinary practice of epistemic evaluation, this does not happen. Subordinate questions will just 'occur' to us as relevant, and we can ignore those that do not occur to us. Their 'occurring' to us generally has a passive character and reflects our character and education; they are influenced by the habits and capacities that we have described as virtues. Judgement is usually involved in determining which questions occur to us as relevant: these judgements are made against an extensive background of background knowledge and experience at carrying out similar kinds of inquiries. The appropriateness of a question is always a function of one's whole cognitive position in the particular case with which we are involved. Success in inquiry thus depends upon the wisdom embodied in our judgements and upon the cognitive habits and skills we have acquired through education, experience, and training. Success depends upon our epistemic 'character'. How observant I am will influence whether relevant evidence grabs my attention; and how intellectually honest I am will influence whether I generally come to doubt propositions once presented with sufficient counter-evidence to them.

If this is how our practice works, then our normal reluctance to take sceptical arguments seriously does not threaten our practice of epistemic evaluation. If we are confident in our possession of epistemic virtues, we can treat it as a sign of our epistemic wisdom. We are not required to reflect upon the bases of all of our beliefs and, in very many cases, we are not able to do so. For a virtue-based account of epistemic evaluation, this is just what is to be expected. Our practice gives us no reason to take sceptical arguments seriously for we are already aware of the shallowness of reflection, of the need to trust our habits of evaluation if we are to inquire well.

To draw these ideas together: why should we talk about virtues? In making judgements, we rely on traits of character, habits and dispositions. If we are genuinely virtuous, we will ask the right questions, and this explains our successes in inquiry. Confidence in our possession of virtuous capacities is required for us to possess confidence in the intuitive judgements that we rely upon in directing our inquiries. And, as we have seen, this confidence is required if we are to be confident of the outcomes of our inquiries. If we possess virtue, and we are confident that we possess virtue, the fact that various reflective questions are not raised can be seen as a symptom of our rationality rather than as a sign of our reluctance to do what epistemic responsibility requires. And this legitimates the avoidance of sceptical problems about whether our reflections have gone sufficiently far, about whether we can ever deal with every question that needs to be addressed. Moreover, so far, nothing has been said about knowledge or justified belief: it is an additional question whether confidence in our ability to inquire depends upon confidence that we possess knowledge or justified belief. Even if it transpires that the concepts of knowledge and justified belief are as important as most philosophers suppose, this is an epistemological *conclusion* rather than being something which is definitive of the discipline from the beginning.

Answer I assumes that *knowledge* is our most fundamental term of epistemic appraisal, perhaps involved in setting the aims of serious inquiries. This may be so, but it is useful to notice that this is not self-evidently the case. Some philosophers—Popper is an example—hold that neither justified belief nor personal knowledge has any importance for epistemology; and they hold that our success as inquirers is not diminished by this fact. Others may hold that 'knows' is a very specialized term of epistemic appraisal, with a role, perhaps, in identifying informants or reliable sources of testimony. Unless we had an interest in learning who was the US president, we would have no interest in establishing who knows who holds that office. If we are interested in whether *we* possess knowledge, this may only be because we hope that others can rely upon our testimony.[22] A defender of the standard view could respond by following Williamson and Peacocke in arguing that inquiry aims to issue in *assertion*, and, when we assert propositions we present ourselves as possessing knowledge of them.[23] But it seems clear that all of these views are controversial, and that they are issues that arise internally to the more fundamental issue of how we can be responsible and effective inquirers. Similar remarks could be made about justified belief.

When virtue ethics entered debates in analytical metaethics during the 1950s, it was often accompanied by claims that moral philosophy had been distorted by focusing on a limited evaluative vocabulary—perhaps just 'good' and 'ought'. Indeed Elizabeth Anscombe argued that the moral 'ought' and

---

[22] See Craig (1990) and Hookway (1990: ch. 10).
[23] Williamson (1996) and Peacocke (1999: 34).

the related idea of moral *obligation* should be expunged from moral thought, reflecting thought about ethics which took for granted a divine lawgiver.[24] I have tried to make attractive a similar possibility in epistemology, although I have not presented a detailed argument in its support. A virtue epistemologist can describe our practice of epistemic evaluation and elucidate the fundamental vocabulary of epistemic evaluation without giving a central role to *knowledge* and *justification*. And she can help us to understand the successes of that practice without taking familiar kinds of sceptical challenges seriously. They do not threaten our confidence in our ability to inquire successfully.[25]

[24] Anscombe (1958).

[25] I have been helped by discussions when I gave this chapter as a paper at the conference at the University of Notre Dame and to the departmental seminar in Sheffield. I am grateful to all those who participated in those discussions, and also for helpful comments on other occasions from Jennifer Saul, Anna Sherratt, Ian White, and Harry Witzhum.

# 9

# Understanding 'Virtue' and the Virtue of Understanding

## Wayne D. Riggs

## I. Introduction

Virtue theories are popular in epistemology these days, but they are a diverse lot. It is sometimes hard to see what they all have in common besides the appropriation of the term 'virtue'. However, one can divide them very broadly into two groups: those theories that really put the analysis of epistemic virtues at the centre of the epistemological enterprise, and those that make use of virtues or virtue-talk along the way to analysing other terms and concepts that they take to be central to epistemology. Examples of the first kind are somewhat rarer than examples of the second. Jonathan Kvanvig, in his book on epistemic virtue theories,[1] makes a clear plea for epistemologists to take the idea of epistemic virtues seriously in their own right. He proposes the radical notion of abandoning what he calls the 'Cartesian perspective' in favour of a different approach that places the intellectual virtues in the foreground of theoretical study. Where evaluations from the Cartesian perspective are synchronic in nature and focused on the individual, Kvanvig argues that social and cross-temporal factors are relevant to important epistemic evaluations.[2] Kvanvig thinks that a genuine focus on intellectual virtues will bring such factors into the mix of epistemological theories.

[1] Kvanvig (1992: esp. ch. 7).   [2] Ibid. 167 ff.

Though Kvanvig does not develop such a theory of his own, Linda Zagzebski takes a few steps in the direction of the new perspective urged by Kvanvig. She does not cast off the Cartesian perspective entirely, but she does develop a detailed account of the intellectual virtues in their own right. Because she accepts a generally Aristotelian conception of virtue, her account includes some social and cross-temporal factors as relevant to having the various intellectual virtues. Virtues are generally acquired over time, and much of our success at being virtuous will depend upon facts about our parents, our society and culture, and other social factors. Thus, Zagzebski's account of virtue makes some room for these influences.

James Montmarquet also presents an epistemological virtue theory in his *Epistemic Virtue and Doxastic Responsibility*.[3] He, too, considers the nature of intellectual virtue in its own right, though his theory is much less Aristotelian and differs widely from Zagzebski's view. He takes 'epistemic conscientiousness' to be the primary intellectual virtue. His view differs most markedly from other theories of epistemic virtue in that he does not make reliability a necessary condition of virtue. One can be virtuous yet fail to get to the truth very often.

This approach contrasts most sharply with those of Ernest Sosa and John Greco, both of whom at one time or another have identified themselves as virtue theorists. Though each of these philosophers has his own distinct account of epistemic virtue, they share a common commitment to the importance of epistemic reliability.[4] They hold that being epistemically virtuous is largely a matter of having cognitive equipment that reliably reports the truth. One possible explanation for this common feature is that each of these epistemologists takes epistemic virtue to be important primarily as a tool to offer an adequate account of knowledge. Epistemic virtues enter the picture by way of their theories of knowledge. Perhaps they began with a commitment to some form of reliabilism, and developing this theory led them to include virtues in their theories to account for certain intuitions about knowledge, or to avoid persistent counterexamples.

But despite the diversity of these approaches to 'virtue epistemology', there is one point of agreement—namely, that epistemic virtues, whatever they may be, are defined either teleologically or instrumentally (or both) in terms of our epistemic ends. Accordingly, a character trait of an agent is an epistemic

---

[3] Montmarquet (1993).

[4] Linda Zagzebski's view also has this requirement, but I don't include her in this group because she does not fit the characterization of Sosa, Goldman, and Greco that I give in the following paragraph.

virtue only if, by the operation of that trait, one is either 'aiming at' some epistemic end or one is actually likely to obtain it (or both). Thus, the definition of 'epistemic virtue' one arrives at on this common picture depends on both (i) the specification of our epistemic ends, and (ii) the characterization of the relationship that must obtain between a cognitive trait and those ends for such a trait to count as an epistemic virtue. In this essay, I will speak to both of these issues. First, I will argue that one recently proposed relationship between cognitive traits and epistemic ends is not an appropriate condition on a trait's being an epistemic virtue. Then I shall turn to the question of our epistemic ends. What ends must we accept in order to capture the traits we normally take to be epistemically virtuous? My answer will depart from the standard line among virtue theorists and other epistemologists alike.

## II. A methodological prelude

Obviously, much of the literature in 'virtue epistemology' is inspired, directly or indirectly, by Aristotle's ethical theory and contemporary developments of similar 'eudaimonistic' ethical theories. I think that this eudaimonistic theory of moral virtue offers a good model for accounting for intellectual virtues. For one thing, it is standard in the literature to speak in explicitly teleological terms about cognitive or epistemic 'ends'. Indeed, until recently there was a fairly strong consensus about just what those ends were: maximizing truth while minimizing error. Though I think this particular account of our cognitive ends is mistaken, I agree that the best way to go about theorizing in epistemology is to specify the goals or ends that define the limits of the field. Having done so, it seems eminently reasonable to define intellectual virtues in terms of just those ends.

A highly simplified version of Aristotle's view goes something like this: (1) *eudaimonia* is the highest good for humans. (2) Whatever contributes to a life of *eudaimonia* is good by virtue of that fact. (3) The members of the standard list of virtues (courage, justice, benevolence, etc.) contribute to a life of *eudaimonia*. (4) So, the virtues are good because they contribute to a life of *eudaimonia*.

On this schematic account of Aristotle's view, the ultimate list of the virtues is driven by his conception of *eudaimonia*, often translated as 'flourishing'. Contributing to human flourishing is both necessary and sufficient for a character trait to count as a moral virtue. One potential advantage this sort of view holds over non-*eudaimonistic* virtue theories is that once you've settled on a description of 'flourishing', you can go out into the world and *see* what character traits are necessary and sufficient for it. You don't have to rely on unreliable bare intuition or on culturally relative conceptions of virtue to make one's list of the virtues. This approach 'grounds' the virtues in a conception of flourishing that, in principle at least, determines for us what can count as a virtue.[5]

I said that this is an advantage for this approach to a *eudaimonistic* virtue theory, but it is also a disadvantage. If we were willing to go wherever human flourishing takes us, so to speak, then this method of determining the moral virtues would be fine. However, in practice any theory that purports to account for the moral virtues simply must include certain specific virtues or it is ruled out from the start. For example, no one would be willing to accept a theory that failed to count courage as a moral virtue. Even if one could argue flawlessly that this followed from a reasonable conception of human flourishing, it would be assumed that the theory was seriously flawed *simply because it failed to count courage as a moral virtue*. Similarly, any theory of epistemic virtues that failed to count open-mindedness, say, as an epistemic virtue would be equally implausible.

In this regard, virtue theories in ethics are in a position no different from that of other moral theories. Any theory of right action, for example, simply must count the brutal acts of torture and rape committed by soldiers in the Bosnian war as wrong in order to be taken seriously. Theories in ethics, as well as in many other areas of philosophy, are constrained by certain commonly held intuitions that we hold dear. On the other hand, certain general principles are equally central to our theorizing. Any theory that did not count the killing of innocents as at least prima facie wrong will also get short shrift. Deeply held general moral principles as well as common intuitions about particular cases constrain ethical theorizing.

Similarly, I think it is unrealistic to propose a virtue theory that claims to derive the actual list of virtues from an account of flourishing. In the actual construction of the theory, the prior intuitions of the philosopher about what traits are really virtues will be driving the account of flourishing at least as much as the other way around. Thus, I will explicitly pursue a strategy of reflective equilibrium in developing the sketch of a theory of intellectual virtue that follows. I am committed to the existence and value of intellectual virtues, regardless of whether any particular theory of them, including my

---

[5] Thanks to Hugh Benson for many conversations stressing this point.

own, succeeds in making good sense of them. On the other hand, I am not so intuition-driven that just any account of what I will call 'intellectual flourishing' will do so long as it captures my intuitions correctly. I will argue in the following sections that we can make sense of the nature and value of various intellectual virtues by placing the notion of 'understanding' at the centre of our account of human intellectual flourishing. This not only captures certain important intuitions about what the intellectual virtues are, but it also seems just the right sort of thing to be central to intellectual flourishing. As complications arise in fitting our intuitions about intellectual virtue to a rough and ready idea of 'understanding', the give and take of reflective equilibrium will guide our modifications as necessary.

## III. Intellectual virtue and success

As I mentioned in the introduction, most current proponents of a 'virtue theory' in epistemology take reliability at producing true beliefs to be a necessary condition for a character trait to be a virtue. This is most obvious with regard to 'virtue reliabilists' like Ernest Sosa and John Greco. For example, Sosa defines a virtue as follows.

A subject S's intellectual virtue V relative to an 'environment' E may be defined as S's disposition to believe correctly propositions in a field F relative to which S stands in conditions C, in 'environment' E.[6]

Somewhat more simply, Sosa's definition states that S's intellectual virtue V is a disposition to have true beliefs about propositions in a field F when in environment E and conditions C. Thus, for example, properly functioning perceptual faculties (operating in a 'normal' environment under 'normal' conditions) are intellectual virtues according to Sosa.

The fact that Sosa's definition of a virtue leaves it relative to a specified environment and conditions is quite significant. An actual 'track record' of success is not necessary for one to have a virtue on his account. Nor is even a disposition to believe correctly in the environment and conditions one finds oneself in necessary to have an intellectual virtue. So, for example, if a cognitively and perceptually normal human being were transported to an evil demon world, this person would not cease to have whatever epistemic virtues she had before,

---

[6] Sosa (1991: 140).

despite the fact that those very dispositions no longer produce mostly true beliefs. The reliability of the disposition is indexed to our (presumably) 'normal' world. Since this kind of reliability is less demanding than the kind to be considered in a moment, I shall call this 'weak' reliability.

Though she does not label herself a reliabilist, Linda Zagzebski also thinks it important to build reliability into the definition of a virtue.

> A **virtue**, then, can be defined as **a deep and enduring acquired excellence of a person, involving a characteristic motivation to produce a certain desired end and reliable success in bringing about that end.**[7]

On this view, though the right sort of motivation is required to have a virtue, one fails to have the virtue unless such motivated action reliably yields the end toward which the motivation is directed. So, unlike Sosa, Zagzebski does require a successful 'track record' of coming to hold true beliefs in order for a trait to count as an intellectual virtue. This is, of course, a much more demanding condition to satisfy. Consequently, I shall call this condition of Zagzebski's above definition 'strong' reliability.

Which version of reliability one builds into one's definition of 'virtue' has major implications for the tenability of one's theory of the virtues, whether those virtues be moral or epistemic. As I shall argue below, strong reliability is indeed much too strong to serve as a condition of virtue—epistemic or moral. Weak reliability escapes these criticisms, and may well be a part of a complete account of epistemic virtue.

## A. The secret of 'success'

Julia Annas argues against what I have called a strong reliability or 'success' component in theories of virtue *ethics*.[8] I will briefly present her argument, and then propose that the same objections to a success component in virtue ethics hold against a reliability requirement in virtue epistemology.

Annas acknowledges that both the Aristotelian and the Stoic traditions of virtue ethics seem to hold that having a virtue requires that one be successful in achieving the aim of that virtue.[9] However, these traditions come apart when one considers an ambiguity in the specification of the 'aim' of a virtue.

---

[7] Zagzebski (1996: 137); emphasis in bold in original.
[8] Annas (this volume), pp. 15–33.   [9] Annas (this volume), p. 23.

But what is the virtuous person's aim in acting? She has two. One is her *telos* or overall aim, of living virtuously and acting from motives of virtue. Virtue, after all, is a settled state of the person, with the overall aim of making the person's life as a whole be one way rather than another, virtuous rather than evil or complacent...The virtuous person's other aim is what the Stoics call her *skopos* or immediate target, which is what is aimed at in any particular case of acting virtuously. The target of a just distribution will be everyone's getting what they are entitled to, . . . and so on.[10]

According to Annas, every virtuous act is aimed both at living a virtuous life overall, as well as whatever state of affairs constitutes the virtuous outcome in the particular instance. If a virtue ethics has a success component, it must specify which of the two kinds of aim (or both) one must reliably achieve. Much rides on this decision. Aristotle focused on the reliability of one's achievement of the immediate target, the *skopos*, as necessary for virtue. The Stoics, Annas argues, chose rather the achievement of the overall aim, the *telos*, to be necessary for virtue. There turns out to be good reason to side with the Stoics on this matter.

Virtue ethics is concerned with the person's life as a whole, with character and the kind of person you are. The right perspective on an action, therefore, will for virtue ethics be the one which asks about success in achieving the overall goal, rather than success in achieving the immediate target...To the extent that success in achieving the immediate target depends on factors over which the person has no control—moral luck of various kinds—it will be of less interest to virtue ethics.[11]

On this issue the Stoic view is much clearer and more defensible than Aristotle's. Of course it is often not up to me whether my action achieves the immediate target; but is it up to me whether I succeed or fail in acting virtuously—that is, with the right motives, from a developed disposition and with the right reasoning? If it is not, then it is not up to me whether or not I can become a moral person; and the Stoics are not alone in finding this an unacceptable position.[12]

Aristotle's requirement that the virtuous person must reliably succeed in achieving the 'immediate target' of a virtue in order to have that virtue places an onerous burden on the would-be virtuous agent. To modify one of Annas's examples, a firefighter might have the virtue of courage as displayed by her continued willingness to enter burning houses to save the lives of the occupants. If, as it turns out, most of these people die later of complications, or even if she usually finds them already dead, the rescuer's courage is not

---

[10] Annas (this volume), p. 24.   [11] Annas (this volume), p. 25.
[12] Annas (this volume), p. 27.

diminished, either in the individual actions themselves, or in her character more generally. The rescuer is courageous, despite generally failing to accomplish the immediate targets of her actions—saving individuals' lives. Yet a virtue theory that has a success requirement on the achievement of the immediate target will fail to count such an individual (or her actions) as courageous.

J. L. A. Garcia has similar worries, though he illustrates the problem with an appeal to the familiar evil demon scenario.

Few of us will feel justified in withholding the classifications benevolent, compassionate, generous, just or honest from someone just because she is unlucky or even inept in her efforts. Consider some possibilities.

In a world wherein an evil demon systematically rendered all someone's efforts to help ineffectual, we should still consider them (and her) to be...virtuous.

The claim that virtue has a necessary component of reliably successful behavior seems also to have a distasteful implication. If one must try to help others with reliable success in order to be benevolent, say, then it is hard to see how those severely incapacitated either physically or mentally can be virtuous...This conclusion is both counter-intuitive and morally repugnant.[13]

Here Garcia argues that the strong reliability condition on virtue not only has the counter-intuitive result that clear cases of virtuous actions and people would fail to make the grade, but also that virtue would be in principle inaccessible to whole classes of people who were physically incapable of certain kinds of actions. I'm not sure that this latter point is as obviously counter-intuitive as Garcia thinks it is, but his evil demon scenario complements nicely the arguments of Annas presented previously. And if one does find the latter point seriously wrong-headed, then so much the worse for the strong reliability condition on virtue that would imply it.

So far all this discussion has taken place within the sphere of *moral* virtue. Are there similar problem cases for a strong reliability requirement in one's account of *epistemic* virtue? Certainly, as the following discussion will illustrate.

## B. On the shoulders of virtuous giants

The epistemic analogue to Annas's objection to the incorporation of strong reliability into the notion of an intellectual virtue is stated nicely by James Montmarquet.

[13] Garcia (1997: 34–5).

[I]f we are to appraise the relative worth or 'virtue' of epistemic agents by the truth-conduciveness of their intellectual dispositions, then how are we to accommodate the approximate *equality* of epistemic virtue we find in such diverse agents as Aristotle, Ptolemy, Albertus Magnus, Galileo, Newton, and Einstein? From our current vantage point, we recognize these thinkers as differing greatly in the truth of their respective beliefs and systems of belief...How can such rough equality in virtue be reconciled with this verific diversity?[14]

Montmarquet puts his point in terms of the rough equality in intellectual virtue of our intellectual heroes of times past. I find it slightly more helpful to recast this thought in terms of a criterion of adequacy for a theory of intellectual virtue. I propose that any theory of intellectual virtue that does not *clearly and definitively* count the likes of Aristotle, Newton, Galileo, etc. as being intellectually virtuous does not capture what we mean by 'intellectual virtue'. These individuals (among many others) are our exemplars of intellectual achievement and of intellectual virtue. It is hard to imagine a theory of intellectual virtue that could otherwise be so plausible that we would be willing to give up counting these individuals among the cognitive elite of our shared intellectual history.

And yet, as we now know, a great deal of Aristotle's science and philosophy was mistaken. It may even be that he was wrong about more of these things than he was right. It is, of course, impossible to take such measurements now, but the mere significant possibility will suffice for our current purposes. For suppose we were somehow to discover that, overall, despite Aristotle's careful observation, his meticulous study, his insightful explanatory hypotheses, the rigorous examination of his arguments, and so on, he nonetheless believed more falsehoods about the nature of reality (both physical and metaphysical) than truths. Would this unfortunate finding cause us to remove the mantle of intellectual virtue from Aristotle's shoulders? I think the correct answer is 'clearly not'.

Part of the reasoning behind this reaction is that Aristotle was hindered in his theory construction by the absence of the kinds of technological and theoretical innovations that we have had the benefit of in our own time. Had Aristotle had a microscope, a telescope, a better understanding of human psychology, and so on, we are confident that those very same intellectual character traits that led him astray in his own time (we are assuming for the moment) would have led him to theories much more like the more accurate (we hope!) theories of today.

---

[14] Montmarquet (1993: 21).

This point can be generalized to all major figures in our intellectual history. The greatest and most virtuous intellects in our shared human history all laboured under what we now know to be mistaken assumptions, inaccurate or imprecise measurements, faulty methods, and a whole host of other disadvantages. These factors limited what these figures were able to accomplish in terms of their immediate targets—understanding the nature of reality—but not the degree to which they could develop the intellectual character traits for which we rightly admire them. The very fact that we unhesitatingly ascribe intellectual virtue to these intellectual giants, despite their often spectacularly mistaken views, is eloquent testimony to the fact that success at accomplishing the immediate targets of cognition or inquiry, true belief, is not necessary for intellectual virtue.

This conclusion, if correct, rules out as non-starters any theory of intellectual virtue that requires strong reliability, or truth-conduciveness, of a trait before it can count as such. Such great thinkers as Aristotle and Newton were simply wrong about a great number of things they took to be true descriptions of reality. To deny them intellectual virtue because of this 'failure' seems so outrageous as to constitute a *reductio* of any view that implies it.

Even if successfully 'producing' truths cannot be made a requirement on intellectual virtues, it does not follow that considerations of truth and falsity are irrelevant to them. Far from it. Indeed, it might seem that the solution to this problem is simply to retract the 'success condition' vis à vis the immediate target (true belief), and instead allow that one can have a virtue so long as one has a stable disposition to be appropriately motivated to acquire true beliefs (and avoid false ones). In other words, we could replace the instrumental relationship between intellectual virtue and true belief with a teleological one.

Garcia seems to suggest just such an account of moral virtue, according to which the courageous or benevolent person need not have a successful 'record' of lives saved or suffering relieved, so long as she has a stable disposition to act appropriately in relevant circumstances. Similarly, one need not have a successful record of switching allegiance from false views to true ones heard about later in order to have the virtue of open-mindedness. In both these cases, luck plays too large a role in determining the particular circumstances that determine whether the right sort of action at the right time to the right degree will actually succeed in attaining the immediate target. If virtue theory is to survive at all, we must assume that people have sufficient control over the development of their own virtue, moral or intellectual, to be responsible for their moral and epistemic character. Thus, we cannot allow luck to play such a large role in determining the presence or absence of virtue. Something less than strong reliability must be found to serve its role in the correct account of virtue.

Does this pave the way for a definition of virtue in terms of weak reliability? Not necessarily. It may be that even weak reliability will be too strong for someone like Garcia. One may think that even the propensity to be successful in one's putative virtuous acts under the right conditions and in the proper environment places too onerous a burden on the would-be virtuous. Even so, one won't be able to make the same case against weak reliability that Garcia does against strong reliability. But my point is simply that there are alternative possible accounts of virtue that reject reliability altogether.

## IV. Love of wisdom

In general, this move away from a strong 'immediate target' (e.g. true beliefs) success condition for intellectual virtues seems the right moral to draw from the arguments in the last two sections. However, this alone is not sufficient to resolve the two issues with which this essay began. The task of specifying the set of our epistemic ends remains. I have thus far mentioned only the two goals of having true beliefs and avoiding false beliefs. In this I follow standard practice among epistemologists. But it is a genuine question whether the goal of maintaining a high truth/falsity ratio among one's beliefs is the goal that defines the set of intellectual virtues. In other words, does the set of stable dispositions to be motivated towards the truth and away from falsity capture all and only the intellectual virtues?

There are some strong preliminary reasons to suppose it does not. First, many traits that aim at truth are not candidates for epistemic virtues. For example, a stable disposition to collect trivial information and memorize it would, if done carefully, have as its end the acquisition of truths. Similarly, extreme scepticism about even common-sense and perceptual beliefs would be aimed at the avoidance of falsehoods. Nonetheless, we are not tempted to cite phonebook-memorizers and solipsists as paragons of intellectual virtue. Epistemologists periodically cite this as a worry for the view that the goal of maintaining a high truth/falsity ratio among our beliefs is the overarching value or goal in epistemology, but beyond a brief bout of hand-wringing, little is generally said or done about it.

While such an avoidance strategy *might* be acceptable when developing a theory of knowledge (though I doubt it[15]), I think devising a theory of intellectual virtues around this conception of epistemic value is unpromising because it leaves out of account values that lie at the very core of our conceptions of ourselves as inquirers and cognitive beings. We are not collectors of random or trivial truths. Nor does the acquisition of knowledge exhaust our epistemological pursuits. Much of our most intellectually satisfying effort is directed towards understanding *why* things appear or happen as they do. As I shall suggest below, this kind of understanding need not be propositional, and so would be lost in a theory that focused entirely on knowledge or on truth.

But rather than attacking further the adequacy of the truth/falsity ratio account of our epistemic values, I will instead offer an alternative picture. It will, of necessity, be sketchy, but I think even in its broad outlines one can see the advantages that my approach offers for developing an interesting and plausible account of intellectual virtue.

In section II, I offered a simplified version of an Aristotelian virtue theory of ethics in order to clarify my purposes and method. This sketch will come in handy again as a kind of template for developing a theory of intellectual virtues, so let us look at it again.

1. *Eudaimonia* is the highest good for humans.
2. Whatever contributes to a life of *eudaimonia* is good by virtue of that fact.
3. The members of the standard list of virtues (courage, justice, benevolence, etc.) contribute to a life of *eudaimonia*.
4. So, the virtues are good because they contribute to a life of *eudaimonia*.

To provide a theory of intellectual virtue of this sort, one must specify a plausible candidate for the epistemic 'highest good' to play the role that *eudaimonia* plays in the moral theory. As I mention above, I do not think that the standard 'truth goal' will serve such a theory well. The onus, then, is on me to provide an alternative. I shall, in the remainder of this essay, suggest just such an alternative, and say a few things about it. As the title of this essay suggests, the achievement of 'understanding' will loom large in the account that follows. However, it is not necessary for me to defend the strong claim that understanding alone *is* the highest epistemic good. All that is required is to show that achieving understanding is at least *partially* constitutive of the

---

[15] See Riggs (2002).

highest epistemic good. For now, I will say no more about this, but for ease of expression later, let us call the highest epistemic good, whatever exactly it may be, 'wisdom'.

Using the simplified version of the *eudaimonistic* theory above as a model, the initial version of my theory of intellectual virtue looks like this:

1. *Wisdom* is the highest epistemic good for humans.
2. Whatever contributes to a life of *wisdom* is good by virtue of that fact.
3. The members of the standard list of intellectual virtues (intellectual integrity, intellectual creativity, epistemic responsibility, open-mindedness, inquisitiveness, self-reflection, intellectual honesty, etc.) contribute to the achievement of wisdom.
4. So, the intellectual virtues are good because they contribute to a life of wisdom.

The plausibility of my view rests on the soundness of this argument. Premiss (1) is a stipulative definition, and so requires no further defence. Recall that 'wisdom' is simply the term I have chosen to refer to the highest epistemic good, whatever that may turn out to be. Premiss (2) is no more than a statement of the teleological value structure implicit in this entire approach. This is not the place to give a general defence of teleological theories, so I shall also have nothing further to say on behalf of premiss (2). Hence, the remainder of this chapter will address the plausibility of premiss (3).

One further preliminary remark: obviously, this theory is not being developed in a vacuum. It is being developed against a tradition, though perhaps only a fairly recent one, of treating truth as the sole aim of epistemology. Because of this, my arguments below will be at least partially directed at showing why understanding, *rather than mere truth alone*, is a necessary component of the highest epistemic good.

To begin, I shall describe what I take to be some necessary components of wisdom. I am explicitly *not* trying to capture what any particular philosopher has meant by the term 'wisdom', at least not in any detail. If this strikes someone as contentious, then he or she may simply read 'highest epistemic good' wherever I use 'wisdom'. My first aim is to show that having understanding adds something of epistemic value even to a person who already has a high truth/falsity ratio among her beliefs. If this is correct, then wisdom must include understanding as well as a high truth/falsity ratio, in addition to whatever else may be required.

## V. Understanding wisdom

Wisdom, then, on my view is given the following (partial) definition:

(D1)  S has wisdom only if
   (1) S has a grasp of the truth about the subjects that are most important, and
   (2) S has *understanding* of these subjects as well.

Bear in mind that I take having wisdom to be very much a matter of degree, and I take it to be obvious that no human being has ever achieved a state of 'maximal' wisdom. There are simply too many 'important things' to grasp for anyone to come to understand them all. This definition is still quite vague, and there are at least three points of ambiguity. Before going on to the next section, I will explain briefly what I mean by a 'grasp of the truth', by the 'most important' subjects, and by 'understanding'.

My main reason for using the vague phrase 'grasp the truth' to describe the first condition of having wisdom is that I do not want to require that S has to *know* the truth about the subject in order to have wisdom. This is primarily because of controversies surrounding the nature of knowledge, and the uncertainty of any particular account of it. Thus, I use the phrase 'grasp the truth' as a kind of placeholder for some connection between the agent and the world that is stronger than merely accidentally believing the truth, yet perhaps not always identical with knowing the truth. Obviously, a full development of this view would require a much more detailed analysis of this phrase, but for now I am only listing necessary conditions of wisdom, not sufficient ones.

Moving on, which subjects are the 'most important' ones? I think there are two viable alternative approaches to answering this question, each of which suggests a slightly different development of the theory. On the one hand, one might offer a relativistic answer. One could take the actual interests and values of the agent to determine what the most important subjects are. Wisdom, then, would become grasping the truth about those subjects most important to the agent, while having understanding of it as well (more on this in a moment). On the other hand, one might give a more absolutist answer to the question. One might say that there is a set of subjects that is somehow objectively more important than the rest. For instance, one might think that the subject of morality and ethical conduct was such a subject; or perhaps the ultimate nature of reality; or the nature of the self; the list goes on.

These sound like the sorts of candidates a philosopher might suggest as describing the most important subjects of human inquiry, thought, and debate. Nonetheless, claiming such a privileged set of important subjects would require an argument, to be sure. On the one hand, it seems to me that any understanding, even of some subject matter we may consider trivial or mundane, contributes to the epistemic value of one's life. Yet at the same time it is hard to resist the tug of the intuition that understanding some things is simply much more important than understanding others. But perhaps this is due simply to a confusion between epistemic value and some more general prudential or moral value. For my purposes here, I am content to remain officially agnostic, though I am inclined towards a mixed account, according to which certain subjects are objectively among the most important, but others may achieve that status by way of the subject's deep interest in them.

And finally, what do I mean by 'understanding'? This is a term that is rarely bandied about in epistemological circles,[16] yet it seems on the face of it a richly normative epistemic term. Why the long-standing bias in favour of knowledge, justification, and the like at the expense of understanding? I suspect that at least one reason is that understanding is a harder phenomenon to account for and describe precisely than the aforementioned others. Fortunately, I think that we have a fairly robust intuitive idea of 'understanding', and I will make a few observations about it that, I think, are sufficient to determine the general contours of the phenomenon I have in mind.

'Understanding' has a range of meanings, some of which fall outside the boundaries of what I have in mind. The kind of understanding I have in mind is the appreciation or grasp of order, pattern, and how things 'hang together'. Understanding has a multitude of appropriate objects, among them complicated machines, people, subject disciplines, mathematical proofs, and so on. Understanding something like this requires a deep appreciation, grasp, or awareness of how its parts fit together, what role each one plays in the context of the whole, and of the role it plays in the larger scheme of things.

It is important to realize that being in a state of 'understanding-S' is fundamentally different in kind from being in other epistemic states, in particular from the state of knowing-that-$p$. One of the more significant differences between understanding and knowledge is that knowledge is a species of belief, but understanding is not (at least not necessarily). Furthermore, the kind of knowledge that epistemologists are concerned with is always *knowledge that p*, or

[16] A recent exception is Zagzebski (2001*b*).

'propositional knowledge'. But there are good reasons for doubting that understanding is always propositional. That is, the actual content of one's understanding might not be fully explicable in terms of beliefs plausibly attributable to the agent. This amounts to a denial that the phenomenon of understanding can be reduced simply to a collection of true beliefs, or to some special kind of knowledge.

An important difference between merely believing a bunch of true statements within subject matter M, and having understanding of M (or some part of M), is that one somehow sees the way things 'fit together'. There is a pattern discerned within all the individual bits of information or knowledge. This is, of course, fairly uninformative. Unfortunately, there is very little literature on this notion of understanding, as distinct from the kind of understanding one has of a language. However, the epistemological notion of 'coherence' and the idea of 'explanatory coherence' in particular seem to be getting very close to something characteristic of understanding.

In fact, the literature in the philosophy of science can be of some help here. Philosophers such as Michael Friedman and Philip Kitcher[17] have explicitly identified scientific explanation as the sort of thing that provides scientific understanding. I think it is fairly reasonable to extrapolate from this claim to the broader claim that explanations in general are the sorts of things that provide understanding in general. Sometimes we come to understand some phenomenon through learning about its causal provenance. At other times we come to understand by seeing how some property or event is part of a wider pattern regulated by some lawlike statement. And sometimes we come to understand what something is or why it is present by finding out what its function is. All of these are kinds of scientific explanation, and each has analogues in ordinary reasoning.

But what about truth? Does an explanation have to be true to provide understanding? This is a vexed question for several reasons. First, an explanation might come in some non-propositional form, such as a chart or graph, which might or might not be reducible to a set of propositions which are either true or false, and are believed by the person who gains understanding. Again, we run up against the possibility that understanding might sometimes be non-propositional. But more importantly, there are good reasons to think that understanding and literal truth are sometimes at cross purposes to one

---

[17] See Friedman (1974) and Kitcher (1981). For a more recent and detailed presentation of Kitcher's views, see Kitcher (1993).

another. Understanding is often best achieved by abstracting away from or 'idealizing' the actual situation. Nancy Cartwright has gone so far as to argue that the explanatory force of the laws of physics depends crucially on the fact that they are false, and known to be so![18] Only laws that ignore the messiness of the 'real world' and our observations of it are sufficiently general to provide explanations of the actual phenomena one encounters in the world.

I think this trade-off between explanatory power on the one hand, which aids understanding, and literal and specific truth on the other is present in the lives of ordinary cognizers as well. Perhaps even more so. If so, then often our epistemic ends will be best served by believing things that are literally false, but are close enough to the truth not to be too misleading, and general enough to let us see deeper, more revealing truths. Of course, this raises a whole host of questions about the precise nature of the trade-off. What are the relative weights of these two considerations? How much inaccuracy can one risk for a given degree of explanatory power? Is there an absolute threshold for how inaccurate one's world-view can be and still provide understanding?

Pursuing these ideas further would lead me too far astray from my current topic, but it is worth mentioning that the relationship between understanding and truth may be more complicated than it appears at first blush. However, it is safe to say that while some degree of falsehood (or 'inaccuracy') might be compatible with understanding, anyone whose picture of the world is radically mistaken will not have understanding. So there is at least a moderate, if not strong, condition of verisimilitude on having understanding. This has the consequence of rendering the first clause of my characterization of wisdom somewhat redundant. If having understanding of M entails that one is largely 'correct' in one's overall representation of M, then we can characterize 'wisdom' as follows:

(D2)  S has wisdom only if S has *understanding* of the subjects that are most important.

I will conclude my brief remarks regarding 'understanding' with a couple of examples I take to be paradigmatic of the phenomenon. First consider someone who understands, say, a complicated machine. Such a person will display a number of typical features. She will typically have a lot of knowledge about what different parts of the machine do, what the controls are for, etc. But anyone who reads the manual can get this information. Her *understanding* of the machine is captured by other things. For example, she might be able to

---

[18] Cartwright (1983).

predict erratic behaviour based on the sounds coming from the machine; or she might be able to diagnose problems that arise in an intuitive and highly reliable manner; or she might know just how hard one can push *this* machine past its specifications, versus that other one over there. Anyone who is blessed with an experienced and talented car mechanic has seen just these abilities being displayed. Someone who truly understands cars is able to do the kinds of things mentioned above, primarily because such a person knows *why* the parts of the car do what they do, and *why* the end result is (or isn't, as the case may be) transportation. These sorts of abilities are indicative of a high degree of understanding, and often cannot be acquired or explained in terms of propositional knowledge. This hardly demonstrates that understanding is distinct from knowledge, but it is suggestive.

Turning to a more obviously epistemic example, imagine someone who has a deep understanding of, say, a certain period in the history of a nation. Such a person will, again, have a great deal of 'knowledge' about who the major political and military figures of the time were. She will 'know' what language was spoken, what kinds of political and social institutions existed at the time, and so on. But, as with the gifted mechanic, this person will display her understanding of the historical period in ways that go beyond the mere grasp of various facts. The historian will be able to imagine (and, presumably, discuss) different possible outcomes of the historical period, assuming certain key figures or facts were different. For example, a historian of the Second World War might discuss what would have happened if Hitler had not invaded the Soviet Union; or if Hitler had been assassinated before the Normandy invasion. Of course, anyone can speculate about such things, but someone with the requisite historical understanding will be able to do so intelligently, and in a way that is much more likely to reflect the genuine possibilities than will the musings of an amateur. Once again, this is because the historian knows (as far as it is possible for us to know such things) *why* events unfolded as they did.

This concludes my rough sketch of what I mean by a state of 'understanding'. My defence of the partial definition of wisdom, (D2), that I proffer must rest on the reader's judgement that what I describe is closer to being the ideal epistemic situation than the mere possession of a set of beliefs, even a *large* set of beliefs, the members of which are predominantly true. Even if some of the details about what constitutes understanding or how we determine the important subjects are wrong, the overall picture is, I think, quite compelling. In contrast, merely having a high truth/falsity ratio among one's beliefs seems rather shallow. If this is unaccompanied by genuine understanding, then one lacks a crucial kind of insight into reality. Merely having at one's disposal a plethora of true beliefs does not satisfy our natural curiosity about *why* things are the way they are. And surely the state of highest epistemic good must include such satisfaction. And best of all, since achieving understanding of M entails that one's account or explanation or 'picture' of M be substantially correct, it requires that one's beliefs about it be predominantly true. Thus, we do not have to abandon the idea that has gripped epistemology for so long that having true beliefs and avoiding false ones is central to the epistemic enterprise. It is, but it is not enough by itself.

## VI. Understanding virtue

This brings us, finally, to the defence of premiss (3) of the argument for the value of the intellectual virtues. I will take this defence in two stages. First, I will make plain the connection between intellectual virtue and wisdom that allows the former to derive its value from the latter. Then, I will briefly point out some of the benefits of taking the 'highest epistemic good' to include understanding as well as more specifically truth-related ends.

### A. The virtue–wisdom connection

How is it, then, that intellectual virtues derive their value from the 'highest epistemic good'? Premiss (3) asserts that the intellectual virtues contribute to wisdom. The answer to our question lies in the nature of this connection. I have argued having wisdom entails understanding the things that are most important, and such understanding requires that one's beliefs about those matters be mostly true and that the non-propositional components of that understanding, if there are any, be 'accurate'. How do the intellectual virtues contribute to this? One obvious answer is to say that they *provide* such truth and understanding. One's possession of such understanding is *due to* one's having some degree of intellectual virtue. The connection, on this view, between intellectual virtue and understanding would be instrumental. The virtues would be a means to the end of understanding.

But this response is clearly unacceptable, for it would require that the means be reliably successful in reaching the end. A means that rarely achieves its end derives little value thereby. Moreover, the first half of this chapter was directed at showing that such an instrumental relationship cannot be all there is to the connection between intellectual virtue and understanding. There must be some alternative relationship between intellectual virtue and understanding that explains the *consistent* value of those virtues, even when they are unsuccessful at achieving their ends. I suggest that this relationship is a teleological rather than an instrumental one.

Any trait that is directed or aimed at some good end derives some goodness teleologically from its end. This value is independent of whether the trait is generally, or even ever, successful at reaching its end. What this boils down to is that any character trait that disposes one to pursue, as best one knows how, some good end *thereby* gains some value—even if the pursuit itself is flawed and unsuccessful. This explains, at least in part, why Annas's firefighter example and Garcia's evil demon victims example have the force that they do. Though these people fail to achieve the immediate targets of many of their actions, they nonetheless have something of value that is exemplified by their actions in the cases described. It is *good* to be disposed to be courageous, or benevolent, or just, even when, for whatever reason, one rarely succeeds in attaining the goods at which these virtues characteristically aim. Similarly, it is *good* to be disposed to be clear-headed, open-minded, disinterested, etc. even when this fails to yield a high dividend in true beliefs or understanding.

Imagine someone who has a vast store of true beliefs, very few false ones, and also has a deep, profound, and broad understanding of the world, herself, other people, etc. The above considerations show that such a person is not in the state of wisdom if she does not also have intellectual virtue. The value derived by intellectual virtues is epistemic, and if she lacks this value she has surely not achieved the 'highest epistemic good'. This is not to deny that having the knowledge and the understanding is also good. Quite the contrary. But the best epistemic position to be in is to have all that and be virtuous as well. The added value derives teleologically from the goals one pursues as an intellectually virtuous agent, as shown above.

Intellectual virtues, then, derive their value from their contribution to wisdom. Their contributions are various. First and foremost, they are partly constitutive of wisdom. One simply cannot have wisdom without having the intellectual virtues. Thus, they partake of the value of the ultimate epistemic end itself. But they also derive value both teleologically and (sometimes) instrumentally from that end. So to achieve wisdom one must have understanding of the most important things as well as having the intellectual virtues. These are conceptually independent, though in the best cases causally related. Having the virtues without understanding is still valuable because aimed at the good. Having understanding somehow without the virtues is also still valuable. But neither situation is as valuable as achieving understanding by way of one's own intellectual virtue.

## B. The benefits of understanding

One of the major motivations behind offering a theory of intellectual virtue is the desire to have a theoretical normative structure onto which we can map the intellectual traits and practices that we intuitively admire or, conversely, that we deplore. I will conclude this section by arguing that taking understanding to be a necessary component of wisdom allows us to make better sense of such things. Admirable intellectual traits that seem hard to accommodate among truth-oriented virtues become natural candidates for virtues on an understanding-oriented approach. Indeed, even those virtues that can be easily accommodated on alternative approaches are given a better account on this view. We gain a deeper understanding of why these traits are virtuous, and of why some traits, while intellectually virtuous, are less so than others.

Wisdom is clearly the kind of thing that comes in degrees, and is probably not attainable in full by ordinary human beings. I have argued that one cannot achieve wisdom without having understanding of the most important things. If we take this to be at least partly constitutive of wisdom, then any trait of character that has as its end the attainment of such understanding will be, prima facie, an epistemic or intellectual virtue. As explained above, having understanding of some subject matter will generally, if not always, require that we have some true beliefs about it. Moreover, it will require that the preponderance of such beliefs as we do have about it be true ones. Thus, as a rule, any trait that has as its end the attainment of true beliefs will be a virtue on this picture. But so will any trait that has as its end the more enigmatic goal of the grasp of pattern within chaos, of finding coherence among apparently disparate elements. These traits often do not have handy names in our ordinary vocabulary, but they are nonetheless crucial to achieving understanding.

Searching for hypotheses to explain one's observations, whether made in the laboratory or on one's walk through the park; trying to discern the motivations and feelings of someone whose behaviour seems random or inexplicable; trying to figure out why one's car makes that sound only when it is first started in the morning, but not when it is started later in the day—all these are examples of searching for pattern and coherence in one's experiences and beliefs. Sometimes the search is prompted by pure intellectual curiosity, and other times by more practical needs. But any time one engages in this sort of intellectual activity, one is exercising an epistemic trait that has as its end putting things together into a more coherent whole.

Having virtues mainly directed at truth without having virtues mainly directed at making sense of things, or vice versa, leaves one well shy of the state of wisdom. If one has the virtues of, say, careful observation, thoroughness, and disinterested evaluation of alternative views, but not the virtues listed in the last paragraph, then one might well achieve a preponderance of true beliefs, but they will be disjointed and often trivial, even to oneself. On the other hand, someone who has a penchant for making up explanatory stories without much regard for being careful about what they believe will be much like the kind of person who indulges himself with vast, complex webs of conspiracy theories. These people typically have an explanation for everything within the domain they concern themselves with. For example, someone who thinks the United Nations is secretly plotting to take over the world will have all kinds of hypotheses to explain the apparent weakness of the UN, the lack of motivation for any nation in the world to cooperate with this plan, the apparent dearth of evidence for any such plan, and so on. Constructing these theories can require a great deal of effort and cleverness. It also requires that one be extremely fast and loose with what one is willing to believe. For example, these people typically disregard the standard national news media while taking as gospel the rumours reported in small newsletters run by other extremists. Only someone who displays a blatant disregard for believing the truth (even when it is not what they want it to be) could indulge in such theories.

Thus, neither the virtues directed mainly at truth nor the virtues directed mainly at coherence are sufficient alone to achieve understanding. But if we take understanding to be a component of the highest epistemic end, then all the standard intellectual virtues remain, and we can also give a deeper account of why they are valuable. Some are valuable merely because they are aimed at making sure, as best we can, that our beliefs are true. Others are valuable because they are aimed at making sense of our world, or of some part of it in which we have a specific interest. Many are aimed at both, and are thus doubly valuable. This explains why we take figures like the ones mentioned earlier in this chapter—Aristotle, Newton, Galileo, Einstein—to be such exemplars of epistemic virtue. Not only were they very careful in their observations and thought, but they all directed their intellectual energies towards making sense of it all. Each of these leading intellectual figures was successful at making some sense of the world while meeting, and often exceeding, the general standards of epistemic rigour prevalent in their times. For this, we admire them even more. But their intellectual virtue resides in their being the kind of people who sincerely and conscientiously attempt to find out the truth about things that provide us with a deeper explanation of why those things are the way they are, even when their results ultimately do not turn out to be correct.

Before closing, there is one loose end that I feel obliged to acknowledge, if not actually tidy up. Throughout this discussion of intellectual virtues, I have not really considered the place of our perceptual faculties. Perceptual processes have typically been counted among the virtues on truth-centred virtue theories. Observation is an activity that requires attention and concentration, but mere perception is, or can be, much more passive and casual. Would such things as seeing, hearing, etc. count as virtues on my account? It depends on how one understands such perception. Ernest Sosa takes even ordinary and casual human perception to include an element of control and active participation, even though any given perception may 'pass through', so to speak, to belief without conscious consideration. This distinguishes us from 'beasts' who also have perceptual beliefs, but who are not capable of exercising virtue.

> Note that no human blessed with reason has merely animal knowledge of the sort attainable by beasts. For even when perceptual belief derives as directly as it ever does from sensory stimuli, it is still relevant that one has *not* perceived the signs of contrary testimony. A reason-endowed being automatically monitors his background information and his sensory input for contrary evidence and automatically opts for the most coherent hypothesis even when he responds most directly to sensory stimuli… The beliefs of a *rational* animal hence would seem never to issue from *unaided* introspection, memory, or perception. For reason is always at least a silent partner on the watch for other relevant data, a silent partner whose very *silence* is a contributing cause of the belief outcome.[19]   (all emphasis in original)

If we accept Sosa's account of the role of reason in even our most direct perceptual beliefs, there seems room to count these 'processes' as traits of character. Presumably, some people 'monitor' their perceptual field more carefully than others. Such 'monitoring' seems to be the sort of thing one can train oneself to do better and more carefully, so it may well be sufficiently under our control to consider this monitoring a character trait. If, on the other hand, we reject this reason-suffused account of perception, I think we

---

[19] Sosa (1991: 240).

must leave 'mere' perception out of the realm of virtue, unless in some sort of derivative sense that lacks full normative import.

I find Sosa's account of perception compelling, but I do not feel the need to wed my view of intellectual virtue to it necessarily. I am happy to live with perceptual faculties failing to be counted as virtues, if that is how things turn out. As I suggest above, this does not rule out more conscious, careful *observation* from counting as an intellectual virtue. And this is enough, I think, to capture the important idea that perception provides us with most of the raw material of the intellect, and therefore must to some extent be accounted for among the intellectual virtues.

## VI. Conclusion

Evidently, a great deal more remains to be said on the topic of understanding and its relationship to intellectual virtue. My project here has been primarily to show that an alternative to the standard truth-centred, success-oriented virtue theories is necessary, and what general direction might be fruitful to explore. I am confident that theories of intellectual virtue will soon occupy a central place in epistemology, if indeed they do not already. However, if they are to fulfil their promise, virtue theorists need to consider the intellectual or epistemic virtues seriously in their own right. When we do so, it becomes clear that the focus on propositions, truth, justification, and knowledge that has been the mainstay of epistemology for some time is not appropriate to the subject of epistemic virtue. Our epistemic aspirations go beyond the mere collection of true propositions, even beyond the acquisition of knowledge. I would argue that this is true, not only for head-in-the-clouds philosophers or theoretical scientists, but for nearly everyone.[20]

---

[20] Thanks to Karen Antell, John Greco, and Linda Zagzebski for helpful comments on early drafts of this chapter. Also many thanks to Hugh Benson, Linda Zagzebski, and the attendees of a presentation of these ideas in the philosophy department at the University of Oklahoma for much helpful discussion.

# 10

# Knowing Cognitive Selves

## Christine McKinnon

Epistemologists have traditionally focused on knowledge claims best captured by sentences of the form, '*S* knows that *p*', where *S* is the knowing agent, *p* is some fact[1] to be known, and *S* stands in some privileged epistemic relation to *p*. The nature of that privileged relation gets glossed differently according to different stories. But *something* epistemically noteworthy about *S*'s relation to *p*—often thought to be ideally captured by a set of necessary and sufficient conditions—marks off *S*'s claim to know that *p* from *S*'s claim to believe that *p*. Further, *p* is usually assumed to be the case independently of the investigation by the knowing agent, to be knowable by all those in the appropriate epistemic relation, and to remain unaltered by the investigation. Methodological ideals of objectivity and impartiality bolster this account of knowledge, thereby minimizing the role of the knowing agent. The less the subjectivity of the knowing agent intrudes, the more unsullied and more value-neutral the facts are, and the purer the knowledge is. The facts are there to be detected and the preferred epistemic relation will make minimal reference to the knower's identity, interests, or subjective perspective. The epistemic focus can then be directed towards the conditions under which a knowledge claim can legitimately be made.[2]

These conditions have been developed in two principal ways: beliefs are shown to be justified either because some of them (often observational or

---

[1] I will talk about facts to be known (to be the case) rather than propositions known (to be true). I do not intend anything epistemologically significant to hang on this.

[2] The focus on conditions and not persons is no accident: the *S* in the '*S* knows that *p*' is simply a place-holder for some anonymous, featureless investigator.

introspective ones) assume a foundational role with others being derived from these, or because they cohere within systems of other beliefs whose status is—if only temporarily and for the purposes of the investigation—taken to be secure. Ernest Sosa's 1980 article, 'The Raft and the Pyramid: Coherence versus Foundations in the Theory of Knowledge',[3] has been widely acknowledged as having exposed serious shortcomings in both the coherentist and the foundationalist approaches to grounding knowledge. In stressing the importance of the logical relations among beliefs, the coherentist strategy fails to grant sufficient due to perceptual beliefs, which standardly have few ties to the remainder of the knower's beliefs. But the foundationalist strategy fares little better: while apparently able to have sensory experience play a role in justifying beliefs, the foundationalist in fact has to appeal to a multitude of fundamental—and disparate—principles to ground the different kinds of beliefs gained through different sensory modalities or by creatures with different kinds of sensory apparatuses. Its claim to appeal to ultimate foundations is thereby rendered suspect.

Since the publication of Sosa's article, attention has turned to a kind of epistemological investigation that attempts to account for the normative features of beliefs and systems of beliefs, not in the logical relations among the propositions expressing them or in the epistemically privileged relations in which cognitive agents stand to these propositions, but in the cognitive agents themselves and in their proper exercise of intellectual virtues. Agents' beliefs are more or less well justified and qualify or fail to qualify as knowledge to the degree that agents do or do not arrive at them through a judicious exercise of intellectual virtues. Virtue epistemologists differ on just what counts as an intellectual virtue (in particular, there is much debate about whether all human excellences—including perceptual faculties—potentially directed towards finding out about the world should qualify) and why. They also differ regarding what it is about the exercise of the appropriate virtues that justifies the claim that the agent *knows*. But they are united in their attempt to ground the relevant epistemically normative properties of beliefs in more fundamental properties of cognitive agents.

Virtue epistemologies have developed in different ways, the two most prominent of which include versions of reliabilism and responsibilism. Reliabilism,[4] in its most general form, argues that beliefs are justified if and

---

[3] Sosa (1980).

[4] Reliabilism comes in a variety of forms, from process reliabilism to faculty reliabilism to proper functionalism to agent reliabilism. While there are important differences among these distinct versions, they do all appear to be consequentialist in structure.

only if the processes leading to them are reliable. Reliabilist virtue epistemologists take the exercise of intellectual virtues to be implicated in these reliable cognitive processes. Abnormal conditions of the kind that feature in Gettier-type problems will sometimes prevent a cognitively virtuous agent from achieving knowledge. But on the whole, the proper exercise of intellectual virtues will result in the acquisition of true beliefs, or, more modestly, in the acquisition of a preponderance of true beliefs over false ones. This strategy is clearly consequentialist in structure: the notion of true belief is independently specified, and intellectual virtues are just those things the exercise of which helps agents maximize the former in an epistemically justified way.

Responsibilist virtue epistemologists, on the other hand, argue that criteria for the epistemically best kinds of beliefs cannot be specified independently of the notion of the proper exercise of intellectual virtues. Just as 'good action' is specified, according to certain forms of virtue ethics, in terms of what the morally good agent would choose to do under the circumstances, so too is 'justified true belief' specified in terms of what the epistemically virtuous agent would believe under the circumstances. This sketch no doubt presents the contrast too starkly, but it serves to distinguish in a preliminary fashion the major players in the current debates among virtue epistemologists.

One complaint, often voiced by feminist philosophers, is that traditional epistemology has marginalized and devalued certain kinds of knowledge, including knowledge of other persons. Epistemologists' interest in knowledge of the self has often been framed in terms of a kind of Cartesian first-person incorrigible, unmediated, indubitable, and privileged access to one's private mental states. This privileged relation of the agent to his own mental states is what is meant to ground his knowledge about himself. Next to the paradigm of certainty that this kind of access is meant to offer, every other kind of claim to knowledge—in particular, knowledge of other persons—has invited sceptical worries of varying degrees of severity. But if first-person access to our mental states is neither unmediated nor infallible, then it cannot provide the kind of evidence that on its own could ground our claims about our characters, dispositional traits, motivational economies, capacities, and notions of what is valuable and worthwhile in our lives. These latter are what are centrally involved in knowing ourselves.

If we are to take seriously the claim of virtue epistemologists that the normative properties of beliefs must be located in properties of cognitive agents, then it will be important to know how we make and justify claims about ourselves and others *as* cognitive agents. Epistemic excellence will have to do with cognitive agents' attitudes or orientations towards the world, including towards themselves as cognitive agents. Understanding these attitudes will be central to knowing agents' cognitive selves. I do not wish to argue that knowledge of agents' cognitive selves assumes some kind of priority among epistemological investigations, nor that all kinds of knowledge claims be grounded in a single way. But seeing in what ways we make and justify claims about ourselves and others and in what ways assessments of cognitive selves can contribute to justifications of beliefs highlights some interesting points of intersection between virtue ethics and virtue epistemology and may thereby shed some light on methodological issues in contemporary epistemology.

## I. Knowledge of other persons

I will begin with an appeal to the arguments of some feminist epistemologists to broaden epistemology so as to include knowledge of other persons as at least one paradigm form of knowledge. (Many of these arguments are clearly formulated in works by Lorraine Code.[5]) Then I will use the conclusions of this discussion to focus on knowledge of our own selves, including our cognitive selves. This shift necessarily renders things even more complicated: in the case of knowledge of oneself, not only is there the spectre of privileged access, the inquiries are necessarily self-reflexive and the motivation to know oneself is coloured by motivations to approve of the self one knows. Looking at the case of knowledge of oneself will underscore the point that the demands of infallibility, impartiality, and passivity are inappropriate for some kinds of knowledge claims. Further, it will suggest ways in which the epistemic community is important in our justifications of our knowledge claims: knowledge of our own and others' cognitive selves and of the kinds of agency involved in the best kinds of epistemic investigations requires mastery of a theory in the context of communally entrenched practices.

The feminist project of trying to introduce a wider range of knowledge claims for epistemological consideration has, no doubt, been fuelled by many political aims. Unless one wants to argue that searches for an 'epistemic ideal of unrealisable clarity'[6] must always be politically motivated, the political aims can take a temporary back seat. Focusing on the kinds of knowledge at play in

---

[5] See Code (1984), (1988), (1991), (1993).     [6] Code (1988: 187).

our daily interactions with friends, children, parents, and partners (sometimes thought of as typifying 'women's experience') helps expose the politically motivated and power-fuelled exclusions of traditional epistemology. It also helps expose other—no doubt related—kinds of exclusions: those reflecting the desires and demands for clarity, for sets of necessary and sufficient conditions circumscribing knowledge, for knowledge as a set of objective, static beliefs to which idealized knowers stand in epistemically privileged relations.

Feminist epistemologists argue that these desiderata, which collectively postulate objectivity and disinterestedness as epistemological ideals, are misguided and that a focus on the kinds of knowledge central to 'women's experience' shows them to be misguided. In this latter kind of knowledge, the facts under investigation cannot be thought to be unaffected by the knower's quest to know them: they are not static. Both our attempts to make ourselves more transparent to others by citing our reasons for acting or believing and our responses to others' assessments of our reasons invite the kind of reflexive scrutiny that might well prefigure modifications to moral or cognitive selves. Further, the knower cannot pretend to be disinterested in her investigations: her attempts to understand other persons will be frustrated unless she invests a certain amount of herself into the pursuit. She cannot think of herself as an anonymous place-holder, lacking a particular identity. The 'view from nowhere' is not the view from which to come to know other persons.

Standards for truth, justification, evidence, and verification—and, arguably, the central metaphor of observation—have been adopted wholesale from the cases of the purest sciences into other kinds of cognitive investigations. These standards seem to suit very badly the common-place inquiries into persons that characterize our daily lives and many of our cognitive practices. One real contribution of the feminist call to look at knowledge claims about persons has been to find a way of showing how epistemic responsibility has, as Code puts it, 'the potential to play a regulatory role in cognitive activity'.[7] The appeal to epistemic responsibility highlights the important roles that the active agency of the knower and her epistemological circumstances—both her individual and her communal circumstances—play in the acquisition and justification of her knowledge claims.

The knowledge of other persons that some feminist philosophers have urged epistemologists to take seriously includes beliefs about a wide range of kinds of properties. For present purposes, a rough and ready folk distinction

---

[7] Ibid. 188.

between what we think of as physical and what we think of as non-physical properties will probably suffice. An inquiry into a person's physical properties might seem to meet all the requirements of standard scientific-type investigative procedures: the subject best comes to know the way things really are by adopting the most objective stance possible; the properties are there to be discovered; they are available to all careful epistemic agents correctly situated; they remain unaffected by the inquiry. But persons' physical properties are not always perceived by them—or by others—to be value-free. What the possession of a particular physical property (being beautiful, being deaf, being tall, etc.) *means* to someone may not be apparent in an investigation constrained by requirements of objectivity and impartiality. The possession of a physical property by someone can affect who she is *as* a person. Thus, seeing someone *as* a person must inform our beliefs about her, including about her physical properties. It will also inform criteria surrounding what count as justified beliefs.

If a detached impartial stance is inadequate for achieving the kind of knowledge of the physical properties of persons that helps us come to know them, how much more so is this true when we are investigating the biographical, social, psychological, emotional, cognitive, or moral properties that help constitute them—and that are relevant to the ways, including the epistemic ways, they interact with their environment. Like the physical properties, the biographical and social properties, although there for the scrutiny of careful observers, do not speak for themselves: they get interpreted and reinterpreted, assume more or less importance, according to how the person wants or does not want them to fit into the particular self-image she is cultivating or into the particular stories those close to her are telling her. And some of the psychological, emotional, cognitive, and moral properties—dispositions, settled patterns of response, emotional repertoires, capacities, what kinds of things she values, and what kind of person she wishes to be—come into existence only as the person becomes self-consciously aware and makes evaluations about preferred kinds of lives.

Seeing persons as self-conscious, self-reflexively aware beings who become who they are as they discover more about the world and themselves and as they come to understand better how to value these discoveries requires that we acknowledge the hazards of supposing that certain of their properties are available to objective, disinterested observers. There is a subjective involvement and investment in coming to know other persons that is quite alien to the standard scientific investigation.[8] Coming to know persons means engaging

---

[8] As Code puts it, 'Knowing other people...is an ongoing, communicative, interpretive process...[in which the] knower's subjectivity is implicated' (Code 1991: 38).

with them: trying on their point of view, identifying their presuppositions, challenging their interpretations, helping them make sense of their narrative, etc. In cases where the knowing agent stands in a particularly close relation to the person she is trying to get to know, the latter is unlikely to remain unaffected by the investigation. So there may well be some fluidity in the person known. But it is not mere fluidity which makes things epistemically complicated. It is also the necessary interest with which the knowing subject scrutinizes the person to be known, as well as the value-laden nature of the properties under investigation.

Knowledge of these kinds of properties comprises our knowledge of other persons. While facts about persons are not always detectable by observation, need not be value-free, either to the investigator or to the person being investigated, and may even be 'socially constructed', with their importance and sometimes even whether they obtain being relative to some contingently entrenched practice, they are nonetheless facts for which evidence can be procured. And our practices of making claims about other persons' moral and cognitive selves suppose that these claims are more or less well justified, approximate more or less well the truth. Persons' commentaries on their actions and their beliefs—their explanations, their justifications, their rationalizations—as well as their behaviour serve as readily available data and can be used to generate and test verifiable and falsifiable hypotheses about them. These hypotheses cover not just predictions about how persons will act or what they will believe; they also include claims about their motivations and about what kinds of reasons they find compelling and hence about what kinds of things they value. The fact that the explanatory hypotheses are themselves embedded in a theory which is value-laden further complicates—but does not undermine—the attempt to secure for knowledge of other persons a genuine place in epistemological inquiries.

Of course, if there are good reasons to suppose that other persons cannot be known, then the motivation to extend our epistemological projects to incorporate this kind of knowledge is missing. There are two versions of the worry which might seem to undermine the possibility that we can have knowledge of persons, either in the first-person case or in the third-person case. I will dismiss these two versions rather summarily and then introduce a third worry which supposes that whatever knowledge we can have of other persons is inferior relative to the knowledge we can have of ourselves.

The first version of the worry suggests that our folk psychological knowledge of others does not count as real knowledge. The latter will be had through further research into neuroscience, with its appeal to neurons and synapses, or to a Freudian-inspired psychoanalysis, with its claims about the unconscious. Many of our desires and our reasons for acting may seem to be transparent to ourselves and to others, but neuroscientific or psychoanalytic 'experts' are required to unearth our real motivations. Even if it were to turn out that the claims of neuroscience or Freudian psychoanalysis are verifiable or falsifiable in the best scientific traditions, it is not obvious that this more 'scientific' knowledge would be knowledge of *persons*—of moral and cognitive selves—in any useful sense. The kind of knowledge we currently have of ourselves and others as intentional agents acting for reasons and holding beliefs of which we and they are—or can be made to be—aware underpins our cognitive and moral interactions with others very well. It permits us to see the contents of cognitive and moral selves as constraining what reasons agents find compelling for believing what they believe and for doing what they do. Further, this kind of knowledge is susceptible to judgements of relative justification and groundlessness.

The second version of the worry might be thought to be more serious: we self-consciously post-modern selves have been taught to think of the notion of a unified, non-fragmented self as a conceit. There is no self there to be known, either by the subject or by those with whom she interacts. This worry might suggest, not that we happen to lack the scientifically or conceptually sophisticated machinery to understand other persons, but that other persons resist understanding. Their very elusive, transient, non-essential nature makes them philosophically unmanageable. This objection, in its own way, also supposes an inappropriate ideal for knowledge claims about ourselves and others.

Persons may well be the kinds of beings who construct their selves as they lead their lives and reflect upon their experiences and their interactions with others, in particular, upon the ways in which those others respond to their explanations of their behaviour and their justifications of their beliefs. They may well lack an essence, instead being the kinds of beings who are constantly constituting themselves as they interact with their environment, with all its physical, social, emotional, cognitive, and moral dimensions. This need not mean that persons are not the kinds of things that can be known; rather, it suggests that the criteria for knowledge of persons will not be the same as those for knowledge of those features of our environment whose nature is immune to self-reflexive awareness and whose properties are less value-laden. To take seriously the claim that persons cannot be known would be to undermine the credibility of many disciplines in the humanities and the social sciences and to force upon us a scepticism about the many low-level accounts of one another's reasons for acting that make communal living possible. The preferred alternative is to readjust our expectations for what counts as knowledge of persons.

This dismissal of two very influential kinds of sceptical thinking about the possibility of knowledge of other persons is admittedly cavalier. I introduce these worries—and dismiss them in this fashion—only because I want to claim that what passes in everyday circles for knowledge of others should be considered a perfectly respectable kind of knowledge. Knowledge of other persons will not meet the same requirements that epistemologists posit for knowledge claims about the physical world. But neither are persons just constituents of the physical world. Nor do knowers stand in the same kinds of relations to other persons as they do to objects in the physical world. We clearly do make, evaluate, and justify knowledge claims about ourselves and others. This alone provides an excellent reason for epistemologists to take seriously this kind of knowledge.

What is known is not always stable and unchanging and can often be modified *by* the very investigation. The knower's subjective perspective may be relevant in her acquisition of knowledge: an impartial objective view may not be the optimum perspective through which to know everything. Criteria for justification must be identified against certain background practices. All this can be acknowledged—and without succumbing to the threat of an epistemic relativism—if we see the normative role the possession and exercise of intellectual virtues can have in the justification of our knowledge claims. The third version of the worry alluded to above is that we can each attain knowledge of our own selves, but that we should be sceptical about the prospects of attaining knowledge of other persons. I will now turn to examine what epistemological ideals have made this position seem tempting and how, once they are resisted, the way becomes clear to see how judgements about cognitive agents can feature in normative assessments of beliefs.

## II. From knowledge of other persons to knowledge of oneself

When it is knowledge of other persons that is in question, we have seen that there are good reasons *not* to insist on the impartiality of the knower. Indeed, in these kinds of quest, the identity and many of the interests of the investigating cognitive agent will be relevant. Her subjective perspective, the contexts in which she interacts with those others, and the extent to which she has invested herself in the well-being of those others will all play a role. These interests do not determine the truth about those others; nor do they justify her beliefs. But neither the cognitive agent's undertaking—which is informed along the many dimensions of her character—nor the criteria for the success of her undertaking—which can be provided only against the background of the relevant communal practices—can be understood unless the role of her subjective perspective and her relation to those others is taken into account. A parent's impartial attitude towards his children will impede his getting to know them. It may also inhibit his children from getting to know themselves.

When the knower stands in a close relation to the ones known (as a friend, parent, or caregiver), her investigations may well serve to initiate or precipitate changes in these others. When the scrutiny is self-directed, the chances that the self-reflexive investigation will result in changes to the self being investigated are even greater. In this case, the criteria of success of the epistemological project have to respect the contributions of the subjective perspective of the knowing subject and to recognize the reflexive responses of the self to the investigation. The plausibility of the claim that we need to expand the traditionally narrow purview of epistemology rests upon being able to show how we make and justify knowledge claims about ourselves and others, that is, how we make and justify knowledge claims in cognitive endeavours where the ideals of objectivity and impartiality are inappropriate.

The knowledge one has in one's own case is supposed to be superior to the knowledge one can have of others. There is both a pre-philosophical and a philosophical presumption in favour of a privileged first-person authority. The pre-philosophical presumption finds its voice in the worry that no one understands one (as well as one does oneself) and in the conviction that one cannot be mistaken about what one is feeling or thinking. The philosophical presumption owes much to Descartes's granting of epistemic privilege to first-person introspective reports.

Descartes held that the contents of one's mind are available to one in a direct, unmediated way and that the sincere claims one makes about them are indubitable and incorrigible. Given the indirect access one has to other persons' minds, any knowledge one has of others is therefore necessarily inferior. This is not the place to establish the various misconceptions upon which this account is grounded. I do want, however, to argue that the project of coming to know oneself is a cognitive project, much like any other, with its public criteria of success and failure and with differential capabilities revealed across different cognitive agents. What complicates the project of coming to know ourselves may not be the special access we each have to our own mental states; it may be instead our self-constituting natures and the ways in which our motivations to discern our own characters are tied up with our motivations to approve of those findings. There is much at stake in self-directed cognitive endeavours. Conceding this does not make epistemological investigations into knowledge of cognitive selves any neater or easier; it does oblige us to acknowledge the role of agents' motivations in our assessments of some of their cognitive endeavours.

Cartesian certainty about the contents of one's own mind has been upset at least since Wittgenstein's private language argument, one lesson of which is that individual agents cannot recognize or identify the contents of their minds without some sort of conceptual equipment with which to do so and without familiarity with the practices in which that conceptual equipment is embedded.[9] The phenomenology of the inner states alone will not suffice, because what *seems* to be 'the same' will have to count as 'the same': phenomenological feels could be distinct for each person across time as well as distinct across persons.[10] As long as there is no difference between something *seeming* to be the same and *being* the same, we have no criteria for correct identification and reidentification. The conceptual equipment requires a grounding in something other than the immediate phenomenal awareness of the contents of one's mind. The metaphysical point is that mental states are not objects. The epistemological point is that privileged access alone does not secure indubitable truth or even justified belief. The phenomenology of the mental is of enormous philosophical interest, but unmediated access to the contents of one's mind cannot be the sort of thing that secures knowledge claims about oneself of the sort at stake here. Likewise, the fact that we lack immediate, privileged access to others' mental states does not make knowledge of other persons suspect.

The best current account of how we come to make belief- and desire-attributions to ourselves and others is the theory-theory story.[11] According to this account, children begin to formulate a theory of mind in their first few years of social interaction with other persons: on the basis of behaviour observed,

---

[9] Famously, if a lion could talk—could provide commentary on its actions and beliefs—we would not understand it. We lack familiarity with the practices that characterize lions' forms of life. See Wittgenstein (1953: 223).   [10] Ibid. sec. 293.

[11] The only other real contender at present seems to be the simulation-theory account. This is less plausible than the theory-theory story, relying as it does on the possibility of 'Cartesian' first-person knowledge to account for our ability to simulate mental states in others.

explanations offered, emotions displayed, environmental influences detected, etc., children soon learn to craft hypotheses to account for and predict the behaviours—including the cognitive behaviours—of those around them by linking behaviours with desires and beliefs. The theory–theory account then has the child invoking this theory—acquired in the first instance to explain and predict behaviour of others by linking it with their desires and motivations and reasons for acting and believing—to permit him to explain and predict his own behaviour. He learns to identify in his own case the desires, emotions, motivations, and capacities that are implicated in these behaviours and that serve partially to constitute his own self.

There is, of course, much boot-strapping according to this picture: starting from a proto-self with minimal content, the child has to begin to tell himself stories—which get tested in the public forum—about reasons other people cite for their actions and beliefs, about the plausibility of these explanations, and about how the reasons are related to actions and beliefs and to underlying desires, motivations, capacities, and dispositions. As these stories become richer, more coherent, and more consistent, and as the child's own self-reflexive capacities improve, he begins to identify in himself certain incipient motivational patterns. He learns to evaluate these dispositions by coming to recognize which ones conduce to the leading of a good life, an ability which is acquired in the context of living in a community in which certain kinds of lives can be seen to be going well and others less well. He may then begin to modify or entrench these patterns, which he comes to see as partially constituting who he is.

The theory of mind within which the developing agent formulates and tests his explanations of others' behaviour also constrains the possible narratives he can plausibly offer to himself. Although the investigation of coming to know oneself is self-reflexive and responsive to the fruits of the inquiry, because it is carried out within the framework of a theory of mind, there are quite clear—and objective—constraints on possible explanations and on what counts as supporting evidence in favour of one explanation over another. Further, because the theory of mind is a theory that has currency within the epistemic community, the question of individual cognitive agents' success at mastery of the theory is one to be answered in a public context.

The incentive to grant epistemic privilege to the private is undermined to the extent that we do indeed learn to become self-consciously aware of and able to individuate and identify our mental states and our emotions and to make claims about our moral and cognitive selves only as we gradually acquire a folk psychological theory about human behaviour through being socialized in the practice of relating behaviour to explanations of behaviour and beliefs to justifications of belief. The access we have to our own mental states may indeed be privileged, but it is not an access that can ground the kind of knowledge about ourselves that is cited in our assessments of ourselves as cognitive or moral agents.

Explanations of behaviour and justifications of beliefs are offered in a communal context. It is within that context that we learn what counts as a reasonable explanation and what counts as a justified ascription of an emotion, a dispositional property, or a character trait to persons, including ourselves. Persons' commentaries on their own and others' moral and cognitive behaviour teach us what kinds of evidence to look for: 'He said that because he was angry, jealous, impatient, etc.' or 'She believes that because she is so optimistic, narrow-minded, cautious, etc.' These commentaries help us master a theory, which we apply in the first case to others and gradually to ourselves. Empirical findings showing that we make similar—and systematic—kinds of attribution errors in the first-person case as in the third-person case[12] support the view that the claims we make about others and about ourselves result from the mastery—sometimes imperfect—of a theory of mind. If coming to know ourselves—including learning to individuate, identify, and reidentify our desires, emotions, motivations, and capacities and seeing how these help constitute us as persons—comes only *as a result* of mastering the theory, then the privileged access we think we have to the contents of our own minds is something acquired and certainly not the kind of access that could perform the sort of foundational work often attributed to it.

Getting to know ourselves means getting to know both our cognitive and our moral characters, as well as the various ways in which they inform one another. This may be possible only if we have the resources of communal practices to which to appeal. In a recent article, Hilary Kornblith[13] argues that some of our non-cognitive traits may well inform our cognitive characters (and hence be relevant to our epistemic evaluations of ourselves), but not in any way that is available to us from our subjective perspective. He provides an example of Jack, who is insecure and defensive. Jack has many inaccurate beliefs about the external world and in particular about the motives and desires of those people with whom he interacts. Jack has these false beliefs *because* he is defensive and insecure. His whole way of perceiving the world is

---

[12] Nisbett and Wilson (1977). [13] Kornblith (1998).

coloured by certain non-cognitive dispositions of his. Not surprisingly, Jack is unaware of these traits in himself; in fact, he has a very distorted self-image and is unable to identify correctly his emotions or his character traits. He is also completely unaware that his non-cognitive character traits play a role in his belief-acquisition. He cannot detect these traits or their influence from the inside because there is nothing about the phenomenology of his mental state identification to give it away. He cannot be informed about their presence or their role by others because these very traits lead him to misinterpret all his friends' interventions. And if we were to ask Jack to *infer* his cognitive dispositions (by explicitly applying the folk psychological theory), he would get it wrong, because his character traits impede his mastering the theory.

Now, Jack does have a privileged perspective on his inner life or the contents of his mind. Further, he has no reason to suspect that his privileged perspective does not deliver to him an accurate representation of the way he is. Jack provides us with an example of someone who is mistaken about the way he is, including about many of his emotions and character traits, but who seems much less well placed than we are to know this. He cannot correctly assess his cognitive faculties as unreliable means of belief-acquisition. Jack does have something we lack: direct access. But he also lacks something we have: the ability to evaluate correctly certain of his cognitive capacities, including his introspective faculties, as reliable or otherwise. And he lacks this ability because of the very unreliability of those capacities. There are no introspective clues permitting him to detect the unreliability from the inside, and the manner in which he identifies his mental states will seem to him to be completely phenomenologically simple.[14]

This example might be thought to warrant a widespread scepticism about our knowledge of ourselves. If we believe that Jack is unable to evaluate correctly his introspective faculties as reliable or otherwise, what grounds do we have for thinking that any of us is able to do so? Here, I think, an appeal to the epistemic community can help. The reliability of one's belief-acquisition faculties and traits can be detected only in the context of one's successes in the community of persons who make attributions of reasons, emotions, dispositions, capacities, and traits to themselves and others. If agents' beliefs are

---

[14] Kornblith notes that this argument can be run through in the perceptual case as well. The colour-blind person has no reason to doubt the reliability of his colour pronouncements *from the inside*. The reasons for doubt occur only when he runs up against the claims of others in his community.

justified at least in part because they know that the means whereby they arrived at them are in general reliable, and if they can know the latter only to the extent that they can appeal to successes within the epistemic community, then the immediacy of the contents of their own minds to their subjective awarenesses does not secure these latter the right kind of epistemic advantage. Epistemological investigations that ignore the central and active role that the epistemic community must play in determining what will count as justification and reliability will be unable to handle those many cognitive practices in which subjective perspectives and self-reflexive considerations are relevant. This appeal to the epistemic community and communally entrenched practices as providing standards for reliability might seem to give the advantage to reliabilist versions of virtue epistemology over responsibilist versions; I will return in the next section to see why this is not so.

Implicit in the theory-theory story is the claim that we *become* persons as we master the folk psychological theory which permits us to link reasons with desires, motivations, dispositions, capacities, and traits. These identifications will not be value-free; the project of becoming a person is permeated with the desire to become a kind of person who can lead a good human life. Neither will the evaluations be along strictly moral dimensions. Given human nature and the human condition, leading a good kind of life requires, among other things, that one become a good cognitive agent. Virtue epistemologies, because of their claim that the normative properties of beliefs flow from properties of cognitive agents, require that we be able to assess these cognitive selves, both in our own cases and in the case of others. This cannot be done using the resources of introspection alone; it has to be done in the context of an appeal to the epistemic community in which the standards for success are located.

Annette Baier argues that persons are essentially what she calls 'second persons': 'A person, perhaps, is best seen as one who was long enough dependent on other persons to acquire the essential arts of personhood. Persons essentially are *second* persons, who grow up with other persons.'[15] The arts of personhood include many normative dimensions. We acquire maturity as cognitive and emotional and moral agents only as we learn to interact with those around us. We come to know ourselves—and come to know what counts as knowledge of the self—only by mastering a folk theory which permits us to come to know others and to assess the claims that persons make about themselves and others. The kind of reflexive self-awareness that permits

[15] Baier (1985: 84).

agents to make judgements about their own desires, emotions, dispositions, capacities, and reasons for acting is a self-awareness acquired in a social context involving close and interactive contact with other persons, especially perhaps with other persons whose judgement they respect.

Certainly, there are asymmetries between knowledge of oneself and knowledge of other selves. They appear to have more to do with the relative wealth of evidence gleaned and with the initiatives to effect change which we are often motivated to undertake in our own case. The constant stream of inner monologues, critical appraisals, rationalizations, and behaviour (both verbal and non-verbal) to which we are privy in our own case is not qualitatively superior; there is just a lot more of it. And the human desire to have one's reasons for acting endorsed by those whose judgements one respects can set in action a feedback loop which can have different kinds of results. The desire for favourable self-assessments can inspire agents to try to modify their characters by attempting both to suppress those traits of which they have come to disapprove and to inculcate those traits of which they have come to approve. It can thereby serve a beneficial purpose. Equally, the feedback loop permits a level of self-deception which is inimical to true knowledge of ourselves. Favourable self-assessments can sometimes be sought dishonestly: rather than work to change the evidence upon which self-assessments are based, the agent may simply deny the evidence or grant to it a different role.

Our knowledge of others (their characters and their reasons for acting and believing) permeates our attempts to lead good human lives. This knowledge is not value-free, neither in our own case nor in the case of others. Our folk psychological explanations are not merely descriptive. Instead, they inform us about norms for intentionality and for responsible agency. They provide criteria for what count as good reasons for acting or believing. In doing so, they serve to constrain which dispositions—moral and cognitive—will be exercised in the best kinds of human lives. They thus have an inherently evaluative component. Our assessments of our own and others' cognitive and moral selves are made in the context of normative criteria for responsible, intentional agency implicit in our folk psychological theories. We need to guard against the very real dangers of wishful thinking, but our assessments of our characters may be in part self-constituting: we can sometimes exercise the required agency to *be* certain kinds of persons. The presence of a feedback loop in our own cases, made possible by our self-reflexive nature, may reveal the real role for first-person authority: sometimes one has, in one's own case, the capacity to *be* a certain kind of person, to be moved by certain kinds of reasons, to hone certain capacities, or to value or exercise one's abilities in a certain manner.[16]

The theory–theory story can be seen to account for a way in which we *earn* first-person privileged authority. In coming to master the folk psychological theory, we learn to identify and reidentify mental states, emotions, and feelings, until, after much practice, our own eventually strike us as immediately available to introspection.[17] The asymmetries between the first- and third-person cases have to do with quantity and with the agency exercised in the first-person case. What makes our pronouncements about ourselves authoritative (when they are) is in part the fact that we can sometimes *become* who we pronounce ourselves to be. Our judgements about ourselves are in part self-constituting. This reminds us of their value-laden nature.

The cognitive project of coming to know other persons is continuous with the project upon which each self-reflexively aware human is embarked of becoming a certain kind of person. This in turn is continuous with the project of learning how to justify different kinds of claims by learning what sorts of reasons count as good reasons and which methods of belief-acquisition are superior. These lessons are learnt in the context of the normative folk psychological theory specifying what counts as responsible, intentional agency. Although we come to know ourselves in much the same way that we come to know other persons, there are differences in the wealth of evidence available, differences in the motivations we have to know other persons or ourselves, and differences in the degree to which the knowledge earned is likely to affect the subject of inquiry. These are not the differences usually cited between first-person knowledge and knowledge of other persons. And they do little to support a scepticism about knowledge of other persons.

---

[16] See McGeer (1996). McGeer argues that self-ascriptions are, similar to promises, often 'commissive', rather than descriptive. More generally, she builds an interesting case for the claim that 'a primary use of folk psychology is normative—to teach and also to remind each other to be what we think of as competent intentional agents' (Ibid. 512).

[17] Peter Carruthers (2000) argues that we can come to acquire recognitional capacities for some of our mental states, but that they are recognitional applications of folk theoretical concepts. He allows that some recognitional concepts, once acquired, could be hived off from their theoretical base to become bare recognitional concepts. This could account for much of what seems to be the phenomenologically immediate nature of our knowledge of our own minds.

## III. Responsible knowers

We have seen that the paradigms and standards traditionally adopted by epistemologists force us to ignore many kinds of knowledge claims that are central to our lives. Further, traditional approaches to justification lead us to assume that knowledge claims can be justified in the absence of assessments of ourselves and others as cognitive agents. Even where the knowledge claims are not about ourselves, given that *we* are the ones who hold and justify our beliefs, it would seem that knowing our cognitive selves—including the reliability of our faculties and the general efficacy of our cognitive dispositions, as well as the manner in which we exercise them—would be relevant to justifying these claims.[18] This should be conceded even from the vantage point of a traditional epistemology, where the aim is to minimize the intrusive influences of the cognitive agent: in such investigations it will surely be incumbent upon individual agents as well as upon the epistemic community to know more precisely in what ways particular kinds of subjective awarenesses detract from claims to know.

Part of what informs our interactions with other persons is the conviction that they are responsible for their actions and their beliefs. Our practice of holding agents responsible for their actions and beliefs supposes—minimally—that these actions and beliefs have not been coerced. It also reveals the kind of human agency that is implicated in these actions and beliefs, as well as in their subsequent justifications: one that is autonomous and that requires capacities to know the emotions, desires, dispositions, capacities, and reasons by appeal to which agents choose, explain, and justify their actions and beliefs. Judgements of responsible agency rest upon the possibility of persons knowing their own and others' moral and cognitive selves.

It is cognitive agents who have beliefs and who assess the epistemic merits or otherwise of these beliefs. They do so against the normative backgrounds provided by the communal practices of the cognitive communities within which they function. These backgrounds provide standards for evidence, reliability, and justification, as well as criteria for what counts as responsible exercise of cognitive capacities. If assessments of cognitive selves are to play

---

[18] As Code notes: 'I think it is just because self tends to obtrude so insistently in all human activity, all attempts to be "objective", that self-knowledge is essential. It is important to know whether the concept of self that is obtrusive is in fact valid; and important to know oneself if one is to achieve a just estimation of the degree to which one does know, believe justifiably, deceive oneself, or fail in epistemic responsibility' (Code 1984: 43).

a central role in our epistemological evaluations, we require an account of which capacities and traits are implicated in reliably acquiring the best beliefs about different aspects of the world. And because the capacities are ones that humans *use* (and have to exercise judgement regarding what counts as appropriate use), we also require an account of what would count as the responsible exercise of these capacities. This is not the place to tackle the first question directly, but I would like to say something about how we should understand the requirement of responsible exercise of our cognitive capacities and then suggest that this makes responsibilist versions of virtue epistemology attractive—at least for some kinds of knowledge claims.

Responsibilist virtue epistemologists argue that reliabilism has not gone far enough towards locating the epistemic value of knowledge in normative properties of agents. In particular, there is the concern that appealing to reliable processes as a means to maximize truth and minimize falsehood fails to distinguish knowledge from true belief. Knowledge is meant to be epistemically superior to true belief, in part because a true belief can be arrived at quite accidentally. But it is unclear why a belief that is arrived at by a reliable process is epistemically better than a belief that is arrived at by accident. The epistemic value would not seem to carry over from the reliable process to the belief.[19]

Responsibilists urge that knowledge gains its epistemic superiority over true belief in virtue of the way the agent arrived at it *and* because the agent was motivated by a desire to find out how things really are. The epistemic advantage thus derives from properties of the agent's cognitive character, in particular from the agent's responsible exercise of her cognitive virtues. Just as the most commendable kinds of moral acts are those performed by agents who exercise their moral virtues judiciously *and* who are motivated by a desire to do what is best, so too are the most commendable kinds of epistemic acts those performed by agents who exercise in a cognitively responsible manner those belief-acquiring dispositions or faculties deemed to be reliable *and* who are motivated to do so by a desire to know how things are in the world.

Virtue epistemologies are correct to focus on cognitive virtues as the source of normative evaluations of beliefs, but the virtues have to be seen in the context of agents' cognitive selves. These selves reveal the manner in which and

---

[19] See Zagzebski (1999*a*). Zagzebski argues that all forms of reliabilism—with the possible exception of the 'mixed strategy' employed by John Greco in his 'agent reliabilism'—suffer the 'value problem': the superior epistemic value that knowledge has over true belief cannot be extracted from the reliability or proper functioning of some process, but must arise from a valuable epistemic property of the *believer*.

the reasons for which agents rely upon their cognitive faculties and dispositions. Stories about epistemically virtuous agents will thus have to appeal to higher-order regulatory dispositions that help monitor and sometimes adjust first-order cognitive traits. These regulatory dispositions reflect communal decisions about what counts as responsible exercise of cognitive faculties and traits. The decisions are not arbitrary: they are made in the context of the normative practices of the epistemic community and the obligations to act in a cognitively responsible manner that membership in an epistemic community imposes.

Neither introspection on its own nor perception on its own delivers infallible knowledge claims that can serve a foundational role; neither on its own, as Kornblith's argument showed, can reveal those cases in which these faculties lead us to error. It is only within the context of the epistemic community that we can come to master the conceptual apparatus that permits us to make any judgements based upon our introspective or perceptual awarenesses. Further, we are unable to assess the reliability of our introspective or perceptual faculties except in the context of the normative practices of the cognitive communities in which we learn to exercise them and in which we can test their pronouncements. This does not mean that numerical consensus in the epistemic community determines the criteria for correct and incorrect use of the concepts, or that consistency with the majority view is the best test for reliability of faculties or belief-acquisition methods.

Some commentators[20] have taken Wittgenstein's discussion of rule-following to grant to linguistic or epistemic communities just this kind of authority: criteria for correctness or reliability are determined by what the majority of the community says counts as correct rule-following or by what it says counts as the right kind of evidence or justification. It is easy to misunderstand claims about the authoritative role of the community. The authority that the linguistic or epistemic community has is not an authority of numbers; what counts as correct rule-following or the right kind of evidence is not a function of what the majority of rule-followers says. The majority of rule-followers could be wrong about their pronouncements, for example, their colour pronouncements. Likewise, the majority of believers could be wrong about how reliable their belief-acquisition methods are.

Having the majority of language users confidently assert that a colour swatch is red is no guarantee that the colour swatch is indeed red. Unbeknownst to

---

[20] See, especially, Kripke (1982).

them, the lighting conditions could be abnormal, or, more fancifully, their colour receptors could have been systematically tampered with, thereby presenting them with the phenomenological awareness apparently consistent with that which they used to experience when presented with red swatches—only this time it is green swatches which elicit the 'red' awareness.

The same is true for other claims based less immediately in contents of our phenomenal awareness. We can imagine the vast majority of users having their measuring instruments (for example, their speedometers) recalibrated—unbeknownst to them—in systematic ways. It does not follow that just because most people think they are driving at or below the posted legal speed limit that they are. The majority of drivers can be mistaken about whether they are in fact speeding. This would be true if *everyone* had their speedometers recalibrated. We cannot simply read off from the majority pronouncements criteria for correctness or justification. Criteria, being normative, cannot arise simply from the results of a head count. This is true for claims about correct rule-following, optimal justifications, reliable processes, and responsible agency.

Kornblith's point that Jack can't assess his own methods of finding out about the world as reliable or otherwise suggested that individual knowers need some external standards against which to assess both the justifiability of their claims and the reliability of their belief-acquisition processes. But it is equally mistaken to suppose that standards of reliability can be determined simply by appeal to what the majority of the community says. That is to conflate descriptions of practices with normative accounts that—implicitly or explicitly—lay down standards for correctness.

The reliabilist, in granting centre stage to reliability of belief-acquiring methods, fails to acknowledge that normative criteria have to be grounded in questions of use, questions that necessarily appeal to intentional agency and that make reference to reasoned decisions to adopt this method or that one. What is missing from the reliabilist account is the normative force that appeals to intentional agency can provide—and that responsibilist versions of virtue epistemology achieve through their appeal to responsible cognitive agency. According to the latter account, the best kinds of cognitive agents are those who use the most reliable belief-acquisition methods available (appropriate to their pursuit), who are motivated to use these optimal methods by a desire to achieve the best kind of cognitive contact with reality, and who use these methods carefully, attentively, and responsibly. The criteria for reliability of method cannot be specified by individual users; neither are they determined by majority consensus. Instead, the criteria are to be found in the stories regarding responsible cognitive agency that permeate our normative folk psychological stories about justified beliefs. In making judgements of cognitive selves central to assessments of the epistemic properties of beliefs, responsibilism correctly stresses the active agency of believers making claims within cognitive contexts.

Talk of responsibility invites worries, however. Neither cognitive dispositions (much less perceptual faculties) nor individual beliefs seem to be voluntary or to be the sorts of things that can be chosen. If the epistemic evaluations attach to agents, or to the manner in which agents act cognitively, then it will be important to see what grounds judgements of responsible agency. Here accounts of the self that underpin many versions of virtue ethics may provide some help to virtue epistemology.

We hold persons responsible for being who they are (for having the moral and cognitive selves they have) and, in a different way, for doing what they do and for believing what they believe. How they are affects what they do and what they believe—and, more importantly, affects what reasons they have for doing what they do and for believing what they believe. Holding agents responsible for their actions and their beliefs is plausible only if agents can also be held responsible for being the kinds of persons for whom certain kinds of moral and cognitive reasons are or are not compelling. This latter may not require that agents' dispositions and traits all be freely chosen. It may require only the kind of second-order agency characteristic of persons that permits an awareness of first-order dispositions and capacities both to evaluate the merits of those dispositions and to decide to try to be motivated by or to rely upon the ones deemed to be optimal. Although it is usually conceded that some persons are born with temperaments that make the acquisition of certain virtues easier and that some persons have favourable moral climates in which to be nourished and better moral role models to emulate, such contingencies are not usually thought to undermine the claim that persons are responsible for their moral characters.[21] They represent one aspect of the multiplicity of ways in which luck intervenes in our moral lives.

Similar kinds of luck intervene in cognitive contexts: some people have natural faculties that function well below the norm; some people have natural traits (both cognitive and non-cognitive) that make the honing of certain

---

[21] Susan Wolf (1987) argues that sanity is a precondition for being responsible for the choices that underlie one's character. This may be one kind of contingency the lack of which does absolve agents of responsibility.

cognitive skills easier; some people are exposed to better teachers and role models; some people inhabit cognitive communities in which judgements of reliability of belief-acquisition methods are problematic. Assessments of the cognitive characters of agents will have to concede the role of luck, both the luck of the individual draw and the luck of the communal draw. But what is taken to be the insidious role of luck in our evaluations of others' cognitive characters is minimized if epistemic praise attaches to the responsible exercise of the best kinds of cognitive dispositions or faculties available to the agent. Agents who are visually impaired, for example, will not be blameworthy for their lack of vision; they will be held culpable—in cases where they had means of ascertaining the unreliability of their vision—for relying on their defective faculty for acquiring certain beliefs about the world. Likewise, conceding this element of epistemic luck will mean that certain cognitive communities will have greater claims to knowledge than will others. We can hold people responsible for their beliefs if the culpability attaches to the manner in which they rely on various faculties, or to their recognition of the epistemic merits of certain processes, or to their judicious exercise of certain belief-acquiring dispositions. Beliefs may still not occur to agents voluntarily,[22] but the ascriptions of responsibility are justified if they attach to the identification with higher-order desires to be motivated to employ those belief-acquisition methods deemed to be cognitively optimal (whether the latter are natural or cultivated) and to do so in a responsible manner.

Locating the normative properties of beliefs in the cognitive characters of agents suggests that we should not expect that every agent be equally good at acquiring knowledge. It does not mean, however, that the standards for belief-justification are relative to each cognitive agent. Being a cognitive agent means being part of a cognitive community. We *learn* whom and what to trust. And we do so, in part, by learning about our own and others' cognitive selves. While we may not be able to choose to improve many of our faculties, we can choose to be sceptical about them, to override them, to ignore them.[23] Further, we can choose to utilize them carefully and in appropriate ways. The normative

---

[22] There may be an analogous apparent lack of choice to act in moral contexts: virtuous agents do not *choose* the right action after considering all possible alternative actions. Given their characters, certain actions strike them as required, and certain actions never occur to them. Situations can *impose* requirements on persons' behaviour and beliefs, given their moral and cognitive sensibilities and dispositions. They are responsible for their behaviours and beliefs because they are responsible for being the kinds of persons whose sensibilities and dispositions make the behaviour or belief seem required.

[23] The beliefs of someone who has poor vision or poor hearing are unlikely to be either true or well justified; it is their choice not to wear glasses or a hearing aid which might, in some cognitive contexts, be deemed irresponsible.

standards implicit in the communal practices show us what counts as careful and appropriate exercise.

The extent of voluntary control over our virtues—both moral and cognitive—is variable. Those firmly grounded in natural traits or faculties may be part of our natural make-up; those more responsive to higher-order regulatory control may be more susceptible to a disciplined and self-conscious cultivation. While one cannot try to have better natural faculties like vision, one can try to be more careful, more open-minded, more rigorous, more imaginative, etc. Responsibilist versions of virtue epistemology require, not that everyone be capable of freely cultivating all cognitive virtues, but that cognitively praiseworthy agents exercise their cognitive dispositions in responsible ways and have the right cognitive orientations towards the world and towards themselves as cognitive agents. This requires a degree of attentiveness and care and a particular kind of self-reflexive awareness. Agents who exercise their optimal cognitive dispositions in careful and attentive manners *because* they have appreciated the epistemic value of so doing are more cognitively virtuous. This is the analogue of the virtue ethicists' claim that the morally best agents are those motivated by those dispositions they have correctly deemed to be optimal and who wish to do that which their practical wisdom tells them is the morally best thing to do in the circumstances.

It is persons who have beliefs, and to the extent that they care about the normative properties of their beliefs (and they need not always), they have particular cognitive ends in mind. But the cognitive ends cannot always be specified independently of the kinds of lives agents lead and the kinds of purposes they are pursuing. Where the cognitive ends are understanding other persons, the purposes are no doubt complex. One aspect of these purposes is that we want to be able to predict the behaviour of other persons. Another aspect is that we want to be able to evaluate the merits of certain desires, dispositions, capacities, and reasons for acting and believing. These evaluations cannot take place except within communal practices. Real lived lives inform our collective deliberations about what count as moral virtues (they permit us to see which kinds of lives are going well morally) and about what count as cognitive virtues (they permit us to see which kinds of lives are going well cognitively). One of the lessons of responsibilist versions of virtue epistemology is that the epistemic properties of beliefs have to be assessed within the well-entrenched practices in which they are held by cognitive agents. Standards for cognitive excellence may differ as the ends of the practices differ or as the nature of the things known differs. The judgements as to whether agents are acting in a cognitively responsible manner are still objective judgements, even though they may be relative to the practices in which the beliefs are held, and even though many of the criteria are pragmatic. They still reflect normative criteria for good reasons, good explanations, and good justifications.

## IV. Conclusion

The kinds of knowledge claims and justifications thereof we make of other persons and ourselves do not meet the ideals of objectivity, impartiality, and value-neutrality traditionally employed by epistemologists. Yet these knowledge claims comprise an important part of our cognitive activities. They are important because they aid us in navigating our complex social, moral, political, and emotional worlds. But, virtue epistemologists claim, they should also be important to epistemology because it is by appeal to cognitive selves—our own and others'—that we can assess the epistemic merits of many of our claims. If assessments of cognitive selves are relevant to many of our normative evaluations of beliefs, then epistemology should concern itself with how we make and justify claims about others' and our own cognitive selves.

We saw that agents come to know themselves in much the same way that they come to know others, namely, by mastering a folk psychological theory. When they apply the theory to themselves, they necessarily engage in a self-reflexive and self-constituting activity. They are motivated to know themselves as moral and as cognitive agents, and the motive to know themselves is closely tied to the motive to approve of themselves, which can sometimes prompt efforts to become a certain kind of person. Judgements of cognitive—and moral—selves are made and justified all the time. I have tried to give some sense of how the mastery of a folk theory—which is possible only within a cognitive community—permits these kinds of judgements. The communal practices provide the norms for evidence and justification as well as the standards for what count as reliable belief-acquisition methods and their responsible use.

Responsibilism seems to have a methodological advantage over reliabilism in that the latter supposes that reliability can be determined independently of the ways in which, and the reasons for which, agents employ certain methods of belief-acquisition.[24] Reliabilists thereby miss the extent to which responsible

---

[24] As noted above, John Greco's 'agent reliabilism' attempts to address this criticism by talking about the reliability of the agent, rather than the reliability of the process employed. See Greco (1999*a*).

agency is implicated in the development of the best cognitive selves and subsequently in our endorsements of optimal ways of finding out about the world. Judgements of responsibility do not take place in a vacuum, and they are judgements about the manners in which cognitive agents investigate the world and justify their claims. Many of our ways of finding out about the world involve mastery of a theory and are context-dependent. It is not until the theory has been mastered or the context has been identified that a particular process or method can be judged to be reliable. The process or method still has to be *used*, and it has to be used by cognitive agents acting in more or less commendable and responsible ways.

Judgements about responsible agency suppose we can know about our own and others' cognitive selves. The motive to know oneself serves the epistemic end of becoming cognitively more virtuous. This requires that one assess the extent to which one has acted in a cognitively responsible manner, in particular, that one determine the reliability of one's epistemic capacities and the extent to which one is exercising them appropriately, attentively, and mindfully.[25] Similarly, the desire to know others—their cognitive character and the manner in which they are exercising their cognitive dispositions—is connected to the desire to evaluate the manner in which others arrive at their beliefs, and thereby, the epistemic merits of those beliefs.

Epistemological stories that focus on the privileged relation in which the knower stands to a fact minimize the role that the cognitive agent plays, undermine the importance of the subjective perspective of the agent, suppose that the facts remain unaffected by the investigation, and fail to see that the normative criteria for truth and justification must be located in actual cognitive practices with their standards for intentional and responsible agency. Looking at the case of knowledge of persons and, in particular, of knowledge of ourselves showed how insisting on criteria of objectivity and impartiality excludes from epistemological interest certain kinds of knowledge central to our cognitive lives. The case of knowledge of persons reminds us that the thing under investigation often changes as a result of the inquiry; criteria for truth and justification for these kinds of knowledge claims have to concede this. If virtue epistemologies are correct to locate the normative features of beliefs in properties of cognitive agents, then it will be important to see how we make and justify claims about our own and others' cognitive selves. I have

---

[25] As Code notes: 'Intellectual virtue is, primarily, a matter of orientation toward the world, and toward oneself as a knowledge-seeker in the world' (Code 1984: 44).

tried to show that for assessments of cognitive selves to be relevant to evaluations of the epistemic merits of belief, appeal has to be made to the responsible exercise of the cognitively optimal capacities of the agents holding the beliefs. These assessments of responsible agency can be made only against the background practices in which the justifications of our beliefs have their point.[26]

[26] I am very grateful to the editors of this anthology for their critical comments, their patience, and their encouragement.

Part Five

*Applying Virtue to Epistemology:
An Intellectual Virtue Examined*

# 11

# Humility and Epistemic Goods

## Robert C. Roberts and W. Jay Wood

## I. Introduction

Virtue epistemology, as we understand it, explores dispositional properties of persons that bear on the acquisition, maintenance, transmission, or application of knowledge and allied epistemic goods such as truth, justification, warrant, coherence and interpretative fineness. Personal traits that regularly promote such goods are virtues, and ones that impede or undermine them are vices. Relevant dispositional properties are of at least two kinds. One kind are excellences and defects of faculties: good and bad eyesight and hearing, high and low talent for discriminating good from bad inferences, and the like. The other kind are dispositional properties that tend to the moral but make people better or worse epistemic agents: honesty, charity, fairness, humility, and the like. We are interested primarily in the latter kind of properties and think that they fit the concept of a virtue better than faculty properties do. To speak of exploration is to suggest that our craft is like the cartographer's. It aims to produce a perspicuous representation of a complex and irregular territory—the mind and heart of knowers. It is an a posteriori normative conceptual discipline; it aims to describe knowers at their best, so it describes an ideal. But the concept of an excellent epistemic agent does not follow deductively from the concept of knowledge. It must be developed by observing ourselves engaging in epistemic pursuits so as to gauge what capacities and dispositions best fit us for epistemic success. Thus, while it is a normative and conceptual discipline, empirical investigation is relevant to it.

We are going to explore a small part of the territory in question, intellectual humility. Like many other epistemic virtues, humility has a wider than merely intellectual sphere. So our strategy will be first to explore it in its broader, moral application, and then to carry what we have learned into a discussion of the intellectual life.

Often, virtues are best described in connection with their vice-counterparts, and this is especially important with humility, which seems to have a negative character that we will comment on later. Humility is opposite a number of vices, including arrogance, vanity, conceit, egotism, grandiosity, pretentiousness, snobbishness, impertinence (presumption), haughtiness, self-righteousness, domination, selfish ambition, and self-complacency. Despite differing from one another in various ways, these vices are all opposites of humility, and therefore definitive of it; we might sum up all of them as 'improper pride'. So a perfectly fastidious and rich account of humility would require us to explore them all. But we think that a fair approximation of the virtue can be achieved by looking primarily at two of its vice counterparts: vanity and arrogance. In this chapter our strategy will be to explore humility chiefly as the opposite of these two vices, with briefer auxiliary comments on a couple of others. We will then clarify why humility is an intellectual virtue by identifying some of the epistemic goods that accrue to the humble person, and end by heading off an objection to our account.

Before we start, however, to give ourselves and our readers a broader orientation in this field we'd like to give very brief sketches of some of the other important vices that help to define humility. Conceit is the dispositions of thought, action, and emotion that stem from an unwarrantedly high opinion of oneself. Egotism is a disposition to exaggerate the importance of, and focus attention on, oneself and one's own interests, to the neglect of others and their interests. Grandiosity is a disposition, in thought and self-presentation, to exaggerate one's greatness. Pretentiousness is a disposition to claim, in action and demeanour, higher dignity or merit than one possesses. Snobbishness is a disposition to associate oneself, in thought and practice, with persons of high social rank, intellect, or taste, and to shun or contemn persons of lower rank. Impertinence or presumption is a disposition to act without proper respect for the limits of one's competence or social station. Haughtiness is a disposition to treat others as hardly worthy of one's attention or respect. Self-righteousness is a disposition to ascribe to oneself a greater moral excellence than one possesses, especially in acts of comparing oneself with others. Domination is a disposition to excessive exertion and enjoyment of control over others. Selfish ambition is a disposition to advance one's own long-term interests to the exclusion or detriment of others' interests. Self-complacency is a disposition to approve uncritically of one's own abilities and accomplishments. Most of these vices have intellectual variants.

## II. Humility as opposed to vanity

Vanity is an excessive concern to be well regarded by other people, and thus a hypersensitivity to the view others take of oneself. Its emotional marks are anxiety about how one appears, joy at making a good appearance, embarrassment or shame at making a bad appearance, resentment of those who criticize or withhold the prescribed admiration, etc. Since part of making a good appearance may be to give the appearance of not caring what sort of appearance one makes, the vain person may cover up these emotions, for others or himself or both.

Not just any concern to make a good appearance is vanity. It is no sign of vanity if you are embarrassed upon discovering that you have lectured for an hour with a gaping fly. You are painfully affected by others' viewing you in an unflattering light, but the concern on which your emotion is based is only to meet a minimum standard of propriety of appearance, not to glitter or outdo someone else. It seems that, to be vanity, your concern must be to appear in some respect excellent; but there is nothing excellent about having your fly closed. Again, you may desire to make a good appearance so as to make money or get promoted, or as evidence of some excellence in yourself. Only if you are concerned to make a good appearance *for the positive social status it entails* is the concern vanity. This is why vanity is typically selective of audience: the vain person may not care to make a good appearance for people among whom he is not concerned for status. For example, a vain philosopher might not mind appearing stupid before an audience of sugar beet farmers; a woman who is vain of her beauty might not mind appearing ugly to her children. These vain people do not mind making a bad appearance before these audiences because approval from such audiences does not seem to them to confer any important status on themselves. In the vain person's view, *the approval of certain others confers value on himself*.

Some vanity may seem to want attention for attention's sake, but the attention that vanity truly seeks is *affirmative of the subject's value as a person*. The sought-for attention may be negative, but the vain individual may see even strongly disapproving attention as having an approving aspect, in particular as showing at least that the subject is important enough to pay this attention to.

(A vain person may have other motives than vanity for seeking attention, such as boredom; and such other motives might not be for approval in any sense. But such motives are not the ones that justify the attribution of vanity.)

It is hard to say exactly what constitutes an excessive concern to put in a good appearance for the sake of positive social status. But it is clear that people are not vain simply for having some such concern. Just about everyone, including people we would not in the least call vain, will feel embarrassed or ashamed upon perceiving that others are shocked at their behaviour, and will regret the loss of status if that occurs, and enjoy the status conferred by others' approval. The vain person, by contrast, is hurt by smaller failings and elated about successful appearances that the humbler person hardly pauses to note. The vain person is preoccupied with his status-relevant appearances. Robustly healthy and virtuous people are a little bothered by others' not taking them seriously, slighting them in society, thinking they are not worth much; but the vain person is very bothered by such things. We are inclined to say that the vain person is enslaved to others' approval of him, or at any rate unduly beholden to it. He demands to be very well thought of, wishes to be adulated, adored, and honoured; and feels nervous and unfulfilled unless he is getting this extraordinary sort of attention.

Some issues of value are typical vanity-issues; others are not typical but are vanity-issues for some people; other issues seem not to be possible vanity-issues. In the first class we have values that are essentially ones of appearance. For example, dress, physical beauty, linguistic accent, beauty of home and car. In the second class we have intelligence, strength, and various kinds of skills. These are not essentially appearance issues, but in vanity a person treats them as sources of appearance (this is not to say that he treats them only as sources of appearance). Wittgenstein published his *Philosophical Investigations* to stop 'mangled or watered down' versions of his ideas from being attributed to him. 'This stung my vanity and I had difficulty quieting it.'[1] Consider morality as an example of value in the third class. We do not think that excessive concern for moral reputation is reason for calling a person vain. Perhaps this is because we consider a moral reputation so important that it is nearly impossible to be too concerned about it; if a person is concerned only about his reputation and not about his actual morality, he is defective, but we are inclined to call him, not vain, but a hypocrite or morally stupid. Someone might take a vain delight in unearned praises of his character, but these are not the kind of plaudits characteristically

---

[1] Wittgenstein (1953: preface, pp. ix–x).

and assiduously pursued by the vain person; and we might say that people who are vain about their moral reputation treat their ethical character in an 'aesthetic' rather than an ethical light.

Vain people may seem to be unvain when in fact they are just in a situation that feeds their vanity enough to satisfy it, so they achieve a certain equilibrium and equanimity. The vanity comes out in emotions when the level of perceived approval goes markedly down or up.

Perhaps we have said enough about vanity to start on the humility that is its opposite. The humble person is unvain, but it is not quite enough to say that the humble person lacks vanity. He does not merely lack it, but veers in the other direction. We have said that vanity is an excessive concern to be well regarded by other people, and thus a hypersensitivity to the view others take of oneself. Humility, as vanity's opposite, is a striking or unusual *un*concern to be well regarded by others, and thus a kind of emotional *in*sensitivity to the issues of status. Julia Driver takes something like this line in her paper 'The Virtues of Ignorance', but she talks not about concerns and emotions, but about beliefs. Thus, for her the virtue of modesty is 'a dogmatic disposition' to underestimate one's worth.[2] She says modesty is not mere ignorance of one's worth, but a resistance to believing it: if the excellent but modest person is presented all the evidence of her excellences, she refuses to believe it. Thus the moral virtue of modesty is an intellectual vice. This undesirable conclusion can be avoided, while doing justice to the intuition behind Driver's mistake. The humble person is not ignorant of her value or status, but unconcerned about it and therefore inattentive to it. She may appear to be ignorant of her excellence or status, but if she needs to assess herself she can give as accurate an account as the next person; she is just not very interested in such an assessment, thus not much inclined to inquire about it, and the evidence for it is not particularly salient for her.

We think that in the cases where humility is clearly a virtue, and not merely the absence of a vice, a certain kind of story can be told about the basis of the unconcern and inattentiveness. We propose that the concern for status is swamped or displaced or put on hold by some overriding virtuous concern. In the Christian moral tradition Jesus Christ, the Son of God, is the paradigm of humility. The Apostle Paul commends humility to the church at Philippi: 'Let the same mind be in you that was in Christ Jesus, who, though he was in the form of God, did not regard equality with God as something to be grasped, but

---

[2] Driver (1989: 378).

emptied himself, taking the form of a slave, being born in human likeness' (Philippians 2.5–7). The Son of God has a very high status, which we might, a priori, expect him to insist on and be preoccupied with. But his love for humankind and for accomplishing his Father's will overrides the concern for his status and moves him to make himself vulnerable to some very unlordly humiliation: 'And being found in human form, he humbled himself and became obedient to the point of death—even death on a cross' (Philippians 2.8). In his status-ignoring love Jesus Christ is at the opposite extreme from the vain person who grasps after recognition and status as though it is the breath of life. So is the Christian disciple who imitates the Lord. As Paul says, 'Do nothing from selfish conceit, but in humility count others better than yourselves' (Philippians 2.3). Following our analysis of humility, when the humble person 'counts' others as better than herself, she does nothing so foolish as to *believe* that they are better than she—say, better cellists, or of higher social status, or more intelligent or beautiful—if they are not. Instead, whatever status she possesses or does not possess matters little to her, impresses her little, in comparison with the value of these persons as ones for whom Christ died, whom she therefore honours and respects highly, 'forgetting' herself.

Consider now a case of intellectual humility that fits the same pattern. Alice Ambrose describes G. E. Moore as a teacher:

> Moore in his lectures was self-effacing. Criticisms he put forward of claims he himself had made, say in a previous lecture, could as well have been directed to an anonymous philosopher whose mistakes called for correction. For example, in discussing truth, Moore had examined the two propositional forms, 'it is true that *p*' and '*p*', maintaining that they meant the same and therefore that 'it is true that' has no meaning because 'it is true that' is redundant. His comment in the next lecture: 'My present view is that so far from its being the case that from the fact that it is redundant it follows that it has no meaning, it follows that if it is redundant *it has got meaning*. No phrase can be redundant in an expression without having a meaning.' Some lectures later he notified his class: 'I am going to make a jump now because I do not know how to go on.'[3]

Is 'self-effacing' the right word? Moore does not seem to efface himself, but just to pay little attention to himself because he has more important things to look after. Self-effacement is a step removed from the kind of humility Moore evinces, in that it involves self-preoccupation, a self that needs to be effaced because it obtrudes or intrudes. The self-effacing person says 'I am no good',

---

[3] Ambrose (1989: 107–8).

'I am unworthy', 'How stupid I am!', thus showing preoccupation with himself. (Wittgenstein often did this.) By contrast, status is 'not an issue' for Moore; to its exclusion, the truth about truth preoccupies him. He has not literally lost track of who he is, nor have we any reason to think he regards himself as undeserving of his position: he goes to the front of the class and lectures, showing that he knows and accepts that he is the professor. But his lack of concern with status is evinced by the fact that his criticisms 'could as well have been directed to an anonymous philosopher whose mistakes called for correction'.

So we see in Jesus of Nazareth and Moore of Cambridge a common motivational pattern of humility: an unusually low concern for status coordinated with an intense concern for some apparent[4] good. This pattern may be regarded as virtuous for at least two reasons. First, the concern for status often weakens and confuses more important concerns, with bad behavioural and epistemic consequences; humility as a motivational configuration leaves the more important concern pure and free of such interference. Second, in some moral outlooks—in particular, highly egalitarian ones like Christianity—the concern for status is regarded with moral suspicion. Hierarchical human relations may be necessary to social order, but dominant status does not motivate the best sort of person.

Another vice opposed to humility, one that involves something like a strong concern for status but less orientated than vanity to others' view of oneself, is domination, mentioned earlier. Here the concern is to have power or influence over others, or even just to have power over things. (Though persons with the vice of domination are interested in dominating—owning and controlling—things primarily as a way of dominating other people.) The intellectual variant of this vice is an inordinate concern to be the determiner of other people's opinions, to take special pleasure in shaping others' minds. Most of us teachers probably have some degree of this concern, but some are very competitive for disciples and feel desolate when disciples defect. Sigmund Freud is said to have reacted violently to the defection of his disciples. Richard Rorty, following Harold Bloom, discusses a particularly grandiose form of intellectual domination (though he does not bill it as a vice) under the title of 'the anxiety of influence', which he attributes to 'strong poets'. Philosophers and

---

[4] We say 'apparent' because a person might be unmindful of status, and thus in this sense humble, in the pursuit of some horrendous evil, such as the extermination of a racial group. Thus humility, like courage, is a virtue that can be possessed by otherwise horrendously vicious persons. If it is to be a virtue in the fullest sense, it must depend on genuinely virtuous concerns. It must stand in a kind of interlocking unity with other virtues (see section VI of this chapter).

scientists may be strongly motivated by the desire to be discussed by future generations, but their claim to fame, if they have any, will be that they somehow got reality *right*. The strong poet's goal is even more ambitious: to create reality for himself and personally to dominate past and future generations by authoring their realities as well. Rorty comments:

> although strong poets are, like all other animals, causal products of natural forces, they are products capable of telling the story of their own production in words never used before. The line between weakness and strength is thus the line between using language which is familiar and universal and producing language which, though initially unfamiliar and idiosyncratic, somehow makes tangible the blind impress all one's behavings bear. With luck—the sort of luck which makes the difference between genius and eccentricity—that language will also strike the next generation as inevitable. *Their* behavings will bear that impress.[5]

In other words, the domineering strong poet wants so to impress his individuality on others that their 'individuality' will not really be theirs, but his. His anxiety is that he will be unable to make his attempted self-imposition stick, that he will fail in his role of creator of other persons. The anxiety of influence stands in the greatest possible contrast with the self-ignoring humility of Moore and with a whole truth-seeking tradition of the ethics of intellect:

> The wonder in which Aristotle believed philosophy to begin was wonder at finding oneself in a world larger, stronger, nobler than oneself. The fear in which Bloom's poets begin is the fear that one might end one's days in such a world, a world one never made, an inherited world. The hope of such a poet is that what the past tried to do to her she will succeed in doing to the past: to make the past itself, including those very causal processes which blindly impressed all her own behavings, bear *her* impress.[6]

The domination that would appear to Moore and Aristotle as an intellectual vice appears to Rorty and his forebear Nietzsche as an inevitable trait of the most developed human beings. We see the relevance of metaphysics to virtue epistemology.

Intellectual humility as the opposite of intellectual domination would perhaps be exemplified most radically by Socrates, who was contented to regard himself as only a midwife, a facilitator, of his pupils' relation to the truth. The doctrine of recollection implies that the whole idea of discipleship, in the sense of intellectual dependency, is a big mistake. Intellectual humility, in this connection, would be a disposition to rejoice in the progress of one's students,

---

[5] Rorty (1989: 28f).   [6] Ibid. 29.

especially, perhaps, when they advance beyond oneself; and it would be an emotional indifference to the question of the extent of one's own influence on them. As the unvain is unconcerned about, and thus inattentive to, whether he is making a good impression on others, the undominating is unconcerned, and thus inattentive to his influence on others.

## III. Humility as opposed to arrogance

Arrogance is a disposition to 'infer' some illicit entitlement claim from a supposition of one's superiority, and to think, act, and feel on the basis of that claim. Examples: the Hollywood star who enters a restaurant unannounced expecting to be given the best table in the house in priority over people who have been waiting for forty-five minutes. The supposed *ius primae noctis*, the 'right' of a feudal nobleman to sleep with the women of his realm on the first night of their marriage. The college president with two doctorates who thinks himself competent to speak with correcting authority in all the fields of his faculty. Typical response to arrogant behaviour: 'Who does he think he is?'

Albert Schweitzer was superior to nearly all the people in his social world with respect to his moral character, his learning, and his musicianship, and the detail in his autobiography suggests he was quite aware of this fact about himself (a failure to believe it, given his social world, would evince some weird epistemic defect). This belief does not by itself make him arrogant. Some 'inference' from it, to the effect that his superiority entitles him to treat his inferiors with disrespect (say, neglect, condescension, or disdain), or to the effect that he is entitled to special treatment or exempted from ordinary responsibilities, seems required to qualify him as arrogant.

The inferred entitlement needs to be illicit. Schweitzer might, without exhibiting arrogance, infer from his medical superiority that he is entitled to the best surgical equipment available in Africa and that he is exempt from the tasks ordinarily assigned to men in the village, because this claim to entitlement is justified by his medical superiority, conjoined with the medical needs of the community. (Presumably the supposed inference from *I am superior in X way* to *I am entitled to treat others with disrespect*[7] is always invalid.) Sometimes

---

[7] Notice that 'treat others with disrespect' is an essentially attitudinal description. Imagine that because of cultural conventions where Schweitzer labours, he will get the community to cooperate with his work only if he treats its members with what in Europe would count as disrespectful (say, condescending, authoritarian) behaviour. He may produce this behaviour without arrogance, in case *he* does not thereby express disrespect, and therewith a false entitlement claim.

arrogance is thought to involve by definition an exaggerated self-estimate. But if Schweitzer did infer from his superiority that he was entitled to treat others with disrespect, he would be arrogant even if he did not exaggerate his qualities—say, his musical and medical superiority to others. Thus arrogance does not require a false superiority claim. It is true that one might want to include in the notion of self-estimate the 'inference' to the false entitlement claim. The inference shows what the self-estimate 'means' to the subject. But we think it is clearer, for purposes of analysis, to keep the premiss and the conclusion distinct. The feudal lord who insists on his *ius primae noctis* is not wrong about being a lord, but he is wrong about what being a lord entitles him to.

One motive for running premiss and conclusion together is the fact that no explicit inference is necessary. To indicate this we have been writing 'infer' in scare-quotes from time to time. If asked why he makes the entitlement claims he does, an articulate and self-aware arrogant person would be able to trace the claims to his sense of superiority, but the arrogant person need not be self-aware or articulate, nor does even the articulate arrogant person need to say or think 'I am superior, therefore I am entitled...'. It may also seem contrary to our analysis that arrogant behaviour and attitudes are sometimes strategies to bolster a low self-estimate. In this case, the entitlement claim is not based on a high self-estimate, but a falsely high self-estimate is 'based' on the entitlement claim. Yes, but even here, the logic of arrogance is in the other direction: the arrogant person who bolsters low self-esteem by acting and thinking arrogantly is trading on the supposition that high self-value warrants the behaviour in question. The self-estimate (which may not rise to the level of belief) is psychologically 'based' on the arrogant behaviour. This is artificial or derivative arrogance (however common it may be as a form of arrogance).

Like us, Valery Tiberius and John Walker analyse arrogance as involving an inference: 'the arrogant person has a high opinion of himself. He differs from the self-confident person [by concluding]... that he is a better person according to the general standards governing what counts as a successful human specimen.'[8] Thus the inference they detect is not from superiority to entitlement, but from superiority in some respect to superiority as a human being. They point out the kind of disrespectful behaviour and attitude characteristic of arrogance, but seem to think this is automatically included in taking oneself to be superior as a human specimen. We hold that a person can be arrogant without thinking himself superior as a human specimen (the arrogant person's claim

---

[8] Tiberius and Walker (1998: 382).

to superiority may be more limited), and that one can think oneself a superior human specimen (as presumably Schweitzer and many other virtuous and intelligent people have done) without being arrogant.

Might Schweitzer infer a false entitlement claim from his superiority, without thus showing arrogance? Imagine that, ignorant of a medical missionary compound on the edge of his territory, Schweitzer falsely believes himself to be the best doctor in the region, and so falsely claims entitlement to the best of some scarce medical equipment. Here we want to ask how he is disposed to respond when his premiss is corrected. If he easily gives up his entitlement claim when corrected, we are inclined to say that the claim does not show arrogance; but if he insists on it, despite the correction, he is arrogant. This seems to fit our formula: arrogance is a disposition to 'infer' illicit entitlement claims from a judgement of one's own superiority. If Schweitzer easily gives up the false entitlement claim as soon as the premiss on which he bases it is falsified, he does not have the disposition that we have identified as arrogance. This kind of case calls for refinement of our notion of disposition. A 'disposition' that consists just in the falsity of one's premiss, plus an ability to make valid inferences to entitlement claims, is not arrogance. Arrogance includes a certain resistance to correction. It is a *motivated* disposition to infer false entitlements. What might the motive be?

It might be sensuality. We can well imagine a feudal lord who is reluctant to give up his '*ius*' claim even after seeing very clearly that being lord does not entitle him to deflower every virgin in his domain. Another motive for drawing the illicit conclusion might be vanity—the preoccupation with the status that is conferred (supposedly) by the superiority. Special entitlement confers personal importance. Claiming entitlement, especially but not necessarily if one gets away with it, is delicious to the vain person. The more conscious kind of arrogant person thinks in terms of special entitlement, and entitlement has a special *meaning* for him (it follows from his superiority).

The humble person might want the very same things as the arrogant person arrogates to himself by entitlement, but does not think of himself as entitled to them, or if he does, entitlement does not have the same ego-expanding meaning for him. Preoccupation with one's own entitlements is self-exalting, but the humble person is not much disposed to that kind of thinking. If his humility is of the most virtuous kind, entangled with other virtues, this inattention is in favour of some noble concern—typically for something outside himself like the health of the community, the excellence of the music, the truth of philosophical claims. Perhaps we can generalize that arrogance never goes it alone as an anti-humility trait. It is abetted by (and abets?) such other traits as vanity, conceit, snobbery, grandiosity, and pretentiousness, as well as others that are not intrinsically anti-humility, such as sensuality and acquisitiveness.

We said that the humility that is opposed to vanity is not merely the absence of vanity, but 'goes in the other direction'. Shall we say something analogous about arrogance? Shall we say that humility is not merely the disposition not to exaggerate one's entitlements based on one's superiorities, but is the disposition to *under*rate them? If we think of humility as a disposition to be inattentive to entitlements, it would be easy for the opposite of arrogance to become a disabling trait and thus a vice, if it became very pronounced. If, for example, Schweitzer did not notice his entitlements to medical equipment, his work as a doctor might be harmed. But it is not quite right to describe this kind of humility as inattentiveness to one's entitlements. The person with the humility of unarrogance may be as attentive to his entitlements as any other alert and rational person. The difference between him and persons who are less humble is that he is relatively inattentive to the ego-exalting potency of his entitlements. Schweitzer may, in humility, insist on his entitlements as an excellent doctor, or as a first-class Bach scholar or theologian, if his interest in those entitlements is 'pure', which is to say to the point of medicine, Bach scholarship, or theology, and not to the point of making him important.

But it would not be right to make ego-exaltation a necessary condition of arrogance. We have allowed that non-anti-humility motives like sensuality and acquisitiveness may be enough to make an overreaching entitlement claim arrogant. The feudal lord who insists on his *ius primae noctis* is arrogant even if his motivation does not include the consideration that the exercise of this entitlement exalts him; sheer sensuality would be enough. And in a moment we will come to a case in which we may want to ascribe intellectual arrogance to Aristotle where he makes an overreaching entitlement claim in the absence of any vicious motive whatsoever. These considerations lead us to propose a three-tiered analysis of arrogance: (1) In the most characteristic cases, arrogant thought and behaviour are motivated by self-exaltation; (2) less characteristic cases have a vicious, but not viciously self-exalting, motive; (3) some cases which are on the outer edges of the class are ones in which the 'arrogant' behaviour is not motivated viciously.

Let us turn now to a different example, which will also bring us closer to intellectual arrogance. Oscar Wilde had undoubtedly an impressive intellect, superior to that of most of his contemporaries, though less so than he claims in *De Profundis*. Wilde details his greatness:

> I had genius, a distinguished name, high social position, brilliancy, intellectual daring: I made art a philosophy, and philosophy an art: I altered the minds of men and the colours of things: there was nothing I said or did that did not make people wonder: I took the drama, the most objective form known to art, and made it as personal a mode of expression as the lyric or the sonnet, at the same time that I widened its range and enriched its characterisation: drama, novel, poem in rhyme, poem in prose, subtle or fantastic dialogue, whatever I touched I made beautiful in a new mode of beauty: to truth itself I gave what is false no less than what is true as its rightful province, and showed that the false and the true are merely forms of intellectual existence. I treated Art as the supreme reality, and life as a mere mode of fiction: I awoke the imagination of my century so that it created myth and legend around me: I summed up all systems in a phrase, and all existence in an epigram.

This is not by itself arrogance, though it may be rampant conceit, and we detect not a little of the Nietzschean 'virtue' of domination and its auxiliary anxiety of influence. However, Wilde does exhibit arrogance, ironically in connection with his claim to have learned humility in prison. A biographer comments that the climax of *De Profundis*,

> doubtless premeditated from the start, was a section dealing with Wilde's discovery in prison of Christ. This too is less humble than it seems, since Wilde not only describes Christ without recognizing his divinity, but blends Christianity with aestheticism, as long before he told André Gide he would do. Christ appears here as the supreme individualist, uniting personality and perfection, saying beautiful things, making of his life the most wonderful of poems by creating himself out of his own imagination. He sympathizes with sinners as Wilde in 'The Soul of Man Under Socialism' sympathizes with criminals, and recognizes no morality but that of sympathy. Christ is a precursor of the romantic movement, a supreme artist, a master of paradox, a type of Wilde in the ancient world.[9]

It is not simple exaggeration of his importance that signals Wilde's arrogance, but his implicit claim of entitlement to remake Jesus Christ in his own image. And the act of doing so does signal arrogance, because Wilde's talents and

---

[9] Ellmann (1988: 514f.). Arrogance and vanity are often comic, as here. The raillery that Kierkegaard directs at Hegelian philosophers' pretensions to 'pure thought', to 'starting with nothing', to 'making an advance on faith', etc. is a response to these philosophers' pretentiousness, which is another in the family of traits opposed to humility. The quotation from Wilde is at Wilde (1996: 44f.).

accomplishments fail to justify his entitlement, because in remaking Jesus he shows colossal disrespect, and thus the outrageous extent of his entitlement claim, and because the subsumption of Christ under the categories of his own invention is ego-exalting for Wilde.

The Wilde case illustrates the relativity of concepts of arrogance and humility to moral outlooks. We read Wilde as arrogant in his treatment of Jesus as an ancient (albeit somewhat less amusing and artistic) forerunner of Oscar Wilde. But this judgement is morally located. It is a Christian judgement. What Christians regard as arrogant, an 'aesthete' or a Nietzschean may not, because we have different ideas about what entitlement-inferences are valid. A Nietzschean or aesthete believes that a creative genius like Wilde is perfectly entitled to remake Jesus in his own image, because making is what human life is about, and genius carries with it this kind of entitlement. Christians don't think so. Thus what we take to be arrogant behaviour, intellectual or otherwise, depends on a lot of other controversial beliefs. To take another example, in Aristotle's framework it would not be arrogant for citizens to regard themselves, on the basis of their superiority to natural slaves, as entitled to treat the slaves merely as means to ends and not as beings who have their own ends that must be considered, because this would be a valid inference; while in Kant's framework the inference would necessarily be false, and would thus qualify as arrogance.

We can illustrate our point while moving still closer to intellectual arrogance and humility by considering Alasdair MacIntyre's recent comments on Aristotle's self-limitation of informants for his political dialectic. Unlike Locke or Descartes, Aristotle is not an epistemic Lone Ranger. His approach to knowledge is highly collegial, and to this extent humble: as part of his investigation he is careful to consult the opinions of those who are most likely to know about a subject matter. But some of his beliefs about human nature led him to limit his informants and discussion partners in a way that we would be less likely to do.

For while Aristotle understood very well the importance of the relevant kinds of experience for rational practice—'we see,' he wrote, 'that the experienced are more effective than those who have reason, but lack experience' (*Metaphysics* A 981a14–15)—in neither ethics nor politics did he give any weight to the experience of those for whom the facts of affliction and dependence are most likely to be undeniable: women, slaves, and servants, those engaged in the productive labor of farmers, fishing crews, and manufacture.[10]

---

[10] MacIntyre (1999: 6).

Aristotle's intellectual conduct assumes that slaves and women need not be consulted when asking ethical and political questions, because they have no insight or information of importance to contribute. For someone who occupies a Christian perspective, or some other non-elitist one, this intellectual policy evinces a false 'inference' along the following lines: slaves and workers are inferior human beings, compared to us investigators, so we are entitled to ignore these people as sources of ethical and political information. MacIntyre's point is that this policy is a blinding or information-impeding one. And our point is that the policy expresses something like the vice of intellectual arrogance. Here the conclusion is not obviously ego-exalting, nor motivated by sensuality, greed, or any other vice; so it is only third-tier arrogance.

## IV. Intellectual humility

What, then, is intellectual humility? The foregoing analysis suggests it is an unusually low dispositional concern for the kind of status that accrues to persons who are viewed by their intellectual communities as intellectually talented, accomplished, and skilled, especially where such concern is muted or sidelined by intrinsic intellectual concerns—in particular the concern for knowledge with its various attributes of truth, justification, warrant, coherence, precision, and significance. It is also a very low concern for intellectual domination in the form of leaving the stamp of one's mind on disciples, one's field, and future intellectual generations. As the opposite of intellectual arrogance, humility is a disposition not to make unwarranted intellectual entitlement claims on the basis of one's (supposed) superiority or excellence.

## V. Humility and epistemic goods

We now propose an empirical hypothesis, one which we will not establish empirically, but will try to make plausible. The thesis is that intellectual humility fosters certain intellectual ends when it is conjoined, in a personality, with other epistemic virtues. Our claim is not that all people who lack humility will be in all respects epistemic failures; we even think that vanity, arrogance, and other anti-humility vices can on occasion contribute to the acquisition, refinement, and communication of knowledge. Rather, we claim that over the long run, just about everybody will be epistemically better off for having, and having associates who have, epistemic humility. Nor do we think that epistemic humility gets all of its claim to virtue-status from the narrowly epistemic advantages it affords. It is a virtue because the acquisition, maintenance, transmission, and application of knowledge are integral parts of human life, and a life characterized by humility with respect to these activities, as well as many other activities, is a more excellent life than one that lacks it. The humility that is the opposite of intellectual vanity and arrogance has the primarily negative role of preventing or circumventing certain obstacles to acquiring, refining, and transmitting knowledge. Vanity and arrogance are epistemic liabilities with which most people are somewhat beset, and the intellectually humble person stands out in his or her freedom from these impediments.

Much acquisition, refinement, and communication of knowledge occurs in a live social setting whose mood and interpersonal dynamics strongly affect these epistemic processes. Research is often pursued by collaborative teams, and even scholars who spend most of their working days alone consult from time to time with colleagues and come together in professional meetings to share and test their findings. Classrooms, where at least some knowledge is developed and exchanged, are obviously social settings. Epistemic humility seems to promote these processes in two dimensions: in the epistemic functioning of the individual who possesses the virtue, and in the functioning of the social context with which he or she is interacting—colleagues, teachers, and pupils.

The intellectually vain person is overly concerned with how he 'looks' to the people who count: he wants to impress, and is very concerned not to look silly at conferences and in front of his bright students. This concern may incline him not to admit, and maybe not even to notice, when someone has raised a good objection to his views. It may also incline him to fudge arguments when he thinks he can make them look good enough to get away with. The intellectually vain person may be genuinely concerned to accomplish intrinsic epistemic ends: to figure out what's what and to give his students a good education. But he *also* has the extrinsic concern to look good intellectually, and we are saying that this is in general an epistemic liability. By contrast, the lack of concern to look good frees the intellectually humble person to pursue intellectual goods simply and undistractedly (think of G. E. Moore). He has one obstacle less to the correction of his views, especially in public and 'competitive' contexts like philosophy colloquia. The humble person will be free to test his ideas against the strongest objections. His humility may also make for intellectual adventure: he will not be afraid to try out ideas that others may ridicule (here, if one lacks humility, courage may be a substitute).

The intellectually arrogant person is inclined to act on a supposed entitlement to dismiss without consideration the views of persons he regards as his intellectual inferiors. Young 'analytic' philosophers sometimes exemplify this vice vis-à-vis 'continental' or informal philosophy, just as young 'continental' philosophers sometimes suppose the profundity of their school to warrant dismissing the work of their 'analytic' counterparts as superficial technical gamesmanship. Highly reputed older scientists may dismiss out of hand the unorthodox proposals of their graduate students or younger colleagues. Subramanyan Chandrasekhar was once asked why he was able to do innovative work in physics well past the age at which most people retire, while most physicists do their innovative work only while they are young. He said:

For a lack of a better word, there seems to be a certain arrogance toward nature that people develop. These people have had great insights and made profound discoveries. They imagine afterwards that the fact that they succeeded so triumphantly in one area means they have a special way of looking at science which must be right. But science doesn't permit that. Nature has shown over and over again that the kinds of truth which underlie nature transcend the most powerful minds.[11]

In face of reality's capacity to surprise even the smartest of us, a certain scepticism about one's entitlement to disregard the views of minorities, of the unorthodox, and of the young may be a significant epistemic asset. As MacIntyre's comments on Aristotle suggest, the humble inquirer has more potential teachers than his less humble counterparts. And this is due not just to numbers, but also to what we might call absorbancy: in interacting with persons whose minds are somewhat alien to his own, the strongly unarrogant person is better able, in the words of James Sterba, 'to achieve the sympathetic understanding of [their] views necessary for recognizing what is valuable in those views and what, therefore, needs to be incorporated into [his] own views'.[12]

Consider now how humility is likely to abet three epistemic desiderata as construed by recent writers in epistemology. First, consider justification. John Stuart Mill argues that competition of ideas promotes truth and justification. Just to the extent that we bar the views of others from consideration, either through political means or simply by turning a deaf ear, we risk cutting ourselves off from beliefs that might be true, or might provide better reasons for the views we already hold. Helen Longino writes that:

Justificatory reasoning is part of a practice of challenge and response: challenge to a claim is met by the offering of reasons to believe it, which reasons can then be

---

[11] Quoted in Hammond (1984: 5).   [12] Sterba (1998: 4).

challenged on grounds both of truth and of relevance, provoking additional reasoning. Reasoning, thus, gets its point in a social context—a context of interaction among individuals, rather than of interaction between an individual and the object of her or his cogitations.[13]

Even externalist views, which do not make evidence a condition of justification, require that we respond to defeaters of our beliefs. Dissertation committees, colloquia, professional meetings, efforts at experimental replication, and journal reviews all serve justification by ensuring that our beliefs pass the refiner's fire.

A major function of such intellectual institutions is to forestall the adverse effects of intellectual vanity and arrogance, which tend to undermine justification by making people less than vigilant in the criticism of their own favourite beliefs. But intellectual humility has the same effect, with the added advantage that it is, as we might say, an internal rather than external control. The humble intellectual carries this power of justification with him in all his work, day in and day out. This is not to say that intellectual humility is a substitute for commentators on papers at conferences or for dissertation committees. These are not merely correctors for vanity and arrogance. But notice also the difference between the intellectually humble and those who are not, in the use that they are positioned to make of the institutions of criticism. Whereas the arrogant may feel entitled to dismiss out of hand a criticism that comes from an 'inferior' quarter, the humble is more likely to consider it carefully, and thus reap whatever intellectual advantages it may afford. Whereas the vain may be so anxious to put in a good appearance before his colleagues that he grasps for any sophistical device that may save him face when confronted with hostile or even friendly criticism, the humble will be free to hear the criticism accurately and engage with it honestly. Furthermore, the demeanour of an intellectually humble person in a social context of challenge and criticism will tend to reduce the ruthlessness of 'competition' in the other participants, and to induce a spirit of good will, cooperation, and honesty.

Another epistemic desideratum is warrant, which Alvin Plantinga defines as that property enough of which turns true beliefs into knowledge. Beliefs have warrant, on Plantinga's view, in so far as they have been formed by properly functioning faculties in congenial epistemic environments.[14] In addition to memory, perception, introspection, and other powers, Plantinga includes among our intellectual faculties a credulity disposition, a capacity to acquire beliefs on the testimony of others. If you have a warranted belief that $p$ and I come to believe $p$

---

[13] Longino (1994: 141).    [14] Plantinga (1993a).

on the strength of your testimony, then I too may come to have a warranted belief that $p$.[15] Warrant comes in degrees. Some beliefs have more of it than others, and the degree of warrant a given belief has depends on the strength of the subject's 'felt inclination' to believe. Thus if I believe that Kant was born in 1724 on the testimony of somebody who is warranted in believing it, but I believe it hesitantly, the belief will be less warranted than if I wholeheartedly accepted it. Intellectual humility could be regarded as a liberation of the credulity disposition against unwarranted intellectual suspicion and distrust, and thus as a disposition promoting warrant in testimony-circumstances.

Philosophers like Locke and Hume hold that we should not accept the testimony of others unless we have, ourselves, some independent reason for thinking the testimony reliable. Richard Foley calls people in this tradition epistemic egoists. Such people will (if they are 'good' egoists), receive much testimony with suspicious hesitation, since it so often happens that we do not have independent justification for accepting testimony. If Plantinga is right about warrant, epistemic egoists are liable to fall short on it, where beliefs based on testimony are concerned. Their character flaw is not exactly arrogance or vanity; perhaps it is an epistemic snobbery. But it does seem that the virtue of epistemic humility would be an actualization, or what the medievals would call a 'perfection', of the credulity disposition that philosophers like Plantinga and Thomas Reid find written into basic human nature.

Consider rationality as a third epistemic desideratum. Richard Foley has proposed that:

> Rationality is a function of an individual pursuing his goals in a way that on reflection he would take to be effective. Since epistemic rationality is concerned with the epistemic goal of now believing truths and now not believing falsehoods, . . . it is epistemically rational for an individual S to believe p just if he on reflection would think that believing p is an effective means to his epistemic goal.[16]

Defining epistemic rationality in terms of what a truth-seeker, upon reflection, would consider an effective means to his end allows for some pretty strange cases of rationality. On this view it is logically possible, though unlikely, that someone be rational in believing his head is made of glass, that other persons are mere projections of his own mental activity, and that the world was created five minutes ago. So too, persons may be found who, on reflection, deny that they have intellectual peers, deliberately insulate their

---

[15] Plantinga (1993b: ch. 4, 'Other Persons and Testimony').   [16] Foley (1987: 66).

views from helpful criticism, and habitually excuse themselves from dialogue with others that would in fact further their pursuit of the truth. But if it is true that intellectual vanity, arrogance, domination, and snobbery tend to impede the pursuit of true beliefs, the person with these traits is to that extent irrational and the person of epistemic humility rational.

In promoting the acquisition and refinement of knowledge, humility affects not only people who possess the virtue, but also the people they interact with. Every scholar and thinker is indebted to others for ideas and information, and often these others are alive, and alive to how their contributions are being used or abused, and by whom. They care about their work and its career in the world, and are likely to respond to kindly acknowledgement with friendly collegial feelings and a disposition to help, to grudging acknowledgement with ironic distance, and to theft or unfair attack with anger and retribution. Unlike the intellectual *prima donna* or the easy dismisser of others' views, the humble person will be free to treat the work of others fairly and charitably, and to acknowledge his intellectual debts, thus promoting gratitude and trust in the hearts of his peers. It seems reasonable to suppose that our own prospects of intellectual progress are better if our colleagues are feeling generous towards us. They are more likely to notice, and to tip us off, to lines of argument that would promote our work, and to writings of interest; they are more likely to introduce us to their friends and acquaintances and invite us to participate in their discussions.

Self-knowledge is undermined by self-righteousness in a different way than scientific or historical knowledge is undermined by vanity. In the case of ordinary external knowledge, the issue is one's status as a knower. Knowledge, especially if displayed before others, confers status (satisfied vanity), while ignorance and confusion confer the opposite (wounded vanity). But in self-knowledge, what satisfies or wounds self-righteousness is the character of one's self—the object of the knowledge. It is satisfying to have a righteous, excellent, virtuous, and in-control self (especially if it is displayed as such before others), and it is wounding to have a guilty, mediocre, slovenly, and out-of-control self (especially if it is displayed as such before others). So the unhumble resist criticism or negative judgements about themselves, not primarily as intellectuals, but as selves. A person might pride himself on his precision as a self-knower, and offer as evidence of his excellence that he knows and acknowledges the worst about himself; but this is an unusual kind of case. The humility that frees the way for self-knowledge is a non-insistence on one's own righteousness. It is not, however, the same as not caring about one's righteousness. This is why Christianity, with its doctrine of alien righteousness in Christ, is especially well suited to the virtue of moral humility in connection with self-knowledge.

We have been noting how humility may aid a person in acquiring and refining her knowledge. It is also an asset in the transmission of knowledge to others. We think that vanity is often behind the obscure and esoteric character of much academic writing and speaking. Unnecessary technicality and impenetrable jargon whose only fruit is to make correction difficult, and allusions whose only value is to impress other guild members, limit one's audience and reduce the understanding even of insiders.[17] The humble intellectual will not hide behind or exalt herself with such devices, but will communicate in the simplest and most effective way she can. We also think vanity and arrogance are often behind the ill-advised straining after originality that characterizes so many conferences and journals of philosophy or literary criticism. By contrast the humble intellectual will let originality, if it comes, be a felicitous by-product of honest work, and not an end in itself. Humility will thus make her a more valuable member of her intellectual community.

Humility fosters the communication of knowledge in another way. Arrogance and vanity tend to engender a one-upping down-putting spirit in the classroom or other community that makes learners nervous, defensive, and cut-throat. Intellectual humility is a teaching asset, since self-forgetful pursuit of a subject tends to subdue the vanity and arrogance of the learners, and thus to free them for fruitful inquiry.

## VI. Intellectual humility and the unity of the virtues

We have construed humility negatively—as a relative lack of concern to appear excellent to others, as a disposition not to make illegitimate entitlement claims on the basis of one's superiority, as a relative weakness of desire to be the author of other people's minds, as a disposition not to ascribe to oneself a greater moral excellence than one possesses, especially in acts of comparing oneself with others. And so forth. But by itself, none of these lacks and negations amounts to a virtue. A person with a certain kind of damage to the frontal lobes of his brain lacks completely both the concern to appear excellent to others and the

---

[17] They also affect the subject's own acquisition and refinement of knowledge by making it harder for her mistakes to be detected, thus reducing the likelihood of collegial instruction.

desire to be the author of other people's minds,[18] but this does not give him any kind of virtuous humility. In describing the humility of Jesus and that of G. E. Moore, we said that the lack of concern for status is coordinated with another virtue, in Jesus love for humanity, in Moore a passion for philosophical insight. And we think this fact represents a general feature of humility—that it is internally connected, in the personality of the virtuous person, with other virtues. For example, lack of self-righteousness is a virtue only in someone who has moral concerns, among them the concern for his own righteousness.

The virtues that are most likely to come to mind on reading our litany of intellectual humility's epistemic advantages are intellectual daring and self-confidence. People can be debilitated not only by intellectual vanity and arrogance, but also by timidity and diffidence. To be the most advancing of knowers, people need to be willing to think outside the presuppositions of their intellectual communities, to doubt authorities and imagine unheard of possibilities. And it seems intuitively clear that intellectual timidity and diffidence hinder such activities. We might worry that an inquirer who markedly lacks intellectual vanity, arrogance, domination, and grandiosity is very unlikely to be daring and self-confident.

We admit that these intellectual vices can sometimes substitute for virtues. The terror of appearing foolish before members of her profession may prompt a scholar to extreme care and thoroughness. Brash and illegitimate claiming of intellectual entitlement by bright graduate students is sometimes a crucial stage on the road to epistemic success. Given the pervasiveness of human vice, such biographies of knowledge may even be the norm, in a statistical sense. But intellectual daring and self-confidence are not tied by any necessity to these vices. Moore was an unusually energetic and venturesome epistemic agent who seems not to have depended on vanity and arrogance. Einstein and Socrates are perhaps other examples.

We do not think that intellectual humility, as we have begun to explore it, is uncombinable, in a single personality, with intellectual daring and self-confidence. One does not, in going beyond one's teachers, have to arrogate false intellectual entitlements; if one's intellectual community is fairly virtuous, the going beyond one's teachers may be legitimated by hearty endorsement. Nor must one, to be intellectually energetic, make one's own reputation a central motivation; intrinsic intellectual enthusiasm is possible, even if somewhat rare.

---

[18] See Damasio (1994: ch. 3).

The combinability of intellectual humility with intellectual daring and self-confidence may be made more plausible by a general observation about the nature of virtues. Virtues are dispositional and situation-tailored. Mercy and justice may seem to be opposed to one another, and there are situations in which an agent cannot exemplify both virtues at the same time. But since they are dispositions, they may both be exemplified, at least on different occasions, by the same agent. They are combinable in a personality, because they are dispositions to act in different ways in response to different features of situations. For example, mercy may override justice when doing strict justice to a criminal would bring unbearable hardships on his family or when he is genuinely repentant; but strict justice may be called for when the situation lacks such features. The kind of indication of situational difference that we have just given is rough, and actual situations may be very ambiguous. Practical wisdom is the power of judgement, internal to virtues, by which virtuous agents make the fine situational discriminations that determine which virtue is particularly exemplified.

Even the most intellectually daring and self-confident—even the Einsteins and Descartes of the world—will confront situations of inquiry and teaching in which the appropriate response is caution and diffidence. The humble intellectual—that is, the one who lacks to an unusual extent the impulses of vanity, arrogance, domination, self-complacency, and the like—will have a special freedom and suppleness of action and judgement that promote his or her epistemic ends.

# REFERENCES

ADAMS, R. (1999), *Finite and Infinite Goods* (Oxford: Oxford University Press).
ALSTON, W. (2000), 'Virtue and Knowledge', *Philosophy and Phenomenological Research* 60: 185–9.
AMBROSE, A. (1989), 'Moore and Wittgenstein as Teachers', *Teaching Philosophy*, 12: 107–13.
ANNAS, J. (1993), *The Morality of Happiness* (Oxford: Oxford University Press).
——(1995), 'Virtue as a Skill', *International Journal of Philosophical Studies*, 3: 227–43.
——(1996), 'Aristotle and Kant on Morality and Practical Reasoning', in S. Engstrom and J. Whiting (eds.), *Aristotle, Kant and the Stoics* (Cambridge: Cambridge University Press), 237–58.
——(1998a), 'Virtue and Eudaimonism', in E. F. Paul, F. D. Miller, and J. Paul (eds.), *Virtue and Vice* (Cambridge: Cambridge University Press), 37–55.
——(1998b), 'Doing without objective values: ancient and modern strategies', in S. Everson (ed.), *Companions to Ancient Thought 4: Ethics* (New York: Cambridge University Press), 193–220.
——(2000), 'The Structure of Virtue', Paper presented at a University of Notre Dame conference on Intellectual Virtue, September 2000.
ANSCOMBE, G. E. M. (1958), 'Modern Moral Philosophy', *Philosophy*, 33: 1–19.
AXTELL, G. (ed.). (1997), 'Recent Work in Virtue Epistemology', *American Philosophical Quarterly*, 34(1): 1–26.
——(2000), *Knowledge, Belief and Character: Readings in Virtue Epistemology* (New York: Rowman and Littlefield Publishers).
AYER, A. (1952), *Language, Truth and Logic* (New York: Dover).
BAIER, A. (1985), 'Cartesian Persons', *Postures of the Mind* (Minneapolis: University of Minnesota Press).
BAIER, K. (1988), 'Radical Virtue Ethics', *Midwest Studies in Philosophy*, 13: 126–35.
BEAUCHAMP, T. (1995), 'Principlism and its Alleged Competitors', *Kennedy Institute of Ethics Journal*, 5: 181–98.
—— and CHILDRESS, J. (2001), *The Principles of Biomedical Ethics* (Oxford: Oxford University Press).
BLOOMFIELD, P. (2000), 'Virtue Epistemology and the Epistemology of Virtue', *Philosophy and Phenomenological Research*, 60: 23–43.
BONJOUR, L. (1985), *The Structure of Empirical Knowledge* (Cambridge, MA: Harvard University Press).
——(1995), 'Sosa on Knowledge, Justification, and Aptness', *Philosophical Studies*, 78: 207–20.

# References

BRADLEY, F. H. (1914), 'On Truth and Copying', *Essays on Truth and Reality* (London: Oxford University Press), 107–26.

CARRUTHERS, P. (2000), *Phenomenal Consciousness: A Naturalistic Explanation* (Cambridge: Cambridge University Press).

CARTWRIGHT, N. (1983), *How the Laws of Physics Lie* (New York: Oxford University Press).

CHISHOLM, R. (1969), *Perceiving: A Philosophical Study*. (Ithaca: Cornell University Press).

—— (1977), *Theory of Knowledge*, 2nd edn. (Englewood Cliffs, NJ: Prentice-Hall, Inc).

CLARKE, M. (1985), 'Doxastic Voluntarism and Forced Belief', *Philosophical Studies*, 50: 39–51.

CLARKE, S. and SIMPSON, E. (1989) (eds.), *Anti-Theory in Ethics and Moral Conservatism* (Albany: Suny Press).

CODE, L. (1984), 'Toward a "Responsibilist" Epistemology', *Philosophy and Phenomenological Research*, 65: 29–50.

—— (1987), *Epistemic Responsibility* (Hanover, NH: University Press of New England).

—— (1988), 'Experience, Knowledge, and Responsibility', in M. Griffiths and M. Whitford (eds.), *Feminist Perspectives in Philosophy* (Basingstoke: MacMillan), 187–204.

—— (1991), *What Can She Know?* (Ithaca: Cornell University Press).

—— (1993), 'Taking Subjectivity into Account', in L. Alcoff and E. Potter (eds.), *Feminist Epistemologies* (New York: Routledge), 15–48.

COHEN, S. (1988), 'How to Be a Fallibilist', *Philosophical Perspectives*, 2: 91–123.

—— (forthcoming), 'Contextualist Solutions to Epistemic Problems: Skepticism, Gettier and the Lottery', *Australasian Journal of Philosophy*.

COOPER, J. (1985), 'Aristotle on the Goods of Fortune', *Philosophical Review*, 94: 173–97.

—— and PROCOPE, J. (1995), *Seneca, Moral and Political Essays*, translation and notes (Cambridge: Cambridge University Press).

COOPER, N. (1994), 'The Intellectual Virtues', *Philosophy*, 69: 459–69.

CRAIG, E. (1990), *Knowledge and the State of Nature* (Oxford: Oxford University Press).

DAMASIO, A. (1994), *Descartes' Error* (New York: Avon Books).

DANCY, J. (1995), 'Supervenience, Virtues and Consequences: A Commentary on Knowledge in Perspective by Ernest Sosa', *Philosophical Studies*, 78: 189–205.

DAVID, M. (2001), 'Truth as the Epistemic Goal', in M. Steup (ed.), *Knowledge, Truth, and Duty. Essays on Epistemic Justification, Responsibility, and Virtue* (Oxford: Oxford University Press), 151–69.

DEPAUL, M. (1993), *Balance and Refinement* (London and New York: Routledge).

—— (2000), 'Character Traits, Virtues and Vices: Are There None?' in B. Elevitch (ed.), *Proceedings of the Twentieth World Congress of Philosophy*, IX: *Philosophy of Mind and Philosophy of Psychology* (Bowling Green, OH: Philosophy Documentation Center), 141–57.

—— (2001), 'Value Monism in Epistemology', in M. Steup (ed.), *Knowledge, Truth, and Duty. Essays on Epistemic Justification, Responsibility, and Virtue* (Oxford: Oxford University Press), 170–83.

DEROSE, K. (1995), 'Solving the Skeptical Problem', *Philosophical Review*, 104: 1–52.

DRIVER, J. (1989), 'The Virtues of Ignorance', *The Journal of Philosophy*, 373–84.

DUMMETT, M. (1978), 'Truth', in *Truth and Other Enigmas* (Cambridge, MA: Harvard University Press).

ELLMANN, R. (1988), *Oscar Wilde* (New York: Alfred A. Knopf).

ENGEL, M. (1992), 'Is Epistemic Luck Compatible with Knowledge?' *The Southern Journal of Philosophy*, 30: 59–75.

FAIRWEATHER, A. and ZAGZEBSKI, L. (2001) (eds.), *Virtue Epistemology: Essays on Epistemic Virtue and Responsibility* (Oxford: Oxford University Press).

FEINBERG, J. (1970), *Doing and Deserving: Essays in the Theory of Responsibility* (Princeton: Princeton University Press).

FOLEY, R. (1987), *The Theory of Epistemic Rationality* (Cambridge, MA: Harvard University Press).

FOOT, P. (1978), *Virtues and Vices* (Oxford: Blackwell Press).

FRANKENA, W. (1963), *Ethics* (Englewood Cliffs, NJ: Prentice-Hall, Inc.).

FREUD, S. (1926), 'Inhibitions, symptoms and anxiety', *SE* 20: 77–172.

FRIEDMAN, M. (1974), 'Explanation and Scientific Understanding', *The Journal of Philosophy*, 71: 5–19.

GARCIA, J. (1986), 'Evaluator Relativity and the Theory of Value', *Mind*, 95: 242–5.

—— (1987), 'Goods and Evils', *Philosophy and Phenomenological Research*, 47: 385–412.

—— (1993), 'The New Critique of Anti-Consequentialist Moral Theory', *Philosophical Studies*, 71: 1–32.

—— (1997), 'Interpersonal Virtues: Whose Interest Do They Serve?' *American Catholic Philosophical Association Proceedings*, 71: 31–60.

—— (1998), 'Lies and the Vices of Deception', *Faith and Philosophy*, 15: 514–37.

GEACH, P. (1956), 'Good and Evil', *Analysis*, 17: 33–42.

GLOVER, J. (2000), *Humanity* (New Haven: Yale University Press).

GOLDMAN, A. (1976), 'Discrimination and Perceptual Knowledge', *Journal of Philosophy*, 73: 771–91.

—— (1992), *Liaisons: Philosophy Meets the Cognitive and Social Sciences* (Cambridge, MA: MIT Press).

—— (1993a), 'Epistemic Folkways and Scientific Epistemology', in A. Goldman (ed.), *Readings in Philosophy and Cognitive Science* (Cambridge, MA: The MIT Press), 95–116.

—— (1993b), *Philosophical Applications of Cognitive Science* (Boulder, CO: Westview Press).

—— and KIM, J. (1978) (eds.), *Values and Morals: Essays in Honor of William Frankena, Charles Stevenson, and Richard Brandt* (Boston, MA: D. Reidel Publishing).

GRECO, J. (1990), 'Internalism and Epistemically Responsible Belief', *Synthese*, 85: 245–77.

—— (1994), 'Jonathan Kvanvig's *The Intellectual Virtues and the Life of the Mind*', *Philosophy and Phenomenological Research*, 54: 973–6.

—— (1995), 'A Second Paradox Concerning Responsibility and Luck', *Metaphilosophy*, 26: 81–96.

—— (1999a), 'Agent Reliabilism', J. Tomberlin (ed.), *Philosophical Perspectives, 13, Epistemology* (Atascadero, CA: Ridgeview Publishing Co.), 273–96.

## 284 / References

GRECO, J. (1999b). 'Virtue Epistemology', *Stanford Encyclopedia of Philosophy*. http://plato.stanford.edu/entries/epistemology-virtue.html

—— (2000a), 'Two Kinds of Intellectual Virtue', *Philosophy and Phenomenological Research*, 60: 179–84.

—— (2000b), *Putting Skeptics in their Place* (New York: Cambridge University Press).

—— and SOSA, E. (1999) (eds.), *The Blackwell Guide to Epistemology* (Malden, MA: Blackwell Publishers).

HAMMOND, A. (1984) (ed.), *A Passion to Know: Twenty Profiles in Science* (New York: Charles Scribner's Sons).

HARE, R. (1963), *Freedom and Reason* (Oxford: Oxford University Press).

—— (1973a). 'Rawls' Theory of Justice: Part I', *Philosophical Quarterly*, 23: 144–55.

—— (1973b). 'Rawls' Theory of Justice: Part II', *Philosophical Quarterly*, 23: 241–52.

HAMPSHIRE, S. (1974), 'A New Philosophy of the Just Society' (Review of Rawls's *Theory of Justice*), *The New York Review of Books*, 24 Jan.

HARMAN, G. (1974), *Thought* (Princeton: Princeton University Press).

HEIL, J. (1983), 'Doxastic Agency', *Philosophical Studies*, 43: 355–64.

HERMAN, B. (1993), *The Practice of Moral Judgment* (Cambridge, MA: Harvard University Press).

HILL, T. (1992), *Dignity and Practical Reason in Kant's Moral Theory* (Ithaca, NY: Cornell University Press).

HOOKWAY, C. (1990), *Scepticism* (London: Routledge).

—— (1994), 'Cognitive Virtues and Epistemic Evaluation', *International Journal of Philosophical Studies*, 2: 211–27.

—— (1999) 'Epistemic Norms and Theoretical Deliberation', *Ratio* 12: 380–97.

—— (2001), 'Epistemic Akrasia and Epistemic Virtue', in A. Fairweather and L. Zagzebski (eds.), *Virtue Epistemology: Essays on Epistemic Virtue and Responsibility* (Oxford: Oxford University Press).

HURSTHOUSE, R. (1996), 'Normative Virtue Ethics', in R. Crisp (ed.), *How Should One Live?* (Oxford: Oxford University Press), 19–36.

—— (1999), *On Virtue Ethics* (Oxford: Oxford University Press).

INWOOD, B. (1986), 'Goal and Target in Stoicism', *Journal of Philosophy*, 83: 547–57.

—— and GERSON, L. (1997), *Hellenistic Philosophy*, 2nd edn. (Indianapolis: Hackett).

IRWIN, T. (1985a), *Aristotle's Nicomachean Ethics*, translation and notes (Indianapolis: Hackett).

—— (1985b), 'Permanent Happiness: Aristotle and Solon', *Oxford Studies in Ancient Philosophy*, iii (Oxford: Oxford University Press), 89–124.

—— (1990), 'Virtue, Praise and Success', *The Monist*, 73: 59–79.

—— (1998), 'Socratic Paradox and Stoic Theory', in S. Everson (ed.), *Companions to Ancient Thought 4: Ethics* (Cambridge: Cambridge University Press), 151–92.

JAMES, W. (1979), 'The Will to Believe', in F. Burkhardt, F. Bowers and I. Skrupskelis. (eds.), *The Will to Believe and Other Essays in Popular Philosophy* (Cambridge, MA: Harvard University Press).

JONES, W. (1997), 'Why Do We Value Knowledge?' *American Philosophical Quarterly*, 34: 423–39.

KAGAN, S. (1989), *The Limits of Morality*. (New York: Clarendon Press).

KANT, I. (1994), 'On a Supposed Right to Lie Because of Philanthropic Concerns', in J. Ellington (trans.), *Kant, Ethical Philosophy*, 2nd edn. (Indianapolis: Hackett), 162–6.

KENNEDY, G. (1991), *Aristotle: On Rhetoric*, translation, notes and appendixes (Oxford: Oxford University Press).

KITCHER, P. (1981), 'Explanatory Unification', *Philosophy of Science*, 48: 507–31.

——(1993), *The Advancement of Science* (New York: Oxford University Press).

KORSGAARD, C. (1996), *The Sources of Normativity* (Cambridge: Cambridge University Press).

KORNBLITH, H. (1998) 'What Is It Like to be Me?', *Australasian Journal of Philosophy*, 76: 48–60.

——(2000), 'Linda Zagzebski's *Virtues of the Mind*', *Philosophy and Phenomenological Research*, 60: 197–201.

KRIPKE, S. (1982), *Wittgenstein: On Rules and Private Language* (Oxford: Blackwell).

KVANVIG, J. (1992), *The Intellectual Virtues and the Life of the Mind: On the Place of the Virtues in Epistemology* (Savage, MD: Rowman and Littlefield).

——(1998), 'Why Should Inquiring Minds Want to Know? *Meno* Problems and Epistemological Axiology', *The Monist*, 81: 426–51.

——(2000), 'Zagzebski on Justification', *Philosophy and Phenomenological Research*, 60: 191–6.

LEHRER, K. (1965), 'Knowledge, Truth and Evidence', *Analysis*, 25: 168–75.

——(2000), *Theory of Knowledge*, 2nd edn. (Boulder, CO: Westview Press).

LITTLE, M. (1995), 'Seeing and Caring: The Role of Affect in Feminist Moral Epistemology', *Hypatia*, 10(3): 117–37.

——(1997), 'Virtue as Knowledge: Objections from the Philosophy of Mind', *Noûs*, 31(1): 59–79.

LONGINO, H. (1994), 'The Fate of Knowledge in Social Theories of Science', in F. Schmitt (ed.), *Socializing Epistemology* (Lanham, MD: Roman and Littlefield), 135–57.

LONG, A. and SEDLEY, D. (1987) (eds.), *The Hellenistic Philosophers*, i (Cambridge: Cambridge University Press).

MACINTYRE, A. (1981), *After Virtue* (London: Duckworth).

——(1990), *First Principles, Final Ends, and Contemporary Philosophical Issues* (Milwaukee: Marquette University Press).

——(1999), *Dependent Rational Animals* (Chicago and La Salle: Open Court).

——(2001), 'Virtue Ethics', in C. Becker and L. Becker (eds.), *Encyclopedia of Ethics* (London: Routledge), 1757–63.

MCDOWELL, J. (1979), 'Virtue and Reason', *Monist*, 62(3): 331–50. Reprinted N. Sherman (ed.), *Aristotle's Ethics: Critical Essays* (Lanham, MD: Rowman and Littlefield, 1999).

MCGEER, V. (1996), 'Is "Self-Knowledge" an Empirical Problem? Renegotiating the Space of Philosophical Explanation', *The Journal of Philosophy*, 93: 483–515.

MEYER, S. (1993), *Aristotle on Moral Responsibility: Character and Cause* (Cambridge, MA: Blackwell Publishers).

MEYER, S. (1998), 'Moral responsibility: Aristotle and After', in S. Everson (ed.), *Companions to Ancient Thought 4: Ethics* (Cambridge: Cambridge University Press), 221–40.

MILL, J. S. (1957), *Utilitarianism*, ed. O. Piest (Indianapolis: Bobbs-Merrill).

MONTMARQUET, J. (1987a), 'Epistemic Virtue', *Mind*, 96(384): 482–97.

——(1987b), 'Belief: Spontaneous and Reflective', *Pacific Philosophical Quarterly*, 68: 94–103.

——(1992a). 'Epistemic Virtue and Doxastic Responsibility', *American Philosophical Quarterly*, 29(4): 331–41.

——(1992b), 'Epistemic Virtue', in J. Dancy and E. Sosa (eds.), *A Companion to Epistemology* (Cambridge, MA: Blackwell Publishers), 116–17.

——(1993), *Epistemic Virtue and Doxastic Responsibility* (Lanham, MD: Rowman and Littlefield).

MOORE, G. (1903), *Principia Ethica* (Cambridge: Cambridge University Press).

MURPHY, M. (forthcoming), *Alasdair MacIntyre* (Cambridge: Cambridge University Press).

NAGEL, T. (1979), 'Moral Luck', in *Mortal Questions* (Cambridge: Cambridge University Press).

——(1986), *The View from Nowhere* (Oxford: Oxford University Press).

NAYLOR, M. (1985), 'Voluntary Belief', *Philosophy and Phenomenological Research*, 45: 427–36.

NISBETT, R., and WILSON, T. D. (1977), 'Telling More than We Can Know: Verbal Reports on Mental Processes', *Psychological Review*, 84: 231–59.

NOZICK, R. (1981), *Philosophical Explanations* (Cambridge, MA: Harvard University Press).

NUSSBAUM, M. (1986), *The Fragility of Goodness: Luck and Ethics in Greek Tragedy and Philosophy* (Cambridge: Cambridge University Press).

——(2001–2), 'When She Was Good: A Review of Peter Conradi's "Iris Murdoch: a Life" ', *New Republic*, double issue of 31 Dec. and 7 Jan.: 28–34.

OATLEY, K. (1992), *Best Laid Schemes* (Cambridge: Cambridge University Press).

PARFIT, D. (1984), *Reasons and Persons* (Oxford: Oxford University Press).

PEACOCKE, C. (1999), *Being Known* (Oxford: Oxford University Press).

PELLEGRINO, E. (1995), 'Toward a Virtue-Based Normative Ethics', *Kennedy Institute of Ethics Journal*, 5: 253–77.

PERRY, M. (1998), *The Idea of Human Rights* (Oxford: Oxford University Press).

PETERS, R. (1975), 'Reason and Passion', in R. Dearden *et al.* (eds.), *Reason: Part 2 of Education and the Development of Reason* (Boston, MA: Routledge and Kegan Paul).

PLANTINGA, A. (1993a). *Warrant: The Current Debate* (New York: Oxford University Press).

——(1993b). *Warrant and Proper Function* (New York: Oxford University Press).

POLANYI, M. (1958), *Personal Knowledge: Towards a Post-Critical Philosophy* (Chicago: The University of Chicago Press).

PORTMORE, D. (2001), 'Can an Act-Consequentialist Theory Be Agent Relative?' *American Philosophical Quarterly*, 38: 363–77.

PRICE, H. (1954), 'Belief and Will', *Proceedings of the Aristotelian Society Supplementary Volume 28*: 1–26.

PUTNAM, H. (1981), *Reason, Truth and History* (Cambridge: Cambridge University Press).

RAWLS, J. (1972), *A Theory of Justice* (Cambridge, MA: Harvard University Press).

RICHARDSON, H. (2000), 'Specifying, Balancing, and Interpreting Bioethical Principles', *Journal of Medicine & Philosophy*, 85: 285–307.
RIGGS, W. (1998), 'What are the "Chances" of Being Justified?', *The Monist*, 81: 452–72.
——(2002), 'Reliability and the Value of Knowledge', *Philosophy and Phenomenological Research*, 64: 79–96.
ROLFE, J. (1927) (trans.), *The Attic Nights of Aulus Gellius*, iii (London: Heinemann).
RORTY, A. (2000), 'Distinctive Measures of Epistemic Evaluation: Character as the Configuration of Traits', *Philosophy and Phenomenological Research*, 60: 203–6.
RORTY, R. (1989), *Contingency, Irony, and Solidarity* (Cambridge: Cambridge University Press).
ROSS, L. and NISBETT, R. (1991), *The Person and the Situation* (New York: McGraw-Hill).
RUSSELL, B. (1948), *Human Knowledge: Its Scope and Limits* (New York: Simon and Schuster).
SCHEFFLER, I. (1982), *Science and Subjectivity* (Indianapolis: Hackett).
SCHEFFLER, S. (1982), *The Rejection of Consequentialism: A Philosophical Investigation of the Considerations Underlying Moral Conceptions* (Oxford: Clarendon Press).
SCHNEEWIND, J. (1977), *Sidwick and Victorian Moral Philosophy* (Oxford: Clarendon Press).
SEN, A. (1982), 'Rights and Agency', *Philosophy and Public Affairs*, 11: 3–39.
——(1985), 'Well-being, Agency, and Freedom', *Journal of Philosophy*, 82: 169–221.
——(1987), *On Ethics and Economics* (Oxford: Blackwell).
——(1999a), *Development as Freedom* (New York: Doubleday/Anchor).
——(1999b), *Reason before Identity: The Romanes Lecture for 1998* (Oxford: Oxford University Press).
——(2000a), 'East and West: the Reach of Reason', *New York Review of Books*, 20 July: 33–8.
——(2000b), 'Consequential Evaluation and Practical Reason', *Journal of Philosophy*, 97: 477–502.
——(2000c), 'Liberty vs. Equality: Oh, Really?' (Lecture at Boston University's Institute on Race and Social Division, Spring).
——(2000d), 'Other People', *New Republic*, 18 Dec.: 23–30.
SHERMAN, N. (1989), *The Fabric of Character: Aristotle's Theory of Virtue* (New York: Clarendon Press).
——(1997), *Making a Necessity of Virtue: Aristotle and Kant on Virtue* (Cambridge: Cambridge University Press).
SIDGWICK, H. (1966), *Methods of Ethics* (New York: Dover Publishing).
SINGER, P. (1973), 'Philosophers Back on the Job', *New York Times Magazine*, 17 Oct.
SLOTE, M. (1992), *From Morality to Virtue* (Oxford: Oxford University Press).
SMITH, A. (1976), *Theory of Moral Sentiments* (Indianapolis, IN: Liberty Classics).
SMITH, H. (1983), 'Culpable Ignorance', *The Philosophical Review*, 92(4): 543–71.
SOLOMON, D. (1988), 'Internal Objections to Virtue Ethics', *Midwest Studies in Philosophy*, 13: 428–41.
——(1999), 'Keeping Virtue in its Place: A Critique of Subordinating Strategies', *Recovering Nature: Essays in Natural Philosophy, Ethics, and Metaphysics in Honor of Ralph McInerny* (Notre Dame: University of Notre Dame Press).

# 288 / References

Sosa, E. (1980), 'The Raft and the Pyramid: Coherence versus Foundations in the Theory of Knowledge', *Midwest Studies in Philosophy*, 5: 3–25.

——(1988), 'Beyond Skepticism, to the Best of our Knowledge', *Mind*, 97: 153–89.

——(1991), *Knowledge in Perspective* (Cambridge: Cambridge University Press).

——(1994), 'Virtue Perspectivism: A Response to Foley and Fumerton', in E. Villanueva (ed.), *Truth and Rationality* (Atascadero: Ridgeview Press), 29–50.

——(1995), 'Perspectives in Virtue Epistemology: A Response to Dancy and BonJour', *Philosophical Studies*, 78: 221–35.

——(1997), 'Reflective Knowledge in the Best Circles', *Journal of Philosophy*, 94: 410–30.

——(1999a), 'How Must Knowledge be Modally Related to What is Known', *Philosophical Topics*, 26: 373–84.

——(1999b), 'How to Defeat Opposition to Moore', *Philosophical Perspectives*, 13: 141–55.

——(2000a), 'Skepticism and Contextualism', *Philosophical Issues*, 10: 1–18.

——(2000b), 'Reply to Critics', *Philosophical Issues*, 10: 38–42.

——(2001), 'For the Love of Truth?', in A. Fairweather and L. Zagzebski (eds.), *Virtue Epistemology: Essays on Epistemic Virtue and Responsibility* (Oxford: Oxford University Press), ch. 4.

Sterba, J. (1998), *Justice for Here and Now* (Cambridge: Cambridge University Press).

Steup, M. (2001) (ed.), *Knowledge, Truth, and Duty. Essays on Epistemic Justification, Responsibility, and Virtue* (Oxford: Oxford University Press).

Stevenson, C. (1944), *Ethics and Language* (New Haven, CT: Yale University Press).

Stine, G. (1976), 'Skepticism, Relevant Alternatives, and Deductive Closure', *Philosophical Studies*, 29: 249–61.

Stocker, M. (1982), 'Responsibility especially for Beliefs', *Mind* 91: 398–417.

Stubblefield, A. (2000), 'Anti-Black Oppression and the Ethical Significance of African American Identity' (Ph.D. dissertation, Rutgers University).

Thomson, J. (1991), 'Self-Defense', *Philosophy and Public Affairs*, 20: 283–310.

——(1997), 'The Right and the Good', *Journal of Philosophy*, 94: 273–98.

——(1999), 'Goodness, Rightness' (Tanner lectures at Princeton University. March).

——(2001), *Goodness and Advice* (Princeton: Princeton University Press).

Tiberius, V. and Walker, J. (1998), 'Arrogance', *American Philosophical Quarterly*, 35: 379–90.

Velleman, D. (2000), *The Possibility of Practical Reason* (Oxford: Oxford University Press).

Vogel, J. (1987), 'Tracking, Closure, and Inductive Knowledge' in S. Luper-Foy (ed.), *The Possibility of Knowledge* (Totowa, NJ: Rowman and Littlefield), 197–215.

Walker, M. (1991), 'Moral Luck and the Virtues of Impure Agency', *Metaphilosophy*, 22: 14–27.

Wallace, J. (1978), *Virtues and Vices* (Ithaca: Cornell University Press).

——(1988), 'Ethics and the Craft Analogy', in P. French *et al.* (eds.), *Ethical Theory: Character and Virtue, Midwest Studies in Philosophy* 13 (Notre Dame: University of Notre Dame Press), 222–32.

WILDE, O. (1996), *De Profundis* (Mineola, NY: Dover Publishing).

WILLIAMS, B. (1973a), 'Egoism and Altruism', *Problems of the Self* (Cambridge: Cambridge University Press), 250–65.

——(1973b), 'A Critique of Utilitarianism', in J. Smart and B. Williams (eds.), *Utilitarianism: For and Against* (Cambridge: Cambridge University Press), 77–150.

——(1985), *Ethics and the Limits of Philosophy* (London: Fontana).

WILLIAMSON, T. (1996), 'Knowing and Asserting', *Philosophical Review*, 105: 489–523.

WITTGENSTEIN, L. (1953), *Philosophical Investigations*, trans. G. Anscombe (New York: Macmillan).

WOLF, S. (1987), 'Sanity and the Metaphysics of Responsibility', in F. Schoeman (ed.), *Responsibility, Character, and the Emotions* (Cambridge: Cambridge University Press), 46–62.

WOOD, W. (1998), *Epistemology: Becoming Intellectually Virtuous* (Downers Grove, Illinois: InterVarsity Press).

WOODRUFF, P. (1990), 'Plato's Early Theory of Knowledge', in S. Everson (ed.), *Epistemology, Companions to Ancient Thought I* (Cambridge: Cambridge University Press), 60–84.

ZAGZEBSKI, L. (1996), *Virtues of the Mind* (Cambridge, Cambridge University Press).

——(1999a), 'From Reliabilism to Virtue Epistemology', in R. Coff-Steven (ed.), *Proceedings of the Twentieth World Congress of Philosophy* (Boston, 1998) v: *Epistemology* (Bowling Green, OH: Philosophy Documentation Center), 173–9.

——(1999b), 'What is Knowledge?', in J. Greco and E. Sosa (eds.), *The Blackwell Guide to Epistemology* (Oxford: Blackwell), 92–116.

——(1999c), *Phronesis* and Christian Belief', in G. Brüntrup (ed.), *The Rationality of Theism* (Dordrecht: Kluwer), 177–94.

——(2000a), 'Précis of Virtue of the Mind', *Philosophy and Phenomenological Research*, 60: 169–77.

——(2000b), 'Responses', *Philosophy and Phenomenological Research*, 60: 207–19.

——(2000c), '*Phronesis* and Religious Belief', in G. Axtell (ed.), *Knowledge, Belief and Character: Readings in Virtue Epistemology* (New York: Rowman and Littlefield Publishers), 205–20.

——(2001a), 'Must Knowers Be Agents?', in A. Fairweather and L. Zagzebski (eds.), *Virtue Epistemology: Essays on Epistemic Virtue and Responsibility* (Oxford: Oxford University Press), 142–57.

——(2001b), 'Recovering Understanding', in M. Steup (ed.), *Knowledge, Truth, and Duty. Essays on Epistemic Justification, Responsibility, and Virtue* (Oxford: Oxford University Press), 235–51.

ZIMMERMAN, M. (2001), *The Nature of Intrinsic Value* (Lanham, MD: Rowman & Littlefield).

# INDEX

Adams, R. 147
affect 5, 34; *see also* emotion
agency 167–168, 248–250
agent-relativity 91–94
Alexander 48 n33
alignment problem 139
Alston, W. 15 n1
ambition 258
Ambrose, A. 262
Andronicus 45 n28
Annas, J. 4–5, 16 n3, 17 n6, 18 n8, 19 n10, 20 n12, 21 n16, 26 n28, 26 n31, 30 n41, 50 n39, 87 n11, 208–210, 222
Anscombe, E. 58 n3, 61, 62, 65–66, 68, 76, 201–202
Antell, K. 226 n20
anti-theory 2, 2 n7, 6, 77
anxiety of influence *see* domination
*apatheia* 44–45
apt belief 155–160
Aquinas 82, 89, 90 n21, 137
Aristotle 2, 5, 89, 134, 155, 189, 264, 270–271; on emotion and virtue 35–44; on *eudiamonia* and truth 22, 140–141, 174; on *eudiamonia* and virtue 205–206; on happiness 6, 26–27, 50–51; on luck 6, 50–51; on virtue and skill 16–19; on virtue and success 23, 26–27, 208–210
arrogance 11–12, 265–271, 273, 274, 278
assessment of cognitive selves 244–245, 251–253

atrocities *see* preventing atrocities and practical reason
attributably believing 171–172
attributably ø-ing 168, 170
Audi, R. 111 n
Axtell, G. 161 n3, 183 n2, 186, 188–189, 191
Ayer, A. J. 62, 63, 65

Baier, A. 241
Baier, K. 65
Battaly, H. 111 n
Beauchamp, T. 70 n22, 71
belief; acts and 8, 137; responsibility for 137, 143; voluntary control of and responsibility for 5, 43–44, 170–171, 248–250; *see also* apt belief; false belief; true belief
Benson, H. 206 n5, 226 n20
Bergman, M. 111 n, 131 n31
blame 7, 117–121
Bloom, H. 263–264
Bloomfield, P. 20
Bloomsbury Circle 63 n13
BonJour, L. 199
Bradley, F. 52 n44, 58, 63, 65
Brentano, F. 103

Carruthers, P. 243 n17
Cartwright, N. 219
causal explanation 132; *see also* causal responsibility

chance *see* luck
Chandrasekhar, S. 273
character; as a cause of action 120–121, 122; cognitive *see* intellectual virtue
Childress, J. 70 n22
Chisholm, R. 12, 130
Christ 261–262, 269–270, 278
Chrysippus 45, 49 n37
Cicero 26 n28
Clarke, S. 2 n7, 77
Code, L. 2 n5, 79, 230–232, 244 n18, 252 n25
Cohen, S. 111 n, 112, 114–115, 124 n20, 124 n21, 125 n22
collegiality in pursuit of knowledge 276
Comesaña, J. 159 n2
community 6, 68; epistemic 230, 238–242, 244, 246–247, 249–250
competition of ideas 273
compassion 146–148
conceit 258
consequences *see* consequence-insensitive moral theory
consequentialism 6–7, 58, 68–69, 82, 84–85, 90–96, 102, 104, 138; *see also* preventing atrocities and practical reason; accommodating/assimilating/subordinating virtue
contextualism 114–115, 126–127
Cooper, J. 47 n31, 50 n39
Craig, E. 201 n22
credit 7–8, 121–122
Cudworth 34

Damasio, A. 278 n18
Dancy, J. 38 n13, 38 n16
daring 278–279
David, M. 161 n3
deliberation 10
DePaul, M. 8 n8, 121 n18, 161 n3
DeRose, K. 111 n, 115 n11, 125 n22
Descartes 52, 196, 236–237

Dewey, J. 63, 153
diffidence 278
Diogenes Laertius 45 n29, 46, 48 n35
disinterested observation *see* objectivity
domination 258, 263–264, 269, 278
Driver, J. 261
Dummett, M. 52

egotism 258
Einstein, A. 278
Ellmann, R. 269
emotion; cognitive view of 5, 37, 45; intellectual virtue and 5, 21, 37–44, 46, 49; moral virtue and 21, 35; motivation and 146; perception and 36; responsibility for 43–44; *see also* Stoic view of emotion
end; epistemic 204–205, 213–221; *see also* true belief; truth; intentional 141–146; motive and 146; natural 140–141
Engel, M. 131 n31
Epictetus 47 n32, 48 n36, 51
epistemic evaluation 193–200
epistemic value monism 161
epistemic virtue *see* intellectual virtue
epistemology; as part of ethics 33; central problems of 9–10, 184–186, 192–198, 201; difficulty using ethical concepts in 59–60; feminist 229, 230–231; relation to ethics 60–61; *see also* virtue epistemology
ethical concepts; concrete v. abstract 68; *see also* conceptual priority of virtue
ethical theory; revolutions in 61–65
ethics; normative v. meta- 63–64, 3 n14; semantic turn in 63–64; *see also* epistemology as part of ethics; moral philosophy; virtue ethics
*eudaimonia* 8; *see also* Aristotle on *eudaimonia* and truth; Aristotle on *eudaimonia* and virtue

evaluation of instruments, tools, etc. 168–170
expertise 17–18
explanatory coherence and understanding 218

Fairweather, A. 106, 183 n2
fallibilism 7, 52–53, 112, 115
false belief; aversion to 148–149
fanaticism 104
Feinberg, J. 7, 117–121
first-person introspective reports 236–237, 242–243
Foley, R. 275
Foot, P. 58 n3, 66 n17, 76
Formichelli, M. 81 n
Frankena, W. 71
Freud, S. 36 n6, 263
Friedman, M. 218
friendship 86, 87–88

Garcia, J. 6–7, 85 n8, 91 n23, 93 n28, 98 n39, 100 n45, 210, 212–211, 222
Geach, P. 76
Gendler, T. 111 n, 132 n33
Gerson, L. 23 n21
Gettier problem 7, 115–117, 127–132
Glover, J. 83, 84
Goldman, A. 2 n2, 130 n27, 183, 204 n4
goods; epistemic 10, 215–221; external 5, 26–27, 34, 49
grandiosity 258, 278
Greco, J. 2 n4, 7–8, 15 n1, 16 n3, 117 n13, 127 n24, 132 n32, 140, 161 n3, 188, 204, 207–208, 226 n20, 245 n19, 251 n24
Griffin, J. 83–84 n5
Grimm, S. 111 n

Hammond, A. 273 n11
Hampshire, S. 64 n15
Hare, R. M. 62, 63, 64, 65, 104

Harman, G. 124 n21
haughtiness 258
hedonism, monistic 161–163
Herman, B. 58 n3, 66
Hill, T. 58 n3
Hitler, A. 84
Hookway, C. 9–10, 184 n5, 194 n16, 195 n17, 197 n18, 198 n19, 199 n20, 201 n22
horrors *see* preventing atrocities and practical reason
Hume, D. 83, 106, 275
humility 11–12, 257–258; epistemic goods and 271–277; intellectual 271, 277–279; opposed to arrogance 267–268; opposed to domination 264–265; opposed to vanity 261–263
Hursthouse, R. 58 n3, 66 n17, 89

illucutionary force of knowledge attributions 7, 111, 116–117
impartiality 10, 232–233, 235–237, 252
impertinence 258
important subjects 216–217
indifferents 45
inductive knowledge 112
inhumanities *see* preventing atrocities and practical reason
inquiry; normative regulation of 199–200; *see also* inquiry and intellectual virtue
intellectual vices; contributing to acquisition of knowledge 271, 278
intellectual heroes 211–212
intellectual virtue(s) 2, 5, 128–131, 204–205; as character traits 87–188; as reliable skills, capacities or traits 187, 207–208, 210–213; as traits aimed at coherence 223–224; as traits aimed at truth 224; as traits aimed at understanding 223–224;

intellectual virtue(s) (cont.)
diversity of 20–21; goodness of 7, 107, 160, 221, 224–225; inquiry and 10, 187–188, 194, 199–201; interconnectedness of 278–279; moral virtue and 20–23, 28, 106–107; of communities 189; of hypotheses and theories 189–190; practical reason and 90, 106; sufficiency for truth 52–53; see also intellectual humility; intellectual virtue and emotion; *prudentia*
internalism and externalism 184
Inwood, B. 23 n21, 51 n32
Irwin, T. 26 n31, 28, 50 n39, 51 n32

James, W. 138
Jones, W. 161 n3
justice 279
justification 9–10, 32; centrality for epistemology of 193–198; objective 128; subjective 127–128

Kagan, S. 58 n3, 66
Kant, I. 100
killing 101–103
Kitcher, P. 218
knowledge 10, 227–228; analysis or definition of 5, 7–8, 9–10, 127–131, 150, 191; as credit for true belief 111, 123; as success term 23–24, 28–29; better than true belief see value problem; centrality for epistemology of 193–198, 201–202; closed under entailment 125; conflicting attributions of 132–133; of other persons 230–236; of self 236–237, 276–277; of self and others 10, 229–230, 237–243, 252; safety account of 113–114, 159–160; tracking account of 112–113; transmission 277; understanding v. 217–218; Zagzebski's definition of 29–31; see also knowledge and luck
Korsgaard, C. 58 n3
Kornblith, H. 15 n1, 239–240, 246, 247
Kripke, S. 246 n20
Kvanvig, J. 15 n1, 80, 161 n3, 203–204

Laches 18
Lehrer, K. 116 n12, 117 n13, 130
Little, M. 34 n1, 34 n2
Locke, J. 275
Long, A. 23 n21
Longino, H. 273–274
lottery problem 7, 111–115, 116–117, 123–127, 248–249
luck 5, 34, 122–123, 164, 170, 173, 212–213; happiness and 6, 49–51; knowledge and 6, 7–8, 52–3, 111, 116–117, 123–127, 131, 133, 151; moral 132, 209

MacIntyre, A. 58 n3, 59, 62, 64, 65–66, 68, 76, 80, 81, 106 n54, 270–271
magnificence 26–27
Maritain, J. 63
maximization see practical reason
McDowell, J. 36 n8
McGeer, V. 243 n16
McKinnon, C. 10–11
McMullin, E. 189 n14
Meinong, A. 104
mercy 279
metaethics; classical 64; see also ethics
Mill, J.S. 138, 273
minimax 82
modernity; critique of 6, 66, 68
modesty see humility
Montmarquet, J. 2 n5, 34 n2, 38 n16, 42 n24, 53 n46, 79, 204, 210–211
Moore, G.E. 58, 62, 63, 65, 262–264, 278
moral conflicts 98–103

moral conviction  81, 82, 104
moral education  96
moral philosophy; ambitions and cultural position of  63–64; central problems of  185, 193, 195, 201–202
moral theory; consequence-insensitive  96–97; input-driven  7, 82, 85–86, 88, 93–96, 98, 103; normative  57–58; patient-focused  7, 82, 86, 87–88, 103; requirements on  74–75; role-centered  7, 82, 86, 91–92, 97, 98, 100–103, 105–106; suspicion of  6, 68, 69, 76–78; virtues-based  86, 87, 91–92, 94–96, 99–103
motivation  8; virtuous  30–31
motives  146–150; *see also* true belief as motive
Murphy, M.  105 n 52

Nagel, T  58 n 3, 91, 132 n 32
narrative structure of life  6, 68
neo-Aristotelian virtue theory  58
neo-Kantian normative theory  58, 68–69; *see also* accomodating/assimilating/subordinating virtue
Nietzsche, F.  264
Nisbett, R.  121 n 18, 239 n 12
Nolan, D.  111 n, 132 n 33
norm-specification  82, 99–100, 103
Nozick, R.  112–113
Nussbaum, M.  50 n 39, 58 n 3, 66 n 17

Oatley, K.  7
objectivity  231–232, 252
outrages *see* preventing atrocities and practical reason

Parfit, D.  58 n 3, 65
passivity  10
Paul  261–262
Peacocke, C.  201
Pellegrino, E.  71

perception  225–226
Perry, M.  83–84 n 5
persons  241–242
*phronesis*  2, 82, 149–150
Plantinga  2 n 3, 174 n 9, 274–275
Plato; on *eudiamonia* and truth  22; on virtue and skill  16, 18–19
Plutarch  48 n 36, 49 n 37
Polani, M.  38 n 17
Popper, K.  201
Portmore, D.  81 n, 91 n 22
practical reason  6–7, 69; instrumental conception of  6–7, 69, 81–82, 84–85; preventing atrocities and  83–85, 90–91
practical wisdom *see phronesis*
pretentiousness  258
Prichard, H.  63, 65
private language argument  237
Procopé, J.  47 n 31
proper function  2 n 3
*prudentia*  82
Putnam, H.  52
Pyrrhonists  196–197

Quinn, P.  32 n 43, 111 n, 125 n 23

rationality  275–276
Rawls, J.  58, 62, 63, 65
reason; strong belief and  103–104; *see also* practical reason
reflection  197–199
reflective equilibrium  206–207
Reid, T.  275
reliabilism  1, 9, 138–140, 160–161; agent  2 n 4
respect  84–85
responsibility; causal  118–120; for being the person one is  248; *see also* voluntary control of and responsibility for belief; blame; credit
result-optimization  82

Richardson, H. 81n, 82, 99
Riggs, W. 10, 111n, 111n1, 134n35, 151n16, 161n3, 214n15
rights 7; violation of 93–94, 101
Roberts, R. 11–12
Rolfe, J. 47n32
Rorty, A. 15n1
Rorty, R. 263–264
Ross, L. 121n18
Ross, W. D. 63, 65
rule-following 246
Russell, B. 130

salience 118–119, 125–126; of intellectual virtue 129
Sartre, J. 63
Saul, J. 202n25
scepticism 4, 9, 196–201
Scheffler, I. 38n17
Scheffler, S. 58n3
Scheler, M. 103
Schneewind, J. 63n12
Schweitzer, A. 265–267
Sedley, D. 23n21
self-complacency 258–259
self-confidence 278–279
self-righteousness 258, 276–277, 278
Sen, A. 6–7, 81n, 81–85, 90–96, 98, 99, 100–101, 103–106
Seneca 46, 48
Sherman, N. 5–6, 35n4, 35n5, 39n19, 40n21
Sherratt, A, 202n25
Sider, T. 111n
Sidgwick, H. 58, 62, 63, 65, 84, 86, 140
Simpson, E. 2n7, 77
Singer, P. 64n15
skill 5, 16; articulate understanding and 18–19; holistic understanding and 17–18; in living 19–20; teachability of 17

*skopos* 5, 209; of virtuous action 24–25
Slote, M. 66
Smith, A. 83, 85–86, 106
snobbishness 258
Socrates 264, 278; defence speech of 27–28
Solomon, D. 6, 70n21, 73n27, 75n29
Sosa, E. 1, 2n3, 38n15, 79, 111n, 111n1, 112n3, 113–114, 117n13, 129, 130n28, 142–145, 159n2, 161n3, 183n1, 188n13, 193, 204, 207–208, 225–226, 228
special relationships 69
Spencer, H. 58, 63, 65
Stalin, J. 84
Sterba, J. 273
Steup, M. 161n3
Stevenson, C. 62, 63, 65
Stewart, T. 32n43
Stoic; doctrine of *eupatheiai* (good feelings) 46; sage 5, 44, 46; view of emotion 5, 44–49; view of knowledge 52
Stoics 5, 87n11; on happiness and luck 6, 51; on virtue and skill 16, 19–20; on virtue and success 23–27, 208–210
Strobaeus 45n27, 45n29
strong poet 263–264
Stubblefield, A. 95n33
Stump, E. 111n
subjectivity 10
success 5, 10, 23–7, 207–213
sympathy 6–7, 81, 81–86, 103–106

Taylor, J. 81n
*telos* 5, 209; of virtuous person 24, 50
testimony 274–275
theory-theory 237–239
Thomson, J. 94n30, 96n36, 97n37, 101n47
Tiberius, V. 266

# Index / 297

timidity 278
Toner, C. 79 n33
tradition 105
true belief; aimed at as such 142–145; as fundamental epistemic value 160–161, 173, 177–179; as end 140–146, 205; as epistemic goal 156–160, 213–214; attributable 172–173, 174–175; credit for 8, 116–117, 123, 133; *see also* attributably believing; value of 8, 135–137, 156–157, 160–161, 174–175; *see also* intellectual virtue(s) as reliable skills and capacities; knowledge and luck; truth
truth 135–136; as aim 5, 8, 21–22, 136, 141–146; coherence theory of 52; love of 146–150, 151–152; understanding and 218–219; verifiability and 52; *see also* intellectual virtue(s) as reliable skills and capacities; knowledge and luck; true belief

understanding 10, 214–221; *see also* understanding v. knowledge; understanding and truth

value; conferred by motives 146–150, 151–152; consequentialist 138–140; instrumental 9, 161–163, 169; intellectual 32; intrinsic 9, 161–163; of agents, performances and products 163–170; performance 9, 175–178; pluralism 98, 99; position relative 90–96; praxical 162–163, 172–174; teleological 8, 140–146, 222
value problem 8, 9, 133–134, 150–153, 160–161, 163–164, 173–178, 245
values-balancing 82, 98 n38, 99
vanity 11, 259–261, 272, 274, 277, 278

Velleman, D. 136 n2
vices opposed to humility 258–159
virtue; accommodating/assimilating/subordinating 66, 70–73; act of 29–31, 152; conceptual priority of 6, 7, 9–10, 67–68, 76–77, 89, 186, 190; end or aim of 21–22, 204–205; happiness and 6; moral 2, 5; practical reason and 89–90; priority of 190–192; as skill of living 19–20; success and 23–28, 208–213; *see also* intellectual virtue
virtue epistemology 1, 9–10, 59, 106, 183–186, 203–205, 228–230; eudaimonist 178–179; radical 80; reliabilist 163–164, 179, 188–189, 207–208, 228, 247–248, 251–252; responsibilist 188–189, 229, 245–252; routine 78–80
virtue ethics 2, 58–59; broad v. narrow agenda 77–78; disagreement with opponents 67–69; happiness based 20 n12; radical 6, 65–66, 68–70, 73–75; recurrent objections 73–75; routine 6, 65, 66, 67–68, 73; *see also* central problems of moral philosophy; virtues based moral theory
virtue reliabilism 79
virtue responsibilism 79
Vogel, J. 113 n5
voluntary assent to emotion 46–47

Walker, J. 266
Walker, M. 132 n32
Wallace, J. 17 n4
Warfield, F. 111 n
warrant 2 n3, 274–275
Watkins Tate, M. 79 n33
White, H. 5–6
White, I. 202 n25

Wilde, O. 268–270
Williams, B. 74, 77, 100
Williamson, T. 201
Wilson, T. 239 n12
wisdom 10, 215–221, 223
wise action 170–171
Wittgenstein, L. 63 n13, 237, 246, 260, 263
Witzhum, H. 202 n25
Wolf, S. 248 n21
Wood, W. 11–12, 38 n17
Woodruff, P. 19 n10

Zagzebski, L. 2 n5, 2 n6, 8–9, 8 n8, 15, 16 n3, 17 n4, 20 n12, 20 n14, 22, 23 n19, 23 n20, 24, 26 n35, 28 n36, 34 n2, 37 n9, 38 n14, 38 n16, 39 n19, 42 n25, 80, 81 n, 90 n20, 106, 111 n, 111 n1, 117 n13, 128 n25, 133, 139 n7, 142 n10, 150 n15, 152 n17, 154 n19, 161 n3, 183 n1, 183 n2, 184 n4, 188, 204, 208, 217 n16, 226 n20, 245 n19
Zimmerman, M. 93 n28